VIKING FUND PUBLICATIONS IN ANTHROPOLOGY

edited by Sol Tax

Number Thirty-Two

COURSES TOWARD URBAN LIFE

COURSES TOWARD URBAN LIFE

ARCHEOLOGICAL CONSIDERATIONS OF
SOME CULTURAL ALTERNATES

Edited by

ROBERT J. BRAIDWOOD

and

GORDON R. WILLEY

ALDINE PUBLISHING COMPANY · CHICAGO

This volume comprises one of a series of publications on research in general anthropology published by the Wenner-Gren Foundation for Anthropological Research, Incorporated, a foundation created and endowed at the instance of Axel L. Wenner-Gren for scientific, educational, and charitable purposes. The reports, numbered consecutively as independent contributions, appear at irregular intervals.

INTRODUCTION

ROBERT J. BRAIDWOOD AND GORDON R. WILLEY

THE CONTENTS of this volume result from a symposium held at the European headquarters of the Wenner-Gren Foundation for Anthropological Research at Burg Wartenstein, Austria, July 3–11, 1960. The separate papers were prepared by the participants before the symposium. Revision of the papers has since been accomplished by all the authors who were able to participate in the deliberations of the symposium. Unfortunately, Professors A. P. Okladnikov and Hasmukh D. Sankalia were not able to come to Burg Wartenstein; their papers stand as we received them, save for minor editing.

The idea for the symposium grew out of our discussions concerning a seminar sponsored by the Wenner-Gren Foundation in the Chicago Natural History Museum in 1958 (Gabel, 1960). We presented the idea in 1959 to Dr. Paul Fejos, President and Director of Research of the Foundation, with the general notion that it might take place during the summer of 1961 at Wartenstein. Dr. Fejos' response not only gratified us greatly, but also took our breaths away—he definitely wanted the symposium, and he wanted it in the summer of 1960. Both of us were involved with field work during the 1959–60 academic year, Braidwood in Iran and Willey in Guatemala. Had we had the extra year for more careful preparation and for detailed correspondence with the other participants, the symposium might have been somewhat different; but we are not—in retrospect—assured that it would have been any better. We might have made our preparations too formal, and could thus have stifled the natural tendency for individual interests and discussions to flow in uncharted and often very useful directions.

A further consequence of the rather short notice and long range (Kermanshah–New York–Guatemala City) correspondence involved in the planning was that many of the participants we invited had already made other commitments. Our desires were torn between keeping the size of the symposium to no more than twenty participants and getting as broad a geographic coverage and as diverse a representation of international scholarship as was possible. By the time some of our invitees had declined, it was too late to substitute obviously useful and desirable alternates. We now believe, again in retrospect, that our actual number of fifteen active-minded and interested participants was already the maximum for fluid and easy communication. We are, nevertheless, sorry not to have had the company and benefit of the knowledge of those colleagues who had other commitments, and we apologize to other obviously well-informed and interested colleagues who were not invited because of the complications of short time and long-range planning.

Because of the foregoing circumstances, what we achieved was in no sense a universal and world-wide consideration of the subject matter of our concern. We believe, however, that it was our very good fortune to have had such particular participants and area coverage as we did have.

As it was originally announced, the subject matter of the symposium was proposed to be as follows:

FROM 15,000 B.C. TO THE THRESHOLDS OF URBAN CIVILIZATIONS: A WORLD-WIDE CONSIDERATION OF THE CULTURAL ALTERNATIVES

The symposium is to be concerned with tracing man's history from latest Pleistocene times up to the threshold of the urban civilizations. It is projected on a world-wide basis. It will deal, substantively, with those archeological evidences that reveal the varying degrees of intensification of food-collecting, the transitions from food-collecting to partial or to fully effective food production, and the eventual emergence of city life and civilization. The cultural consequences and accompaniments of these transitions are to be examined closely. Inquiry will be directed not only to those regions where urbanization was first to crystallize but to those more "peripheral" regions that may or may not have attained full urbanism.

Attention will be given to environmental adaptations under differing conditions and to shifts in adaptations either before or following the appearance of food production. The relative roles of environmental factors and migration and/or diffusion in the conversion of hunter-collector cultures to those of food production will also be studied. Interest will center upon those qualities and quantities of cultural intensifications immediately antecedent to the appearance of urban civilizations, analyzing the evidences for such things as settlement patterns, population sizes and groupings, long-range trade, incipient "priesthoods," "kingships," and the institution of warfare. In brief, we will be posing the questions: What can the prehistoric archeologist contribute to the understanding of why urban civilizations came about when and where they did?

.As a working hypothesis we will use the delineations of an urban civilization given by Childe (1950) with Redfield's comments in *The Primitive World and Its Transformations* (1953). The goal of the symposium is not so much the definition of urban civilization as such—or a *post facto* analysis of its genesis via "historic" materials —as a consideration of the varieties of cultural build-ups leading to the thresholds of urban civilizations.

Certainly not all our desiderata were achieved, but it was against this framework of problem that the background papers of the participants were prepared. These papers were circulated in advance among the participants and were not read as such during the sessions of the symposium.

The symposium opened with three and one-half days of panel discussions based upon the background papers. Discussions ranged over possibilities of generalizations about culture change in widely separated world areas. Environmentally similar culture areas were examined (e.g., semitropical areas, semiarid areas, Mediterranean-type areas, continental plains areas, and temperate-arctic woodland areas), and developments within each of these were contrasted with the developments of environmentally different areas. Similarly, "nuclear" and "marginal" area developments were explored for parallels and differences. A day of unprogramed discussions followed, during which five central questions were formulated:

1. In the late glacial and in the early postglacial periods, what major cultural events characterize your area? By what archeological traces are these expressed?
2. Defining incipient cultivation (and/or animal domestication) as a minor or supplementary basis of total subsistence, when and how do such conditions appear?
3. At what point in the cultural sequence of your area do you feel that you can identify effective food production (plant cultivation and/or animal domestication assuming a major subsistence role), and what are its artifactual expressions and social (directly inferred) consequences?
4. Does effective food production appear as part of an indigenous evolution or does it (as revealed archeologically) suggest outside influences? To what extent does the appearance of effective food production (either indigenous or imported) seem explosive ("revolutionary")?
5. Could you use the term "threshold of urbanization" in your area? If so, what would you mean, and what is the evidence for its development?

The remaining four working days of the symposium were devoted to the reworking and redrafting of the background papers in the light of these "thematic" questions. This was done, but in its course many informal talks on all aspects of the symposium subject were held. The final revisions of the papers contain, either implicitly or explicitly, the responses each individual participant believed that he could make to the five "thematic" questions, as he understands and interprets the available archeological evidence in his area (the Okladnikov and Sankalia papers, being the original background papers, did not receive this treatment; unfortunately also Klíma, Pittioni, and Schwabedissen had to leave Wartenstein before the informal discussions were completed).

The shift in the wording of the last phrase of the original subtitle from "cultural alternatives" to "cultural alternates" was discussed by the participants. The change was made because our dictionaries suggested that the word "alternatives" *might* carry the implication of only two possible choices, and we are convinced that the possibilities of cultural choice were never so limited.

We also considered how worthwhile it might be to construct a master map and chart to include here with the papers. The idea was rejected on the ground that it would give our efforts an implication of universality that we are only too conscious we must not claim.

The arrangement of appearance of the papers in this volume follows the organization of the first three and one-half days of the symposium itself; that is, the ordering runs essentially from tropical to boreal. We deny that any *mystique* lies behind this order. Our purpose has been only to choose an arrangement that gives precedent to neither hemisphere nor to any particular focus of nuclearity.

Certain usage inconsistencies in style, spelling, and the capitalization of words inevitably arose. The editors have made such judgments as they saw fit in these matters and assume full responsibility therefor. For the translation of the Okladnikov paper into English, we are indebted to Paul Tolstoy; for those of Klíma, Pittioni, and Schwabedissen to Wolfgang Weissleder and Linda Braidwood.

One further observation about the symposium session itself is perhaps in order. Braidwood took the latter phrase of the original title, "to the Thresholds of Urban Civilizations," to mean only an approach to this threshold. Willey's conviction was that the phenomena of the threshold itself should be discussed. Some of the other participants leaned toward Willey's interpretation, and some toward Braidwood's. This unevenness, of course, showed in the background papers, and it was tacitly agreed that considerations of the threshold itself should be, in the main, postponed for a further symposium. We give some thought to this curious divergence and a possible reason for it in our conclusions.

It only remains for us—and here each of the active participants explicitly expressed the desire to join us—to thank Dr. Fejos, his entire staff, and the Wenner-Gren Foundation for the hospitality and stimulation we received at Burg Wartenstein. Sight (or site [sic]!) unseen, it was difficult for us to believe that Wartenstein could possibly be a place for serious scholarly activity, although we were quite prepared to believe that it might be an excellent place in which to dream. But for some reason that we cannot fully explain, we all felt happily impelled to industriousness and the communication and exchange of ideas. It will be difficult for the reader to catch, from the printed page, the spirit and *élan* of the affair itself. Whether or not these pages appear to be anything more than simply the proceedings of just another symposium, we feel certain that the impact that this session had on that segment of international scholarship represented by the participants themselves has been the important thing. This may, we hope, leave its mark on the development of ideas in future culture-historical scholarship. For this, we are indebted to Burg Wartenstein.

BIBLIOGRAPHY

CHILDE, V. GORDON
  1950. "The Urban Revolution," *Town Planning Rev.*, 21:3–17.
GABEL, CREIGHTON
  1960. "Seminar on Economic Types in Pre-Urban Cultures of Temperate Woodland, Arid, and Tropical Areas," *Current Anthrop.*, 1:437–38.
REDFIELD, ROBERT
  1953. *The Primitive World and Its Transformations*. Ithaca, N. Y.: Cornell University Press.

CONTENTS

COURSES TOWARD URBAN LIFE

AFRICA SOUTH OF THE SAHARA

J. DESMOND CLARK

INTRODUCTION

ANY ASSESSMENT of the rate and trend of the swing from food-collecting to food-producing and so to incipient and then full urbanization must depend fundamentally on the establishment of a sound absolute chronology. There is as yet no such reliable chronology for sub-Saharan Africa. This must be stressed from the start. We have at the most only a handful of C^{14} determinations—suggesting isolated dates—on which to construct our absolute chronology, and we have none of the other dating methods such as, in Europe and America, are derived from varved sediments, postglacial forest development, or dendrochronology. Neither have we had the benefit of such concentrated field work. Prehistorians in Africa are few and far between, and, in fact, it is estimated that there is something less than one prehistorian to every 100,000 square miles of territory. Most of the field work has been exploratory rather than intensive; no complete settlement has been excavated, and many of the patterns are still, from the archeological evidence, mainly conjectural.

Black Africa is, however, rich in ethnographic survivals in microenvironments that emphasize the very gradual and conservative nature of cultural progress in the subcontinent prior to the coming of Western civilization. It is both permissible and illuminating, therefore, to make critical comparisons between later prehistoric cultural assemblages in similar environments and the way of life and material culture of existing, or recently existing, groups living at a similar cultural level. Not infrequently, also, physical anthropology shows that the same physical stock is associated.

The location of sites in the higher rainfall areas is often difficult because of the thickness of the vegetation cover, which prevents, through lack of soil erosion, knowledge of what lies beneath the surface. The greatest number of sites, therefore, is known from the semiarid regions, where natural exposures have permitted a more complete understanding of cultural development. Moreover, the general nature of the environment in sub-Saharan Africa is such that it has always influenced human activity toward mobility rather than long settlement in one place. Structures and dwellings were of the simplest and left few or no remains, while occupation sites, except those in caves or by the waterside, are usually shallow and show little indication of continuity of settlement.

1

The tropical climate and the microfauna have, moreover, destroyed the organic remains in all but a few cases, so that only the more imperishable evidence from stone, bone, or clay remains.

It is therefore small wonder that there are so many blanks and unknown areas on the prehistoric map of Black Africa. Indeed an immense field still awaits properly equipped research. But, bearing in mind these shortcomings, we can say, in all fairness, that a good start has been made, and quite extensive assemblages have been collected in some regions. The approach, however, has almost invariably been the old taxonomic, typological one, so restrictive of wider interpretation, while the great bulk of the material is from the surface, and its homogeneity and position in the time scale are thus open to doubt—so much so that, for example, estimates for the duration of the later stone age in southern Africa have ranged from about 2,000 to 10,000 years.

Except where contamination of the sample has obviously falsified the result, the few radiocarbon determinations now at our disposal are not inconsistent and agree reasonably well with the chronology as previously deduced from an interpretation of the stratigraphical and cultural evidence. A general pattern begins to emerge that, although it will need much amplification and amendment, shows that the later and post-Pleistocene cultural and economic levels of development are still largely determined, on the one hand, by environment and, on the other, by the diffusion of improved methods of food-getting from the north, beyond the Sahara.

The Sahara Desert, with its eastern extensions, and the sudd area of the Nile valley form between them a fairly effective, but never complete, barrier to population movements between the regions to the north and south. In the past, at times of improved climate and more abundant or more evenly distributed rainfall, free movement of peoples and semipermanent settlement were possible in certain parts of the Sahara. These movements affected not only man but also both Ethiopian and palearctic fauna and flora, allowing them to mix. But, with the onset of desiccation, connections between north and south were disrupted and at the maximum ceased entirely (McBurney, 1960; pp. 70–87). It is believed, therefore, that these climatic oscillations played an important part in deciding the pattern of the later prehistoric cultures south of the desert.

Thus at times the desert was unpopulated; at other times it acted as a filter through which cultural traits and economic products were able to pass in both directions. It sometimes also served as a common meeting ground for peoples moving into the Sahara when environmental conditions were more favorable than they are today. An understanding of developments in the desert in early post-Pleistocene times is essential, therefore, to an understanding of the sequence of events in the tropical regions. The general trend appears to have been for peoples to move down into the subcontinent, at least in historical or protohistoric times, though this does not exclude the fact that important movements have taken place in the opposite direction, especially during the warmer and wetter climate that followed the end of the Pleistocene in the Sahara. But most of the later and major cultural movements in sub-Saharan Africa seem to have had their origin in influences that penetrated the subcontinent from the north. Southern Africa may be described as a cul-de-sac, which was very receptive of new ideas—especially when these concerned improved and easier methods of food-getting—but had made no major contribution to human advancement after the end of the middle Pleistocene. The emphasis in this region thus seems to have been on the reception rather than on the dissemination of new cultural ideas.

GEOGRAPHICAL SETTING

Sub-Saharan, or Black, Africa is a vast area of country with great variability in climate and environment. It is populated by many differing racial and cultural groups, living a life of equally varied economies, which have, in their turn, variously affected their natural surroundings.

Africa is a very old land mass, and the greater part of it is uplifted some three to four thousand feet above the coast. This central plateau is usually gently undulating or monotonously flat, though it is relieved in places by mountain ridges of a residual nature or by great synclinal basins, such as Lake Victoria, the Congo, and the Kalahari. Down much of the center of the continent runs the Great Rift Valley, an ecological divide in the bottom of which are situated some of the deepest lakes in the world, flanked on either side by high mountain country and plateaus, which have formed natural highways for population movement. The coastal plains are mainly narrow and usually pass abruptly through rocky escarpment country up to the high mountain ridges that almost everywhere determine the edge of the plateau in the subcontinent. Such a topography prohibits navigation and renders the rivers largely useless as a means of access to the interior.

Most of the rain is strictly seasonal and falls in the southeastern and northwestern parts in a pattern that can be traced back into Pleistocene times and that is reflected in the predominant vegetation zones. These zones have played a major part in determining the zoölogical distributions and the main characteristics of their human populations, at least since the beginning of the upper Pleistocene. Paleobotanical (Bakker, 1960, and in press) and paleontological evidence indicates that, while they have fluctuated in extent, these vegetation zones are basically old, so that the over-all historical pattern is not one of complete replacement of one form of vegetation by another in response to temperature and rainfall variability but rather one of advances and retreats between the different zones.

By the closing stages of the upper Pleistocene the tectonics and volcanicity that had characterized middle Pleistocene and earlier times in eastern and central Africa were at an end, except for purely local movement, and the physiographic and vegetation patterns were in essence the same as those existing today—though the vegetation has, of course, been subject to variability in response to climatic fluctuation.

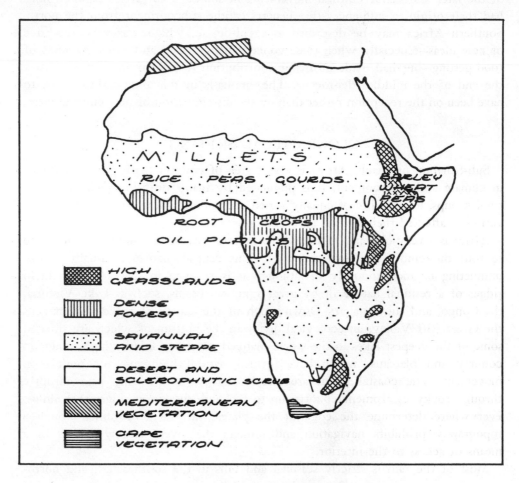

FIGURE 1. Simplified vegetative patterns and main
indigenous plant crops of Africa.
(*After Schnell, 1957*)

There are five main vegetation types (Fig. 1) that have determined human
cultural specialization (C.S.A., n.d.):

1. Lowland, evergreen rain forest in the western half of our region between
10° north and 10° south of the equator. This is dependent on a high and fairly
evenly distributed rainfall and on fairly high temperatures. The rain forest is
best seen in western Africa and the Congo basin, but eastward and southward it
fingers out along the main river valleys in the form of gallery forest separated
by open grasslands.

2. Deciduous woodland savanna, which is very variable in thickness from grass
to open forest and covers the greater part of the subcontinent to the north,
south, and east of the rain forest at altitudes from sea level up to about 5,000

feet. It is characterized by a long dry season and for the most part a semiarid type of rainfall with cool temperatures during the dry season, when surface water may be difficult to come by.

3. Open grasslands in eastern and southeastern Africa and on either side of the Rift Valley are to be found alternating, in the higher parts, with stretches of evergreen montane forest. Such grasslands usually occur at altitudes of over 5,000 feet; the two most extensive regions of this kind are the Abyssinian and east-African plateaus, which lend themselves to the cultivation of cereal crops.

4. Semidesert and true desert occur in western and central Africa north of the savanna and form the southern border of the Sahara. Eastward, in the Horn, the Somalilands are covered by a semiarid sand and rock vegetation that has rendered this region favorable for pastoralists but not for agriculturalists. In the southwestern parts of the continent is found the Kalahari—not a true desert, since much of it is covered by thornbush, but with little permanent surface water. On the southwest coast itself, however, true desert conditions have existed since very early times.

5. All the regions described above have summer rains, but in the extreme south the country between the coast and the Great Escarpment experiences winter rains that give the southwestern parts of Cape Province a Mediterranean type of climate. This region is considered to have formed an important "retreat area" for man when climatic change rendered the semiarid regions to the north too unattractive for permanent settlement.

In the tropical savanna and forest human and animal disease has been a limiting factor to cultural development above the simple, mixed farming level, and the thick vegetation and inadequate methods of transport have generally been further hindrances to the growth of urban centers.

Indigenous economies today are still dictated fairly closely by this pattern of environment. Thus the rain forest supports both sedentary peasant agriculturalists and hunter-collectors; deserts and semideserts support hunter-collectors and pastoral peoples, either fully or seminomadic; in the savanna mainly shifting agriculturalists or mixed farmers are found; in the grasslands live mixed farmers—again in semipermanent settlements—or seminomadic pastoral peoples (Schnell, 1957; pp. 68–73). This pattern is already foreshadowed in later Pleistocene times in the economies of the hunting-collecting peoples (Fig. 2).

In later prehistoric times two "nuclear areas" may be distinguished in sub-Sarahan Africa. The one is the Congo basin northward to Lake Chad; the other is the Abyssinian and east-African high plateaus. To the north both these regions were in contact with influences coming up the Nile. In each, cultural development followed different lines of specialization, and, from both, easy migration routes lead southward to the southern African plateau. However, southern Africa is so rich in natural food resources—in game and wild vegetable foods—that hunting and collecting have always formed a very important part of the economic life of the indigenous populations. Thus there was never complete dependence on stock-raising or agriculture, probably also because, in the one case, the prevalence of the tsetse fly and rinderpest disease and, in the other, the generally poor soils and uncertain rainfall, which usually restricted agricultural practices to the slash-and-burn level, rendered any overspecialization too uncertain or impracticable. It is important to appreciate this in order to understand why greater specialization and more intensive methods of farming did not evolve.

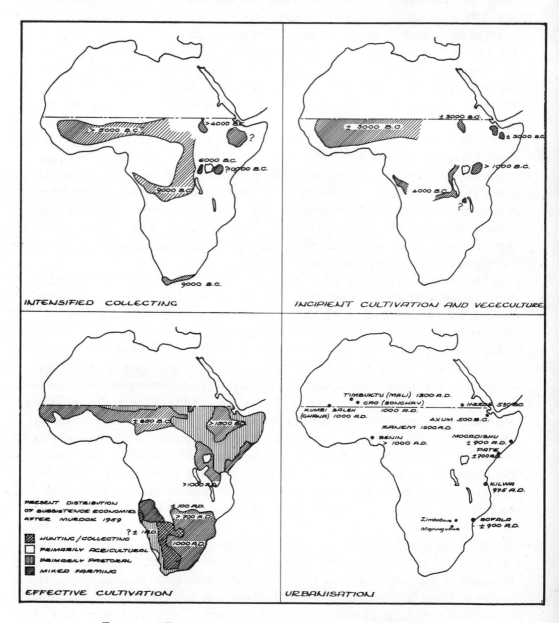

FIGURE 2. The distribution and chronology of early subsistence economies and urbanization in sub-Saharan Africa.

SPECIALIZED AND UNSPECIALIZED HUNTER-COLLECTORS OF THE FINAL PLEISTOCENE

About 15,000 B.C. the cooler temperatures and increased rainfall of the last maximum of the Gamblian pluvial were beginning to be superseded, and the resulting decline must have been reflected in a deterioration of the vegetation pattern as well as in the shrinking of water resources in some of the drier parts of the continent (Korn and Martin, 1957, p. 19; Wayland, 1954, pp. 30, 39; Clark, 1954, p. 149). The rainfall would probably have been about a third as much again as the present mean in and around 15,000 B.C. and probably a similar amount less during the height of the dry period (Bond, 1957, pp. 50–54; Flint, 1959, p. 370), which seems to lie between about 10,000 and 8,000 B.C. (Clark, in press).

Archeological knowledge of human economies at the end of the Pleistocene is based largely on the associated fauna and on the interpretation of the stone equipment, since perishable remains have so seldom been preserved. That the people of these times had leisure to develop their intellectual interests is apparent from the existence of an aesthetic sense, which is seen in the fine craftsmanship exhibited by many of the tools and by the use of ornaments. It is probable also that magicoreligious beliefs had become established, as evidenced, for example, in the existence of pigment for painting and in intentional burial. Moreover, it may be estimated that, in the grasslands and semiarid bush country, larger groupings became possible, if the great number and extent of the sites there is an acceptable indication in a continent where soil erosion is the archeologist's best friend (e.g., Summers and Cooke, 1960, p. 27 and Map 2).

By the last Gamblian maximum (*ca.* 17,000–10,000 B.C.) it would seem that modern man had everywhere replaced the paleoanthropic forms and, with one exception, was practicing a form of evolved middle stone age culture, based on the prepared core and faceted flake and on pressure and controlled percussion flaking for the secondary work. These cultures were widely but locally specialized, so that a number of "regional variants" are distinguishable, which take their pattern from the environment in which they develop. All these people were food-collectors, but there is evidence for believing that, in some cases, the collecting was of the intensified form that has been observed in other parts of the world (e.g., Magdalenian, Hamburgian). If the premise is sound that, the more particular and specialized the food resources of a group, the more specialized the material and technical products of their society, then the most specialized utilization of food resources in our area at this time is to be found, on the one hand, in the gallery forest of Equatoria and, on the other, in the open grasslands, where can be seen intensification of settlement around lakes and rivers and on the seacoasts in the temperate region of the south.

Thus we find semipermanent settlement in caves and rock shelters and a greater concentration of open station sites in favored localities yielding a variously specialized hunting and collecting equipment.

In the arid country of the Horn the emphasis must have been on hunting, as indicated in the Somaliland Stillbay (Clark, 1954, pp. 190–203) by the greater number of and greater specialization in projectile points and knives. In other respects, however, the desert cultures of these times—southwestern Africa or the Kalahari (Fock, 1959, p. 14; Clark, 1959a, p. 41), for example—are less specialized and have few characteristics that distinguish them, unless it be the general absence of pounding or grinding equipment.

In the savanna regions there is evidence of more continuous and more frequent occupation of cave sites and the accumulation of some depth of deposits belonging to these times. The food resources seem to have been more variable, since, besides specialization in projectile and cutting equipment, certain scraping, pounding, and grinding equipment occurs, which suggests that vegetable foods assumed some importance. Such, for example, are the cultural assemblages at Mumbwa (Clark, 1942, pp. 181–83) and Bambata (Armstrong, 1931, pp. 239–75; Jones, 1940, pp. 11–28) in Rhodesia, or Mwulu's Cave (Tobias, 1949, p. 8) in the northern Transvaal.

In the grassland and open savanna cultures the emphasis seems to have been on hunting, and collective hunting at that. If one can judge from the, so to speak, "repetitive" nature of the faunal remains, these groups must have relied for their meat exclusively on some two or three antelope species, zebra and pig (e.g., Twin Rivers, Northern Rhodesia [H. B. S. Cooke, n.d.]; Vlakkraal, O.F.S. [Wells, Cooke and Malan, 1942, pp. 214–32]; Kalkbank, Transvaal [Mason, Dart, and Kitching, 1958]). Although no fauna was present, the remarkable specialization in triangular bifacial points by the later middle stone age group that inhabited the Gorgora rock shelter, at the north end of Lake Tana in Abyssinia (L. S. B. Leakey, 1943, pp. 199–203) indicates that this specialized form was surely dictated by an equally specialized hunting technique. A similar interpretation is suggested by the faunal assemblages from the open sites on the south-African high veld and central-African savanna—for example, Vlaakkraal, Kuruman (Malan and Wells, 1943, pp. 263–70), Katontwe (Anciaux de Faveaux, 1957, pp. 100–01), Twin Rivers, etc.

In the forest and closed savanna, on the other hand, the quantity of woodworking tools suggests a possible emphasis on vegetable foods and perhaps trapping or on more personal hunting by individuals or small groups. Settlement seems to have been concentrated here not in the equatorial rain forest proper, but in the peripheral areas where gallery forest in the valleys alternated with grassland and savanna on the interfluves as in northeast Angola and the Bas-Congo. The restriction of the lowland forest at this time seems to have been due to the cooler temperatures of the later Pleistocene, which may have represented a drop of as much as 5° C. and which permitted the evergreen montane forest to form continuous corridors and to move down some 1,000 feet or more lower than it is found today (Flint, 1959, p. 362). Thus the peoples responsible for the Lupemban culture (note new terminology in Clark, 1959b, pp. 155–58) of the Congo basin lived, on the one hand, from the forest, as evidenced by the great preponderance of chopping and pounding tools, and, on the other hand, from the grasslands, since the highly developed bifacial projectile points stress the importance of meat in their diet and a well-organized hunting machinery. On this basis one may see the Lupemban forest culture or the Stillbay of the Horn, Kenya, and southern Africa as examples of the more specialized economies that can be distinguished at this time. All these regional variants were autochthonous growths from an earlier middle stone age ancestry, but usually part of their nature can be ascribed to external influences.

There was, however, a true blade culture—the Kenya Capsian—present in the grasslands of the eastern Rift during the closing stages of the Pleistocene, and it is claimed that it was established there a good deal earlier. That it is intrusive south of the Sahara—as also in the continent itself—can scarcely be doubted, though the source from which it came is harder to determine. The nature of its stone industry, based on obsidian with numbers of backed blades of Chatel-perron-type, microliths, the presence of a very little pottery, a bone industry including the harpoon, and ornaments of shell suggest that the form represented in the type site at Gamble's Cave in the Nakuru basin (L. S. B. Leakey, 1931, pp. 90–109) can hardly be as old as the tenth millennium B.C. and is most likely to be contemporary with the so-called Khartoum mesolithic, though it is possible that its earlier stages may be as old as 15,000 B.C.

Perhaps one may see in the Kenya Capsian a southern movement, parallel to the Dabba culture of Cyrenaica, which may have entered Africa from south-western Asia about 15,000 B.C. (McBurney, 1960, p. 225) and which reached the Kenya highlands, and perhaps also Abyssinia, via the eastern desert and the Red Sea hills. The nature of its material products and its restricted distribution show that it was as highly selective as collecting groups can be in its choice of environment and that it depended upon an economy based on hunting and fishing (Cole, 1958, pp. 47–51).[1] It is associated with a proto-Hamitic, longheaded, long-faced, physical stock (L. S. B. Leakey, 1935, pp. 47–56), which also seems to be intrusive into the continent, contrasting markedly with the Boskopoid and Australoid forms that are found with the middle stone age cultures south of the Sahara (Clark, 1959b, pp. 88–93).

About 9000–10,000 B.C. (Clark, 1959b) the desiccation that ended the Pleisto-cene had set in, and the stone industries of the final middle stone age underwent fundamental changes. Middle stone age technology began in many places to give place to industries having as their object the production of small and micro-lithic backed blades and lunates; by later stone age times boneworking had been extensively developed, objects of bone, stone, and shell for personal adornment had become abundant, and new techniques for piercing and grinding stone had been introduced. The period of transition evidenced by the various Magosian-type industries, which combine both middle and later stone age technical forms,

---

1. A butt end and central fragment of two bone harpoons, with a single row of barbs similar to forms found with the Early Khartoum and Khartoum Neolithic industries, have also been recovered with the upper Kenya Capsian Phase A from Gamble's Cave.

seems to have lasted from about 9000 to 6000 B.C. and may be termed "the microlithic revolution," for by the end of that time human culture in the sub-continent had entered the later stone age.

The microlithic techniques practiced in sub-Saharan Africa were of three main kinds. First, there were true microblade industries in the highlands of eastern Africa based on the microburin technique and directly evolved, no doubt, from the Kenya Capsian (Cole, 1954, p. 192). Second, a microflake or flake-blade technique (Lowe, 1945, pp. 240–46) based on small, often flat, cores with a platform at one or both ends developed out of the final middle stone age cultures in most other parts except in the high veld of southern Africa, where the existence of indurated shale resulted in the special persistence of macrolithic forms (Goodwin and Lowe, 1929, pp. 151–234). Third, in the equatorial regions microliths of "petit tranchet" type were made from broken sections of macro- and microflakes struck from biconical-type cores. This diversity of technique suggests that it was the idea of "microlithicness" and the improved food-getting efficiency that it represented, rather than any extensive population movement, that was mainly responsible, with ecological pressure, for the changed industrial forms.

There is reason to believe that the climatic deterioration was responsible for a general withdrawal and concentration in certain areas favorable for settlement by reason of the permanent water, since the sites of these times are never as numerous as are those of the preceding and succeeding periods, except in the forest regions. This natural restriction of movement must have resulted in greater specialization in collecting and hunting habits, though this cannot yet be proved. Certainly, however, it seems to have prepared the way for the more intensive collecting habits of the later stone age. In the equatorial forest region, however, the larger extent of the settlements, especially in northeastern Angola and the Congo; the many forms of projectile points (including serrated types); the introduction of tanged and winged points and of the punch technique and pressure flaking; and the evidence of wear, in the form of fine striations, smoothing, and incipient polishing of the working edges, as seen on bifacial adzes, gouges, and chisels, all indicate that the populations of these regions were now able to take greater care in the preparation of their tools and that they could develop special forms for special purposes and use many of these continually, on the sites where they were made, until the tools became too blunt, thus implying that the habitation sites were certainly semipermanent.[2]

These transitional industries in the savanna and grasslands—the regional Magosians—are also, however, associated in some cases with new racial characteristics in southern Africa (Clark, 1959b, pp. 89–92). This suggests that at least some population movement was taking place at that time. It may be supposed that such movements, whether they comprised migration of groups or contacts

2. Unpublished results of field work undertaken in northeastern Angola on behalf of the Companhia de Diamantes de Angola in 1959 and 1960.

only, were instrumental in introducing new techniques and new kinds of tools and weapons. Because of their superiority over the traditional forms, these innovations were absorbed to varying degree from region to region. The use of the composite tool and the barbed projectile point, whether for spear or for bow and arrow, had very considerable advantages, which the indigenous populations cannot have been slow to appreciate. It is possible, but improbable, that this blade and microflake element was diffused to southern and western Africa solely from the Kenya Capsian of the east-African highlands since the more or less simultaneous appearance of other cultural forms, not represented in the Kenya Capsian, shows that other influences were at work here. For example, the tanged, shanked, and hollow-based forms of point or the bored stone,[3] occurring in specific but widely separated associations, suggest the likelihood of northwestern African influences having been in part responsible also for the introduction of these new techniques and forms south of the Sahara.

At the time these northern influences began to make themselves felt in southern Africa, during the drier climate that marks the end of Pleistocene times, sub-Saharan Africa was still in a food-collecting stage of culture. However, by the time of the last major desiccation of the Sahara in the first and second millennia B.C. we can distinguish, besides the food-collectors, other groups at a probable vegecultural stage of development and still others practicing incipient agriculture with domestication of animals.

THE CHANGE-OVER FROM FOOD-COLLECTING

1. THE NORTHERN DRY BELT

Sometime, probably beginning in the seventh millennium B.C., there was a gradual change of climate and an increase in rainfall over the Sahara and subcontinent (the Sahara wet phase: the Makalian wet phase of eastern and south Africa). Paleobotanical evidence shows that a typical Mediterranean flora was established in several parts of the desert (Bakker, 1960). This resulted in a readjustment of the vegetation belts, and peoples from the north and south were able to move into the desert. Cultural elements from the Congo basin and western Africa were able to carry the bifacial technique to the north into the Sahara and to the Nile at Khartoum. Immediately prior to that time the Sahara would appear to have been quite unpopulated (McBurney, 1960, p. 273). Evidence for northward movement from this nuclear area can be seen in the bifacial projectile points and axes; in the crescent adze-flake and the "petit tranchet" arrowhead; in the representations of Negroid peoples in the rock paintings and engravings in the Hoggar (Lhote, 1958, pp. 89, 179) and Fezzan (Mori, 1960); in the presence of fossil remains of Negroids at Early Khartoum (Arkell, 1949a, pp. 31–33), at Asselar (Boule and Vallois, 1946, pp. 455–58) north of Timbuctoo,

3. Bored stones have been found in stratified association with Magosian industries at the type-site of Magosi in northeastern Uganda, at the Kalambo Falls in Northern Rhodesia, and at Khami, Southern Rhodesia.

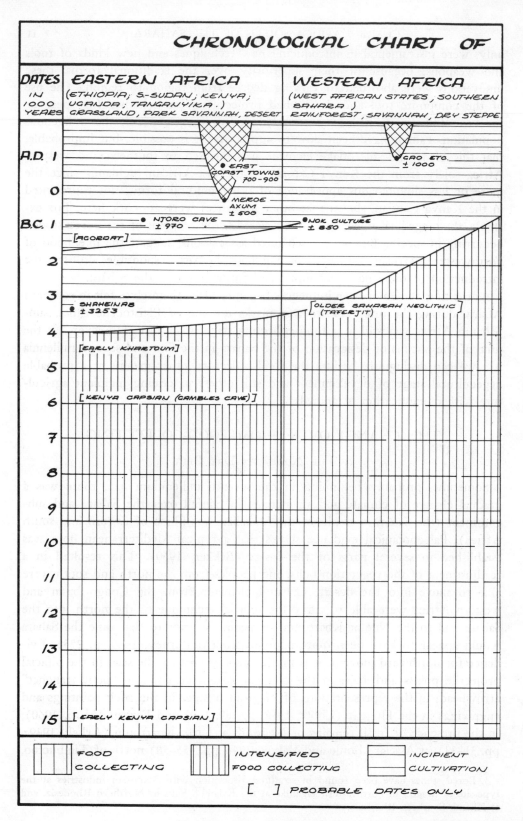

FIGURE 3. This chronological chart is an attempt to show the relationships between regional distribution and the times when major economic changes took place in sub

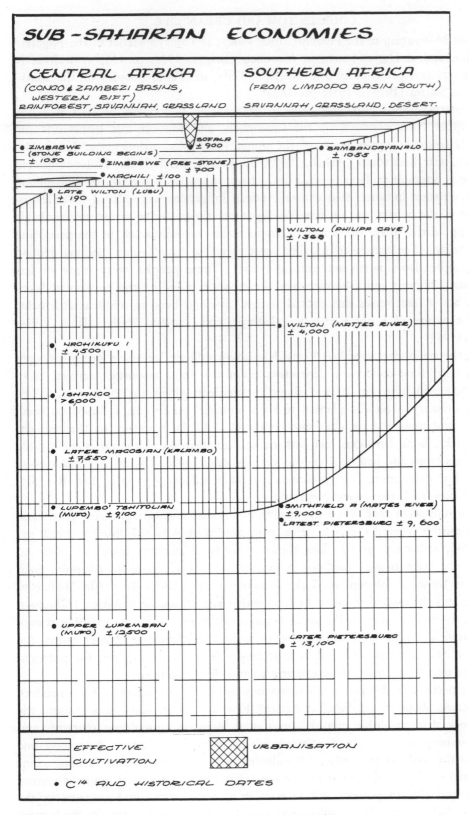

SUB-SAHARAN ECONOMIES

CENTRAL AFRICA (CONGO & ZAMBEZI BASINS, WESTERN RIFT) RAINFOREST, SAVANNAH, GRASSLAND	SOUTHERN AFRICA (FROM LIMPOPO BASIN SOUTH) SAVANNAH, GRASSLAND, DESERT.

● ZIMBABWE (STONE BUILDING BEGINS) ± 1050
● SOFALA ± 900
● ZIMBABWE (PRE-STONE) ± 700
● MACHILI ± 100
● LATE WILTON (LUBU) ± 190

● BAMBANDYANALO ± 1055

● WILTON (PHILIPP CAVE) ± 1368

● WILTON (MATJES RIVER) ± 4,000

● NACHIKUFU I ± 4,500

● ISHANGO ≻6,000

● LATER MAGOSIAN (KALAMBO) ± 7,550

● LUPEMBO' TSHITOLIAN (MUFO) ± 9,100

● SMITHFIELD A (MATJES RIVER) ± 9,000
● LATEST PIETERSBURG ± 9,600

● UPPER LUPEMBAN (MUFO) ± 12,500

● LATER PIETERSBURG ± 13,100

[legend:] EFFECTIVE CULTIVATION   URBANISATION

● C¹⁴ AND HISTORICAL DATES

Saharan Africa. It must be remembered, however, that older subsistence patterns persisted in symbiosis with more evolved forms for long periods and still do today.

at Uan Muhuggiag in the Fezzan (Mori, 1960), at Tamaya Mellet in the Nigerian Sahara, and at Dar-es-Soltan in Morocco (Briggs, 1958, p. 13); as well as in the continued presence of the Negroid Teda, or Tebu, peoples of the south-eastern Sahara (Briggs, 1958, pp. 162–63).

That there must also have been an even earlier movement, at least as far as the upper Nile, is shown by the Lupemban- and Sangoan-like lanceheads and chisels from the upper levels of the upper Pleistocene sediments at Khor Abu Angar, near Khartoum (Arkell, 1949b, pp. 9, 23). Though the evidence quoted above is referable to later times, mainly from the sixth to the fourth millennium, it nevertheless indicates that central-African influences were already well established in the Sahara and on the Nile by those times, and it is not unreasonable to suppose that these influences began to make themselves felt in the preceding millennium. The Sahara at this time must therefore have been a meeting ground for peoples from north and central Africa. These peoples were more or less sedentary hunters and fishermen who were concentrated on the permanent lakes, pans, and watercourses that existed at that time and lived in midden settlements of the nature of Early Khartoum, Taferjit, and Tamaya Mellet (Kelly, 1934, pp. 135–43).

In the mesolithic so-called Early Khartoum culture we see a group of very specialized food-collectors, dependent upon the food resources derived from the Nile and living in large "village" settlements along the river banks. The stone industry, which is adapted to both hunting and fishing, is based on small blades and tools and includes some microliths and large crescents, the crescent adze-flake, bone harpoons, net sinkers, and grindstones. Although these people grew no crops and had no domestic animals, their pottery, with its characteristic wavy-line decoration, is a good indicator of a sedentary type of life. Racially, as has been said, they were Negroids.

It would seem that when the neolithic traits of cultivating cereal crops and stock-raising entered the Nile delta from southwest Asia (McBurney, 1960, pp. 230–44), sedentary groups like those at Early Khartoum were not slow to adopt the revolutionary methods of insuring a more adequate food supply. Such sites as those of Ishango on Lake Edward in the Albert Rift (de Heinzelin, 1957) and the coastal middens of the south coast of southern Africa (Goodwin et al., 1938; Hoffman, 1958) again emphasize the great importance of a water-side milieu in the establishment of permanent settlements in later stone age ("mesolithic") times, and in thus providing a favorable setting for the potential change-over from intensive collecting to full domestication.

Is it possible to determine when and how incipient and effective food production came about in sub-Saharan Africa? Few would probably now dispute the evidence that "neolithic culture"—insofar as incipient agricultural practices and stock-raising are concerned—entered Africa from southwestern Asia sometime late in the sixth or the early fifth millennium B.C. Simple peasant farming communities of Fayum A type occupied the valley of the lower Nile and the eastern oases, and Fayum pottery and bifacial stone tools occur in Cyrenaica in the second half of the fifth millennium B.C., but only much later—in the fourth millennium B.C.—is their influence seen in the Sudan and upper Nile. This seems to exclude Abyssinia as having been the initial center from which food production spread in Africa.

Though it cannot be disputed—both because of the radiocarbon determinations and because no wild wheat is known in Africa—that the wheat cultivation of the earliest agriculturalists in the Nile delta can be derived only from southwestern Asia, and also that the same is true of the domesticated sheep and goat of those times, it is not quite so certain that there may not have been a second center of cattle domestication somewhere in northern Africa. A potential domesticate, *Bos opisthonomus*, existed in northern Africa, and C[14] determinations for Saharan neolithic industries from Tassili, claimed to be associated with the "bovidienne" style of rock paintings, give dates in the mid-third and mid-fourth millennia B.C.,[4] while dates fom Uan Muhuggiag in the Fezzan show that related styles representing domesticated cattle can be ascribed to the mid-fourth and mid-sixth millennia B.C.[5] If the latter date is confirmed, an independent African source for domestic long-horned cattle may be a probability. Indeed, typically African rock engravings showing cattle exist at Kilwa in southern Transjordan and may indicate a first stage of animal domestication coming from Africa, but the age of these engravings is as yet unknown (Perrot, this volume).

Although remains of *Bos* have been recorded from the prepottery neolithic levels at Jericho, it is not yet possible to say whether these are of the domesticated form (Kenyon, personal communication). It would seem that the earliest occurrence of undoubtedly domesticated *Bos* in southern Palestine is with the Ghassulian at Beersheba in an early fourth-millennium context (Perrot, this volume).

That the change to food-producing was a very slow and gradual process— not a sudden and revolutionary one—is well shown at another Khartoum settlement, the neolithic site of Shaheinab. These people were still hunters and fishers, but they now relied also on a small species of domestic goat. The pottery and stone industries show, on the one hand, associations with the mesolithic of the Early Khartoum site and, on the other, associations with the lower Nile neolithic cultures—the Tasian and Badarian. This is evidenced by the polished axes of stone and bone, the pyriform maceheads, and the characteristic gouges and adzes (Arkell, 1953). The Shaheinab C[14] determinations (average) of 3253 ± 415 B.C. for the Khartoum neolithic confirms that its cultural innovations can have come only from the north and not from the Abyssinian plateau. This date also provides an indication of the time taken for cultural influences from Lower Egypt to reach the Sudan, as well as a lower limit when they may be expected to appear in sub-Saharan Africa.

4. Results obtained from charcoal recovered in two different rock shelters at Jabbaren give determinations of 3500 B.C. and 2550 B.C. (H. Lhote, personal communication).

5. Charcoal from two horizons in a rock shelter at Uan Muhuggiag in the Acacus Mountains, western Fezzan, give determinations of 3500 B.C. (associated in the upper layer with the desiccated burial of a Negroid child) and 5500 B.C. The associated industries in each case are presumably of Saharan neolithic form (Mori, 1960).

So-called neolithic industries have been found in many parts of the central and eastern Sahara. There can be no doubt that the people who made them were living at a time when there was a substantial improvement in climatic conditions in the desert. From the few radiocarbon determinations now available it would seem reasonable to equate the main "neolithic" occupation with the warmer and wetter Atlantic period of Europe (5500–2500 B.C.). It is not easy to assess whether these industries were truly neolithic in the economic sense of being food-producing; the presence of various forms of pressure-flaked arrowheads, pottery, and small grindstones[6] are not in themselves sufficient to warrant such a deduction. In any case, it is likely that the communities still obtained most of their meat supply by hunting. However, the industry at the central Saharan lake or pan of Taferjit includes bone harpoons of Khartoum neolithic type, deep concave-based arrowheads of Fayum A type, and a large, double-bladed axe or macehead similar to those on the predynastic Egyptian Lion Hunt Palette. This thus shows that the neolithic culture of the Nile must have spread widely during the optimum climatic conditions in the desert. Such spreading is hardly likely to have come about in the southern Sahara earlier than the fourth millennium B.C.—and perhaps was considerably later—but in this connection the sixth-millennium date from Uan Muhuggiag must not be forgotten.

The various Egyptian and Lybian influences in the cattle paintings that can be seen in the central and northern Saharan art groups are associated with the later Saharan neolithic industries, and McBurney has suggested that they cannot be any earlier than the middle of the first millennium B.C. The later Saharan groups lived by cattle-raising, but the numerous quernstones and rubbers that are found on many of these later Saharan sites, as well as on those of Khartoum neolithic form, and the claim that some of the Tassili paintings depict reaping scenes suggest that some kind of incipient cultivation was being practiced at this time in the desert.

Mauny (1951, p. 83) has recognized a later neolithic with a marked Egyptian influence that was contemporary with a drying climate, and an earlier neolithic with bone harpoons and hollow-based arrowheads that belongs with a wet phase. On the Khartoum neolithic dating the latter cannot be older than the fourth millennium B.C., but the Tassili and Fezzan dates suggest that it extends back at least into the fifth millennium.

2. The East African Desert and High Plateau

Hollow-based arrowheads and other old Saharan forms make their appearance in the drier parts of the Horn of Africa during a wet phase in post-Pleistocene times (Clark, 1954, pp. 203–82), and, if the dates for the earlier Saharan neo-

6. Grindstones, rubbers, and pounders are, of course, known in association with the cultures of the later Pleistocene in sub-Saharan Africa (e.g., Mwulu's Cave, Transvaal; Kalkbank, Transvaal; Kalambo Falls, Northern Rhodesia; etc.), but the forms are essentially of the kind found in use today for working *wild* vegetable foods. The stones associated with grinding cereal crops are all of the saddle and dish quern form. The grindstones associated with the Kenya stone-bowl cultures are flat with shallow dishing.

lithic are confirmed, it may be that the spread of neolithic forms in the Horn is also of fifth-millennium date—though it may well be later. In the Horn, however, there is no indication as yet from these sites that any form of cultivation (quernstones are quite absent) or domestication of animals was practiced, and they are still small settlements of hunter-collectors concentrated round the pans and water holes.

There are, however, indications that influence, which stemmed ultimately from incipient food-producers, may have penetrated the Somalilands and, we may suppose, also to the Abyssinian plateau as early as the fourth millennium B.C. Unfortunately, almost nothing is known of the prehistoric cultures of Abyssinia. Middle stone age cultures gave place at some unspecified post-Pleistocene time to industries such as that from Quiha (Clark, 1954, p. 324) in the Tigre, where long blades and microliths in obsidian are associated with burnished pottery. The blades of this industry resemble the food-collecting Elmenteitan culture of Kenya and the blades associated with the Omerdin industry in eastern Abyssinia (Breuil, et al., 1951, p. 230). As yet, however, there is nothing to show that the Quiha people were anything more than sedentary food-collectors.

Finds of polished axes and adzes, maceheads, stone palettes, and pottery having affinities with the so-called C group culture of Nubia have been described from Agordat in Eritrea (Arkell, 1954) and would seem to be the products of a sedentary and fully agricultural economy. Arkell has suggested a date in the earlier to the middle part of the second millennium B.C. for these assemblages, but with the proviso that they may well be later. Polished axes and adzes have been found also in western Abyssinia on the Tuli Kapi plateau and at Iubdo in Wollega District (M. D. Leakey, 1943, p. 193), but until research on a proper basis is undertaken there, it would be idle to speculate as to when food-producers entered Ethiopia. Paintings, which are themselves late and associated with impoverished microlithic industries in rock shelters in the Somalilands, all show long-horned cattle and pastoral peoples (Clark, 1954, pp. 295–315). These paintings are believed to date to a time before the Christian Era, since the zebu cattle are not represented. Zebu cattle were probably introduced to the Horn from southern Arabia at about that time and are now the only form found in Ethiopia; the suggestion (Naville, 1898) that zebu cattle were introduced to Egypt from Punt (the Horn) during the eighteenth to nineteenth dynasties (1580–1205 B.C.) is not borne out by an examination of the bas-reliefs depicting the Punt cattle.

In the Horn, therefore, specialized hunting groups showing Saharan connections may have been present as early as the fifth millennium and persisted until historic times. In the later stages, they appear to have lived contemporaneously with pastoral—probably Hamitic—peoples showing connections with the Saharan cattle-breeders; as yet this latter group is known only from the paintings, and their connections are obscure. It is not impossible that these hunting groups in the Horn may have acquired their cattle at much the same time as did those in the Sahara, but it seems more likely that the stock-owners entered sometime before the middle of the second millennium B.C., when increasing desiccation dictated the dispersal of population from the central Sahara region.

Peoples living in permanent, semisubterranean houses, practicing ceremonial group burial, and with other traits indicative of a settled food-producing community, were living in the grasslands of the Kenya Rift valley and in northern Tanganyika during the first millennium and certainly earlier (M. D. Leakey, 1945; M. D. and L. S. B. Leakey, 1950). They had domestic cattle and sheep, but, while they made pottery, there is no conclusive evidence as yet of plant cultivation, though it may be suspected from the grinding and mulling equipment. The microlithic and flaked-stone element remains much the same as it was in mesolithic times but is somewhat more impoverished by the falling-out of certain microlithic forms, and this points to the use of some other food source in addition to hunting. Their most characteristic piece of equipment is a shallow stone bowl of lava, sometimes with carbonaceous matter adhering to the inside, which was used, probably—since it is likely to have been of a utilitarian rather than a ceremonial nature—for cooking or roasting. It is suggested that whatever it was that was roasted in the bowls formed part of the staple food of this neolithic "stone-bowl culture," as it has been called. From the pestle stones that very often accompany the bowls, this food would seem to have been pounded before it was used. The stone-bowl cultures are believed to have evolved from the Elmenteitan and the Kenya Capsian (Cole, 1954, pp. 228, 237).

These people were longheaded Hamites, and at least three variants of their culture are known (Cole, 1954, pp. 227–46). The distribution has been only imperfectly established, but the culture occurs on the Kenya high plateau and in the Rift valley and extends certainly as far south as northern Tanganyika. Until it proves possible to determine whether these people planted cereal crops, one can go no further than to say that there is good reason to suppose that the stone-bowl peoples practiced some form of cereal cultivation—probably based on *Eleusine coracana* and other millets—owned domestic stock, and lived in small family groups, but were only semisedentary in their habits and indulged in not a little hunting and gathering. These details we can learn from the Njoro River Cave and Hyrax Hill sites, the former (a late form) giving a C[14] determination of approximately 970 B.C. (L. S. B. Leakey, 1956, p. 28). The remarkable beads of semiprecious stones, bone spacer beads, and some of the polished-stone axe forms (M. D. Leakey, 1943, p. 190) associated with the Kenya stone-bowl cultures point to connections with the Sudan, while the number of workings for bead stone indicate that the bead-making industry was of considerable extent. Such an industry could hardly have been carried on by a people who had advanced no further than the food-collecting level.

That these neolithic stone-bowl cultures continued in some places until quite late times is indicated, however, by the possible occurrence of zebu cattle with the Gumban B variant at Hyrax Hill North-East Village (M. D. Leakey, 1945, p. 365). The continuation is also indicated by the earthwork-protected Lanet site, which is as late as the end of the sixteenth century A.D.[7] and shows, besides

7. C[14] determination of 375 ± 100 years. Posnansky, 1961, p. 186.

the extremely conservative nature of the cultural forms, a contemporaneity with potentially hostile iron age peoples.

It may be suspected, therefore, that neolithic influences from the Sudan penetrated to eastern Africa (probably via Abyssinia) sometime after the beginning of the third millennium B.C. These influences (like those of the Kenya Capsian and Elmenteitan peoples before them) seem to have been restricted to the high grasslands, where the potential for mixed farming was greatest, though pastoral nomads were established in the semiarid parts of the Horn before the end of the first millennium B.C.

Vavilov (1931) has suggested that the Abyssinian high plateau may have been the place where millets and sorghums were first domesticated.[8] But, even if Vavilov's hypothesis is confirmed by archeological investigation, it would seem to be unlikely that the cultivation of the millets (*Eleusine, Pennisetum*) and sorghums can have arisen independently in Abyssinia, since such indirect evidence as is available at present—in particular from radiocarbon determination —indicates that it is much more likely that the use of millet followed the transmission of the basic discovery of plant cultivation in southwest Asia by a process of experiment and selection.

3. THE WEST AND CENTRAL AFRICAN FORESTS

In western Africa the later Sangoan and middle stone age cultures give place —though the intermediate industries are not differentiated—to later stone age cultures of local variation but all showing the same basic elements. These are a microlithic stone industry with many *petit tranchet* forms, flaked- and polished-stone axes and adzes, small grindstones and mullers, and pottery. Perhaps the best-known west coast forms are those from Bosumpra Cave in Ghana (Shaw, 1944), and the Grotte des Singes in Dahomey (Delcroix and Vaufrey, 1939) Recent work has distinguished an earlier and a later neolithic in Ghana and Nigeria: pottery belongs only with the latter (Davies, 1959; Willett, 1959).[9]

In the Congo basin essentially similar industries are found, but usually confined to the more open country peripheral to the rain forest proper. The best

8. This refers, of course, to the African millets *Pennisetum spicatum, Eleusine coracana*, and *Sorghum vulgare*, not to the Asiatic millets *Panicum* and *Setaria*. The latter formed the staple crop of neolithic China (see Chang, in this volume) and presupposes a domestication center independent of the African millets.

9. In Ghana, Davies has found two main neolithic variants: an older form with edge-ground axes, adzes, and hoes but no pottery, which was possibly derived from the northeast; and a later form, perhaps coming from the northwest, characterized by pottery of cardial and pseudo-cardial type and small neatly made celts. The Bosumpra industry belongs with the later stage (Davies, in press). In Nigeria, Willet has similarly found evidence of two neolithic variants, one with pottery and polished axes, e.g., at Rop (Fagg, 1944) and one without these forms as at Old Oyo (Willett, in press). The age of these west-African neolithic variants is as yet unknown. Davies associates both neolithic stages with a wet phase and suggests that the earlier may have commenced about 1300 B.C. There seems little doubt that the neolithic persisted until quite late times in the west-African forests—Davies suggests until the sixteen century A.D.

known are the northern tributaries' (Welle basin) industries (Grenade, 1910), and the Leopoldville and lower Congo forms (Mortelmans, 1957). Basically these industries appear to be those of hunters and collectors, but the "neolithic" elements, especially the stone hoe forms, seem to indicate that a more intensive type of collecting was being practiced here and that some groups had probably taken to cultivation of root crops and a settled village life. In the forest proper and many other parts of the south typical mesolithic-type collecting cultures still persisted.[10]

The more sedentary nature of the industries of the forest margins in terminal and early post-Pleistocene times suggests that exploitation of the food resources of the peripheral forest—such as the oil palm (*Elaeis guineensis*) and other oil-bearing plants, the wild yams (*Dioscorea* sp.), and perhaps *Aframomum*—enabled some of these groups to establish permanent camps and rendered them especially responsive to crop cultivation when influences from the neolithic cultures of northern Africa began to spread south of the Sahara. In fact it is not impossible, though this cannot yet be proved, that some of the mesolithic communities in the Guinea type of forest (e.g., the so-called "Guinea Tumbian" and some of the regional Tshitolian forms) may have already practiced incipient domestication of the wild yam and perhaps other indigenous root plants before a knowledge of cereal cultivation was diffused to western Africa. Certainly the edge-ground axes and adzes could have had a natural derivation from the flaked forms, smoothed and polished by continuous utilization, which are found first with the transitional Lupembo-Tshitolian industries in the tenth millennium B.C. Likewise, no drastic change in the material equipment would have been necessary to change the enonomy to a fully vegecultural level.

Murdock's (1959, p. 67) hypothesis that agriculture was invented independently in Negro Africa by ancestral Mande peoples around the headwaters of the Niger sometime before 4500 B.C., although based on linguistic evidence and a presumed distribution center for the main west African indigenous food crops, is not yet supported by archeological evidence. In fact, as outlined in the present paper, the archeological data point rather to the contrary's being the case, namely, that agriculture in western Africa resulted from experiment following the diffusion of ideas and techniques of crop cultivation from northern Africa, though based quite possibly on an already simple vegecultural level of subsistence.

At what date did the later stone age "neolithic" cultures of the Guinea-type forest and savanna come into being? There are no points of very close resemblance in the material culture with the earlier Saharan neolithic stage except in the bifacial stone element, and it is likely that the "neolithic" traits did not take

10. Purely microlithic industries with *petit tranchets* were noted by the writer at Mutongo near Masisi northwest of Lake Kivu; the Tshitolian of northeastern Angola and the lower Congo also shows no definite indication that the economy had passed out of the hunting-collecting stage.

full effect in the equatorial region until late in Saharan neolithic times, probably only after continued desiccation had driven some of the Saharan groups southward to seek new pasturage and new land for cultivation. It is probable, therefore, that their full effect was not felt before the second millennium B.C. The neolithic people of western Africa are unlikely to have been important stockowners except in the Sahel and Sudan belts, since forest and closed savanna country would not have proved attractive to stock-owning peoples (mainly on account of cattle diseases that would have rendered stock-raising impossible). The main equipment, as we have seen, consists of flaked and polished axes and adzes (some of which were certainly used as hoes), chisels and gouges of various kinds, microliths, grindstones, and pottery. The former tools are in great part the natural, autochthonous development from the percussion-flaked forms, but the latter two and the hoes suggest a more specialized crop production based probably on the millets (*Digitaria, Pennisetum,* and *Sorghum*) or, in Guinea, on *Oryza glaberrima* (Schnell, 1957, pp. 146–47).

The microlithic element shows these people to have done not a little hunting; the many axe forms may indicate a more determined attack on the forest margins by slash-and-burn methods than had ever been made before; while the pottery —occurring in considerable quantity—points to at least a semisedentary life. There is even evidence that these cultures persisted in places in the Cameroons and Congo until quite recent times, and the replacement of stone by iron may have come about as a result of later diffusion without any necessary change in population. Not a little traditional evidence exists to show that some of the so-called axe forms were used on the ends of digging sticks to break up new ground for cultivation, and in regions where iron was scarce these axe forms may have continued in use until quite late times, for example, in the lower Congo and in the Cameroons (Jeffreys, 1957, pp. 262–73).

The later development of the neolithic economy in west Africa is best seen in the so-called Nok Figurine culture of northern Nigeria, which clearly must have been organized on a simple village basis. The Nok culture extends over a wide area—at least 300 miles across the Niger/Benue valley—and is characterized by terra-cotta sculpture of a high artistic standard, polished-stone tools, and stone beads and bracelets (Fagg, 1955). The chronological limits of the culture are believed to fall between 900 B.C. and A.D. 200, and from the associated finds it can be shown that by the terminal period iron was being worked and was replacing stone for axes. Tin had also come into use. Unfortunately, the settlement pattern is not known, since the finds come from the lowest aggradation terraces in the valleys and are being exposed by modern tin-mining operations. The fluted gourd and one or two other crops, as well as hafted axes, are represented on figurines, and carbonized seeds of an oil-bearing tree (*atili*) have been found associated. It also seems probable that millet was cultivated (Willett, personal communication).

4. The Central-African Savanna and Southern African Grasslands

Until about the beginning of the Christian Era the rest of the subcontinent was occupied by locally adapted food-collecting cultures, such as are represented by the Smithfield and Wilton complexes, associated with a remarkable art tradition. Anyone seeing the naturalistic style of this art cannot but be convinced that the artists were hunters with an intimate knowledge of the animals and scenes they portrayed. The leisure they enjoyed in which to do these paintings and engravings bears witness to the specialized collecting habits of the artists. This leisure resulted from intensified collecting practices, the general abundance of game, and the concentration upon one or two animal forms (for instance, the eland and rhebuck by the Basutoland and Drakensberg Wilton and Smithfield C peoples).

The Bushman peoples preserve for us something of the collecting life of the later stone age groups in southern Africa. Dependent essentially on game, they lived in bands of varying size according to the richness or poverty of the resources of their territory. While the game herds were their chief source of food, they supplemented this with vegetable foods and sometimes with fish. Special circumstances permitted the strandlooping groups of the seacoasts to live in fairly permanent camps based on caves and rock shelters or middens in the coastal dunes. They fished with weirs, lines, and the spear; they collected shellfish and trapped and hunted game and were thus enabled to live a more or less sedentary life, interrupted only by a decline in the food supply or by death or disease that forced a move (Clark, 1959b, pp. 217–52). Specialized collecting groups, depending upon hunting, fishing, and shellfish-collecting, are also found around some of the lakes of eastern and central Africa during the later stone age. The people responsible for the Ishango culture on the shores of Lake Edward had developed a specialized fishing equipment based on the harpoon (de Heinzelin, 1957). Although the determination ascribed to them on extrapolated C^{14} evidence is early in the seventh millennium B.C., it is likely that they really belong, in fact, somewhat later and are related to the southern Saharan and upper Nile fishing communities of the early fourth or late fifth millennium. On the other hand, the shell mound Wilton C people of Lake Victoria are a later adaptation to strandlooping, and there is reason to believe that they were contemporary with more efficiently organized "neolithic" groups (L. S. B. Leakey, 1936, pp. 69, 71).

All these groups were never anything more than specialized food-collectors. As such, they persisted in many places, contemporaneously with pastoral and simple farming communities, up to the coming of the European.

The historic Hottentots of southwestern Africa were pastoralists having herds of sheep and zebu-type cattle, but they grew no crops and lived a life of pastoral nomads. There is some evidence to suggest that the pastoral way of life was introduced into southern Africa by a group of longheaded peoples from eastern

Africa, perhaps practicing one of the stone-bowl cultures.[11] At what date they arrived in southwestern Africa is not certainly known as yet, but it may be suggested that their advent there may have been brought about by the super-cession in eastern Africa of the neolithic stone-bowl peoples by iron-age Negroid groups, perhaps during the first millennium A.D.

In south-central, and perhaps also in central Africa (i.e., in Northern Rhodesia and Uganda) the naturalistic art tradition had by the fifth millennium B.C. been replaced, if indeed it had ever existed there in a pure form, by a schematic tradition. This suggests that certain changes had come about in the culture of the later stone age hunting-collecting groups there that could have been asso-ciated with the growing importance of a simple vegecultural economy.

The distribution of the bored stone in central and south-central Africa sug-gests that it may also sometimes accompany a vegecultural, perhaps in the more northern parts even an incipient agricultural, level of economy during later stone age times. It is widely distributed on the high watershed country in Rhodesia and Nyasaland, the high savanna in the Katanga, the high ridge country running west of the Rift Valley in the Congo, and the Sudan-type savanna in Nigeria and the Sudan. It is present in Abyssinia, in a recent context at least, for turning fresh land in millet cultivation (Clark, 1944, pp. 31–32), while the earliest evi-dence from C^{14} of its presence is in an early fifth-millennium context in North-ern Rhodesia (Clark, 1958). The central-African bored-stone forms, while they undoubtedly were put to many different uses, must have served most often as digging-stick weights, and it is by no means improbable that their particular distribution and later associations may be related to millet cultivation, possibly also to cultivation of the wild *Dioscoreas*. Its almost total absence from the neo-lithic and collecting cultures of the Kenya highlands and the Horn, as also from the west-African forest country (where the polished axe replaces it), is surely significant.

The context of the digging-stick weights with a microlithic culture is best seen in Northern Rhodesia, where they appear consistently earlier than the pol-ished axe and adze and continue in later associations with the polished axe until the end of stone age times. The Nachikufan culture, of which they form a part, there is adapted to savanna woodland and provides all the elements usual to a hunting people who rely to a considerable extent on vegetable foods, as evi-denced by the many grinders and mullers (Clark, 1950). Some of the latest Nachikufan peoples may even have cultivated wild root crops and some millet (*vide* Bemba tradition), but the bored stone in southern Africa proper is asso-ciated with food-collecting only.

11. Stone bowls have been found in the northern part of south-west Africa and in south-ern Bechuanaland, and the Kakamas physical type on the middle Orange River is most closely comparable with some of the east African mesolithic stock (Clark, 1959*b*, pp. 99–101, 282).

VILLAGE-FARMING COMMUNITIES AND
INCIPIENT URBANIZATION IN SOUTHERN AFRICA

While the neolithic "stone-bowl" peoples of the east African grasslands were organized in small open villages by at least the beginning of the first millennium B.C., it was not until the introduction of metalworking and mixed farming on a more intensive scale that the southern Africa savanna region supported true village-farming communities of a dispersed, rather than a concentrated, nature.

The earliest metal-users worked iron, and the earliest metalworking peoples in western Africa were Negroes, who presumably acquired the art from the Meroitic Kingdom of the upper Nile in the centuries immediately prior to the beginning of the Christian Era. In south-central Africa the first metalworkers seem to have been basically of the same stock as the Bush-Hottentot people but with Negroid admixture north of the Zambezi. They are believed to have been in Northern Rhodesia in the first century A.D. (Clark, 1959b, p. 311) and to have crossed the Zambezi before A.D. 700—since the site of Zimbabwe was occupied by that time (Summers, 1955; 1961, p. 13)—and the Limpopo by A.D. 1055 (Galloway, 1959, p. xi). They were communities of simple mixed farmers living in circular wattle-and-daub or grass huts, grouped, it is believed, in small open hamlets and villages. They worked iron and copper and also, where these metals occurred, tin and gold. By the tenth century A.D. there was a flourishing gold trade with Arabs at Kilwa and Sofala on the east coast.

It is probable that the knowledge of metalworking was introduced to southern Africa via the Horn, on the one hand, and across the Sahara to the Lake Chad region, on the other, about the beginning of the Christian Era—sometime between the last century B.C. and A.D. 500. These people were farmers and had long-horned cattle and fat-tailed sheep, but apparently not the goat, and are believed to have cultivated millets and sorghums. They made two characteristic forms of well-fired and decorated pottery—Stamped and Channeled wares (Summers, 1960). They depended very considerably on hunting for meat and, certainly, for their clothing also. Like some of their descendants today they seem to have been very loath to kill their stock, and, since the supply of wild meat was so plentiful, there was indeed no valid reason why they should do so except for religious purposes. The settlement sites of these people are not well known, but they seem to have lived in small open villages and sometimes to have used pits for food-storage purposes. The type of country in which they preferred to settle was the more semiarid parkland and grassland. No public or religious buildings existed, and their magicoreligious beliefs seem to have been of a simple animistic form with which clay figurines of a fertility nature are associated.

There can be no doubt in the case of the Channeled wares that their appearance in southern Africa represents a true population movement down the high country flanking the Rift valley from an original center of dispersal, perhaps in the southern Sudan or in Abyssinia. The origins of this ware in Rhodesia can be traced northward to the Katanga and Ruanda-Urundi to Kenya and Uganda, and it seems most probable that this distribution is connected with the tsetse free routes that this high country provided into the drier south African grasslands. It is not known what crops these people cultivated, but one was almost certainly millet (probably *Eleusine coracana*), and they practiced slash-and-burn methods on the forest margins in their gradual progress down the central highway to the south. If the open and higher country was more healthful for man and beast, the opposite was true for the main river valleys, which were generally avoided—except where the economically strategic and environmentally favorable open valleys, such as the Barotse valley on the upper Zambezi, encouraged settlement on mounds in flood plains.

That these people lived in harmony with the hunter-gathering peoples is attested by the general tranquillity of the rock art (Cooke, 1957) and the persistence of the collecting traditions. With the coming of the later iron age peoples, about the beginning of the fifteenth century, adaptation, integration, or annihilation of the hunting groups seems to have begun to take place or to have been speeded up. Later pottery elements and, in some cases, iron slag appear with the collecting cultures in the topmost layers in many of the rock shelters north of the Zambezi, and at the same time there is a marked degeneration in the stone industry, such as is always attendant upon fundamental changes in the economy. North of the Zambezi, at any rate, the evidence of the rock shelters suggests that some of the indigenous collecting peoples had effectively adapted their economy and turned to food-producing and metalworking by this time.

Very little archeological evidence is available for protohistoric times in sub-Saharan Africa, and the best-studied areas are Southern Rhodesia and in east Africa. More efficient methods of warfare, agriculture, and stock-raising were transmitted to the subcontinent during the first millennium A.D. No doubt this was due indirectly to the influence of the establishment of the Ghanian and later empires in western Africa under Meroitic influence and trans-Saharan trade and to the Himyaritic and Amharic empires in the Horn, which captured the maritime trade from the Indian Ocean through the Red Sea. It is now possible to see the Abyssinian highlands and the Congo basin as nuclear areas, so to speak, from which at various times migrations of peoples with more efficiently organized political systems and new cultural traits spread into souhtern Africa.

In the Congo, tribal groupings based on strong centralized authorities rose up and sank again into obscurity with surprising rapidity because of competition resulting from a kind of continual "hiving-off" process of groups moving eastward and southward in search of new land and new wealth. Such movements gave rise to the present-day later Bantu populations of East and South Africa. One movement originating probably from Ethiopia was instrumental in establishing the Zimbabwe-Monomatapa culture in Southern Rhodesia (Caton-Thompson, 1923; Wieschoff, 1941; Sommers, 1961).

The Zimbabwe culture was certainly one of the most highly organized of all the indigenous cultures in sub-Saharan Africa outside the west coast and Abyssinia. These people were warrior agriculturalists and mixed farmers living in large villages and building defensive and perhaps religious structures in stone. They were governed by a centralized political system and had more complex religious beliefs. It cannot, however, be doubted that they owed much of their development and prosperity to "exotic" influences from the east coast, and when these influences began to weaken we find that the Zimbabwe culture decayed and was overrun by later invaders. It was never a truly urbanized society in the strict sense of the term, since there is no indication that classes of professionals or a religious hierarchy, a centralized exchequer or public building programs, ever existed, but it must have come nearer to this form than any other southern African culture. It appears to have been stimulated by racial elements deriving from Ethiopia and the Congo basin, and certainly the later elements have their connections with the southern Congo, where it can be supposed that over-population and the limitation of cultivable land in this nuclear region were the main reasons for the tribal movements into the southeastern savanna (Walton, 1957).

CONCLUSIONS

During the closing stages of the Pleistocene and in early post-Pleistocene times the climatic events that took place between 10,000 and 6000 B.C. led to greater cultural specialization than ever before. There was a general concentration on one or more sources of food instead of on any and every available source, probably because first the desiccation and then, during the Makalian wet phase, the forest encroachment affected the distribution of game and generally limited the range of the hunting territory and the collecting potential.

In the gallery forest country of west-central Africa this concentration can be clearly demonstrated—larger areas of settlement, more specialized and more intensive utilization of the cultural equipment, and the use of two or three staple vegetable foods. Movement to the south African coasts and concentration for the first time on a shellfish diet rich in protein permitted the southern mountain peoples to live for long periods in the same place. That they still practiced transhumance cannot be doubted, especially in the earlier period, but the gradual decline in quanity of animal bones in the food debris and the preponderance of shellfish and later of fish remains shows that these groups could, by the end of the later stone age, have existed permanently from the seafoods available in the immediate vicinity of the settlements. Around the lakes of eastern and central Africa—Nakuru and Ishango, for example—a similar development can be observed, but here the emphasis was on both fishing and hunting and on the development of efficient equipment for both these occupations. In the grasslands the improved forms of projectile points and cutting implements indicate the over-all importance of hunting and the probable dependence on one main food animal. Moreover, the general increase that can be seen in the use of smaller animals as a source of food suggests that traps and snares were now more intensively used than ever before.

The introduction of microlithic forms into the tool kit at this time also emphasizes the importance and superiority of the composite weapon—whether the spear or the bow and arrow—which formed lighter and more efficient piercing and cutting weapons, especially when used with poison, than had been available heretofore. This "microlithicness" may have developed and spread out of the need to adapt hunting equipment to suit the capture of smaller and fleeter animals that followed the extinction of the large beasts on which man had even up to early middle stone age times depended for his main source of meat. The more restricted territorial range that more concentrated settlement would necessitate must also have brought the smaller animals into more important focus.

Thus by about 6000 B.C. we can distinguish two main zones of population concentration: one in the gallery forest country based on staple vegetable foods and hunting, with emphasis on chopping, digging, pounding, and grinding equipment; the other around the lakes and other permanent water in the grasslands and on the seacoasts, with emphasis on bone points, harpoons, hooks, and gorges for fishing and microliths for hunting. Both, when the opportunity occurred, were not slow to make use of the domestication practices that filtered through to them from northern Africa across the Sahara. Each adopted those practices best suited to the natural environment, so that the one led through vegeculture to full cultivation of root crops, while the other developed cereal cultivation and stock-breeding, though both still obtained a high proportion of their meat from hunting.

By the middle of the sixth millennium B.C. it would seem that central-African groups had, by reason of the higher rainfall that probably coincided with the Atlantic period in Europe, been able to penetrate to the northern Sahara, carrying central-African hunting techniques and equipment—in particular the bifacial technique—with them and making their influence felt still farther, as far as the Mediterranean coast and the Nile delta. By contact and exchange with Mediterranean peoples moving southward they acquired a knowledge and experience of crop cultivation, almost certainly wheat (emmer). These mixed Saharan neolithic populations do not seem to have been slow to adopt an incipient form of agriculture, based, we must suppose, on wheat and later on barley, as well as domestication of cattle and sheep. This economy can, however, have been little more than a supplementary basis of subsistence, since, while the cattle and possible reaping scenes in the rock art, together with the sickle blades, show that stock-raising and agriculture were practiced, hunting as a source of food must have assumed almost equal importance, if we can again judge by the rock art and the many associated projectile points. Such an economy in an arid or semiarid environment necessitates mobility of the settlement pattern and a wide range of territory, so it may be expected that the new domesticates must have spread fairly rapidly through the desert.

On the existing archeological evidence, sub-Saharan Africa seems never to have made any major contribution to food production or to any of the higher forms of economy. Perhaps the richest part of any continent in potentially domesticable large mammals, it succeeded in domesticating none of them and received its domestic stock from external sources, and the initial impetus for the cultivation of cereal crops also seems to have come from outside.

If, however, Black Africa seems not to have taken any important lead in domestication, yet it cannot have been slow to experiment and adapt the new potential to the locally available natural resources. Thus it is not difficult to see how simple vegecultural practices, based on the wild yam and oil-bearing plants, could have grown up in the Guinea-type bush of western and central Africa, since many tribes in Africa have the habit of storing any collection of root vegetables—over and above those required for immediate needs—by partially burying them in the ground. Also contact with and observation of the desert peoples and later, because of the desiccation of the Sahara, movements out of that region resulted in population absorption and adjustment.

Plant cultivation and, probably, domestication cannot have arrived at the proportions of effective food production in western Africa until the time of the Nok culture at the beginning of the first millennium B.C., though it is probable that in eastern Africa cultivation of millets and domestic stock were first present in the second millennium B.C. In eastern Africa the new economy manifests itself in the presence of open village settlements of small groups of semi-subterranean houses; in material equipment, such as grinding stones, pestles, stone bowls, platters, and pottery; and in group burial and the presence of domestic animals in the food debris. There can still have been little cohesion between groups, however, and the social and political organization must have been on a simple communal level, with no centralized political authority. In the forested country it is more difficult to assess the settlement patterns, since no occupation sites other than rock shelters have ever been completely excavated. The environment, however, lends itself to greater cohesion of the population into larger but more widely dispersed settlements. From such simple village societies, which must nevertheless have been organized on an effective food-producing level, can be derived the later village-farming communities of southern Africa that are connected today with the Bantu- and semi-Bantu-speaking peoples. In some regions, notably in the more thickly wooded and lower-lying parts of the central plateau, as well as in the rain forest, greater importance seems to have been given to agriculture—as, for example, in the Kisalian culture of the Katanga. In other parts, for example in the dry Bechuanaland grassland and thornveld, cattle-raising predominated, while in the richer soils and higher rainfall areas of the southeast mixed farming was the rule. But all remained essentially mobile as a result of quick exhaustion of suitable agricultural soil and pasture, and all still relied to a considerable extent on hunting and collecting to supplement their diet and, especially, to tide them over famine years.

Thus, effective food production appears as a terminal stage in a long and gradual developmental process that derived from experiment and adaptation in the northern grasslands and forest fringes. From here population movement into the subcontinent caused fully food-producing economies to appear suddenly in some regions from the beginning of the Christian Era onward, while around them, as the result of symbiotic existence, some of the hunting-collecting peoples, by gradual adaptation, became fully food-producing also.

Full urbanization was never achieved in southern Africa, and the main centers of the Zimbabwe-Monomatapa culture can at most represent only the first step in this direction. Though there was a strong centralized political system with a hereditary ruling house and hereditary office-bearers, society was still organized on a dispersed-village basis. The Monomatapa may have been the religious and secular head, but there was no official state religion; neither was there a priestly or, for that matter, any fully professional class dependent upon other groups for their basic needs. There can never have been any great food surplus in a country where insect pests, uncertain rainfall, and war are the contributing factors in restricting food production to a subsistence level and where no intensive forms of agriculture, such as irrigation or selective stock-breeding were widely developed. The population concentrations that were responsible for the large stone-constructed prestige buildings may have had unlimited manpower at their disposal, but the lack of interdependence between specialized communities never enabled them to develop full urbanization, and, as the coastal gold trade decreased, the Monomatapa culture began to disappear. Of course, in western Africa, on the east-African coast, and in Abyssinia full urbanization was achieved, but this came about in historic times as a result of trade—both overland trade routes and maritime trade—which was usually in the hands of foreigners, Berbers, Moors, Persians, and southern Arabians, and so does not rightly fall within the scope of this paper.

The main cause behind this lack of "invention" centers and progression to full urbanization in sub-Saharan Africa is probably the nature of the climate, which did not require any particular exertion on the part of the population to insure survival. Generally it was not difficult to obtain a livelihood, food and other natural resources were abundant, and the incentive to develop any cultural form more elaborate than the simple village-farming community was for the most part absent. On the other hand, if a subsistence level of life is generally easier in the tropics than in temperate or colder conditions, it is also more restrictive. The rapidity of plant growth, malnutrition from an unbalanced diet, famine, disease, and warfare have all combined to act upon the mentality of the people, so, while they are not usually slow to adopt improvements that affect the obtaining of food, such revolutionary inventions and developments as the use of the wheel, irrigation systems, or the growth of classes of professionals or experts seem never to have been adopted. Perhaps the general difficulties of intercommunication have been a contributing factor to those others that probably explain the receptivity but absence of intiative qualities of the sub-Saharan peoples in post-Pleistocene and later times.

BIBLIOGRAPHY

ANCIAUX DE FAVEAUX, DOM A.

1957. "Les Breches ossiferes de Kokontwe." *In* J. D. Clark (ed.), *Proceedings of the Third Pan-African Congress on Prehistory, Livingstone*, pp. 98–101. London: Chatto & Windus.

ARKELL, A. J.

1949a. *Early Khartoum*. London: Oxford University Press.

1949b. "The Old Stone Age in the Anglo-Egyptian Sudan." ("Occ. Papers Sudan Antiq. Serv.," No. 1, pp. 1–52. Cambridge: Deighton Bell.

1953. *Shaheinab*. London: Oxford University Press.

1954. "Four Occupation Sites at Agordat," *Kush.*, 2:33–62.

ARMSTRONG, A. L.

1931. "Rhodesian Archaeological Expedition (1929): Excavation in Bambata Cave," *J.R.A.*, 63:239–75.

BAKKER, E. M. VAN ZINDEREN

1960. "Pollen Analysis and Its Contribution to the Palaeoecology of the Quaternary in Southern Africa." *In* "Palynology in Africa" (6th Rept. covering the years 1958–1959). University of O. F. S., Bloemfontein.

BOND, G.

1957. "The Geology of the Khami Stone Age Sites." ("Occ. Papers at. Mus. S. Rhodesia," No. 21A, 3:44–55.) London: Cambridge University Press.

BOULE, M., and H. V. VALLOIS

1946. *Les hommes fossiles*. 3d ed. Paris: Masson et cie.

BREUIL, H., P. TEILHARD DE CHARDIN, and P. WEINERT

1951. "Le Paleolithique du Harar," *L'Anthropologie*, 55:219–30.

BRIGGS, L. C.

1958. "The Living Races of the Sahara Desert." ("Peabody Museum Papers," Vol. 28, No. 2.) Cambridge, Mass.

CATON-THOMAS, G.

1931. *The Zimbabwe Culture*. London: Oxford University Press.

CLARK, J. D.

1944. "The Use of the Bored Stone in Abyssinia, *Man*, 44:31–32.

1950. "The Newly Discovered Nachikufu Culture of Northern Rhodesia and the Possible Origin of Certain Elements of the South African Smithfield Culture," *S. Afr. Arch. Bull.*, 5:2–15.

1954. *The Prehistoric Cultures of the Horn of Africa*. London: Cambridge University Press.

1958. "Chifubwa Stream Rockshelter, Solwezi, Northern Rhodesia," *ibid.*, 13:21–24.

1959a. "Reflections on the Significance of Prehistoric Cultural Influences in South West Africa," *S. Afr. Mus. Assoc. Bull.*, 7:37–45.

1959b. *The Prehistory of Southern Africa*. Penguin Books.

n.d. "Carbon 14 Chronology in Africa South of the Sahara." (Paper read at the 4th Pan-Afr. Cong. Prehist. Leopoldville, 1959.) (In press.)

COLE, S.

1958. *Early Man in East Africa*. London: Macmillan & Co.

COOKE, C. K.
1957. "The Prehistoric Artist of Southern Matabeleland: His Materials and Techniques as a Basis for Dating." *In* J. D. CLARK (ed.), *1957 Proc. 3d Pan-Afr. Cong. Prehist., Livingstone, 1955*, pp. 282–94. London: Chatto and Windus..

COOKE, H. S. B.
n.d. Unpublished list of fauna from Twin Rivers, Northern Rhodesia.

C.S.A.
n.d. Specialist Meeting on Phyto-geography, Yangambi 1956. (Scientific Council for Africa South of the Sahara [C.S.A.] publ. 22). Hertford: Stephen Austin.

DAVIES, O.
n.d. "Neolithic cultures from Ghana." (Paper read at 4th Pan-Afr. Cong. Prehist. Leopoldville, 1959.) (In press.)

DELCROIX, R., and R. VAUFREY
1944. "Le Toumbien de Guinee Française, *L'Anthropologie*, 49:265–312.

FAGG, B.
1944. "Preliminary Report on a Microlithic Industry at Rop Rock Shelter, Northern Nigeria," *Proc. Prehist. Soc.*, 10:68–69.

1949. "An outline of the Stone Age of the Plateau Minefield," *Proc. Internat. W. Afr. Conf.*

FLINT, R. F.
1959. "Pleistocene Climates in Eastern and Southern Africa," *Bull. Geol. Soc. America*, 70:343–74.

FOCK, G. J.
1959. "Survey of Archaeological Research in South West Africa," *S. Afr. Arch. Bull.*, 14:9–18.

GALLOWAY, A.
1960. *The Skeletal Remains of Bambandyanalo*. Johannesburg: Witwatersrand University Press.

GOODWIN, A. J. H., and C. VAN RIET LOWE
1929. "The Stone Age Cultures of South Africa, *Ann. S. Afr. Mus.*, 27:1–289.

GOODWIN, A. J. H., *et al.*
1938. "Archaeology of the Oakhurst Shelter, George," *Trans. Roy. Soc. S. Afr.*, 25: pp. 229–324.

HEINZELIN, J. DE
1957. *Les Fouilles d'Ishango*. (Publ. No. 2, Inst. Parcs Nati. Congo Belge.) Brussels.

HOFFMAN, A. C.
1958. "New Excavations in the Matjes River Rock Shelter," *S. Afr. Mus. Assoc. Bull.*, No. 6, pp. 342–48.

JEFFREYS, M. D. W.
1957. "Some Notes on the Neolithic of West Africa." *In* J. D. CLARK (ed.), *Proc. 3d Pan-Afr. Cong. Prehist., Livingstone, 1955*. London: Chatto and Windus.

JONES, N.
1940. *Bambata: A Reorientation*. ("Occ. Papers, Nat. Mus. S. Rhodesia," No. 9, pp. 11–28.)

KELLY, H.
1934. "Harpons, objets en os travaille et silex tailles de Taferjit et Tamaya Mellet (Sahara nigerien)," *J. Soc. Africanistes*, 4:135–43.

KORN, H., and H. MARTIN
1957. "The Pleistocene of South West Africa." *In* J. D. CLARK (*ed.*). *Proc. 3d Pan-Afr. Cong. Prehist.* London: Chatto and Windus.

LEAKEY, L. S. B.
1931. *The Stone Age Cultures of Kenya Colony*. London: Cambridge University Press.

1935. *The Stone Age Races of Kenya*. London: Oxford University Press.

1943. "The Industries of the Gorgora Rock Shelter, Lake Tana," *J.E. Afr. & Uganda Nat. Hist. Soc.*, 17:199–203.

1956. *Annual Report of the Coryndon Museum, Nairobi*.

LEAKEY, M. D.
1943. "Notes on the Ground and Polished Stone Axes of East Africa," *J. E. Afr. & Uganda Nat. Hist. Soc.*, 17:182–95.

1945. "Report on the Excavations at Hyrax Hill, Nakuru, Kenya Colony, 1937–1938." *Trans. R. Soc. S. Afr.*, 30:271–409.

LEAKEY, M. D., and L. S. B.
1950. *Excavations at the Njoro River Cave*. London: Oxford University Press.

LHOTE, H.
1958. *A la decouverte des freques du Tassili*. Paris: Arthaud.

LOWE, C. VAN RIET
1945. "The Coastal Smithfield and Bipolar Technique," *S. Afr. J. Sci.*, 42:240–46.

MALAN, B. D., and L. H. WELLS
1943. "A Further Report on the Wonderwerk Cave, Kuruman," *S. Afr. J. Sci.*, 40: 258–70.

MASON, R. J., R. A. DART, and J. W. KITCHING
1958. "Bone Tools at the Kalkbank Middle Stone Age Site and the Makapansgat Australopithecine Locality, Central Transvaal," *S. Afr. Arch. Bull.*, 13:85–116.

MAUNY, R.
1951. "Du nouveau sur la prehistoire et l'archeologie de l'Aouker et du Hodh (Mauritanie)," *Bull. Soc. Prehist. Franç.*, Nos. 1–2, pp. 78–83.

McBURNEY, C. B. M.
1960. *The Stone Age of Northern Africa*. London: Penguin Books.

MORI, F.
1960. *Arte Preistorica del Sahara Libico*. Rome: De Lucca.

MURDOCK, G. P.
1959. *Africa: Its People and Their Culture History*. New York: McGraw-Hill Book Co.

NAVILLE, E.
1898. *The Temple of Deir el Bahari*, Part III. (Publ. Egypt Explor. Fund.) London: Kegan Paul.

OAKLEY, K. P.
1961. "Bone Harpoon from Gamble's Cave," Kenya," *Antiq. Jour.*, 41:86–87.

PERROT, J.
1962. "Palestine–Syria–Cilicia." (This volume.)

POSNANSKY, M.
1961. "Pottery Types from Archaeological sites in East Africa," *Jour. African History*, 2:177–198.

SCHNELL, R.
1957. *Plantes Alimentaires et vie agricole de l'Afrique noire*. Paris: La Rose.

SHAW, C. T.
1944. "Report on Excavations Carried Out in the Cave Known as 'Bosumpra' at Abetifi, Kwahu, Gold Coast Colony," *Proc. Prehist. Soc.*, 10:1–67.

SUMMERS, R. F. H.
1955. "The Dating of the Zimbabwe Ruins," *Antiquity*, No. 114, pp. 107–11.

1961. "The Southern Rhodesian Iron Age," *Jour. African History*, 2:1–13.

n.d. "Iron Age Research in Rhodesia, 1950/1960." (Paper read at the First Federal Science Congress, Salisbury.) In press.

SUMMERS, R. F. H., and C. K. COOKE
1960. *Supplement to the Annual Report of the Commission for the Preservation of Natural and Historical Monuments and Relics.* Salisbury, Southern Rhodesia.

TOBIAS, P. V.
1949. "The Excavation of Mwulu's Cave, Potgietersrust District," *S. Afr. Arch. Bull.* 4:2–13.

VAVILOV, N. I.
1931. *The Problem of the World's Agriculture in the Light of the Latest Investigations.* London.

WALTON, J.
1957. "Some Features of the Monomatapa Culture." *In* J. D. CLARK (ed.), *Proc. 3d Pan-Afr. Cong. Prehist., Livingstone, 1955*, pp. 336–56. London: Chatto and Windus.

WAYLAND, E. J.
1954. "Outline of Prehistory and Stone Age Climatology in the Bechuanaland Protectorate." (Academie Royale des Sciences coloniales, Section Sciences Naturelles et Medicales, Memoires, 25:1–47.)

WELLS, L. H., H. B. S. COOKE, and B. D. MALAN
1942. "The Associated Fauna and Culture of the VlaakKraal Thermal Spring, O.F.S.," *Trans. R. Soc. S. Africa*, 29:203–33.

WIESCHOFF, H. A.
1941. "The Zimbabwe-Monomatapa Culture of South-East Africa." (General Series in Anthropology, No. 8.) Wisconsin: George Banta.

WILLETT, F.
n.d. "Microlithic Industry from Old Oyo, West Nigeria." (Paper read at 4th Pan-Afr. Cong. Prehist., Leopoldville, 1959.) In press.

THE INTERMEDIATE AREA,
AMAZONIA, AND THE CARIBBEAN AREA

IRVING ROUSE[1]

INTRODUCTION

THE THREE regions under consideration, the Intermediate area, Amazonia, and the Caribbean area, are outlined in Figure 1. They may be characterized as follows:

THE INTERMEDIATE AREA

This region takes its name from its geographic position between the two areas of New World civilization, Mesoamerica and the Central Andes (Haberland, 1957). It comprises the lower part of Central America, including eastern Honduras and Nicaragua, Costa Rica, and Panama; all of Colombia and Ecuador except the eastern, Amazonian sections; and the northwestern, Andean corner of Venezuela. It has a central core of mountains, consisting of the local ranges in Central America and of the Andes in northwestern South America. These are bordered by a low coastal strip along the Pacific Ocean in the west and by another such strip along the Caribbean Sea to the north and east.

The mountains occupy the greater part of the region and provide its unifying factor. By contrast, the coastal strips are relatively narrow, except where they extend deeply into the lower Magdalena valley of Colombia and the Maracaibo basin of Venezuela and cut across the peninsulas of Panama and Nicaragua. The mountains tend to be rugged and the coastal strips swampy, with the result that travel and communication through the area are relatively difficult.

The region is characterized by an extreme diversity of climate, flora, and fauna. Although it straddles the equator, there are areas of perpetual snow and of treeless plains, known as *páramos*, on the mountain tops. Moving down to lower altitudes, one enters successively the *tierra fría*, in which potatoes are the principal crop; the *tierra templada*, in which maize grows best; and, finally, the *tierra caliente*, in which tropical root crops such as sweet manioc abound (Cruxent and Rouse, 1958–59, 1:138). The coastal belts and the flood plains of the major rivers are also *tierra caliente*. Here the vegetation varies from semiarid

1. I am indebted to Gerardo Reichel-Dolmatoff and Michael D. Coe for reading this paper and suggesting several additions and corrections, especially as it pertains to their own work.

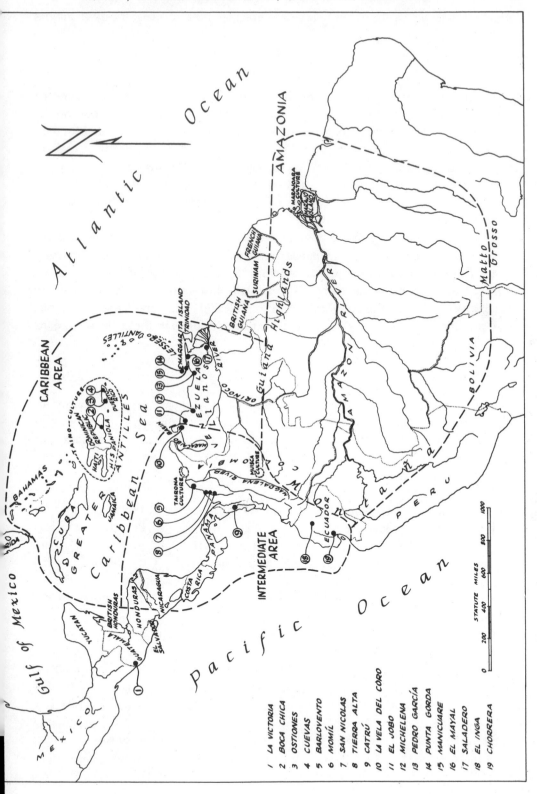

FIGURE 1. Regions considered in the Intermediate area, Amazonia, and in the Caribbean.

1   LA VICTORIA
2   BOCA CHICA
3   OSTIONES
4   CUEVAS
5   BARLOVENTO
6   MOMÍL
7   SAN NICOLAS
8   TIERRA ALTA
9   CATRÚ
10 LA VELA DEL CORO
11 EL JOBO
12 MICHELENA
13 PEDRO GARCÍA
14 PUNTA GORDA
15 MANICUARE
16 EL MAYAL
17 SALADERO
18 EL INGA
19 CHORRERA

scrub growth along the Venezuelan-Colombian border to dense tropical jungles on the Pacific coast.

Amazonia

The Amazon basin extends from the so-called Montaña, or eastern slopes of the Andes, in Bolivia, Peru, Ecuador, and Colombia on the west through northern Brazil to the Atlantic Coast on the east. To the south, the region begins in the vast central Brazilian plateau of Matto Grosso, and, to the north, it ends in the Guiana highlands of southern Venezuela and the Guianas proper. The Atlantic drainages of central Brazil and of the Guianas probably also belong in this region, culturally speaking, but will be omitted here because relatively little is known of their archeology.

This is a region of gentle topography and poor drainage, except in parts of the Montaña and the Guiana highlands. The climate is hot and humid, supporting dense tropical forests, interspersed with savannas in the uplands. The seasonal rains produce heavy floods, which inundate the lowlands and thereby limit the possibilities of habitation. On the other hand, the rivers are large, navigable, and provide an easy means of communication throughout the area, despite its large size.

The Caribbean Area

The term "Caribbean" is employed here not in its ordinary geographical meaning but in a special culture-historical sense. It refers to the region lying east of Mesoamerica and the Intermediate area, north of Amazonia, and southeast of the United States, that is, to central and northeastern Venezuela, the adjacent part of British Guiana, and the West Indies (Fig. 1).

As in the case of Amazonia, the geographical unity of this region is provided by its waterways, including the drainage of the Orinoco River in the interior and the Caribbean Sea along the coast and in the islands. But there are also large numbers of mountains; unlike the Andes, these occur in relatively small, isolated masses, both on the mainland and in the islands. They are surrounded by low, flat areas, the largest of which is the so-called "llanos" or plains of Venezuela, which extend from the coastal mountain range in the north to the Orinoco River on the south.

The region does not have such extremes of environment as the Intermediate area or such uniformity as Amazonia. The mountains are lower and offer only a temperate climate on the upper slopes and a tropical environment lower down. The trade winds blow steadily, cooling the coasts and providing heavy rainfall on the windward sides of the mountains, where tropical jungles flourish. The leeward sides tend to be dry. Vegetation on the coasts varies from semiarid scrub growth to savannas and forests. The Venezuelan llanos consist primarily of grasslands, giving way to open forests in the west.

CONTACT ETHNOLOGY

Steward (1947, pp. 85–86) has distinguished three levels of cultural development within the regions under consideration at the time of first contact with Europeans. These he calls "Marginal," "Tropical Forest," and "Circum-Caribbean," respectively.[2] In the terminology of the symposium, these may be regarded as cultural alternates, adapted to the variations in climate that have just been outlined. Their nature is as follows:

1. MARGINAL ALTERNATE

Scattered through the peripheries of the regions were groups of people who lacked agriculture and subsisted only by hunting, fishing, and gathering. They lived in relatively small camps, building only the flimsiest of huts, if any, and had the simplest kind of social organization and religion. Pottery was usually, though not always, lacking. Since most of the artifacts were of perishable material—even the arrows were tipped with wood rather than with stone—it is difficult to find archeological traces of these people.

Marginal tribes were most widespread around the edges of the Amazon Basin, that is, in parts of the Montaña, Matto Grosso, and the Guiana Highlands. Here they emphasized hunting and gathering in adaptation to an upland forest environment. The Caribbean area also had a considerable Marginal population, living in the swampy areas of western Cuba, in parts of Haiti, in the Orinoco delta, and possibly in the eastern llanos. Here, because of the nature of the environment, there was greater emphasis upon fishing and the gathering of shellfish. On the other hand, Marginal tribes are not reported from the Intermediat area.[3]

2. TROPICAL FOREST ALTERNATE

At the time of first European contact, the greater part of Amazonia was occupied by agriculturalists of the Tropical Forest type. These Indians cultivated primarily bitter manioc and other root crops, which are best adapted to the humid conditions and poorly drained soils of the forests, using the slash-and-burn technique. After harvesting, the manioc root was grated, squeezed in a basketry tube to remove the poisonous juice, and baked on a large circular griddle. Almost all the artifacts employed were made of perishable material; the only ones likely

2. Steward and Faron (1959, pp. 60–64) have recently redefined these three levels as "sociocultural types" and have given them more descriptive names: "nomadic hunters and gatherers," "tropical-forest-village farmers," and "chiefdoms," respectively. This enables the authors to abandon the term "Marginal" and to use "Circum-Caribbean" in a purely areal sense, referring jointly to the two regions here called the Intermediate and the Caribbean areas.

3. For a map of the distribution of Marginal culture see Steward and Faron (1959, p. 375). There the two variants distinguished above are termed "forest hunters and gatherers" and "aquatic nomads," respectively. Steward and Faron, however, include the so-called Ciboney Indians in the former category, whereas we have put them in the latter

to survive archeologically are small pieces of flint that were set into a wooden slab to form the grater and the griddle, which was made of clay.

The Tropical Forest Indians were good potters, frequently using this technique to make burial urns as well as vessels and griddles. Ground-stone axes or celts are also characteristic. Little else is found in the archeological sites, because most of the artifacts were made of perishable materials. The buildings consisted of huts grouped together into villages. The villages tended to be politically independent and to have a relatively simple form of social organization, with little emphasis upon religion.

While the Tropical Forest alternate was most typical of Amazonia, it also occurred widely in the Caribbean area and was the dominant form of life in the Orinoco basin, the Lesser Antilles, and parts of both the Greater Antilles and the north coast of· Venezuela. It also extended into the Intermediate area, where it occupied the western part of the Maracaibo basin, the Pacific coast of Colombia, and the Atlantic coastal plain of Nicaragua.[4]

Bitter manioc was the staple food in the Caribbean area as well as in Amazonia, but in the Intermediate area its place was taken by sweet manioc, which is not poisonous. The Indians boiled or roasted the latter plant, and as a result its use cannot be readily identified from archeological remains. The Tropical Forest Indians of both the Caribbean and the Intermediate areas also relied heavily upon fruits, especially of the *pejivalle* and *moriche* palms, and upon the products of fishing.[5]

3. CIRCUM-CARIBBEAN ALTERNATE

Interspersed among the Tropical Forest tribes, especially in the Intermediate area, were more-advanced farming peoples, characterized by a certain complexity of social and religious life. These Indians lived in larger villages, which were socially stratified, and had chiefs, whose authority typically extended over more than one village. They also possessed priests, who presided over the worship of idols in temples made of the same perishable materials as the houses, since there was little or no monumental architecture.

The Circum-Caribbean alternate was not limited to the Intermediate area but, as its name implies, was also present at scattered points in the northern part of

4. The distribution of Tropical Forest tribes is mapped by Steward and Faron (1959, p. 285). To this map should be added Tropical Forest enclaves along the north coast of Venezuela, as discussed above.

5. The Talamanca Valley of northeastern Costa Rica provides a good example of the difficulties that maize faced in the lowlands. According to Stone (1956), this area was occupied by Tropical Forest people, subsisting primarily upon sweet manioc and the fruit of the *pejivalle* palm, until shortly before the arrival of Europeans. Then the area was invaded by "Mexicans," who presumably introduced maize. This crop never "made too great an impression, whether because the climatical conditions were unfavorable to its cultivation and storage or whether it was a question of taste" (Stone, 1956, p. 192).

Venezuela and among the so-called Taino of the central part of the Greater Antilles. It has not been reported from Amazonia during historic time.[6]

There were several significant differences between the Circum-Caribbean tribes of the Intermediate and of the Caribbean areas. In the first place, maize was the staple food of the Intermediate area, whereas in the Caribbean area the Circum-Caribbean tribes followed the example of their Tropical Forest neighbors in relying primarily upon bitter manioc. Maize was present as a secondary crop among some Caribbean tribes, but they apparently boiled or roasted it instead of grinding it into flour to make bread (Rouse, 1948, p. 523). As a result, one finds metates and manos of stone archeologically only in the Intermediate area; in the Caribbean area, their place is taken by clay griddles for baking cassava.

Sauer (1952, pp. 40–73) theorizes that the Intermediate and Caribbean forms of agriculture constitute separate culture-historical complexes, to which he gives the names "seed" and "vegetative" farming, respectively. We may say that the Circum-Caribbean peoples of the Intermediate area had the seed complex because they relied primarily upon maize and beans, using root crops only secondarily, and that the Circum-Caribbean tribes of the Caribbean area were, instead, vegetative planters because their staple foods were bitter manioc and the sweet potato, with maize being used only secondarily, if at all. There are exceptions to this rule, of course. The Indians of the *tierra fria* in the Intermediate area relied not so much on seed crops, which grow poorly at that altitude, as on the potato, which is a root crop. Similarly, some Indians of the *tierra caliente* seem to have favored sweet manioc, presumably because it grows better than maize in the poorly drained tropical jungles. Wherever the environment was favorable, however, the tribes of the Intermediate area were seed planters.

A second significant difference between the Circum-Caribbean tribes of the Intermediate and the Caribbean areas was that only the former had learned to cast metals. They fashioned gold and other precious metals into ornaments and religious objects of considerable complexity, although not into tools and utensils. These religious objects, together with large amounts of pottery, are now found mainly in graves, especially of the deep-shaft type. Elaborate graves with such a wealth of furniture are absent from the Caribbean area, and it would seem that the Indians who lived there had relatively little interest in burial and in life after death.

Some anthropologists have theorized that the civilizations of Mesoamerica and the Central Andes must have been joined by an as yet undiscovered civilization in the Intermediate area. If it was present, such a civilization would constitute an additional alternate within the area, existing alongside the Tropical Forest and Circum-Caribbean cultures. There is, however, no evidence that this was so, either in the colonial records or in the contemporary studies of the Indians. The

6. For a map of the distribution of Circum-Caribbean culture see Steward and Faron (1959, p. 203).

Muisca (Chibcha) tribe of the Bogotá basin in Colombia is sometimes cited as an example of civilization because of its sedentary form of agriculture and relatively dense population, but the rest of its culture was typically Circum-Caribbean (see, e.g., Steward and Faron, 1959, pp. 212–16). It must be concluded, therefore, that the Indians of the Intermediate area did not attain civilization.

ESTABLISHMENT OF CHRONOLOGY

Of the three regions, only the Caribbean has been adequately covered by archeologists. This region has not only been the scene of intensive local activity, especially in Cuba and Venezuela, but has also benefited from a series of research programs by United States organizations: the Bureau of American Ethnology, Smithsonian Institution; the Museum of the American Indian, Heye Foundation; and, most recently, the Peabody Museum, Yale University. These programs have been well planned and have covered all parts of the area in some detail. One of their principal results has been the establishment of a region-wide chronology, which will be utilized in the present paper (Cruxent and Rouse, 1958–59, Vol. 2, Figs. 6–9, 26, 100, 149, 170).

Research in the Intermediate area, on the other hand, has been relatively unbalanced. Until recently, it was concentrated in the mountainous parts of the region, where most of the modern population lives and where the more elaborate archeological remains are to be found. It was not until the last decade that intensive work was begun on the coast by a few archeologists, notably Bushnell (1951), Estrada (1957a, b, 1958), and Evans and Meggers (1957) in Ecuador; Reichel-Dolmatoff (1954, 1957, 1958) in northern Colombia; and Willey (1958, pp. 358–59) and his students (e.g., McGimsey, 1956, 1958; Ladd, 1957) in Central America. Chronology proved to be difficult to obtain in the highlands, for the refuse sites there are sparse, shallow, and, in the area of most intensive agriculture around Bogotá, Colombia, surprisingly late (Haury, 1953). On the coast, however, the recent work has resulted in the discovery of deep refuse sites with long sequences of occupation. These are still too few in number and too scattered to provide a reliable chronology for the region, but they are a promising beginning.

Amazonia is even less fully covered. Intensive work has been carried out only in the peripheries of the region, that is, in the Montaña (e.g., Bennett, 1936; Lathrap, 1958), the Guianas (Meggers and Evans, 1955), and at the mouth of the Amazon (Meggers and Evans, 1957). We do have chronologies for these peripheral regions, since the sites are deep enough to yield sequences of occupation, but they will not mean much over-all until stratigraphic work is carried out in the central part of the area. The one attempt at synthesis, by Howard (1947), is now out of date.

For purposes of the present paper, it seems advisable to use the Caribbean chonology, since it is region-wide, is based upon the most stratigraphy, and is supplied with the best series of radiocarbon determinations. The scattered chronological sequences in the other two regions will be correlated with it, but the correlations must be considered no more than provisional, since we do not yet possess adequate data for either the Intermediate area or Amazonia.

Figure 2 presents the chronology to be used here, consisting of a Pleistocene and/or early post-Pleistocene period and a Recent one. The latter is subdivided into four parts, arbitrarily numbered from I to IV. The probable values of these periods in absolute time are indicated on the left side of the chart. In order to simplify the presentation, only selected local areas are included in the figure and the lesser cultures have been eliminated. The periods listed in Figure 2 will be discussed in turn and will be illustrated primarily in terms of the cultures named in the figure.

PERIODS		INTERMEDIATE AREA		AMAZONIA		CARIBBEAN AREA	
		COASTAL ECUADOR	NORTHERN COLOMBIA	PERUVIAN MONTAÑA	AMAZON DELTA	EASTERN VENEZUELA	GREATER ANTILLES
IV		HUANCAVILCA	TAIRONA	HUPA-IYA	ARÚA / MARAJOARA	GUARGUAPO	BOCA CHICA
III		QUEVEDO	TIERRA ALTA	SHAKIMU	MANGUEIRAS	LOS BARRANCOS	OSTIONES
II		TEJAR	LOMA	TUTISHCAINYO	ANANATUBA	BARRANCAS	CUEVAS
II		CHORRERA	MOMÍL			SALADERO	
I		VALDIVIA	BARLOVENTO			MANICUARE	LOIZA
I		?	?	?			
PLEISTOCENE (?)			SAN NICOLÁS			EL JOBO	?

Left axis labels: 1500 A.D., 1000 A.D., 200 A.D., 1000 B.C., 5000 B.C.; RECENT spans periods I–IV; PLEISTOCENE(?) at bottom.

FIGURE 2. Chronology of selected areas of the Intermediate area, Amazonia, and the Caribbean.

PLEISTOCENE(?) PERIOD

Early hunters must have been widespread throughout the three regions, but only a single complex—El Jobo—has so far been worked out. This is situated in the west-central part of Venezuela (Cruxent and Rouse, 1958, 1: 68–70). It is known from small, shallow camp sites some distance in the interior, which have yielded only stone implements. Leaf-shaped projectile points of quartzite, finely rechipped over both surfaces, are characteristic. There are also unifacially or bifacially worked knives, scrapers, and choppers. Traces of food are lacking, but it may be presumed that the points, knives, and scrapers were used in hunt-

ing and butchering big game and the choppers, perhaps, in collecting and split-
ting nuts, in the manner described by Desmond Clark (this volume) for nearly
identical tools from Africa.

Some evidence of hunting big game has recently been obtained by Cruxent
(personal communication) at the nearby coastal site of La Vela del Coro. Here
he found typical El Jobo points in association with the bones of various extinct
mammals, including the mastodon, glyptodon, and megatherium. Unfortunately,
the deposit was too disturbed to determine whether this was a kill site, but several bones showed evidence of cutting.

Cruxent (personal communication) has obtained a radiocarbon determination
of 14,000 B.C. for this site, but the date cannot definitely be associated with the
El Jobo complex because of the disturbance there. The typical El Jobo points
are comparable to those found with mammoth bones at Santa Isabel Iztapan in
the Valley of Mexico, which are dated from 14,000 to 9000 B.C. (Willey, this
volume), and to the points of the Ayampitín complex in Argentina, which have
a radiocarbon determination of about 6000 B.C. (Cruxent and Rouse, 1958–59,
1: 70). It is presumed, therefore, that the El Jobo complex dates from either late
Pleistocene or early post-Pleistocene time.

Two other lithic assemblages were discovered recently. At Catrú on the headwaters of the Baudó River in western Colombia, Gerardo and Alicia Reichel-
Dolmatoff (personal communication) obtained "a large series of flake tools, all
fashioned by percussion chipping, mostly uniface scrapers. There is only one
(doubtful) single-shouldered projectile point." Reichel-Dolmatoff adds that Catrú
"is related to San Nicolas, Lower Sinú," which is another lithic site in the Caribbean part of Colombia (Fig. 1).

At El Inga, near the town of Tumbaco in highland Ecuador, Bell and Mayer-
Oakes (1960) encountered a more typical hunting complex, characterized by
fluted points and also by large stemmed specimens comparable to those obtained
by Junius Bird in the bottom level of Fells Cave in Patagonia. These would
place the site in early post-Pleistocene time, since the earliest occupation at
Fells Cave has a radiocarbon determination of 6679 B.C. (Libby, 1955, p. 134).

These scattered finds do little more than indicate the presence of early hunters
in the Intermediate and Caribbean areas. Presumably the hunters migrated southward from Mesoamerica, but the time of their arrival, the directions in which
they moved, and the duration of their occupation remain to be determined (cf.
Collier, this volume).

PERIOD I

The first of the Recent periods is so far known almost entirely from a series
of shell middens along the coast and on the adjacent islands, which indicate a
change in the principal means of subsistence from hunting to fishing and the
gathering of shellfish. A number of cultural complexes have been recognized,

and these may be divided into two groups, depending upon whether or not pottery is present. The six best-documented non-ceramic complexes and all three known ceramic complexes are listed in Table 1, with their radiocarbon determinations. It will be seen that Period I lasted from about 5000 to 1000 B.C.

TABLE 1

THE PRINCIPAL COMPLEXES OF PERIOD I WITH THEIR RADIOCARBON DETERMINATIONS

Complex	Location	Determination (B.C.)	Sources for the Complex and Its Determination
1. Cerro Mangote	Pacific coast of Panama	4850 ± 100	McGimsey, 1956, 1958
2. El Heneal	Central coast of Venezuela	1440 ± 120	Cruxent and Rouse, 1958–59, 1: 75–76
3. Cubagua	East coast of Venezuela	2190 ± 80	*Ibid.*, pp. 46–49
4. Manicuare	East coast of Venezuela	1610 ± 130 1090 ± 80	*Ibid.*, pp. 49–53 *Ibid.*, pp. 111–13
5. Loiza	Eastern Puerto Rico	——	Alegría, Nicholson, and Willey, 1955
6. Couri	Haiti	——	Rouse, 1941, pp. 24–53
7. Monagrillo	Pacific coast of Panama	2130 ± 70	Willey and McGimsey, 1954; Deevey, Gralenski, and Hoffren, 1959, pp. 166–67
8. Valdivia	Coastal Ecuador	——	Estrada, 1956
9. Barlovento	Caribbean coast of Colombia	1510 ± 70 1180 ± 120 1020 ± 120	Reichel-Dolmatoff, 1955, personal communication

Note. The first six complexes lack pottery. The last three have it.

The origin of the complexes is not known, but there is reason to think that it was diverse (Rouse, 1960). As Table 4 indicates, the non-ceramic complexes are widespread in both Intermediate and Caribbean areas. The Manicuare complex, in eastern Venezuela (Fig 2), is a typical example. It has been found in a large number of shell middens on the peninsula of Araya and on the islands of Cubagua and Margarita offshore. Most sites are situated just back of sandy beaches, where agriculture would be difficult if not impossible but where fishing could easily be carried out. Occupation must have been relatively permanent, since the deposits range up to 15 feet in depth. The presence of large numbers of fish bones, shells, and especially echinoderm remains confirm the importance of sea food in the diet. Projectile points are made of bone rather than stone; there are also biconical sling(?) stones. Gouges are the commonest implements of shell and are thought to have been used in the manufacture of dugout canoes, which the Manicuare peoples must have had in order to be able to travel from island to island. Burials are directly in the refuse, without grave objects. No religious structures or other evidences of ceremonialism have been encountered.

The ceramic complexes have so far been found only in the Intermediate area.

Barlovento, in northern Colombia (Fig. 2), may serve as an example. Its sites are very similar to the shell heaps of the Manicuare complex and, like them, are situated in areas where agriculture is virtually impossible but where there is good fishing. The few non-ceramic artifacts include hammerstones and possible net-sinkers. Potsherds are considerably more common; they come from sub-globular bowls with broad-line incised designs. Similar decoration occurs in the other complexes, and it may be that, despite very considerable differences in the details of material, shape, and design, all the pottery came from a single, as yet undetermined, source, spreading from this source to the preceramic peoples in advance of agriculture.

The absence of agriculture from these complexes is of interest because Period I was the time when incipient farming made its appearance in Mesoamerica to the north and the Central Andes to the south. Instead of being in the line of agricultural development, the complexes just described must be regarded as a distinct, non-agricultural alternate that had become specialized on the marine food available along the coast. At least in the two examples described, the necessary preconditions for incipient agriculture seem to have been lacking. Wild vegetable foods were rare, judging from modern conditions and from the paucity of milling stones in the sites. There may have been little incentive to turn to these foods anyway, since products of the sea were so easily obtainable. Even in later periods, many of the coastal people seem to have been loath to accept agriculture, for non-agricultural shell heaps continued through Periods II, III, and IV, as will be discussed below, and the culture of these sites leads directly into the Marginal culture of historic time.

Since the coastal people of Period I seem to have been ancestral to the Marginal tribes of historic time and since they had a similar mode of life, we will apply the term "Marginal" to them. It signifies that they had specialized away from the direction of incipient agriculture, which was developing elsewhere during Period I.

If we are to find incipient agriculture in the regions under consideration, we must look for it in the interior rather than on the coast. Unfortunately, it has not yet been possible to locate sites dating from Period I in the interior, with the possible exception of Michelena, in the Valencia basin of northern Venezuela, where workmen constructing a factory found milling stones, pestles, axes, and hammerstones two meters deep, together with traces of ash, which may indicate habitation (Cruxent and Rouse, 1958–59, 1: 171–72). One might speculate that the milling stones and pestles were used to prepare wild or cultivated vegetables, although they are not typical of the historic agriculture in the area.

Sauer (1952, pp. 45–46) has theorized that there was a center of plant domestication in the llanos or plains of central Venezuela, in which the Indians first cultivated manioc, which subsequently became their staple. One can imagine this taking place where the forests border the llanos, especially along the galleries on the banks of the Orinoco River. Presumably, these forest galleries were inhabited at the beginning of Period I by people who fished in the Orinoco, collected wild vegetable foods in the galleries, and at the same time continued to hunt upon the savannas, like some modern tribes in South Africa (Clark, this volume). From collecting manioc roots and palm fruits wild, it would have been an easy step to start cultivating them, that is, to develop incipient agriculture of the vegetative type.

We would suggest, then, that incipient vegetative agriculture may have developed on the llanos in the interior of Venezuela during Period I as an alternate to the Marginal fishing cultures that were emerging on the coast at the same time. But we must also consider the possibility of a third alternate that is even more speculative. Incipient seed agriculture may have spread along the Pacific coast of Central America, Colombia, and Ecuador from either of the two known centers of its development, Mesoamerica to the north and Peru to the south. Finally, it is probable that some of the Pleistocene hunting cultures persisted into Period I as a fourth alternate, although with a shift from large to small game. This is particularly likely to have been true of Amazonia, since Marginal hunting tribes still survive there, but it has yet to be demonstrated archeologically.[7]

PERIOD II

Period II is the time of first appearance of effective food production. Here we are on firmer ground. Vegetative agriculture is well represented in archeological sites of the Caribbean area during this period, and seed agriculture in archeological sites of the Intermediate area. In addition, we have good evidence of a continuation of the Marginal fishing alternate of Period I in the peripheries of the Caribbean area.

The principal cultures of the period are listed in Table 2, beginning with the Marginal complexes and continuing with those characterized first by vegetative agriculture and then by seed agriculture. Radiocarbon determinations are included where known. It will be seen that Period II lasted from *ca.* 1000 B.C. to A.D. 200, that is, during approximately the same time that effective agriculture was making its appearance in Mesoamerica to the north and the Central Andes to the south.

Little need be said about the Marginal complexes, since they continue the form of life already described for Period I. Punta Gorda, for example, is simply an offshoot of the Manicuare culture, already discussed, from which it differs mainly in having a greater elaboration of shellwork. It also contains a few potsherds, but these are so rare and technologically so fine as to indicate that

7. Willey (1960, Fig. 2) has recently published a chart in which he postulates the coexistence of all four of these alternates, as suggested above, except that he shows the fishing alternate only along the south coast of Brazil (not covered here) and omits it from the Caribbean area.

TABLE 2
THE PRINCIPAL CULTURES OF PERIOD II WITH THEIR RADIOCARBON DETERMINATIONS

Culture	Location	Determination	Sources for the Culture and Its Determination
1. Punta Gorda	East coast of Venezuela	——	Cruxent and Rouse, 1958–59, pp. 53–56
2. Ortoire	Trinidad	800 ± 130 B.C. 790 ± 130 B.C.	Rouse, 1953, pp. 94–96; Cruxent and Rouse, 1958–59, Table 2
3. Saladero	Middle-lower Orinoco River, Venezuela	910 ± 130 B.C. 740 ± 130 B.C. 610 ± 130 B.C.	Cruxent and Rouse, 1958–59, 1: 213–23
4. Barrancas	Lower Orinoco River, Venezuela	890 ± 120 B.C. 860 ± 80 B.C. 840 ± 150 B.C.	*Ibid.*, pp. 223–27
5. El Mayal	Northeast coast of Venezuela	A.D. 165 ± 80	*Ibid.*, pp. 119–21
6. Cedros	Trinidad	——	Rouse, 1953
7. Cuevas	Puerto Rico	——	Rouse, 1952, pp. 336–40
8. Tutishcainyo	Montaña of Peru	——	Lathrap, 1958
9. Anantuba	Mouth of the Amazon	——	Meggers and Evans, 1957
10. Momíl I–II	Caribbean lowlands of Colombia	——	Reichel-Dolmatoff, G. and A., 1956
11. Monte Fresco	Pacific coast of Costa Rica	A.D. 90 ± 200 A.D. 430 ± 280	Michael D. Coe, personal communication
12. Sarigua	Pacific coast of Panama	——	Willey and McGimsey, 1954
13. Chorrera	Coastal Ecuador	——	Evans and Meggers, 1957
14. Tejar	Coastal Ecuador	——	*Ibid.*, 1957
15. Loma	Caribbean lowlands of Colombia	——	Reichel-Dolmatoff, G. and A., 1951
16. Tocuyano	Western Venezuela	220 ± 300 B.C.	Cruxent and Rouse, 1958–59, 1: 152–55
17. Cerro Machado	Central Venezuela	A.D. 30 ± 70	*Ibid.*, pp. 93–95

Note. The first two cultures are Marginal, Nos. 3–9 have vegetative agriculture, 10 apparently has a succession of vegetative and seed agriculture, and 11–17 have only seed agriculture.

they were not locally manufactured but were traded in, probably from the El Mayal culture (Table 2, No. 5), which has similar pottery.[8]

8. It is perhaps also worth noting that the Ortoire complex, on the island of Trinidad, and the related El Conchal and El Peñon complexes, on the east coast of Venezuela, have large numbers of tiny stone chips (Rouse, 1953, pp. 94–96; Cruxent and Rouse, 1958–59, 1:113–14, 128–29). These could have been used in manioc graters, but, in view of the absence of pottery griddles, I am more inclined to believe that agriculture was lacking.

Theoretically, effective vegetative agriculture should have originated some-where around the Venezuelan llanos about the beginning of Period II, arising out of the hypothetical incipient form of agriculture postulated for the previous period. Alternatively, it may have spread to the Orinoco as the result of a migra-tion from Amazonia or the Intermediate area. Unfortunately, we know nothing about its origin. There can be little doubt, however, that it was present in the lower Orinoco valley by 800 B.C. We have six radiocarbon determinations clus-tering around that time (Table 2, Nos. 3 and 4), and all are associated with clay griddles like those still used in the area today for the preparation of manioc bread. Metates and manos indicative of maize agriculture are absent. Accom-panying the earliest griddles is a relatively fine, white-on-red painted pottery, to which we have given the name of the Saladoid tradition (Cruxent and Rouse, 1958–59, 1: 26).

The Saladoid pottery is widespread in eastern Venezuela and the West Indies. Study of its distribution, resemblances, and the sequence of radiocarbon deter-minations presented in Table 2 has led to the following historical reconstruction. Saladoid potters, with effective vegetative agriculture, made their appearance in the Orinoco valley during the first millennium B.C. By the time of Christ, they had spread to the northeastern coast of Venezuela, where they supposedly ac-quired the ability to navigate by sea from the already extant Marginal peoples of the Manicuaroid tradition. With this new skill, they were able to move out into the West Indies during the first centuries after Christ (Cruxent and Rouse, 1958–59, 1: 244–45). They apparently proceeded only as far as Puerto Rico at this time, since we do not find the white-on-red pottery diagnostic of Period II in any other parts of the Greater Antilles. The Marginal peoples must have survived in the other islands, such as Hispaniola and Cuba (Rouse, 1951, Fig. 2).

The Cuevas culture of Puerto Rico may be discussed as an example of the Saladoid development. A survey of Puerto Rico has revealed that Cuevas sites are limited to the seashore and to the banks of the major rivers near the shore (Rouse, 1952, Table 13). Most are close to sheltered beaches, from which fish-ing could have been undertaken, and contain large amounts of crab and shell remains. It would seem, therefore, that not only agriculture but also fishing and shell fishing contributed to the diet.

Since the sites are considerably larger than in the previous period, we may assume that the Cuevas people were living in more or less settled villages, all of which appear to have been of approximately the same size. There are no cere-monial structures, and the burials consist simply of skeletons in the refuse, usually without any grave objects.

Cuevas potsherds are technologically better than any of the latter material, are more complicated in shape, and are characteristically decorated with fine, white-on-red painted designs. Few other artifacts have been found in the sites, and these are all relatively plain and utilitarian. They include clay griddles for baking cassava, stone adzes and celts, bone awls, and beads and pendants of stone, bone, and shell. No ceremonial artifacts have been recovered, nor are there any recognizable evidences of warfare or trade. One gains the impression of simple, peasant villages, existing in relative isolation.

This way of life corresponds to Steward's Tropical Forest alternate of historic time, and indeed most, if not all, of the historic Tropical Forest Indians of the Caribbean area seem to have developed out of the Saladoid tradition or out of the corresponding Barrancoid tradition, which also makes its appearance in eastern Venezuela during Period II, accompanied by vegetative agriculture (Table 2, No. 4). There are likewise evidences of Tropical Forest culture in Amazonia that may be this early (Table 2, Nos. 8 and 9), although its relationships are not known.[9] If Sauer's theory is correct, effective vegetative agriculture should have spread from Venezuela to Amazonia during Period II, with Tropical Forest people expanding there, too, at the expense of the previous Marginal inhabitants.

To the west, in the northern Andes, a different picture is beginning to emerge. Coe (1960) has found pottery in the Ocos phase at the site of La Victoria on the Pacific coast of Guatemala that is surprisingly similar to that of the Chorrera culture on the coast of Ecuador (Table 2, No. 13). He postulates a southward diffusion of this pottery from Guatemala to Peru, accompanied by the first fully effective cultivation of maize, that is, the first effective seed agriculture. Whether this diffusion took place as a result of contacts along the Pacific coasts of Central America, Colombia, and Ecuador or is due to direct, overwater movement from Guatemala to Ecuador is a problem currently under investigation as a project of the Institute of Andean Research.

According to Manglesdorf, MacNeish, and Willey (MS), this southward diffusion of effective seed agriculture began in Mesoamerica about 1000 B.C. It apparently reached the Central Andes during the Cupisnique period, that is, about 750 B.C. (Collier, this volume). Hence, it paralleled the spread of effective vegetative agriculture through the Caribbean area to the east, where, as we have seen, the earliest dates are *ca.* 800 B.C.

The western area of effective seed agriculture overlaps the eastern area of effective vegetative agriculture at the site of Momíl, near the Caribbean coast of northwestern Colombia (Table 2, No. 10). In the lower half of this site— Momíl I—Reichel-Dolmatoff (1957, pp. 233–34) found a local style of pottery accompanied by clay griddles, which he, too, considers indicative of vegetative agriculture. In the upper half—Momíl II—griddles are replaced by metates and manos, and the pottery begins to show stronger Mesoamerican influences. The exact age of the site of Momíl is not known, but, from the other dates listed in Table 2, it may be inferred that seed agriculture, together with Mesoamerican ceramic influences, reached Momíl about 500 B.C.

From Momíl, Mesoamerican-like pottery, presumably accompanied by seed agriculture, spread eastward through cultures such as Loma in northeastern Colombia to Tocuyano in the interior of western Venezuela, where it has a radiocarbon determination of *ca.* 220 B.C. (Table 2, No. 16). It subsequently reached

---

9. The dates given in Table 2 for Nos. 8 and 9 are based upon Willey (1958, Fig. 9). Evans and Meggers (personal communication) consider these dates too early.

the Caribbean coast of central Venezuela *ca.* A.D. 30 (Table 2, No. 17). Here it is obviously intrusive and lasted for only a short period of time, for subsequent cultures in the central part of Venezuela have local, Caribbean pottery of the Saladoid and Barrancoid traditions, accompanied by griddles indicative of vegetative agriculture (Cruxent and Rouse, 1958–59, 1: 93–98).

There is an interesting parallel between this spread of effective seed agriculture eastward through the northern part of South America and its diffusion northward from Mesoamerica into the southwestern part of the United States (Haury, this volume). Both events seem to have taken place at about the same time, and both seem to have stopped abruptly, the South American spread in the face of Tropical Forest culture, which was already well established in the Caribbean area, and the North American one in the face of non-agricultural alternates, which prevailed in California and the Great Basin.

Momíl II culture of northern Colombia may be described as an example of the form of life that resulted from the introduction of effective seed agriculture into northwestern South America. The Momíl site is composed of refuse but without the remains of sea food so characteristic of the Tropical Forest cultures, even though sea shells were used in making artifacts. There is a greater variety of pottery than in the Tropical Forest cultures, such as bowls, jars, and storage vessels with incised, rocker dentate stamped, and polychrome decoration. The Mesoamerican traits include basal flanged bowls, tripod vessels, and mammiform supports. There is a much greater variety of other artifacts than in the Tropical Forest cultures: clay spindle whorls, figurines, stamps, and whistles; stone axes, metates, and manos; rechipped flint points, scrapers, and microliths; bone awls and needles; and shell buttons and pendants. Many of these artifacts, like the pottery, indicate Mesoamerican influence, and they also testify to a ceremonial development that is lacking in Tropical Forest cultures. This ceremonial development, like the pottery and cultivation of maize, may have had its origin in Mesoamerica (Reichel-Dolmatoff, 1957, p. 233).

From the standpoint of Steward's classification of the historic tribes, cultures like Momíl II must be considered Circum-Caribbean because of their evidences of ceremonial (and presumably also social) development.[10] In other words, we would equate Momíl II with the Circum-Caribbean tribes that occupied the Intermediate area during historic time.

Theoretically, there should also have been Tropical Forest tribes in the Intermediate area during Period II, since they were there at the time Europeans arrived. No traces of them have yet been reported, however. Momíl I does not qualify, despite its vegetative agriculture, because it already has evidences of ceremonialism. We must look for sites with Momíl I's economy but without its

10. The term "Circum-Caribbean" is used here in place of "Formative," which is preferred by many archeologists (e.g., Collier, this volume), for two reasons: it makes for easier correlation with the ethnology and applies equally to all the periods and regions under discussion, whereas there is a tendency to restrict "Formative" to the spread of effective seed agriculture from Mesoamerica during Period II (e.g., Evans and Meggers, 1957; Reichel-Dolmatoff, 1957).

evidences of Mesoamerican influence, which, in effect, make it transitional between the Tropical Forest and the Circum-Caribbean form of life.

PERIOD III

The distinction between Marginal, Tropical Forest, and Circum-Caribbean alternates continues into Period III. The principal cultures indicative of each of these alternates are listed in Table 3, with their radiocarbon determinations. It will be seen that the period lasted from *ca.* A.D. 200 to A.D. 1000.

TABLE 3

SELECTED CULTURES OF PERIOD III WITH THEIR RADIOCARBON DETERMINATIONS

Culture	Location	Determination A.D.	Sources for the Culture and Its Determination
1. Pedro García	Northeast coast of Venezuela		Cruxent and Rouse, 1958–59, 1: 105–7
2. Los Barrancos	Lower Orinoco River, Venezuela	590 ± 90	*Ibid.*, pp. 227–30
3. Chuare	Northeast coast of Venezuela	605 ± 80	*Ibid.*, pp. 121–23
4. Irapa	Northeast coast of Venezuela	380 ± 40	*Ibid.*, pp. 129–31
5. Erin	Trinidad	——	Rouse, 1953
6. Troumassée	St. Lucia, Lesser Antilles	740 ± 110	Marshall McKusick, personal communication
7. Ostiones	Puerto Rico	——	Rouse, 1952, pp. 340–44
8. Santa Elena	Puerto Rico	——	*Ibid.*, pp. 344–47
9. Meillac	Haiti	——	*Ibid.*, pp. 54–113
10. Shakimu	Montaña of Peru	——	Lathrap, 1958
11. Mangueiras	Mouth of the Amazon	——	Meggers and Evans, 1957
12. Matapolo	Pacific coast of Costa Rica	565 ± 90	Michael D. Coe, personal communication
13. Venado Beach	Pacific coast of Panama	210 ± 60	Deevey, Gralenski, and Hoffren, 1959, p. 166
14. Quevedo	Coastal Ecuador	——	Estrada, 1957*b*
15. Tierra Alta	Caribbean lowlands of Colombia	——	Reichel-Dolmatoff, G. and A., 1958
16. La Pitia	Western Venezuela	——	Cruxent and Rouse, 1958–59, 1: 63–66

Note. The first culture is Marginal, cultures 2–11 are Tropical Forest, and cultures 12–15 are Circum-Caribbean.

Only a single Marginal culture, Pedro García in northeastern Venezuela, can be listed in Table 3. However, it is probable that similar cultures persisted in the Greater Antilles and in Amazonia, since they were still there during historic time. In the Greater Antilles, the Marginal Indians may be said to have retreated into the positions they occupied historically, for we find the Tropical Forest sites extending beyond Puerto Rico, which had been their limit during Period II, into most of the rest of the Greater Antilles.

Tropical Forest culture is well represented archeologically in both Amazonia and the Caribbean area. As in the case of Period II, however, it has not yet been reported from the northern Andes, although it should be there. All the known cultures of the latter area may be identified as Circum-Caribbean (Table 3).

The known Tropical Forest cultures show very little advance over the previous period, with one significant exception. During late Period III a geographically restricted group of cultures in Puerto Rico and the neighboring islands began a ceremonial development that was to culminate later, during Period IV, in the eastern variety of Circum-Caribbean culture. The Ostiones culture, which succeeded Cuevas in Puerto Rico (Table 3, No. 7) will serve to illustrate this development. Ostiones sites are found throughout the major river valleys as well as on the coast, indicating that at least some of the inhabitants were relying more on agriculture and less upon fishing. The villages are still of the relatively small, peasant type; whatever increase of population there may have been was apparently siphoned off by expansion into the interior of the island and seizure of the neighboring islands to the west from Marginal peoples. The earlier sites still contain no ceremonial structures, but the later ones have ball courts, consisting of flat areas surrounded by stone slabs. Burial continues to be directly in the refuse, with few, if any, grave objects.

The earlier Ostiones pottery is largely undecorated, the white-on-red designs of the previous period having died out; but lugs modeled in the form of human and animal heads are added to it during the latter part of the period. To judge from the customs of historic time, these were intended to portray the Indian deities, called *zemis*, and hence they support the evidence of the ball courts in indicating that the Circum-Caribbean religious development of historic time had its origin in this period. Representations of the *zemis* also began to be carved on ornaments and implements of stone, bone, and shell during the latter part of Period III. Otherwise, the artifacts are little more complex than in the previous period. A few trade sherds have been found but no evidences of warfare.

The Circum-Caribbean cultures of the Intermediate area show equally little advance during Period III. It was at this time that the Indians to the north and the south, in Mesoamerica and the Central Andes, achieved civilization, but the local Indians now fell behind. In effect, they stagnated, as compared with their neighbors who had crossed the threshold of civilization.

The culture of Tierra Alta, in the Atlantic lowlands of Colombia, may be cited as an example of Circum-Caribbean life in the west during Period III (Table 3, No. 15). Reichel-Dolmatoff (1958, pp. 481–82) reports that the people of this culture expanded up the rivers and their tributaries in a manner analogous to that in Puerto Rico. At the same time, the villages along the larger streams increased in size and clearly became differentiated from the lesser hamlets in more remote areas, something which did not happen in Puerto Rico. Burial was now in urns, accompanied by some grave objects, but religious structures are not known.

Tierra Alta pottery is typically incised and modeled. Most of the other types of artifacts listed for the preceding Momíl culture persisted, but clay figurines were replaced by effigy vessels. Gold ornaments appear for the first time.

PERIOD IV

Selected cultures of the final period are listed in Table 4. We do not have many radiocarbon determinations for them but estimate that the period began about A.D. 1000 and persisted into historic time.

TABLE 4

SELECTED CULTURES OF PERIOD IV WITH THEIR RADIOCARBON DETERMINATIONS

Culture	Location	Determination A.D.	Sources for the Culture and Its Determination
1. Cayo Redondo	Cuba	1000 ± 60	Osgood, 1942; E. S. Deevey, personal communication
2. Guarguapo	Lower Orinoco River, Venezuela	1660 ± 50	Cruxent and Rouse, 1958–59, 1: 230–34
3. El Morro	Northeast coast of Venezuela	1670 ± 70 1245 ± 70	Ibid., pp. 123–25
4. Baní	Central Cuba	——	Rouse, 1942
5. Hupa-iya	Montaña of Peru	——	Lathrap, 1958
6. Arua	Mouth of the Amazon	——	Meggers and Evans, 1957
7. Esperanza	Eastern Puerto Rico	——	Rouse, 1952, pp. 352–54
8. Boca Chica	Dominican Republic	——	Boyrie Moya, 1955
9. Valencia	Central Venezuela	——	Cruxent and Rouse, 1958–59, 1: 175–79
10. Marajoara	Mouth of the Amazon	——	Meggers and Evans, 1957
11. Guetar	Highlands of Costa Rica	——	Lothrop, 1926
12. Coclé	Pacific coast of Panama	——	Lothrop, 1937–42
13. Chibcha	Andes of Colombia	——	Haury and Cubillos, 1953
14. Huancavilca	Coastal Ecuador	——	Estrada, 1957a
15. Tairona	Caribbean slope of Colombia	——	Mason, 1931–39; Reichel-Dolmatoff, G. and A., 1954
16. Mirinday	Andes of Venezuela	1380 ± 50	Cruxent and Rouse, 1958–59, 1: 148–51

Note. Culture 1 is Marginal, cultures 2–6 are Tropical Forest, and 7–16 can be considered Circum-Caribbean.

So far as is known, the distributions of the Marginal, Tropical Forest, and Circum-Caribbean cultures relative to each other remained the same during Period IV with an important exception. Circum-Caribbean culture now penetrated the Caribbean area and Amazonia, from which it had previously been absent.

This penetration can be demonstrated archeologically at three points: in the Greater Antilles, central Venezuela, and at the mouth of the Amazon (Table 4, Nos. 7, 8, 9, and 10, respectively). The first of these is simply the culmination of a local development that began during the previous period, as discussed above, very probably under the stimulation of Mesoamerican influences, which will be described below. The second may well have developed in a similar manner, under influences from the Intermediate area rather than from Mesoamerica. The third is a different matter. Meggers and Evans (1957) conclude that Marajoara, the Circum-Caribbean culture at the mouth of the Amazon, was intrusive from up river—from as far away as the Intermediate area, according to them— and that it lasted only briefly.

It is interesting to speculate why the Antillean and Venezuelan developments survived whereas the Amazonian did not. Meggers and Evans (1957) theorize that Marajoara culture failed because it was poorly adapted to the tropical-forest conditions at the mouth of the Amazon. However, the Circum-Caribbean cultures of the Greater Antilles and central Venezuela flourished in the same kind of environment. We would suggest that a difference in agriculture may have been the determining factor. Both the Greater Antillean and central Venezuelan cultures were built upon vegetative agriculture, which was well adapted to Tropical Forest conditions, whereas Marajoara culture, if it did come from Colombia, was probably based upon seed agriculture, which could not be efficiently carried on in the jungles of Amazonia.[11]

There were, then, two kinds of Circum-Caribbean people in the regions under consideration at the close of Period IV: isolated groups of vegetative planters in the Caribbean area and a much larger mass of seed planters in the Intermediate area. Boca Chica culture, of the Dominican Republic (Fig. 2), will serve to illustrate the life of the vegetative planters. Boca Chica is the culture of the Taino Indians, who were encountered by Columbus (Lovén, 1935). Its sites vary considerably in size, and the larger ones are accompanied by ceremonial plazas and ball courts, usually surrounded by stone slabs set on edge. Stone pillars, carved with figures of the zemis, or Indian deities, were set up in the centers of the plazas. Burials are frequently accompanied by pottery vessels, although there are still no ornaments or other ceremonial artifacts, such as are found in the Intermediate area. It may be assumed that the larger sites were inhabited by more important chiefs and that considerable trade and social stratification were also present, since both have been described by the first European explorers. On the other hand, the Taino were not warlike.

The pottery is elaborately decorated with modeled-incised heads, which, according to the historic sources, represented zemis. Carvings of the zemis also

11. One wonders, though, why the Marajoara people did not shift from seed to vegetative agriculture when they entered the tropical forests, as the Mexicans who migrated into the Talamanca valley apparently did (see n. 5 above).

appear on celts, pestles, and ornaments of various kinds and are reproduced as idols of clay, stone, and wood. The last come out of caves, which the Indians used as shrines. The caves have also yielded carved wooden stools, which were a sign of rank, and several of these are inlaid with gold—the only use of that metal known for the culture. Finally, there are a number of unique types of carved-stone artifacts, including collars, "elbow stones," three-pointed stones, and balls, most of which also bear representations of the zemis.

The historic sources indicate a dense population and refer to the use of irrigation among the Taino, but this cannot have been extensive, since no traces of it have been found archeologically. The cultivation of maize is also recorded, but it was secondary to bitter manioc. As already noted, the Taino apparently did not grind maize into flour to make bread.

Not only maize but also the ball game and certain ceremonial objects, such as stone collars, and elbow stones, look Mesoamerican. Lovén (1935) has suggested that the Taino obtained the basic elements of their religion through diffusion directly from Mesoamerica, although this would have required long over-water voyages of several thousand miles.

The highest development of Circum-Caribbean culture among the seed planters was achieved by the Tairona Indians in northern Colombia (Fig. 2). Reichel-Dolmatoff (1958, p. 483) terms Tairona an urban culture—the only one in the three regions under discussion here—but it cannot be considered a civilization, since it lacks many of the other elements in Childe's (1950) definition, such as monumental buildings, writing, and science. The sites consist of "large urban centers grouped around one or various ceremonial sites." There are foundations of stone masonry—presumably for temples as well as dwellings—ceremonial courts, reservoirs, irrigation canals, agricultural terraces, stone bridges, paved stone roads and stairways, and stelae. Burial was in urns, shaft graves, or slab-lined cists, accompanied, as is typically the case in the Intermediate area, by pottery vessels and ornaments of various kinds, including some of metal. Pottery is complex in shape and is decorated mainly by simple modeling or incision. Other artifacts of clay include pestles, whorls, rattles, stamps, whistles, and, more rarely, figurines. Stone was used not only for utilitarian artifacts, such as metates and manos, but also for ceremonial objects, for example, batons, small seats or tables, amulets, and figurines. The last two were also carved out of bone. The Tairona Indians knew how to smelt gold, copper, and the alloy of the two called *tumbaga*, using these materials for ornaments but not for implements. According to the historic sources, the government was theocratic; there was marked social stratification; and warfare, if not trade, was well developed.

The Tairona sites are situated on the northern and western slopes of the Sierra Nevada de Santa Marta. One might expect them to be limited to, or at least concentrated in, the *tierra templada*, or temperate zone, but such is not the case. Most of them lie in the lower, tropical zone. Reichel-Dolmatoff (1958, p. 483) believes that the Tairona Indians originated in the Caribbean lowlands, probably in a culture like Tierra Alta, which has been described above for Period III.

CONCLUSIONS

Three features stand out in the foregoing account of the culture history of the Intermediate area, Amazonia, and the Caribbean area. One is the fact that all the cultural alternates survived until historic time (Fig. 3). True, the early hunters must have shifted from large to small game as the latter became extinct at the close of the Pleistocene, but otherwise the Marginal tribes who lived in the peripheries of Amazonia during historic time apparently carried on much the same form of life as their Pleistocene predecessors. The fishing peoples who arose in the Caribbean area during Period I similarly survived in places like western

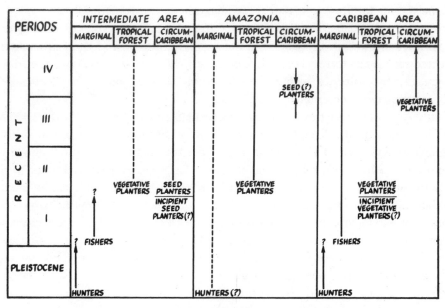

FIGURE 3. Summary of the culture history of the Intermediate
area, Amazonia, and the Caribbean.

Cuba until the time of Columbus; and both the Tropical Forest and Circum-Caribbean alternates, which developed during Period II, were still widespread when the first Europeans arrived.

This survival of earlier forms of life recalls the situation in Negro Africa and in Siberia (Clark and Okladnikov, both in this volume). As in the latter areas, it may be due to the varying nature of the environment, which in effect supplies a number of different ecological niches, many of them better suited to earlier forms of life. The absence of civilization is also probably a factor. If it had been present, the less advanced peoples would presumably have been drawn into its economic and political web, becoming a part of the larger whole, even though they might, at the same time, have retained many of their local customs and their peculiar means of subsistence.

A second interesting feature of the culture history just discussed is the way in which the Intermediate area, in the west, diverged from Amazonia and the Caribbean area, in the east, after the appearance of effective agriculture. The Tropical Forest cultures of the first part of Period II in the east give us our first evidence of effective vegetative agriculture. The situation in the west at this time is uncertain. (Momíl I, with its vegetative agriculture, may or may not be typical of the west.) Sometime during Period II, effective seed agriculture seems to have entered the Intermediate area from Mesoamerica, accompanied by ceremonial traits that have led us to classify the new cultures as Circum-Caribbean. These traits apparently did not penetrate either Amazonia or the Caribbean area, which remained on the less advanced, Tropical Forest level of development (Fig. 3).

One reason for this divergence may have been the remoteness of the eastern regions from Mesoamerica. Another may have been the persistence of vegetative agriculture in the east. In effect, the Indians of Amazonia and the Caribbean area rejected seed agriculture, presumably because they were satisfied with the form of agriculture they already had, and, in rejecting it, they may also have rejected the accompanying ceremonial developments.

Both Amazonia and the Caribbean area, then, lagged behind the Intermediate area in achieving the Circum-Caribbean level of development. It did not arise in either area until Period IV, though it had been present in the Intermediate area two periods earlier. Moreover, the Indians of Amazonia achieved it only temporarily—in the form of Marajoara culture at the mouth of the Amazon—and the Caribbean Indians only sporadically. We have speculated that the latter were more successful with it than the former because they based it upon their own vegetative agriculture rather than upon seed agriculture.

A third significant feature brought out by our survey is the failure of the Indians of the Intermediate area to develop civilization. They acquired the basis for it when they adopted seed agriculture during Period II but then stagnated during Periods III and IV, long after their neighbors in Mesoamerica and the Central Andes had crossed the threshold of civilization.

This stagnation cannot have been for lack of knowledge of civilization, for we find many evidences of contact between the Indians of the Intermediate area and their neighbors to the north and south (e.g., Willey, 1959, pp. 188–89). The extremes of environment and difficulties of communication within the Intermediate area, to which reference was made at the beginning of this article, may have been factors, but they can hardly have been decisive, for civilization existed in similar, though perhaps less extreme, environments to the north and south.

The relatively low density of population in the Intermediate area was probably also a factor, although this may have been a symptom of the stagnation rather than a cause. So far as we know, only isolated groups of Period IV Indians, notably the Tairona and Muisca in Colombia and the Taino in the Greater Antilles, attained a significant degree of population density. One wonders whether these Indians would have gone on to develop civilizations if the Europeans had not arrived in America when they did, or whether other factors, such as the scarcity of irrigation, the relative simplicity of social stratification and religion, the lack of specialization by occupation, and the apparent paucity of large-scale trading, would have prevented them from rising beyond the Circum-Caribbean level of development.

BIBLIOGRAPHY

ALEGRÍA, RICARDO; H. B. NICHOLSON; and GORDON R. WILLEY
1955. "The Archaic Tradition in Puerto Rico," *Amer. Antiq.*, 21:113–21.

BELL, ROBERT E., and W. J. MAYER-OAKES
1960. "An Early Lithic Site near Quito, Ecuador." (Paper delivered at the 25th Annual Meeting of the Society for American Archaeology, New Haven.)

BENNETT, WENDELL C.
1936. *Excavations in Bolivia.* ("Anthrop. Papers Amer. Mus. Nat. Hist.," Vol. 35, Part 4.) New York.
1944. *Archeological Regions of Colombia.* ("Yale Univ. Publs. in Anthrop.," No. 30.) New Haven.

BOYRIE MOYA, EMILE DE
1955. *Monumento megalítico y petroglifos de Chacuey, Republica Dominicana.* ("Publs. de la Universidad de Santo Domingo," Ser. 7, Vol. 97, No. 1.) Ciudad Trujillo.

BUSHNELL, GEOFFREY H. S.
1951. *The Archaeology of the Santa Elena Peninsula in Southwest Ecuador.* ("Occ. Publs. Cambridge Univ. Mus. Archaeol. and Ethnol.," No. 1.) Cambridge, England.

CHILDE, V. GORDON
1950. "The Urban Revolution," *Town Planning Review* (Liverpool), 21:3–17.

COE, MICHAEL D.
1960. "Archeological Linkages with North and South America at La Victoria, Guatemala," *Amer. Anthrop.* 62:363–93.

CRUXENT, J. M., and IRVING ROUSE
1958–59. *An Archeological Chronology of Venezuela.* ("Pan American Union, Soc. Sci. Monogs.," No. 6.) 2 vols. Washington.

DEEVEY, EDWARD S., L. J. GRALENSKI, and VÄINÖ HOFFREN
1959. "Yale Natural Radiocarbon Measurements IV," *Amer. J. Sci., Radiocarbon Suppl.*, 1:144–72. New Haven.

ESTRADA, EMILIO
1956. *Valdivia: un sitio arqueológico formativo en la costa de la provincia del Guayas, Ecuador.* ("Publ. Museo Victor Emilio Estrada," No. 1.) Guayaquil.
1957a. *Los Huancavilcas: ultimas civilizaciones pre-históricas de la costa del Guayas.* (*Ibid.*, No. 3.)
1957b. *Ultimas civilizaciones pre-históricas de la cuenca del Río Guayas.* (*Ibid.*, No. 2.)
1958. *Las culturas pre-clásicas, formativas, o arcaicas del Ecuador.* (*Ibid.*, No. 5.)

EVANS, CLIFFORD, and BETTY J. MEGGERS
1957. "Formative Period Cultures in the Guayas Basin, Coastal Ecuador," *Amer. Antiq.*, 22:235–47.

HABERLAND, WOLFGANG
1957. "Black-on-red Painted Ware and Associated Features in Intermediate Area," *Ethnos*, (Stockholm), 22:148–61.

HAURY, EMIL W.
1953. "Some Thoughts on Chibcha Culture in the High Plains of Colombia," *Amer. Antiq.*, 19:76–78.

HAURY, EMIL W., and JULIO CESAR CUBILLOS
1953. *Investigaciones arquelógicas on la Sabana de Bogotá, Colombia (cultura Chibcha)*. (Univ. Ariz., Soc. Sci. Bull., No. 22.) Tucson.

HOWARD, G. D.
1947. *Prehistoric Ceramic Styles of Lowland South America: Their Distribution and History*. ("Yale Univ. Publs. in Anthrop.," No. 37.) New Haven.

LADD, JOHN
1957. "A Stratigraphic Trench at Sitio Conté, Panama," *Amer. Antiq.*, 22:265–71.

LATHRAP, DONALD W.
1958. "The Cultural Sequence at Yarinacocha, Eastern Peru." *Amer. Antiq.*, 23:379–88.

LIBBY, WILLARD F.
1955. *Radiocarbon Dating*. 2d ed. Chicago.

LOVÉN, SVEN
1935. *Origins of the Tainan Culture, West Indies*. Göteborg.

MANGLESDORF, PAUL C., R. S. MACNEISH, and G. R. WILLEY
MS. "Origins of Agriculture in Mesoamerica." In ROBERT WAUCHOPE (ed.), *Handbook of Middle American Indians*, Vol. 1. (In preparation.)

MASON, J. ALDEN
1931–39. *Archaeology of Santa Marta, Colombia: the Tairona Culture*. ("Anthropol. Ser., Field Mus. Nat. Hist.," Vol. 20, Nos. 1–3.) Chicago.

McGIMSEY, C. R., III
1956. "Cerro Mangote: a Preceramic Site in Panama," *Amer. Antiq.*, 22:151–61.
1958. "Further Data and a Date from Cerro Mangote, Panama," *Ibid.*, 23:434–35.

MEGGERS, BETTY J., and CLIFFORD EVANS
1955. "Preliminary Results of Archeological Investigations in British Guiana." (Reprinted from *Timehri: J. Roy. Agric. and Commer. Soc. British Guiana* [Georgetown], No. 34, pp. 1–26.)
1957. *Archeological Investigations at the Mouth of the Amazon*. (Bur. Amer. Ethnol. Bull., No. 167.) Washington.

REICHEL-DOLMATOFF, GERARDO
1954. "A Preliminary Study of Space and Time Perspective in Northern Colombia," *Amer. Antiq.*, 19:352–66.
1955. "Excavaciones en los conchales de la costa de Barlovento," *Revista Colombiana de Antropología* (Bogotá), 4:249–72.
1957. "Momíl: A Formative Sequence from the Sinú Valley, Colombia," *Amer. Antiq.*, 22:226–34.
1958. "Recientes investigaciones arqueológicas en el norte de Colombia," *Miscellanea Paul Rivet, Octagenario Dictada*, 2:471–86. Mexico City.

REICHEL-DOLMATOFF, GERARDO and ALICIA

1951. "Investigaciones arqueológicas en el Depto. del Magdalena, Colombia, 1946–1950," *Boletín de Arqueología*, Vol. 3, Nos. 1–2. Bogotá.

1954. "Investigaciones arqueológicas en la Sierra Nevada de Santa Marta," *Revista Colombiana de Antropología*, 2: 147–207; 3:139–70. Bogotá.

1956. "Momíl, excavaciones en el Sinú," *ibid.*, 5:109–333.

1958. "Reconocimiento arqueológico de la hoya del Río Sinú," *ibid.*, 6:29–158.

ROUSE, IRVING

1941. *Culture of the Ft. Liberté Region, Haiti.* ("Yale Univ. Publs. in Anthrop.," No. 24.) New Haven.

1942. "The Arawak." In JULIAN H. STEWARD (ed.), *Handbook of South American Indians.* (Bur. Amer. Ethnol. Bull. No. 153, 4:507–39.) Washington.

1951. "Areas and Periods of Culture in the Greater Antilles," *Southwestern J. Anthrop.* 7:248–65.

1952. *Puerto Rican Prehistory.* ("N.Y. Acad. Sci. Scient. Surv. of Porto Rico and the Virgin Islands," Vol. 18, Nos. 3–4.) New York.

1953. *Indian Sites in Trinidad.* ("Yale Univ. Publs. in Anthrop.," No. 50, pp. 94–111.) New Haven.

1960. *The Entry of Man into the West Indies. Ibid.*, No. 61.

SAUER, CARL O.

1952. *Agricultural Origins and Dispersals.* New York.

STEWARD, JULIAN

1947. "American Culture History in the Light of South America," *Southwestern J. Anthrop.*, 3:85–107.

STEWARD, JULIAN H., and LOUIS C. FARON

1959. *Native Peoples of South America.* New York.

STONE, DORIS

1956. "Date of Maize in Talamanca, Costa Rica: An Hypothesis," *J. Soc. des Américanistes* (Paris), n.s., 45:189–94.

WILLEY, GORDON R.

1958. "Estimated Correlations and Dating of South and Central American Culture Sequences," *Amer. Antiq.*, 23:353–78.

1959. "The 'Intermediate Area' of Nuclear America: Its Prehistoric Relationships to Middle America and Perú," *Actas del XXXIII Congreso Internacional de Américanistas, San José, 20–27 Julio 1958*, 1:184–94. San José.

1960. "New World Prehistory," *Science*, 131:73–86.

WILLEY, GORDON R., and C. R. McGIMSEY

1954. *The Monagrillo Culture of Panama.* ("Papers Peabody Mus. Archaeol. and Ethnol., Harvard Univ.," Vol. 49, No. 2.) Cambridge.

INDIA

HASMUKH D. SANKALIA

I. INTRODUCTION

BEFORE CALLING our attention to the main theme of the symposium I should like to say a few things regarding, first, the traditional point of view; second, the present view of archeologists in India and outside; third, the method of inquiry and the type of approach necessary for answering the problem, and, fourth, a detailed review of archeological evidence.

Traditionally, it is believed that the centers of early civilization in India were the Gangetic valley, Sind, Sauvīra, Saurāshtra, and Vidharba, south of the Narmadā. It is in these regions only, covering most of northern India and northern Deccan, that cities like Rājagriha, Pātaliputra, Kosāmbi, Hastināpur, Ujjain, Kushasthali, and Kundinapūra existed. Ancient literature describes also very briefly how these centers developed, but we have had no idea of the actual stage of their development: were they really urban centers or merely peasant villages, though called *puras* and *nagaras?*

Archeologists believe that India is on the periphery of culture spread, the main centers where urban civilization developed being the ancient "Fertile Crescent," known as the Near East or Middle East to Western archeologists and as western Asia to Indian archeologists. The belief is probably right; but it must be said that it is also based on insufficient field work done in India so far, and many areas, even potentially rich ones, are left unexplored. To take one instance, only ten years ago it was believed that the vast expanses in India outside the Indus Valley civilization were in a purely food-collecting stage or at best were just emerging from it. Explorations have shown that these areas were not in such a backward condition but were teeming with early peasant villages, some of which might have developed into cities that are not yet discovered. For example, Navdatoli and Nagda in the Narmada and Chambal Valleys of central India, Prakashe in the Tapi, and Nasik, Nevasa, and others in the Godavari-Pravara basin. Again, in the last mentioned valley, the writer thought that since numerous sites have given identical pottery from the basal layers, the Jorwe-Nevasa was the first or the earliest chalcolithic culture. But this view has been belied by the discoveries at Daimabad, only fifteen miles west of Nevasa, where two earlier cultures are found.

METHOD OF INQUIRY

There are three different methods of approach for our inquiry:

1. We may divide India geographically, following Subbarao, into "nuclear" areas or areas of "attraction," areas of "relative isolation," and areas of "isolation."
2. We may discuss the evidence riverwise as follows:
    a) The Indus basin
    b) The Gangetic valley
    c) The Narmadā valley or the Malwa plateau and central India
    d) The valley of the Sarasvatī and Drishadvati in Rājputāna and Sābarmatī in north Gujarat and the Saurāshtra or Kāthiawad peninsula
    e) The valleys of the Tāpī, Godāvari, Krishnā or the upper Deccan plateau (known as Desha) or Mahārāshṭra
    f) The lower Krishnā basin covering parts of Āndhra-Karṇāṭak
    g) The valleys of Kaverī, Tāmbraparṇī etc. in Tāmilnaḍ
    h) The valleys of the Mahānadī, Brahmāṇī etc. in Orissa
3. We may simply divide the subcontinent on a topographical basis into northern India (NI), western India (WI), central India (CI), eastern India (EI) and southern India (SI).

TYPE OF APPROACH

Whatever be the method of approach, it is essential that it should not be biased by different assertions. The conclusions and explanations about the nature of the results should follow from the objective statement and interpretation of archeological facts, rather than taking for granted a particular theory or attitude, and should explain the results from that point of view. The reasons for such an approach are obvious. Our knowledge about the different regions in India is incomplete for various reasons. There is the lack of systematic and planned research, so that some areas are completely neglected, whereas some, for instance Sind and more recently the Deccan, Gujarat, central India, and the United Province are better explored in recent years. Again the nature of the evidence itself, though based on scientific excavations, is fragmentary and therefore incomplete. Excavations and even explorations have been only partial and by no means exhaustive, in any of its aspects.

II. REVIEW OF ARCHEOLOGICAL EVIDENCE

PRIMITIVE TO ADVANCED FOOD-COLLECTING STAGES: FLAKE INDUSTRIES

A regional review is therefore desirable. Almost all parts or divisions of India have now yielded lower paleolithic industries. These are of two types: (1) Soanian and (2) the hand-axe-cleaver type. The former is primarily confined to the Punjab, though tools resembling some of its types, for example, choppers and chopping tools, do occur in the latter.

The handaxe or the biface industry has an all-India distribution, though, owing to perhaps inadequate explorations, it has not been reported so far from Sind, Saurashtra in Western India, Assam in Eastern India, and the extreme south. Everywhere it can be placed typologically and/or stratigraphically in the middle pleistocene period. In the Punjab this is related to the inter-glacial period, while in the rest of India it may be placed in the first pluvial or a period of heavy rain. So far, however, its earlier antecedents are nowhere clearly visible. It may have been introduced from Africa, where a well-marked development is available.

Until recently, the next cultural stage was not clearly discernible, except in the Punjab and to some extent in Kurnool in south India. Work during the last six years has shown that the handaxe culture was followed by a culture in which scrapers, points, blade-like flakes (some of definite Levallois type, but others of nondescript nature) occur.

This culture has a wide distribution, almost co-extensive with the handaxe culture.

Since stratigraphically it succeeds the former—particularly at Nevāsā and other sites in western India and at Maheshwar and other sites in central India—and is assignable in both to Terrace II, it has been called "middle paleolithic" or "Middle Stone Age" or, after the type site "Nevāsa," *Nevasian*. A middle Pleistocene fauna such as that including *Bos namadicus Falconer* has been associated with it at Kālegaon and other sites on the Godavari in western India, but since the culture is typologically so dissimilar to the hand-axe culture and also uses a completely different raw material in western, central, and eastern India, it is advisable to place it in the late Pleistocene. Moreover, it seems to bear a genetic relationship with the later blade cultures, though so far no indisputable stratigraphical evidence is available anywhere. For all these reasons, this culture has been discussed in some detail here (though if it is indeed late middle Pleistocene, it would fall outside the scope of this symposium).

Observations by the writer in western India, central India, and Karnatak and Kurnool in south India and reports from Orissa, United Province, central India, and Rajputana definitely indicate that stratigraphically this culture succeeds the lower paleolithic or the handaxe culture. The raw material, except in Kurnool and Karnatak to some extent, is fine-grained stone-like jasper and agate or flint in southern Rajputana.[1]

The tools indicate a peculiar combination of "free," "controlled," "soft hammer," and "pressure" techniques as well as the (occasional) preparation of the core as in the Levallois technique. But by and large the makers preferred to

---

1. In Kurnool, however, where quartzite is plentiful, the tools continue to be made of this material. And it appeared to the writer, when he recently examined the sites there, that this region might provide a clue to the development or evolution of a middle paleolithic and late paleolithic culture from the lower paleolithic. Elsewhere there appears superficially to be a clean break between the techniques as well as the raw material of the two cultures. It must, however, be mentioned that a tendency toward smaller and neater bifaces, very nearly like points, is visible at a number of sites in western India and central India

use any flat or flattish flake or a suitable nodule and turned it into a "side" or "hollow scraper" or into a point. A recurrent type is a point-cum-hollow scraper. The retouch—sometimes very fine, but often nothing but nibbling—is generally only on one side, the upper or the under, but at times on both. Carefully finished specimens are a thing of beauty—perfectly symmetrical, with retouch, and exhibiting an innate sense of the selection of the material. Points, for instance, are of a multicolored stone (e.g., jasper; Kalegaon, D.C., Poona).

Some of the points also indicate an incipient tang and the use of hafting. Recently this feature was noticed in small hand-axes and cleavers of a late lower paleolithic character from Gangāpur, near Nāsik, western India.

There is also a blade element in this culture, the flakes being thin and narrow and at times quite long, as for example from the Tapi basin in Khāndesh, central India. These are also at times retouched, thus resembling the classical upper paleolithic blades of western Europe.

Thus this new culture, called here "middle paleolithic" or the "Nevasian," has some elements that recall those of Europe and Africa. Two of its most characteristic tool types—the scrapers and points—definitely indicate a change in the hunting method of the people who made them. Bows and arrows and spokeshaves had come into use, in addition to the earlier methods of snaring and capturing the prey. These included *Bos namadicus Falconer* and probably the *Elephas anticuus*, equids, rhinoceros, and the hippopotamus, besides deer, etc. (A fuller list will be available when Mr. C. Tripathi of the Geological Survey of India and Dr. Khatri working on behalf of the C.S.I.R. submit their reports.)

The climate was decidedly wetter than when (owing to increasing dryness) the silt of the first conglomerate phase was deposited but not so wet as to enable the streams to transport large and heavier material. Consequently, the gravels everywhere are smaller in size and often contain markedly different material. For instance, in the Deccan there are medium-sized chunks and occasional pebbles of agate, chalcedony, carnelian, and jasper, and sometimes olive-green pebbles of basalt or olivine dolorite. This feature also indicates that the makers could break the thin veins of the fine-grained rocks that appear in the trap hills.

Another notable feature is that the gravels almost everywhere covered the old conglomerate but did not reach up to the silt, and thus they form a kind of ledge or low terrace against the older formation. This is clearly visible at Maheshwar on the Narmada in central India and Nandur Madhmeshwar on the Godavari in western India. Probably it is for this reason that the gravels are found eroded at a large number of places where these have been examined in India. However, some of the best exposures of this gravel are seen on the Godavari.

Briefly, then, the middle paleolithic culture characterized by scrapers and points and incipient blades may be assigned to the late Pleistocene, when the climate was comparatively less wet than in the middle Pleistocene, when the handaxe culture flourished. The fauna and probably the flora (of which we have no remains) continued the same.

Probably contemporary and perhaps related to this are the late Soan industries of the Punjab. The earlier, late Soan A, belongs to the third glacial period, when T2 was being formed. It is placed in the upper Pleistocene and contains a good deal of Levallois element along with the earlier choppers (which are now smaller and neater) and a small percentage of blades. This last feature definitely indicates a change in the life of the people and occupies a prominent place in late Soan B industries. Thus for our purpose this phase in the Punjab is important. It is associated with the basal portion of the Potwar loessic silt on T2 and placed tentatively in later third interglacial.

Thus both the tools and the climatic conditions—a dry phase as in the rest of India—suggest different environment for man and his activities.

While recent work in India has been able to fill the gap between the middle Pleistocene and the earliest Holocene, there is no clear undisputed stratigraphical evidence for a culture or cultures as in Europe, Palestine, and Africa (?) that can be assigned to the latest Pleistocene times (unless, of course, future research brings down the date of the culture just discussed or the cultures which are about to be mentioned are relegated to this phase of the Pleistocene from the Holocene).

Transition from Food Collection to Food Production: Microlithic Industries

As in Europe, Africa, and several parts of Asia, great climatic changes had taken place in India toward the end of the paleolithic period. These must have had bearing upon the environment of man and his mode of living.

Though there was widespread archeological evidence for this in the shape of microliths, it was not supported by stratigraphical, geochronological, and paleobiological data. Hence the microliths had little cultural significance. This deficiency is being slowly filled up, though not so quickly and in such a planned manner as one would wish.

Within the last twenty years, three or four other regions, besides the classic sites of Cammiade in Kurnool District, have yielded microliths in a geological context. We may say that the whole of India is thus represented. Todd's Khandivli microliths come from the western coast near Bombay and those from Karachi in Sind may be regarded as their continuation.

The evidence from Langhnaj is fully representative of the whole northern and central Gujarat, which lies a little away from the western coast.

In eastern India the evidence is provided by Birbhanpur, Chakradharpur, and Mirzapur, while in south India we have evidence from the *Teri* sites and from surface microliths from Mysore.

Of these, the oldest microlithic industry seems to be that from the *Teri* in the Tinnevelly in south India. The sites lie mostly along the eastern coast of the tip of the peninsula and, though exposed, they are believed to be "derived from a soil profile, now in the process of denudation and forming part of a series of aeolian sands." The sites seem to be associated with a sea level somewhat higher than at present.

On the basis of the available collection, a sequence of three industries is postulated: (1) an earlier Ṭeri industry consisting of flakes and core tools; (2) a later, the main Ṭeri industry, similar to the former but including blades and geometric forms; and (3) a neolithic blade industry, often accompanied by stone axes. In fact nothing much is known about the last, and so it is better left out of consideration.

The first two are generally made on quartz and chert (though why these should be preferred when finer silicate material is locally available is a mystery) and are heavily stained with red, hydrated ferric oxide. The tools comprise a large number of indeterminate flakes, blades, burins, geometric forms like the lunates, trapezes and triangles, scrapers and discoids, small chopping tools, and points of various types, including a few pressure-flaked bifacial ones.

These tools must have been made by hunting and/or fishing people living in temporary camps on or near the coast. The geological context and the presence of certain tool types might make the industry upper paleolithic and might place it toward the close of the late Pleistocene, but provisionally it has been given a date of 4000 B.C., which is certainly very conservative.

The second, and perhaps equally ancient, is the Birbhanpur microlithic industry. Because of the non-occurrence of the trapeze and the triangle it is regarded as non-geometric and includes irregular, free-flaked cores; fluted cores; blades; lunates; points; borers; scrapers; and burins. The material is mostly milky quartz, though occasionally crystal, chert, chalcedony, quartzite, and fossil wood are used. Dr. Lal's (1958, p. 47) geochronologic studies indicate that when the microlithic people occupied the site the climate must have been comparatively dry and mild, following the last wet phase, during which the laterite weathered, and dense forest existed in the region. This mild climatic phase was followed by a period of increasing aridity and violent wind activity, so that the habitation layers were covered with wind-blown sand.

The evidence from Mysore is mostly surface. The only important site is at Jalahalli, near Bangalore. Here Todd found in a reddish soil horizon, beneath the black soil, microliths of quartz and rock crystal and one of red jasper. Dr. Seshadri groups the collection on typological basis into:

1. Jalahalli microlithic industry with a preponderance of crescents, points, and arrowheads, indicating a hunting economy and environment.
2. Brahmagiri microlithic industry, consisting primarily of parallel-sided flakes and Gravettian-like penknife blades, implying a semiurban culture in which arrowhead, crescent, etc., are absent.

There is also a third group, formed by Kibbanahalli in which there are three or four types of scrapers, blades, and highly finished lunates.

Subsequent work elsewhere in India has shown that Brahmagiri microlithic industry indeed forms a part of the vast Chalcolithic culture complex, which was mostly of a peasant village type but had attained an urban stage in Sind, the Punjab, and Saurashtra. Further, while this peasant stage can be approximately dated to 1000 B.C., the purely geometric industry cannot be brought to that date. Probably it is early and truly mesolithic.

The Mirzapur (Singrauli basin) microliths occur about four feet below the upper alluvium along the southern bank of Bālia Nadi near Kolā. They are predominantly of limpid quartz, which is easily available in the vicinity and are "non-geometric denoted by parallel-sided blades, lunates and points. Only a few tools are either finished or retouched." It may be a degenerate, late upper paleolithic blade industry, ascribable to an early mesolithic period, when a gradual dryness came over the area after the end of the paleolithic period.

This brings us to Langhnaj. It is not a solitary site, an oasis, but one of the hundreds (Subbarao lists over 80) in the sandy undulating alluvial plain of northern and central Gujarat. The topography is certainly different from that which one sees in Kurnool, in the heart of the old land mass. Here are miles and miles of flat sandy stretches, where suddenly one finds two or three small hillocks of the same material enclosing an inundation lake that keeps water for almost ten months in a year. The tops and slopes of these small hillocks are strewn with microliths. These, as well as the river banks, were the resorts of the microlithic people. A series of small excavations and examination of the soil by Professor Zeuner suggest that the dunes were formed when at the end of the dry phase (U) a slightly damper phase had followed, which in its turn was succeeded by a drier phase. It was at this phase, sometime in the late Pleistocene, that "more or less isolated dunes were blown over the land surface." A soil developed on these dunes.

The climate was slightly wetter, so that large inundation lakes were formed between the hollows of the dunes. A nomadic, hunting people lived on these mounds and along the river banks. The industry—consisting of blades, lunates, trapezes, triangles, scrapers, points, a few burins, and fluted as well as amorphous cores—may be described as geometric but is on the whole coarse and crude, though the material is chert, agate, carnelian, and only occasionally quartz. Heavy tools so far are very few; only one macehead or weight for a digging stick of quartzite was excavated. The men hunted rhinoceros (*Rhinoceros unicornis* L), hog deer (*Hyelaphus porcimus Zimm*), Indian buffalo, antelope (*Boselaphus tragocamelus Pall*), black buck (*Antelope arvipra*), and dog. All these, including the dog and the buffalo, seem, according to Professor Zeuner's study, to be wild. The fauna is thus of game, and the people were, primarily, hunters and fishers (as, besides animal bones, remains of fish vertebra and tortoise shell have been found).

Along with microliths, a large number of bones, and a negligible quantity of pottery, about twelve human skeletons have so far been found. These are of a fairly tall, thin, dolicocephalic people with a slight prognathism. Their cranial capacity compares with that of the modern Europoid, whereas other skull features suggest Negroid affinities.[2]

2. This is based on a preliminary study by my colleague Dr. (Mrs.) I. Karve as far back as 1948. Since then the human remains have been more fully studied by Dr. (Mrs.) Erhardt of Tubingen University. I hope to bring forward her report at the symposium.

Since a majority of microliths, animal remains, and human skeletons were found more than four feet from the surface, which represents a buried soil phase, the Langhjaj culture is likely to be quite old and may, by further tests and work, turn out to be toward the closing phase of the Pleistocene.

Cammiade's Kurnool sites do not stand isolated now. Extensive explorations by Shri Isaac of the Deccan College have brought to light numerous sites, some even extending into the limestone cave region of the district. This field will be further enlarged when the adjacent regions are similarly explored, thus bringing into our purview those districts of Andhra, Madras, and Mysore States that have similar geomorphological features, implying similar or identical climatic conditions in the past.

The Kurnool microliths may fall into two series—non-geometric and geometric, though as yet a rigid stratigraphical correlation eludes us. The industry comprises parallel-sided blades, lunates, triangles, trapezes, scrapers, backed blades, and burins.

Khandivali microlithic was supposed to mark the end of a rich cultural sequence beginning with the early paleolithic. But recent observations by Lal, McCown, and the writer suggest that the whole is probably a rewash, and more extensive studies of the area are necessary before inferences are made regarding the climatic conditions.

However, there are other sites along the coast and the Thānā creek and along the banks of rivers like the Ulhās in the north and the Ambā in the south of Bombay that definitely suggest that the people inhabited these areas on slightly higher grounds—usually rocks or hillocks—and avoided the thicker jungle in the interior. It is likely that they preferred the region because it grows an abundance of bananas and coconuts and abounds in fish and fowl. Hitherto no remains of their temporary camps have been discovered except microliths. These sites also contain a few heavier tools like the macehead or digging weight and chopper, besides a purely geometric microlithic industry. They may therefore be divided into an earlier and a later series. The former may be derived from the blade and burin industry, dependent primarily on hunting, while the latter, along with geometric forms and heavier tools like the macehead, may point towards a food-producing stage. Todd lists the following groups of tools: microliths (obliquely and wholly blunted), lunates, triangles, trapezes, trapezoids, and drills, five types of cores and scrapers, maceheads, and axes.

This review shows that in a few areas in India the microliths claim a fairly good antiquity. This in Tinnevelley or at Birbhanpur might mean the latest Pleistocene times or the beginning of Holocene. The exact age in years is difficult to guess but may be placed between 10,000–4000 B.C.

In all the regions there was definitely an environmental change, though differing in intensity and nature from region to region. But on the whole a climate drier than in the preceding phase may generally be postulated. Except in northern and central Gujarat, no idea can be had of the contemporary fauna or flora (though even in Gujarat, the evidence for the flora is almost nil). In Gujarat, man was practically a hunter, and almost all the animals on whom he subsisted were wild (or of a huntable type) except perhaps the dog. It is argued from the presence of small flat querns (found, so far, in numerous fragments that cannot be put together and hence no idea can be had of their size) that man probably pounded (wild) grains and might thus be placed on a higher rung of the ladder between a food-collecting and a food-producing stage. This view does not seem to be justified. First, the querns seem to have been too small to pound anything on them; they are more like stones used today for preparing sandalwood and other pastes. Second, the writer, so far, has not come across a single grain in any one of the numerous excavations on the site or elsewhere in the region. The pottery evidence is also negligible. Not more than ten to twenty sherds, not one indicating the probable shape of the vessel, have so far been recovered. Thus the Langhnaj culture must be regarded as a food-collecting one, whatever be its exact antiquity.

The microliths (whether they contain a geometric element or not) might have evolved from the earlier "blade and burin" industry; but nowhere is such an evolution available stratigraphically. The Kurnool evidence is not from one stratified site but from a typological grouping of the collection from a number of sites.

So we may end this section with the observation that the microlithic industries are associated with an environmental change, that they do indicate a change in the mode of life of man in India, but that it is not exactly clear whether the microliths developed out of the earlier "blade and burin" industries or were due to the influence of some external stimuli.

From the Semi-Nomadic and Pastoral Stage to Urbanization through a Peasant Village Stage

Just as we do not get from one single site in India well-documented data for the evolution of man, his environment, and his cultural equipment in the early period, so also the evidence for his further march toward civilization is scattered and hence inadequate for understanding the steps by which this was achieved.

On the one hand, we find several cultures in the foothills of Baluchistan which from the existence of painted pottery (some of which is definitely wheel-made) is an index of a food-producing stage, though among their other equipment are microliths and occasionally figurines of animals, "mother goddess," and rarely burials. However, none of this is fully or even partially excavated, so we have no clear image of the size of settlement or of even one of its houses. Fortunately some sites now have C^{14} determinations, while their pottery definitely indicates Iranian influence. So we know the age of a few of these cultures and how they might have come about.

Immediately east of these peasant cultures, in the fertile valleys of the Indus and in Sind and the Punjab, we suddenly meet face to face a mature urban civilization. Its antecedents are hitherto unknown, though Wheeler's work at Harappa and Khan's at Kot Diji show that there were earlier stages. The civilization had a much wider extension than originally realized; its offshoots are being found as far south as the coast of Gujarat in western India, as far east as Delhi, and in the west beyond the borders of Sind proper.

But this was not the only culture in western and northern India. In the Punjab, as well as in Rajputana, Saurashtra, central India, in the Deccan and Andhra and Mysore and probably in the Uttar Pradesh in the Gangetic valley, traces of peasant or early agricultural communities have been found every year since 1947. The antecedents of these, as well as their relationship with the Harappan, also remain unknown. It is probable that most of the central Indian, Saurashtra, and the upper Deccan painted pottery cultures are later than the original, mature, Harappa civilization in the Punjab and Sind and that they were perhaps responsible for its destruction. But the same is not true of the purely polished-axe cultures of southeastern India. These were in a neolithic stage, practicing primitive agriculture and rearing animals, and partly dependent on hunting and fishing. C^{14} determinations for two of these—Piklihal and Utnoor in Andhra State—give a date of 2100 B.C. (4120 ± 150). They were definitely contemporary with, though far removed from, the Indus civilization.

Thus four different cultures intervene between the mesolithic cultures of the latest Pleistocene or early Holocene and the advent of iron and the second phase of urbanization in about 500 B.C. With this brief introduction, we shall review in detail the size of the settlement, food economy, and industry and affinities of some of the more important and well-documented sites of each of the four cultures mentioned above.

III. EARLY FOOD-PRODUCING CULTURES OF BALUCHISTAN OR INDO-PAKISTAN BORDER

This account is based mainly on the recent work of Fairservis. Prior to it we had only studies of pottery collected by Stein, Piggott, and others. Fairservis' work was confined to small excavations in the Quetta valley and the adjoining eastern area, namely, surveys in the Zhob and Loralai districts of Baluchistan.

Baluchistan, lying between the higher inland plateau of central Asia and the low flat plains of Sind, is indeed a transitional zone. The region is mostly mountainous. The Quetta valley itself is very narrow, not more than six miles in width and running north-south. Since its physiographical features shut out the monsoon winds from the south and east and admit the winds from the northwest, the climate is more akin to that of southern Afghanistan and eastern Iran than to that of Sind and the Punjab. This has had an important bearing upon the growth, development, decay, and affinities of the prehistoric cultures of Baluchistan.

This District of Quetta was extensively inhabited in prehistoric times. The earliest of the inhabitants, some 5,500 years ago (Kili Ghul Mohammad I [C^{14} determination 3100–3500 B.C.]), lived in small huts, perhaps at first of mud and later of mud bricks. They had no pottery but probably used skin bags and had basketry. They had bone and stone tools. It was thus an extremely primitive pastoral society that depended upon plentiful forage and water for their flocks in the central portion of the valley. During the next phase, Kili Ghul Moham-mad II, probably because of the fertility of the soil, the abundant water supply, and the arrival of people and ideas from Iran, we find a fine wheel-made pottery, implying the beginning of agriculture and even an increase in population. This black-on-red pottery might have been locally made or brought in by traders from Iran. Stimulus from the west is also seen in a fine buff wheel-made ware having decorative styles of the Halaf type.

Probably these influences also introduced copper to the inhabitants, which helped them to improve the drainage in the southern part of the valley and enabled its settlement.

From the size of the sites, it is estimated that the villages were large, the houses small, and the passages between them irregular; doors moved on stone sockets, hearths were sunken, and pottery bread ovens were used in every home. Flat stones and pebbles were employed as foundations for the mud walls. The predominant economy was agriculture (probably wheat and barley, though so far no actual grains have been found). Herds of sheep, goats, and cattle must have been kept as before. The emphasis on agriculture is perhaps indicated by small mother goddess figurines, which are regarded as symbols of a fertility cult.

In the third and last phase, owing to the increasing contact with the Indus valley, the original Baluchi culture inspired by Irani migrations and influences underwent a radical change. Both the pottery and houses exhibit this in no uncertain way. The pottery now displays typical Indian designs, such as the Brahmi bull and the pipal leaf, and the houses are equipped with bricks and drains. But the Iranian influence persists, as instanced by the ibex and the desert antelope. Agriculture naturally must have received a great impetus.

However, instead of producing a large homogeneous culture or civilization in the valley, a number of localized cultures came into existence, probably because of regional politics, economic outlets, and social affinities, as has happened so often in India and the East.

At present, in the absence of other evidence, we see only the different ceramic traditions, but there might have been variations, probably minor, in ritual and crafts from region to region.

This study of Baluchi cultures seems to explain the growth of the typical Indus, Sindhi, or the so-called Harappa culture. At first it appeared that there were a number of local cultures, for instance, the Amri, Kot Diji I, and Harappa I, originally perhaps inspired by Iranian sources. But these cultures, being based on a different ecological background from that existing either in Iran or in Baluchistan, took a further step toward urbanization. The fertile alluvial plains, under efficient management, could promise agricultural surplus—the main source of wealth and rise in population. Some genius, who, it is believed, was under Mesopotamian influence where earlier cities existed, turned these rich agricultural villages into fine brick-built towns and cities. This implies also a great organizing and unifying factor—either a simple political figure or a religious-cum-political personality—something like a priest-king of Iraq and Egypt. Whatever it be, the indigenous character of the civilization stands unchallenged. Once having established itself, it affected in turn the Baluchi on the west (e.g., Mehi and Kulli), Sutkagen-dor in the south, and Dabar Kot in the north and soon encompassed on the east almost the whole of north India up to Delhi and the Simla foothills and western India as far Surat. Without some explanation like this, we cannot understand the rise and expansion of the Indus civilization. About the civilization itself, much has been written. It is well known. However, little is known about the method of plowing and irrigation. The traces of the latter might have disappeared in the frequent Indus floods, and plows, if of wood, might have perished.

So far no remains of plows are found in any of the cities, so the exact method by which the agriculture was practiced is not known. Whatever be the methods for plowing and irrigation, it is suggested by some scholars that bunds were extensively prevalent, and it is these that were broken by the Aryans under Indra. It is the traces of these bunds that were noted by Sir Aurel Stein in Baluchistan. There was so much surplus grain that it was stored in large well-built granaries. In fact, this was a special feature of the Indus civilization and has been noticed as far away as Lothal on the Gujarat-Saurashtra border.

This civilization was destroyed by invasion, floods, or drought. In Sind and the Punjab there is a hiatus so far, and we do not know what culture replaced it. At Harappa the Cemetery H culture does not exactly overlie it. It also has a localized distribution, though this may be due to want of field work, whereas at Chanhu-dare the new people—Jhukar—are believed to have come after the Harappan was deserted. So it is doubtful whether Aryans could be held responsible for the destruction. In Rupar another culture succeeds it after a clean break indicated by a thick layer of sand. At Alamgirpur (Ukhliana, District Meerut) a break is indicated by a weathered surface.

Only at Rangpur in Saurashtra does it appear that the original Harappan culture gradually changed into another. And this change was not for a better, still more highly organized urban culture, but probably for a pastoral or, at most, a village culture.[3] Rangpur illustrates what happened in the Punjab and Sind. One cultural cycle ended with the Harappan and another began, which was to take nearly a thousand or more years to reach urbanization—a city civilization once again.

About 2000 B.C. large parts of India outside Sind, the Punjab, Uttar Pradesh, Saurashtra—and even inside these regions—were enjoying a peasant-cum-pastoral culture. This has been sufficiently demonstrated by explorations, followed by small excavations in the Punjab, Uttar Pradesh (that is, the Gangetic valley as far as Bihar), in Rajputana (the valleys of the Sarasvatī, Dṛishadvatī, Beas, Chambal etc.), in central India (the valleys of the Narmada, Chambal, Kṣiprā),

3. Unfortunately all excavations, including that by the writer and Dr. M. G. Dikshit in 1947, were on a small scale, and those carried out by Shri S. R. Rao have not been fully reported.

in northern Deccan (the valleys of the Godavari, Pravarā, Mula), in southern Deccan (the valleys of the Krishṇā), and in Karnatak-Andhra (the valleys of the Krishna and Tungabhadrā).

All these are riverine cultures. Except at two sites—at Nāvdātoli in central India and at Nevāsa in northern Deccan—excavations were nowhere large enough to provide an answer for their rise and growth or to give a definite idea of the size and form of the houses and of the food economy of the people. One does, however, notice a broad relationship between the riverine cultures of central India and southern Rajputana, on one side, and those of central India and Khandesh and northern Deccan, on the other. At the same time, the tendency to develop a highly localized culture, evidenced so far by ceramic features, differing not only from valley to valley but within one river valley itself, has to be mentioned. This may be but a shadow of what was to happen throughout historic times—small and large states dotted over the length and breadth of India. Two exceptions to this may be cited: one is the existence of Jorwe-Nevasa culture, which by 1000 B.C. had spread over a large area, and the other is Malwa or Navdatoli culture, which had covered an equally large area.

What brought about both these riverine cultures? Was it a slow development from the earlier food-gathering-cum-food-collecting stage? Or was it external stimuli, such as colonization by outsiders?

The evidence is so inadequate that no satisfactory answer can be given. It appears probable, however,

1. that around 2500 B.C. a purely neolithic culture flourished in Andhra-Karnatak and possibly extended up to northern Deccan and that its one feature—the polished stone axe—might have been derived from the east or alternatively from the west (?);

2. that Saurashtra, central India, came under Iranian or central Asian influences either because of the actual migration of peoples or because of ideas and contacts and that this led to the colonization or development of village cultures;

3. that these—or some of their branches—migrated farther down and impinged upon the neolithic cultures of the northern Deccan and Karnatak;

4. that the refugees of the Indus culture after its destruction spread out and gave birth to another pottery tradition that bore a vague affinity with the Indus.

Such is a most tentative explanation of the birth of these early village communities. We shall now have a glimpse of their life.

This can be had in some detail from one or two sites in India. Elsewhere the excavations are small, and nothing but pottery, microlithic blades, beads, and some animal bones have been found. Moreover, the reports of these are not yet published, and hence nothing more than a brief reference to them is possible. Something about the food economy of the inhabitants is possible to guess because the excavators have kindly supplied me with the identification of the animal bones.

Presumably, all these settlements—in Sind, the Punjab, Uttar Pradesh, Bihar, Saurashtra, central India, Khandesh, north and south Maharashtra, and even in the granitic regions of Andhra-Karnatak—were clusters of mud huts. But barring Rajputana and the Punjab, where the settlements seem to rest on sandy alluvium, they are on a black soil. This may imply a clearance of the jungle, the black soil itself being a weathering *in situ* of the brownish alluvium, owing to thick vegetation. This is clearly demonstrated at Navdatoli and Nevāsa, the two sites that have so far been horizontally excavated and of which the writer has firsthand knowledge. Navdatoli is situated opposite Maheshwar on the Narmada, about sixty miles south of Indore. It stands on an old crossing of the river, which itself is a great commercial artery dividing India into north and south.

The black soil at Navdatoli, a small hamlet now occupied by boatmen (*nāvḍās*), covers a fairly large area, about 2 × 2 furlongs, and caps the top of four mounds that some 4,000 years ago probably formed a single unit but was later cut up by erosion. This single mound represented the topmost terrace of the Narmada; the river itself presumably was flowing at the foot of its northern extremity, though it now flows at a distance of about three furlongs to the north. The present village of the *nāvḍās* is situated on a still younger terrace.

Excavations on all the four mounds indicate that the entire pre-historic mound was occupied but that some of its parts might have been occupied later than others. For instance, it was revealed during the 1958–59 season that the northeastern extremity of Mound IV was not inhabited before the end of Period II within the chalcolithic.

From the very beginning the inhabitants built round and square or rectangular huts. These houses were raised on thick wooden posts. Around these were put bamboo screens, which were then plastered with clay from outside and inside. The floor was also made of clay mixed with cow dung. Both were then given a thin coating of lime, so the house when first built must have looked spick and span. The size of the largest rectangular room was 20 × 40 feet. But, sometimes, a circular hut was only 3–4 feet in diameter, the largest being 8 feet in diameter. So it is doubtful that the small one was meant for habitation. Such small huts might have been used for storing grain or hay, as the writer recently saw in Kurnool, Andhra State. Normally in Period II, the size of a room was 10 × 8 feet. How many persons lived in a room or a house can only be guessed, but possibly not more than four in a room of 8 × 10 feet. The settlement was so often rebuilt, as evidenced by house floors, that it is difficult to distinguish the house plans by mere occurrences of post holes. Judging from the modern village of Navdatoli, however, one may guess that the prehistoric village might have had about fifty to seventy-five huts, supporting a population of 200.

In the middle of one house was found a well-made rectangular pit (7 ft. × 4 ft. 6 ins.). Its sides are slightly beveled, and around it there are post holes. On either side at some distance is a pot-rest made in the ground, and possibly the remains of a single-mouthed hearth. Inside the pit were found two logs of wood, placed almost at right angles, and the remains of two unique pots. These have a high corrugated neck with everted rim, a ribbed ovalish body with one or two incised bands filled in with lime, and a high hollow base (which looks similar to the mouth, so that until we could reconstruct the pots from this pit we were not certain which was the mouth and which the base).

These houses were built very close to each other. But between a row of four or five houses, there appears to have been an open space, like a Chowk (square). These houses were furnished (as is to be expected at this time, and as we find in a farmer's house even today) with small and large earthen pots for storing, cooking, and drinking. The large storage jars were strong and sturdy but generally decorated with an engraving along the neck. But what surprises us and delights our eye is their "table service," or dinner set. It is this which distinguishes these early Navdatolians from the modern primitives like Santals and other tribes in Chota Nagpur, for instance. The Navdatolians had a large number of pottery vessels, which, according to their fabric, shapes, and designs, fall into four distinctive groups, each having certain shapes and designs associated with a particular period. The most common is a pale red slipped fabric with paintings in black over it. Since this occurs throughout Malwa (an old geographical name for parts of central India), it is called the "Malwa Ware." This occurs as a major pottery fabric right from the first occupation and runs through the entire chalcolithic habitation. However, in the earliest period only certain shapes and designs figure, both becoming more varied later.

There is a sprinkling of black-and-red ware, with paintings in white, generally comprising bowls with gracefully inturned sides and cups. This fabric is confined only to Period I and seems definitely to be an import from the adjoining region of Rajputana, where at Ahar it occurs in profusion.

The third important fabric is the white-slipped one, which is associated with only the first two periods and died out later. It has several gradations in slip and texture, but the finest is smooth, lustrous and slightly greenish-white. Though it copies some of the shapes of the Malwa ware, its own distinctive shapes are a shallow dish with broad, flat rim and stand and a high concave-walled cup with bulging bottom. An almost complete bowl of this in fine white slip recalls a similar vessel from the earliest period at Sialk, in Iran (Ghirshman, "*Fouilles de Sialk*," Vol. I, Frontispiece, 4). A band of running antelopes and dancing human figures seem to be characteristic designs in this fabric.

In Period III occurs, for the first time, a new fabric called "Jorwe" after the "type site" in the Deccan. This has a well-baked core with a metallic ring and a matt red surface. Comparatively limited numbers of shapes and designs figure in this ware. It is also at this time that the most distinctive form of a vessel occurs, the teapot-like bowl in Malwa fabric. In the 1958–59 season we were lucky in getting a complete bowl, which leaves no doubt about its shape and function. It seems to have been a vessel with which ablutions were performed. Since it is without a handle, it must be held in the palms of both hands and the contents (liquid) poured slowly, as in a sacrifice or some such ritual. In order to control the flow of the liquid, a hole was sometimes made at the junction of the spout and the body of the vessel. A similar contrivance may be noticed in the channel-shaped bowls from western Asia.

Besides this important change in pottery, there was another very significant change in the life of the people. For the first couple of hundred years, the inhabitants ate principally wheat. But now other grains—rice, lentil (*Masur*) (*Lens esculenta*), *mung*, peas (*Pisum Satiyum* var. aryense), a kind of broad beans, and *khesari* (*Lathyrus Sativus*)—formed the regular diet of the people.[4] These are the grains that are grown and eaten in the Nimad District today. Our discovery, the first of its kind in India, shows that the food habits of a section of the people of Madhya Pradesh are at least 3,000 years old. Though wheat was known before from Mohenjodaro, these are the earliest examples of rice, *gram, masur, mung, kulathi*, and beans. And though we do not know how these grains were cultivated, for no plows have been found, a number of heavy stone rings that have been discovered may have been used as weights for digging sticks, as some primitive people still do in Orissa. Still, it is obvious that a people who ate so many types of grains and had such a variety of pots and pans, indicating varied needs and uses, were not so primitive as some tribes today.

The stocks of the grains were probably cut with sickles set with stone teeth, since thousands of such stone tools have been found. The grain might not have been ground into flour but merely crushed, either dry or wet, in deep, basin-shaped stone *pāṭās*, called "querns" in English, with the help of a pounder or rubber. The resultant bread will be unleavened, as it is even today in several parts of India. A number of these querns were found as they were left by their users, right on the kitchen floor, near *chulhas* or hearths. These again were quite large, made with clay and thinly plastered with lime. It is, however, not to be presumed that the inhabitants were strictly vegetarians. In the debris of their houses have been found remains of cattle, pig, sheep-goat, and deer. Except the last, all must have been domesticated and eaten. But, since the grains were varied and plentiful, they relied less on animal food, and hence their remains are comparatively few in number as compared to those from Nevasa.

Economically, the early inhabitants of Navdatoli were fairly well off. They were essentially farmers or peasants. They did not yet know iron, they used copper, but sparingly, in the shape of simple, handleless axes, fishhooks, pins, and rings. In a later phase they possibly used daggers or swords with a midrib, as suggested by a fragment found in 1958-59. For their daily needs in cutting vegetables, scraping leather, and piercing stone, they had to rely upon stone tools— with blades so small that we call them "microliths." These were hafted in bone and wooden handles, as we nowadays fix an iron blade into a penknife. Among ornaments, we have thousands of beads of sand coated with a glaze and called "faience," or chalk, and a few of semiprecious stone such as agate and carnelian.

4. Another interesting grain is linseed. This is being studied in the palaeo botanical laboratory in the Birbal Sahni Institute at Lucknow.

These must have been strung into necklaces. Bangles and rings made of clay and copper were also worn.

The earliest farmers in Madhya Pradesh lived, as we know from C^{14} determinations, kindly supplied by the University of Pennsylvania, about 2000 B.C. and continued to live on, with three major destructions by fire, at least up to 700 B.C., when an iron-using people from Ujjain and possibly farther north wiped out their existence and laid the foundation of a new economy in which iron, minted money, houses of bricks, and an altogether new pottery played a dominant part.

The question of who were the first dwellers, whose remains are found all over Malwa, is not yet resolved. Probably they were a people from Iran, as their pottery shows. This is a very important and interesting clue. In that case, they might be a branch of the Aryans. This trail is to be followed up by further detective work across India and Pakistan up to eastern Iran.

While Navdatoli illustrates the settlement pattern in central India, Nevasa helps us to understand the burial practices and their relation to the habitation in northern Maharashtra. Nevasa is the headquarters of a *taluka* of the same name in Ahmadnagar District. It is situated on both the banks of the river Pravara, a tributary of the Godavari, and about 110 miles northeast of Poona.

Perhaps originally there was one large mound, which was later bisected by the river, giving birth to Nevasa Khurd (small) and Nevasa Budrunk (big), which overlook the river. The portion lying on the southern side (or the left bank) is nearly 1½ furlongs long and ½ furlong wide. It is now called "Lādmoḍ," and cut up into three smaller mounds by erosion and man. From the water level it is nearly 70 feet high, the top 30 feet or so containing the debris of four cultural periods from 1500–1000 B.C. to A.D. 1500. It is the first period that concerns us here.

The earliest occupants settled on a thick layer of black soil by effecting an opening in the jungle with the help of copper and polished-stone axes. For the rest of the cutting and clearing activities they used short parallel-sided and Gravette-like blades and points of a limpid chalcedony. Of the earlier microlithic tradition, we find a sparing use of lunates and trapeze. True saws also occur in this assemblage. The technique by which blades were removed has been studied in great detail by Dr. Subbarao. It has been described as a crested ridge and fluted core technique and is a common feature of all the chalcolithic cultures mentioned above. Among the heavier tools, we have occasionally the macehead or weight for digging stick, small querns, mullers, rubbers, and large boat-shaped querns for crushing the grain. But the latter are comparatively very few. This is possibly because agriculture was in its infancy. Negatively, this is confirmed so far, by the absence of any grains, whereas a large amount of animal bones, among which those of cow-ox predominate, underlines the predominance of beef in the diet. Not only their food habits but their pottery is strikingly different from that of Navdatoli. It is generally matte with geometric paintings in black over a red surface. Wheel-made, it is so well baked that it gaves a metallic ring when struck. The shapes are again comparatively limited: carinated bowls of various sizes; vessels with tubular spout and flaring mouth and carinated belly, and vessels with globular body and high neck. Dishes are rare. Among the unpainted group there are sturdy storage jars with fingertip decoration, basins or troughs, and fine black slipped ware with red coating that vanishes on touch.

The people who enjoyed such a material culture lived in mud huts that were generally square or rectangular. These were built with the help of uncut thick wooden posts. The floors were made with lime and clay but at times with a bedding of sand or gravel. The size of the rooms so far found is 9 x 7 feet. A more detailed picture of the alignment of the houses has not yet emerged. But what is remarkable is that the inhabitants buried the dead right in the floor of the houses. Three of four different burial methods were followed: the adults were at times laid right on the black soil, which was smeared with lime; or they were put in a long, large earthen jar, the outlines of the pit being marked with lime; or several jars (five) were used to cover the dead body. Children, as a rule, were interned in double, single, or at times treble wide-mouthed urns, after the remains were probably exposed. For in two cases, the skull is in two parts, and kept separately.

So far an area of 80 x 40 feet and 25 x 200 feet has yielded over ninety skeletons, of which six are adults. Thus little doubt remains about the burial practices of this people. Since similar pottery and remains of urns are found over a large area from Khandesh in the north to Brahmagiri in northern Mysore in the south, a distance of over 500 miles, the extent of this Brahmagiri-Jorwe-Nevasa culture was certainly wide. Its east-west extension is not yet known, nor are its origins. Partly it is derived from the neolithic cultures of Andhra and Karnatak. These seem to have been the substratum over which the copper-knowing, painted-pottery, wheel-using people, slowly impinged from the north in about 1500 B.C. Who they could be, we shall discuss later on. Before that an idea of the neolithic cultures of Andhra-Karnatak is necessary.

The region in which these cultures flourished is now shared by the states of Andhra and Karnatak. Since the raw material was a consideration, the remains of these cultures are found in areas with granatoid hills, with dykes, of fine-grained basalt, the latter being most suitable for polished axes. So far, only two or three sites are very partially excavated. None of these gives an idea of the houses, but it is inferred that the people lived under overhanging rocks and carried on a primitive agriculture in the plains below. By and large, however, they were pastoral and hunters. This has now been proved by the identification of the remains of large cinerary mounds as accumulated heaps of cow dung. Both short-horned and long-horned cattle (Indian buffalo) besides sheep-goat were domesticated.

The principal tools of this people were pointed butt polished stone axes, adzes, chisels, hammerstones, fabricators, and microliths. C^{14} determinations from two sites, Piklihal and Utnoor, would place their culture around 2000 B.C.

IV. TOWARD SECOND URBANIZATION

None of these cultures—whether the chalcolithic of Saurashtra, Rajputana, central India, or northern Deccan or the purely neolithic of southern Deccan—ever developed into an urban civilization. Around 800 B.C., another copper-using culture, with an altogether different pottery tradition called the painted grey ware, spread over the entire Gangetic valley. Traces of it are found in Rajputana and central India. Since it occupies the same position as some of the traditional cities of the *Mahābhārata*, like Hastināpura, Ahichchatra, and later Kosāmbi, it should be, at least in its chief cities, of an urban character. But owing to the smallness of the excavations, nothing can be said about the character of the culture.

Within two or three centuries, however, possibly due to Iranian influence, from the Achaeminian empire, iron came to be introduced. Along with this, the pottery changed into a fine polished, lustrous black, grey, gold or silvery. Its principal center is the Gangetic valley. And here the first cities of the historical period arose, very soon to be followed at Ujjain and Maheshwar in central India, at Nasik and Paithan in northern Deccan, and possibly at Brahmagiri in Mysore. This happened in the wake of iron and a pottery, which is called "black-and-red" but may better be described to as "black-topped," according to the late Professor Childe.

None of these early cities is excavated so that we can have an idea of their size. Mauryan Taxila was irregularly laid with very narrow streets. It is only with the Indo-Greeks that the chessboard-like cities appeared at Charsadda and Taxila in the Punjab, and possibly later at Mathura, Kosambi, Pataliputra, and Ujjain. Thus it took nearly 2,500 years for an old concept to reassert itself in India.

V. CONCLUSIONS

In India, thus, we witness almost the same stages of development from food-gathering stage to urbanization through the intermediate stages of food-producing with food-gathering and early peasant economy. At no one site or region are all the stages of development discernible. The picture is built from a scene here and a scene there. This unequal development might be due to geographical factors. But how was each particular stage of culture reached?

Even the earliest—the hand-axe culture—is believed to have been introduced from Africa, where a well-attested development from a crude pebble culture is available. Looking to the geographical position of Africa and India, and the absence of a stratigraphically earlier stage of hand-axe culture, one has to accept the present hypothesis. The Soan, as is well known, has a limited distribution and is connected with southeast Asia.

The next paleolithic culture, characterized by points and scrapers and called "Nevasian" or middle paleolithic or stone age, has also a great affinity with some of the African cultures. But unless actual tools are available for a comparative study, further comments are unnecessary. From what the writer has seen, the tools seem to evolve after the late acheulian. This was first marked by my pupil and now colleague, Dr. K. D. Banerjee, in Karnatak. It is now being confirmed by our collections from north Deccan, Kurnool, and central India. So, for the advanced food-collecting stage, now witnessed over almost all India, no external influences are at present postulated, though one will have to account for the man's rejection of the old raw material. A different man and/or new ideas should have been on the scene. But whether he or the ideas belonged to India or came from outside requires much deeper studies based on planned explorations.

The same is true of the various microlithic industries. They are believed to have evolved from the earlier blade and burin industries. The classical, well-documented regions are, however, known from outside India, for example, Palestine, and it has been said by writers that the stimulus might have been received from the peripheral area through Palestine. But without further research this remains a mere suggestion.

This position dogs us when we enter the early pastoral and peasant-village stage. The early peasant villages of Sind, like Amri, are believed to have originated under Iranian influence, and later, under Sumerian or Mesopatanian impetus, they achieved a still better and highly efficient urban civilization.

While this may be true, what happened to the early village cultures in the rest of India? Are they all indigenous or do they owe their birth to outside forces? According to one theory based on ceramic evidence from Rangpur in Saurashtra and Navdatoli in central India, we may postulate the existence of these cultures to the arrival of Aryan tribes from Iran. This explains the appearance of almost identical vessels, such as goblets, channel-spouted cups, and fine white-slipped ware, in such profusion at Navdatoli. While the shapes are very similar, the Indian fabrics are inferior. This may be due to the non-availability of the kind of clay found in Iran and elsewhere in central Asia.

Some of the tribes with highly specialized pottery penetrated further south in the Deccan and brought about the Daimabad-Jorwe-Nevasa-Brahmagiri culture. A similar thing seems to have occurred in Saurashtra and Rajputana, where several local cultures came into being.

While all these—Saurashtra, central Indian, and the Deccan tribes—might be thought to stem from one common stock, another Aryan tribe bearing the grey ware entered the Punjab and spread into the Gangetic valley. This pottery with typical Svastika design is traced in the west to Shahitump in southern Baluchistan, while the fabric and color reveal similar patterns in Thessaly.

The theory of Aryan migration in two principal waves may accord with the once held view of Grierson and others of an "outer" and "inner" band of Aryans, the grey-ware people being the former, and the various painted pottery groups representing the "inner." There are, however, two serious weaknesses in this theory. First, if the "Aryans" or whoever the immigrants were, brought the pottery tradition with them, why could not even one of them transplant the advanced metallurgical technology of the west? This argument applies against the

	N.W. INDIA & KASHMIR	CENTRAL INDIA	WESTERN INDIA	SOUTHERN INDIA	EASTERN INDIA
HOLOCENE		PANCHMARI MAHADEO-HILLS ADAMGARH	RANGPUR-A WAI PANCHGANI LANGHNAJ-B KANDIVLI LANGHNAJ-A	MYSORE BELLARY NELLORE GIDDALUR KURNOOL TERI NANDI KANAMA	SINGHBHUM ORISSA SINGRAULI BIRBHANPUR
LATE PLEISTO-CENE	ROHRI-SUKKUR LATE SOAN-B LATE SOAN-A	NEVASIAN-B [SR. III] NEVASIAN-A	NEVASIAN-B [SR. III] NEVASIAN-A	NEVASIAN-B [SR. III] NEVASIAN-A	NEVASIAN-B [SR. III] NEVASIAN-A
MIDDLE PLEISTO-CENE	EARLY SOAN	HAND-AXE CLEAVER	HAND-AXE CLEAVER	HAND-AXE CLEAVER	HAND-AXE CLEAVER

FIGURE 1. From the food-gathering stage to the threshold of the pastoral stage in India.

ECONOMY	BALUCHI-STAN	SIND	PUNJAB	UTTAR-PRADESH	BIHAR	RAJPUTANA
EARLY IRON-AGE URBAN			(NBP & FIRST BRICK BLDG) RUPAR III (C. 400 BC)	HASTINAPUR (C.400 BC) KOSAMBI III (C.400 BC)	PATALIPUTRA RAJAGRIHA (C. 500-400 BC)	
PEA-SANT		JHANGAR JHUKAR	RUPAR (GREY WARE) (C. 700 BC)	KOSAMBI II HASTINAPUR II (C.400 BC) KOSAMBI I		
NOMADIC PAS-TORAL						
BRONZE URBAN	DABARKOT MEHI KULLI SUTKAGEN-DOR	MOHENJODARO CHANHUDARO KOT DIJI II (2125±137 BC)	HARAPPA	ALAMGIRPUR (UKHLIANA)		
CHALCOLITHC EARLY ADVANCED PEASANT PEASANT SMALL LARGE VILLAGE VILLAGE	DAMB SADAAT II-III (2450±165BC) DAMB SADAAT I (2400±190BC)	KOT DIJI I (2463±141 BC) AMRI	PRE-HARAPPA			AHAR
NEO-LITHIC PAS-TORAL	KILI GUL MOHAMMAD (3500±310BC)I					

FIGURE 2. India, from the beginning of the pastoral stage.

SAURASHTRA	CENTRAL-INDIA	KHANDESH	N.MAHA-RASHTRA	S. MAHA-RASHTRA	ANDHRA-KARNATAK	S. INDIA-ORISSA
GIRINAGARA (c. 300 B.C.)	UJJAYINI MAHISHMATI (C. 500 B.C.)		NASIK (C. 300 B.C.) PAITHAN		ISILIPATTANA (BRAHMAGIRI) (C. 300 B.C.)	
LAKHABAWAL SOMANATH RANGPUT II						
RANGPUR LOTHAL						
	NAGDA MAHESHWAR NAVDATOLI (1545±128BC)	PRAKASH BAHAL	NEVASA-JORWE (1148±122 BC) DAIMABAD		MASKI BRAHMAGIRI I	
					PIKHLIHAL SANGANKALLU	

FIGURE 3. India, to the threshold of urban civilization.

Sumerian theory, the urbanization in Sind and the Punjab. For some reason the tools and weapons of the Indus, as well as the later village communities in India, remained of a simple, unsocketed type. It is only when they came into contact with the Indo-Greeks and the Romans, in the early centuries of the Christian Era and a little before, that socketed axes, arrowheads, spearheads, etc., were manufactured.

Second, in the absence of well-marked links between central India and Iran, the theory lacks confirmation. While we are trying to fill up the gap in India, it is the work in Pakistan and on the Indo-Pakistan-Iranian border that may help elucidate the problem.

If we do not accept this Aryan or outside emigration theory for the birth of certain cultures in the Gangetic valley and central India as well as the Deccan, we must credit the known indigenous tribes—such as Kolis, Bhils, Nagas, Pulindas, Nishadas—for their authorship.

This will to some extent nullify the view that India is a peripheral region, for we are postulating an independent origination of cultures. Much of this dilemma, I believe, is due to our ignorance. With planned work in Rajputana, in Saurashtra, and on the Indo-Pakistan-Iranian border, it is probable that a more definite solution can be found.

BIBLIOGRAPHY

BANERJEE, K. D.
1957. "Middle Palaeolithic Cultures of the Deccan." (Ph.D thesis, Poona University, 1957). (Deccan College and Poona University Library.)

BURKITT, M. C., and L. A. CAMMIADE
1930. "Fresh Light on the Stone Age of South-East India," *Antiquity*, 4:327–39.

FAIRSERVIS, WALTER A., JR.
1956. *Excavations in the Quetta Valley, West Pakistan.* ("Anthrop. Papers Amer. Mus. Nat. Hist.," 45:165–402.)

1958. *Archaeological Surveys in the Zhob and Loralai Districts, West Pakistan.* ("Anthrop. Papers Amer. Mus. Nat. Hist.," 47:277–448.)

GHOSH, A. (ed.)
1953–59. *Indian Archaeology: A Review, 1953–54, 1954–55, 1955–56, 1956–57, 1957–58, 1958–59.*

GORDON, D. H.
1950. "The Stone Industries of the Holocene in India and Pakistan," *Ancient India*, No. 6, pp. 64–90.

HARGREAVES, H.
1929. *Excavations in Baluchistan, 1925, Sampur Mound, Mastung and Sohr Damb.* ("Nat. Mem. Archaeol. Surv. India," No. 35.)

KRISHNASWAMI, V. D.
1951. "The Lithic Tool-Industries of the Singrauli Basin," *Ancient India*, No. 7, pp. 40–65.

LAL, B. B.
1954–55. "Excavation at Hastinapur and other Explorations in the Upper Ganga and Sutlej Basins, 1950–52," *Ancient India*, Nos. 10 and 11, pp. 5–151.

1958. "Birbhanpur, a Microlithic Site in the Damodar Valley, West Bengal," *ibid.*, No. 14, pp. 4–48.

MACKAY, ERNEST
1937–38. *Further Excavations at Mohenjo-Daro: Being an Official Account of Archaeological Excavations at Mohenjo-Daro Carried Out by the Government of India between 1927 and 1931.* 2 vols. New Delhi.

1943. *Chanhu-Daro Excavations.* ("Amer. Orient. Ser.," Vol. 20.) New Haven: American Oriental Society.

MARSHALL, JOHN (SIR)
1931. *Mohenjo-Daro and the Indus Civilization: Being an Official Account of Archaeological Excavations at Mohenjo-Daro Carried Out by the Government of India between 1922 and 1927.* 3 vols. London.

PIGGOTT, STUART
1950. *Prehistoric India to 1000 B.C.* (Penguin Books.)

ROSS, E. J.
1946. "A Chalcolithic Site in Northern Baluchistan," *J.N.E.S.*, 5:291–315.

SANKALIA, H. D.
1956. "The Microlithic Industry of Langhnaj, Gujarat," *J. Gujarat Res. Soc.*, 17:275–84.

1956. "Animal Fossils and Palaeolithic Industries from the Pravara Basin, at Nevasa, District Ahmadnagar," *Ancient India*, No. 12, pp. 35–52.

1958. "New Light on the Aryan 'Invasion' of India: Links with Iran of 1000 B.C. Discovered in Central India," *Illustrated London News*, September 20, 1958, pp. 478–79.

1959. "Four-Thousand-Year-Old Links between Iran and Central India: New Excavations at Navdatoli," *ibid.*, September 5, 1959.

SESHADRI, M.
1956. *The Stone-using Cultures of Pre-historic and Proto-historic Mysore*. London.

SOUNDARA, RAJAN, K. V.
1952. "Stone Age Industries near Giddalur, District Kurnool," *Ancient India*, No. 8, pp. 64 ff.

STEIN, AUREL
1904–5. "Report on Archaeological Survey Work, N.W. Frontier and Baluchistan," *Baluchistan District Gazetteer* (Allahabad), 2:44–49.

1929. *An Archaeological Tour in Waziristan and Northern Baluchistan*. ("Mem. Archaeol. Surv. India," No. 37.)

1931. *An Archaeological Tour in Gedrosia* (*Ibid.*, No. 43.)

SUBBARAO, B.
1948. *Stone Age Cultures of Bellary*. (Deccan College Diss. Ser., No. 7) Poona.

1952. "Archaeological Explorations in the Mahi Valley," *J. M. S. Univ. Baroda*, 1:33–69.

1958. *The Personality of India* ("M. S. Univ. Archaeol. Ser.," No. 3.) 2d ed. Baroda.

THAPAR, B. K.
1957. "Maski 1954: A Chalcolithic Site of the Southern Deccan," *Ancient India*, No. 13, pp. 5–142.

TODD, K. R. U.
1948. "A Microlithic Industry in Eastern Mysore," *Man*, 48:28–30.

1939. "Palaeolithic industries of Bombay," *J. Roy. Anthrop. Inst.* 69:257–72.

VATS, MADHO SWARUP
1940. *Excavations at Harappa: Being an Account of the Archaeological Excavations at Harappa Carried Out between 1920–21 and 1933–34*. 2 vols. Delhi.

WHEELER, MORTIMER (SIR)
1953. *Indus Civilization*. (Suppl. vol. to the *Cambridge History of India*.) Cambridge, England.

WHEELER, R. E. M.
1947. "Harappa 1946: The Defence and Cemetery R.37," *Ancient India*, No. 3, pp. 58–130.

ZEUNER, F. E.
1950. *Stone Age and Pleistocene Chronology in Gujarat*. ("Deccan College Monog. Ser.," No. 6.) Poona.

ZEUNER, F. E., and BRIDGET ALLCHIN
1956. "The Microlithic Sites of Tinnevelly District, Madras State," *Ancient India*, No. 12, pp. 4–20.

MESOAMERICA

GORDON R. WILLEY

INTRODUCTION

MESOAMERICA includes the southern two-thirds of mainland Mexico, Guatemala, British Honduras, a western strip of Honduras, Salvador, the Pacific coast of Nicaragua, and northwestern Costa Rica (Fig. 1). These geographical limits define a culture area that began to take form at the beginning of the Precolumbian agricultural era, at about 1500 B.C., and persisted until the Spanish conquest, at A.D. 1520. In this essay we are concerned with this span of time, during which the aboriginal peoples of this part of the New World passed from village agriculture to civilization. We are also concerned with the prehistory of the inhabitants of the same geographical area prior to the threshold of village agriculture. This earlier record goes back as far, perhaps, as 15,000 B.C.

Physiographic, climatic, and vegetational variability within Mesoamerica is tremendous, and almost every generalization may be marked by exceptions. Geologically, it is an area of relatively recent, and even continuing, vulcanism. Two great mountain ranges, the Sierra Madre Occidental and the Sierra Madre Oriental, run from north to south through northern Mexico to join a central highland block in the general region of the Valley of Mexico. There are two other highland massifs, one in Oaxaca and another farther south and east in Chiapas and Guatemala. On the west, the Pacific coastal shelf is relatively narrow; on the Atlantic side there is a wide, low coastal plain. Depending upon altitude, temperature varies from lowland tropical to upland temperate; relating to latitude it changes gradually from temperate in the north to tropical in the south. In general, the north and west are dry lands with sparse vegetation, while the south and east have abundant rains and tropical forests and savannas.

Human history in Mesoamerica may be divided into three major eras of subsistence technology (Fig. 2). The earliest of these eras, lasting from an unknown date up to about 7000 B.C., is designated that of the *Early Hunters*. These hunters pursued and killed big animal game, including large Pleistocene mammals now extinct. Between 7000 and 1500 B.C. is the era of the *Food-Collectors and Incipient Cultivators*. The peoples of this era subsisted by gathering wild seeds and plants, by hunting and snaring small game, and by the cultivation of food plants. Although cultivation was on the increase during this era, it did not assume primary importance as a means of food-getting until the next major era, that of the

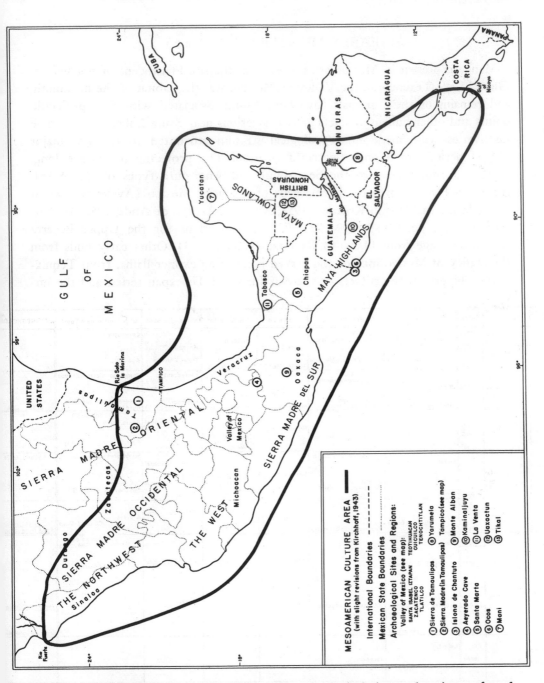

FIGURE 1. Mesoamerica as a culture area with archeological sites and regions referred to in the text. (Area geographic definition follows Kirchhoff [1943] in general, although the northern frontier has been extended somewhat farther north and the southern boundary has been revised to include a portion of Honduras.)

Agriculturists, which extended from 1500 B.C. to the entry of the Spanish into native America in A.D. 1520.

EARLY HUNTERS (?–7000 B.C.)

Man was present in Mesoamerica as early as the late Pleistocene, if not before. Glacial Lake Texcoco, in the Valley of Mexico, was the habitat of the mammoth, and remains of these animals have been found associated with flint projectile points and other human artifacts at two locations near Santa Isabel Iztapan. The discoveries were made in a geological stratum attributed to the last major pluvial period, the Upper Becerra formation. The projectile points are long, stemless forms, similar to the Scottsbluff and Angostura types of the North American Plains and to the Lerma type of northeast Mexico (Aveleyra Arroyo de Anda and Maldonado-Koerdell, 1953; Aveleyra Arroyo de Anda, 1956; Wormington, 1957, pp. 91–99, 199–202). C^{14} determinations for the Upper Becerra formation range from 14,000 to 9000 B.C. (Libby, 1955). Other early finds from the Valley of Mexico include the carved bone of an extinct llama, from Tequixquiac, chipped-stone artifacts of the San Juan and Tepexpan series, and the hu-

SUBSISTENCE ERAS	Periods	Dates	Tamaulipas	Central Mexico	Oaxaca	S. Veracruz-Tab.	Maya Lowlands	Maya Highlands & Coast	"THRESHOLDS"
A G R I C U L T U R I S T S	Post-Classic (late / early)	1500	Los Angeles San Antonio	IV Aztec II (Tenochtitlan)		Soncautla		Chinautla	
		1200			Monte Alban V		Mayapan		
		900	San Lorenzo	Aztec I–Tula-Mazapan	Monte Alban IV	Upper Cerro las Mesas	Toltec Chichen	Ayampuc	
	Classic (late / early)			Coyotlatelco Ahuitzotla–Amantla III B			"Florescent"	Pamplona Cotzumalhuapa	
		600	La Salta	Tlamimilolpa Xolalpan		Lower Upper Cerro las Tres Mesas II Zapotes	Tepeu	Amatle	
		300	Eslabones Palmillas		Monte Alban IIIA		"Regional" Tzakol	Esperanza Chiapa IX Aurora	Urban Life
							Matzanel	Santa Clara Chiapa VII	
	Pre-Classic late	A.D. B.C.		Miccaotli	Monte Alban II	Lower Middle Cerro Tres las Mesas I Zapotes		Arenal Izapa	
		300		Tzacualli Cuicuilco-Ticoman			Yaxund Chicanel	Miraflores Chiapa IV	(Urban Life ?)
	Pre-Classic middle		Laguna La Florida	Middle Zacatenco Tlatilco	Monte Alban I	? Lower Tres Zapotes La Venta ?	Xtampak Mamom	Las Charcas Chiapa II	
		1000				?	Mani	Arevalo	Effective Food Production
	Pre-Classic early	1500	Mesa de Guaje	Early Zacatenco–El Arbolillo I				Chiapa I–Ocos	
INCIPIENT CULTIVATORS and FOOD-COLLECTORS		2000	Almagre Guerra Flacco		Yanhuitlan			Islona de Chantuto	
		3000	La Perra Ocampo					Santa Marta	
		4000							
		5000	Nogales Ocampo	Chalco Aeyerado					Incipient Cultivation
		7000	Infiernillo						(Incipient Cultivation)
EARLY HUNTERS		9000	Lerma Diablo	Iztapan					

FIGURE 2. Mesoamerican subsistence eras, cultural periods, estimated datings, and arrangement of culture phases by regions and chronological positions. (Chronological placements of cultures follow MacNeish [1958]; Willey [1960a]; and Willey, Ekholm, and Millon [Ms, 1960].)

man skeleton known as "Tepexpan Man" (Aveleyra Arroyo de Anda, 1950; De Terra, Romero, and Stewart, 1949; Wormington, 1957, pp. 238–41). Although the antiquity of some of these, particularly the latter, has been challenged, it is probable that they are all of considerable age.

In northeastern Mesoamerica, in Tamaulipas, the Diablo complex may antedate 10,000 B.C. The artifacts consist of crude bifacial knives and choppers and uni-facial side scrapers or knives. Associated animal bones and the small size of the occupation zones suggest small nomadic bands of hunters (MacNeish, 1958, p. 152). The Lerma phase overlies the Diablo and is believed to date at about 8000–7000 B.C.[1] The most characteristic artifact is a lenticular or laurel-leaf-shaped projectile point. It was noted above that a Lerma-like point was found in associa-tion with one of the Iztapan mammoths. Besides the points, snubbed-nose and stemmed end scrapers, large planoconvex end and side scrapers, pebble choppers, and bifacial knives all relate to a hunting economy. Sites of the Lerma phase are small camp stations, including cave locations. Analysis of the refuse suggests that something over half the subsistence of the societies that occupied these sites was based upon game (MacNeish, 1958, pp. 152–53).

A few other discoveries in Mesoamerica tend to substantiate the Valley of Mexico and the Tamaulipas finds in demonstrating that early hunting peoples once roamed the area (Aveleyra Arroyo de Anda, 1950; Bosch-Gimpera, 1959; Coe, 1960a). None of these other data are as definitive in their geological contexts or associations as those of Iztapan, Diablo, and Lerma.

It is noteworthy that almost no clues of the Early Hunters have been found in the lowland, tropical regions of Mesoamerica. Iztapan, Diablo, and Lerma are all in highland, somewhat semiarid regions that were once cooler and more moist than they are today.

The time of the Mexican Early Hunters is believed to correspond to the Man-kato-Valders glacial maximum and to the still wet conditions of the Anathermal climatic stage that immediately followed it. This was the era of the specialized big-game hunters of the North American Plains and Eastern Woodlands, an era characterized, first, by fluted Clovis and Folsom dart points and, later, by those points of the Eden, Yuma, Scottsbluff, and Plainview traditions. Although the early Mesoamerican finds are typologically closer to these last-named North American points, they are found under conditions and with radiocarbon deter-minations more nearly approximating those of Clovis and Folsom. Data are still too few to resolve this contradiction. What is significant in the present context is that nomadic hunters of large grassland game occupied sections of Mesoamerica during and immediately after the close of the last glacial advance, and from what evidence they have left behind it is possible to say that these hunters followed the same pattern of life that characterizes similar groups in many areas of both North and South America at approximately the same time. Although early, this was a pattern of subsistence by no means simple or ineffective. Rather, it was an

1. There is an associated radiocarbon determination of 7320 ± 500 B.C. (Crane and Griffin, 1958a).

adaptation of quite specialized equipment to quite special environmental circumstances (Wormington, 1957; Willey, 1960a, b).

FOOD-COLLECTORS AND INCIPIENT CULTIVATORS (7000–1500 B.C.)

Excavations in caves and open sites in two regions of interior Tamaulipas, on the northeastern periphery of the Mesoamerican area, reveal a long story of food-collecting and experimentation with cultivated plants. Archeological sequences have been developed in the Sierra de Tamaulipas and in the Sierra Madre. Both regions are mountainous, semiarid in part, and in part wooded. Both have fairly good potentials for hunting, plant-collecting, and farming. The Sierra de Tamaulipas is, on the whole, somewhat more favorable for these activities than the drier, higher Sierra Madre country, but the archeological sequences from the two regions are closely related and will be presented together.[2]

The Infiernillo phase is the earliest of the Sierra Madre sequence. It is determined, with the aid of radiocarbon, at 7000 to 5000 B.C. (Crane and Griffin, 1958a). Presumably, it follows the Lerma phase of the Sierra de Tamaulipas in the chronology of the general Tamaulipas region, but Infiernillo displays a subsistence adjustment quite different from that of the Early Hunters. Infiernillo living refuse from dry caves contains vegetal food scraps, mostly from wild plants but with some remains of probable domesticated pumpkins (*Cucurbita pepo*) and possible domesticated peppers (*Capsicum frutescens*). Associated, but definitely wild, plants are the agave, opuntia, and runner bean (*Phaseolus coccineus*). Infiernillo sites are small camps of seminomadic people who were part-time hunters but who settled down seasonally to exploit these plant resources. The chipped-stone implements of these early Food Collectors and Incipient Cultivators include distinctive diamond-shaped or tear-shaped projectile points used with darts or spears, scraping planes, and flake choppers or scrapers. Found also in the caves are snail-shell beads, bird-bone awls, twilled and plaited mats, net-bags, and baskets with rod foundations.

From 5000 to 3000 B.C. this Tamaulipas plant-collecting tradition is traced in the early Ocampo (Sierra Madre) and Nogales (Sierra de Tamaulipas) phases.[3] Subsistence estimates, based upon refuse analyses, are 70–80 per cent of diet from wild-plant collection and 5–8 per cent from domesticated plants. The remainder came from hunting. Yellow seed beans (*Phaseolus vulgaris*) are added to the cultivated plant complex, and there are new varieties of pumpkins that were probably prized for their seeds rather than for their pulp. Sites are larger than those of Infiernillo, but it is still likely that they were occupied only seasonally. Some slight changes in projectile-point types over the preceding phase are noted;

---

2. The discussion of these Tamaulipas sequences follows MacNeish (1958). I have also relied upon an unpublished manuscript by MacNeish (MS, 1959) in preparing this summary.

3. Radiocarbon determinations for Ocampo are: 3700 ± 350 B.C., 3280 ± 350 B.C., and 2630 ± 350 B.C (Crane and Griffin, 1958a).

there is a somewhat greater range of flint scrapers, choppers, and gouges; and stones used for seed-grinding appear. Baskets, nets, and mats are all present.

In the La Perra and late Ocampo phases, ranging from 3000 to 2200 B.C.,[4] domesticated plants make up an estimated 10–15 per cent of total diet, wild plants 70–75 per cent, and game the rest. Settlements are similar to early Ocampo and Nogales. Red beans (*Phaseolus vulgaris*) come into the sequence for the first time. Significantly, a primitive, but nevertheless cultivated, maize appears in the La Perra (Sierra de Tamaulipas) phase. Nogales and late Ocampo artifactual remains differ but little from the preceding phases. Points are still dart types, although there are new forms; mullers and manos are an important part of the artifact complex; and baskets of both twilled and multiple-stitched and warp types, mats, and full-turn coil nets are among the textile remains.

The Flacco (Sierra Madre) and Almagre (Sierra de Tamaulipas) phases existed from 2200 to 1800 B.C.[5] Agriculture increased to perhaps 20 per cent of the total subsistence at the expense of plant-collecting, which drops to 65 per cent. The Bat Cave, or Chapalote, race of corn is found in Flacco sites. Two Almagre sites suggest greater stability of residence than anything previously seen in the sequence. One shows wattle-and-daub house remains, while the other is an open-site location of village dimensions. New projectile-point types with these phases include stemmed and corner-notched forms, apparently used as dart or spear heads. Coiled, twined, and twilled baskets, nets, a large amount of cordage, cotton cloth, and metates and manos for seed-grinding are all present.

The Guerra phase, 1800–1400 B.C., is known only from the Sierra Madre.[6] Both open and cave sites are represented. Another squash (*Cucurbita moschata*) is added to previously known plant domesticates. Cultivated plants are now estimated to have composed 30 per cent of the diet, wild plants 60 per cent, and animals 10 per cent. Projectile points and scrapers show no major innovations, nor do the varieties of baskets and nets. The earliest-known burials of the Tamaulipas sequence are associated with this phase. These were of ordinary flexed form and had been covered with mats and accompanied with baskets. It is at about this point in the Tamaulipas story that incipient cultivation may be said to terminate. Succeeding phases, as will be mentioned farther along, cross the threshold into full village agriculture.

Farther south in Mesoamerica are other, although less fully documented, instances of probable or definite incipient cultivation. In the Valley of Mexico a complex known as the Chalco is dated as about contemporaneous with Nogales

4. La Perra date is from a radiocarbon determination of 2495 ± 280 B.C. (Libby, 1955).

5. The Flacco radiocarbon determination is 1995 ± 334 B.C. (Whitaker, Cutler, and Mac-Neish, 1957). Almagre probably lasts later than Flacco, possibly extending up to 1400 B.C. (MacNeish, MS, 1959).

6. The radiocarbon determination of 2780 ± 300 B.C. for Guerra seems out of line and too early (Crane and Griffin, 1958a). The dating given here follows the stratigraphy and the other radiocarbon determinations of the sequence (MacNeish, MS, 1959).

of the Tamaulipas sequence.[7] Chalco is associated with the hot, dry altithermal climatic stage in western North America. Most Chalco implements are of basalt, including long, leaf-shaped projectile points; grinding stones suggest the utiliza- tion of plant foods. Certain similarities have been pointed out between the Chalco artifacts and those of the Cochise complex of southern Arizona, a contemporane- ous seed-gathering, incipient cultivation, and hunting tradition of the southwest- ern United States desert (De Terra, Romero, and Stewart, 1949; also Haury, this volume). Very recent discoveries in southern Puebla, at Aeyerado Cave, reveal a non-ceramic complex of a typology similar to that of the Ocampo phase of Tamaulipas and, by inference, of the same general time period as Ocampo and Chalco (5000–2000 B.C.). In the lowest levels of Aeyerado Cave were ears of what appears to be an extremely primitive maize—possibly a wild maize.[8] It is indeed possible that this is the earliest complete maize find yet reported for the New World.[9] Significantly, the Puebla cave shows a stratigraphy of maize do- mestication and increasing hybridization leading up and into the first millennium B.C. Still farther south are possible clues to incipient-cultivation levels: the chipped-stone implements from Yanhuitlan, Oaxaca, taken from preceramic levels dating at 2000 B.C. (Lorenzo, 1958); the preceramic shell mound deposits of Islona de Chantuto on the Chiapas coast (Drucker, 1948; Lorenzo, 1955); and a long preceramic sequence in the Santa Marta cave site in interior Chiapas.[10]

Farther afield than Mesoamerica we note that the food-collecting patterns of the Desert peoples of western North America are essentially similar to those from Tamaulipas and farther south. This North American "Desert Pattern" also has its origins as early as 7000 B.C.[11] and incipient cultivation was also an element within it, at least in some regions. Primitive domesticated maize is known from as far north as New Mexico (Mangelsdorf, 1958) and Colorado (Irwin and Irwin, 1959) in the third millennium B.C., and it is found there in contexts comparable to those of the contemporaneous phases of the Tamaulipas caves. In brief, in those millennia between 7000 and 1500 B.C. the uplands of northern and central Mexico appear to have been a part of the much larger North American Desert culture area. It is uncertain as to how far south such "Desert" traditions may have reached. It seems unlikely that the early populations of such tropical regions as coastal Chiapas could be characterized as participating in a "Desert" subsistence pattern. These early inhabitants of the tropical lowlands were apparently food-

7. Radiocarbon determination of 4440 B.C. ± 300 B.C. (Libby, 1955).

8. Personal communication, R. S. MacNeish and P. C. Mangelsdorf, 1960. This cave has since been renamed "Coxcatlán Cave."

9. If radiocarbon determinations (as yet not available) should prove to be in the range of 5000–3000 B.C. The only exception to this would be the maize pollen, certainly wild, in the interglacial deposits of the Valley of Mexico (Barghoorn, Wolfe, and Clisby, 1954).

10. Personal communication, R. S. MacNeish, 1959.

11. Jennings and Norbeck, 1955. There is some evidence that the Desert plant-collecting pattern is even older in certain areas of North America. See Willey (1960a, b) for general discussions of this.

collectors who utilized plants, shellfish, and small game, but there is insufficient information about them to know whether incipient cultivation was practiced.

AGRICULTURISTS (1500 B.C.–A.D.1520)

MESOAMERICA AS A CULTURE AREA

With the transition from incipient to established cultivation—or to effective food production—at about 1500 B.C. Mesoamerica assumes a unity as a culture area (Kirchhoff, 1943). This unity is expressed in a basic agricultural complex of maize, beans, squash, and chili peppers, supplemented by cacao, sweet manioc, agave, and numerous fruits and vegetables and by the slash-and-burn shifting method of farming. It is also expressed in a tradition of massive public ceremonial structures, including platform mounds, which served as pedestals for temples or palaces and which were laid out around rectangular plazas or courts. Certain religious themes or deities characterize the area. Among these are the frequently depicted gods, Tlaloc and Quetzalcoatl, lords of rain and cultural enlightenment. Closely related to religion is an emphasis on astronomy, the calendar, mathematics, and writing. Although there was regional variation in such matters, some ideas were area-wide. Among these is the year calculation of 18 months of 20 days each plus 5 extra days and the 260-day period resulting from the permutation of 13 and 20 numbers and names. Markets and merchandising are also a Mesoamerican specialty. From earliest agricultural times we have archeological evidence of interregional trade, and from the ethnohistoric accounts of the sixteenth century we know that one of the main functions of native cities was as trading centers.

In spite of this common sharing of cultural traditions Precolumbian society and culture in Mesoamerica was also diverse, and this diversity is expressed geographically in several regional divisions. Individual regions are characterized by styles, such as the Maya polychrome style of pottery of the Maya lowlands or the Classic Veracruz style of stone sculpture of central Veracruz. Regions are also set apart by certain emphases in trait patterns. A good example would be the preoccupation with and elaboration of astronomy, calendrics, and writing in the Maya lowlands or the strong tradition of large human figure-modeling in the ceramics of western Mexico.

Three chronological periods generally are recognized within the agricultural era of Precolumbian Mesoamerica: the Preclassic, Classic, and Postclassic (see chart, Fig. 2). Although these terms have carried developmental implications (Armillas, 1948; Brainerd, 1954, 1958; Morley and Brainerd, 1956; Willey and Phillips, 1958), they are used here in a strictly chronological sense. The most objectively determined dates for any of these periods are those beginning the Classic period, for the close of that period, and for the entry of the Spanish into Mesoamerica at the end of the Postclassic period. This last date is A.D. 1520. The other two dates are fixed by the Maya native calendar of the Initial Series or long-count system. By this system the beginning of the Classic is set at A.D. 300, and its end is placed at A.D. 900.[12] Following this, the Postclassic period runs from A.D. 900 to A.D. 1520. Preclassic dates are based largely upon radiocarbon determinations. Unfortunately, these have not given uniform results. In the interpretation used here, the date 1500 B.C. marks the beginning of the Preclassic. However, some radiocarbon determinations suggest Preclassic beginnings nearer the 1000 B.C. dateline.[13]

The Village Agricultural Threshold (Early Preclassic Period)

Village agriculture is defined as sedentary community life based primarily upon plant cultivation. There were two types of village settlements: concentrated and dispersed. In the former, dwellings composed a compact community; in the latter, households occurred at some distance from one another, individually or in small hamlet clusters but with farming lands interspersed between them. The important thing, however, was that the locus of the village, whether concentrated or dispersed, was stable.

The Sierra Madre sequence in southwestern Tamaulipas, in which we have already traced a series of culture phases in a stage of incipient cultivation, is one of the very few places in Mesoamerica where the archeologist may observe a continuous transition from incipient cultivation to village agriculture. The Mesa de Guaje of the early Preclassic period has its inception at about 1500 B.C.,[14] and it is a direct development out of the preceding Guerra phase (MacNeish, 1958, pp. 168–69; MS, 1960). The food plants of Mesa de Guaje include hybridized, as well as Bat-Cave-type maize, yellow and red beans, squash, and pumpkins.

12. The beginning of the Maya Classic period is placed at the Maya calendar katun ending date 8.12.0.0.0. According to the Goodman-Martinez-Thompson calendrical correlation, this katun ending is A.D. 278, or, in round figures, A.D. 300. The close of the Classic period is placed at the katun ending of 10.3.0.0.0 or 10.4.0.0.0, rendered as A.D. 889 and 909, respectively, or, in round figures, A.D. 900. In this presentation we follow the Goodman-Martinez-Thompson interpretation. Following the Spinden correlation of Mayan and Christian calendars, the beginning of the Classic would be put at about A.D. 50 and its close at A.D. 650. Recent radiocarbon tests run by the University of Pennsylvania strongly favor the Goodman-Martinez-Thompson (personal communication, Linton Satterthwaite, Jr., 1960).

13. We cannot review all these determinations. "Early" determinations for the Preclassic include C-885, 886, 879, 884, 887 (Libby, 1955), all from Kaminaljuyu; C-196, 199, 202, 200, 203 (Libby, Ibid.), all from the Valley of Mexico; and GRO-774, 1172, 1512, 1056, 1524, 1525, 1589 (Dixon, 1959, p. 41), all from Chiapas. "Late" determinations for the Preclassic include Y-402, 401, 384, 390, 370, 374, 391, 382, 377, 406 (Deevey, Gralenski, and Hoffren, 1959), all from Kaminaljuyu; and M-662, 612, 611, 664, 663 (Crane and Griffin, 1958a, 1959), Y-437 (Deevey, Gralenski, and Hoffren, 1959), all from the Valley of Mexico. A series of determinations from La Venta, Tabasco, could be interpreted as supporting either an "early" or a "late" dating of the Preclassic, M-535, 529, 534, 532, 531, 530, 528, 533, and 536 (Drucker, Heizer, and Squier, 1957). Two Oaxaca determinations favor the "early" interpretation (C-424, 425 [Libby, 1955]), as does one from Tamaulipas (M-505 [Whitaker, Cutler, and MacNeish, 1957]).

14. Radiocarbon determinations of 1700 ± 250 B.C. and 1490 ± 250 B.C. (Crane and Griffin, 1958a).

These plant foods are estimated as having composed about half the total diet. Metates for corn-grinding are numerous. Pottery appears in the sequence for the first time. The vessel forms are simple (flat-bottomed jars and small-mouthed jars) and without ornamentation. There is a great variety of netting, matting, and basketry; and loom-made cotton cloth is present. Available information on settlement pattern suggests small village areas without special architecture. In brief, Mesa de Guaje appears poised on the basal threshold of effective food production and sedentary village life.

In the Valley of Mexico such early Preclassic period phases as the Early Zacatenco presumably had some antecedents in the Chalco culture, but intervening developmental steps are missing. The Early Zacatenco site is an extensive and deep refuse bed.[15] Located on the shore of an old lake, the inhabitants supplemented their agricultural diet with wild fowl from the marshes and deer from the surrounding mountains. Dwellings were wattle-and-daub huts, but there are no mounds or major constructions that can be interpreted as temple platforms or ceremonial constructions. Thousands of handmade female figurines imply a fertility cult, and pottery and other artifacts found with burials show a concern for the afterlife. Ceramics are of good quality and have variation in form and decoration (Vaillant, 1930). In general, pottery of Early Zacatenco is representative of early Preclassic period pottery elsewhere in Mesoamerica. Monochromes, often polished, predominate, and frequently polished black ware has incised or engraved-line decoration with dry red pigment rubbed into these lines. Plain white and white-on-red vessels are also a diagnostic of the phase. The ollas and the composite silhouette bowls are the common forms, the latter sometimes having tripod legs. Jade, the precious commodity of ancient Mesoamerica, was already in use as ear ornaments.

Other clues to sedentary agricultural village communities, apparently comparable in character and type to Mesa de Guaje and Early Zacatenco, are found on the Gulf Coast, near Tampico, in the early-Preclassic-period Pavon, Ponce, and Aguilar phases (MacNeish, 1954). At the opposite end of Mesoamerica the Yarumela I phase of Honduras provides an example (Canby, 1951), as do the Chiapa I (Dixon, 1959; Lowe, 1959) and Mani (Brainerd, 1958) phases of Chiapas and Yucatan and, probably, the beginnings of the Mamom phase of Uaxactun of the Guatemalan Peten lowlands (A. L. Smith, 1950; R. E. Smith, 1955).

In addition to those listed, certain phases that seem to be equally early in the early Preclassic period are represented by sedentary village sites plus ceremonial mounds. The Arevalo phase of Kaminaljuyu, in the Guatemalan highlands, is a case in point, as may be Ocos, of the Guatemalan Pacific coast.[16] The

15. We estimate an Early Zacatenco date of *ca.* 1500–1000 B.C. There is a radiocarbon determination of 1360 ± 250 B.C. (Libby, 1955) and a conflicting determination of 500 ± 250 B.C. (Crane and Griffin, 1958b).

16. Shook, 1951. Shook (personal communication, 1959) now places Arevalo as earlier than Las Charcas. Radiocarbon determinations on these phases show a wide chronological range (see Libby, 1955 [C-885] and Deevey, Gralenski, and Hoffren, 1959 [Y-401, 402, 384]).

artificial mounds associated with these phases are not large and elaborate, but there can be little question but that they are intentional and special structures markedly different from ordinary house platforms.

As yet we do not know where village agriculture originated in Mesoamerica. Some of the best documented discoveries of incipient cultivation, including maize finds, come from Tamaulipas; but Tamaulipas is at the northeastern periphery of Mesoamerica, and it seems more likely that the earliest agricultural villages are somewhere farther south. The early maize sequence from southern Puebla supports this, and the fact that the earliest ceremonial mounds are in southern Mesoamerica suggests that still earlier simple village levels may be found there.

The Rise of the Temple Center (Middle and Late Preclassic Periods).

The change from the simple sedentary village community to the community of villages-and-center was a significant turning point in Mesoamerican cultural and social history. It occurred over much of the area in the middle and late Preclassic periods, beginning as far back as 1000 B.C. While not as profound a change as that from food-collecting and incipient cultivation to established cultivation, nevertheless, it had far-reaching results. In a sense, it was the beginning of the change from simple to complex society. It is not yet clear from the archeological record as to where this change-over took place. In Tamaulipas, the Valley of Mexico, and other regions the temple center appears subsequent to a preceding level of undifferentiated agricultural villages. In highland Guatemala, on the other hand, the temple center is there at the beginning of the agricultural sequence, at least insofar as the sequence is now known.

It is almost certain that the process of the change from village to villages-and-center was accompanied by a general population increase, probably over most of Mesoamerica. Thus the process might be envisaged as the splitting-off of new village units from old ones as the latter become too large for the available surrounding farm lands. Certain villages then may have remained as the sacred centers of these expanding societies, and, in these, special constructions were put up as shrines, temples, and burial places. These temple or ceremonial centers eventually became the residences of priests and rulers, the seats of market places, and, as the resident leadership grew in power, the foci of art, crafts, and learning.

We have noted the presence of small temple mounds in highland Guatemala in the early Preclassic, but by the end of the middle Preclassic Miraflores phase, the site of Kaminaljuyu, in the Guatemala basin, had become a major ceremonial center. Not only do huge adobe platform mounds pertain to this phase, but the extent of the living refuse around the mounds suggests a population approaching urban proportions. The politicoreligious importance of Kaminaljuyu in the Miraflores phase is dramatized by rich burials of priests or chiefs in the mounds. In one instance hundreds of pottery and marble vessels and fine jades had been piled around the deceased. Another discovery at Kaminaljuyu not only under-

lines the ceremonial significance of the site but symbolizes the dawn of civilization in artistic and intellectual achievement. This is a fragmentary carved-stone
altar taken from a Miraflores context. The carvings are executed in a highly
sophisticated style and include hieroglyphic inscriptions relating to those of the
Classic period lowland Maya as well as to those of early Monte Alban in
Oaxaca.[17]

Temple-center construction in middle and late Preclassic times is also a feature
of other Mesoamerican regions. In Oaxaca, at Monte Alban, great mound architecture is associated with hieroglyphics at this time (Caso, 1938); and La Venta,
of lowland Tabasco, is known as the ceremonial center that served as a focus
for the Preclassic "Olmec" art style. Several mound groups occur at the La
Venta site, and the largest mound is 32 meters high. Other features are court-
yards, stone cist graves covered by mounds, carved stelae and altars, and huge
carved human heads. Temple-building is also known for the Maya lowland Preclassic period. The temple of E-VII-sub, at Uaxactun, is a famous late Preclassic
example (Ricketson and Ricketson, 1937), and in Yucatan there is a middle
Preclassic mound of impressive size at Yaxuná (Brainerd, 1951). In the Tlatilco
phase, which succeeds the Early Zacatenco in the Valley of Mexico, are hints of
specialized architecture in plastered terraces and stairways (Porter, 1953; Covarrubias, 1957, pp. 17–35), although the construction of large ceremonial mounds
is somewhat later—in the Cuicuilco phase (Cummings, 1933; Heizer and Bennyhoff, 1958). Also in the Teotihuacan site zone a platform mound and plaza area
have been discovered to date definitely from the late Preclassic Tzacualli phase;
and the Tzacualli phase refuse is found over a large district, indicating the beginnings of urban development (Armillas, 1950; Millon, 1957a).

Finally, it is of interest to return to the Tamaulipas sequence to observe the
changes occurring there following the establishment of village agriculture in
the Mesa de Guaje phase. La Florida succeeds Mesa de Guaje and is largely a
development out of it, but it is also clear that by late Preclassic times Tamaulipas
is the peripheral recipient of traits diffused from regions to the south. The agricultural complex of La Florida includes three races of hybridized maize, in addition to other plants known previously. The Laguna phase, contemporaneous
with La Florida (500 B.C.–A.D. 0) but in the Sierra de Tamaulipas rather than
the Sierra Madre region, has settlements with numerous house platforms grouped
around larger, presumably ceremonial, mounds or pyramids. These community
nuclei are surrounded, at some distance, by smaller villages or hamlet clusters of
house platforms. Pottery is found in a wide variety of forms, including tripod
and effigy vessels; and handmade pottery figurines are a part of the complex.
Ground-stone implements are better fashioned than previously and include not
only manos and metates but celts, adzes, and barkbeaters (MacNeish, 1958).

What sociopolitical and religious inferences may be drawn from the phenomenon of the rise of the temple centers during the middle and late Preclassic

17. Shook and Kidder, 1952; material in the National Museum, Guatemala City.

period? First, the presence of more archeological sites, larger sites, and public
works all imply an increase in general population from earlier periods. Second,
we have clues to the beginning and increasing complexity of the social order in
the ceremonial centers themselves, in the monumental arts and hieroglyphics,
and in the signs of rank and status associated with richly furnished burials.
Clearly, an aristocracy was being differentiated out of the general farming population at this time. Third, relating again to the evidences in the temples, the
representations of deities and the associations of calendrics and writing with
these representations strongly suggest an organized religion and a specialized
priesthood in charge of complex ritual and learning. Fourth, the material achievements in arts and crafts during the middle and late Preclassic periods imply full-
time craftsmen. Fifth, the raw materials and manufactured goods that are found
at great distances from their places of origin indicate important patterns of trade
linking together much of the Mesoamerican area.

The Threshold of Urban Civilization (Preclassic to Classic Periods)

Cities and civilization have been defined by the following criteria insofar as
these may be inferred from archeological data: (1) extensive and densely populated settlements, (2) specialization of crafts and labors, (3) concentration of
capital wealth, (4) monumental public architecture, (5) a class-structured society, (6) writing and systems of notation, (7) the beginnings of true science,
(8) great art styles, (9) long-distance trade, and (10) the formation of the state
(Childe, 1950). It is difficult to determine the exact point in an archeological
sequence at which such criteria may be said to make their first appearance. Some
of these traits are as early as the Mesoamerican middle Preclassic period; others
are present in the late Preclassic or are in process of development during that
period to climax later in the Classic.

The conditions of urban living seem to have been attained more fully in the
upland valleys of Mesoamerica than in any other type of environment. The
basins of Guatemala, Oaxaca, and the Valley of Mexico are the outstanding examples. Urban settlements appear early in these regions, and in the Valley of
Mexico, at least, they persist throughout later Precolumbian times. In the Guatemala basin the Kaminaljuyu site zone extended over several square kilometers
during the late Preclassic period. This was also the time of greatest cultural vigor
at Kaminaljuyu, and certainly the succeeding Classic period phases give no
greater evidence of urbanism and civilization (Shook and Proskouriakoff, 1956).
The urban maximum in the Guatemalan highlands thus comes relatively early in
the sequence. Of the other criteria of civilization that we have enumerated,
Kaminaljuyu of the late Preclassic would have met the greater part of them.
For true science and state formation only are there no definite clues.

Monte Alban, in the Valley of Oaxaca, reached its urban zenith at the beginning of the Classic period.[18] Although Monte Alban is known mainly as a mam-

18. Caso, 1938. This was its III A phase.

moth ceremonial center of pyramids and temples perched on top of a natural hill overlooking a fertile valley floor, it was almost certainly an urban center. Hundreds of small artificial house terraces dot the flanks of the main hill as well as all the nearby hills.

The vast ruins of Teotihuacan, in the Valley of Mexico, are the remains of what was once the largest city of native Mesoamerica. Even in the late Preclassic Tzacualli phase the site was extensive, and at the height of its power, in the Classic period Xolalpan-Tlamimilolpa phases, the residence zone of Teotihuacan was spread over ten square kilometers (Armillas, 1950; Millon, 1957a). One of the problems in connection with the site is how its sizable population, probably in excess of 50,000 persons (Sanders, 1956), was sustained. The immediate locale of the site is barren, cultivation is impossible today without irrigation, and there is no reason to believe that the environment and climate have changed within the last 2,000 to 3,000 years. We know that canal irrigation was in operation in the vicinity of Teotihuacan at the Spanish conquest and that *chinampa*, or "floating garden," intensive cultivation was also practiced at that time in the Valley of Mexico. Although secure evidence has not yet been adduced to demonstrate contemporaneity of either of these techniques with the Teotihuacan Classic period, it is a reasonable possibility that they did exist at that time in view of the demographic conditions of the region (Millon, 1954, 1957a; Armillas, Palerm, and Wolf, 1956; Wolf and Palerm, 1955).

The monuments of Teotihuacan qualify fully as "monumental." The largest pyramid at the site, built either at the close of the Preclassic or the beginning of the Classic period, is 64 meters high and 210 meters square at the base, easily one of the biggest man-made structures in the native New World. Social classes, division of labor, concentration of capital wealth, and great art styles are all inferable or evident. Furthermore, Teotihuacan was the center of one of the greatest networks of trade and influence in ancient Mesoamerica, and there are reasons to believe that some of the goods and cultural influences that radiated out of that site during the early Classic period were carried on waves of military expansion (Kidder, Jennings, and Shook, 1946). If so, Teotihuacan must be considered a forerunner of the Mesoamerican conquest states of the Postclassic period. Those civilizational criteria that are rare or lacking at Teotihuacan are writing and evidences of astronomical science and calendrics, such as were developed elsewhere in Mesoamerica.

If the cities of the upland valleys of Mesoamerica are defined as "concentrated urban" settlements, the term "dispersed urban" might be applied to the great centers of the Maya lowlands. Yet the term is a contradiction. To be dispersed is not to be urban in the sense of the true city. Perhaps the phase "civilization without cities" approximates more closely the settlement and sociopolitical qualities of the lowland Maya of the Classic period.[19] This settlement difference in the development of upland and lowland civilizations may have a natural environ-

19. The term and concept of "civilization without cities" is borrowed from John Wilson, who applied it to ancient Egypt (see Kraeling and Adams [eds.], 1960).

mental origin. Dense, close-packed settlement is, perhaps, more feasible in the uplands, with their deeper, richer soils and possibilities for intensive cultivation, while scattered and shifting settlement may be a correlate of the tropical forests and of "slash-and-burn" agriculture. There are other differences between the upland and lowland civilizations in Mesoamerica, although these are not easily derived from the natural settings. For instance, the great ceremonial centers of the Maya lowlands, such as Tikal, excelled in those very criteria of civilization that are rare or lacking in Teotihuacan: writing, calendrics, and astronomy. Conversely, there is little in the Maya Classic remains to suggest the kind of state power and expansive force that characterizes Teotihuacan.

The growth of the late Preclassic ceremonial centers and the ensuing attainments of Classic period civilization did not occur contemporaneously in all parts of Mesoamerica. The Valley of Mexico appears to be the northernmost boundary for civilization in Classic period times. The archeology of the west—Michoacan, Guanajuato, Colima, and Jalisco—is only beginning to be known; but, as yet, there are few indications of ceremonial-center construction or urban sites in these regions that can be dated with certainty as belonging to the Preclassic or Classic periods. This is also true of northwestern and northeastern Mexico. In the latter region, the Tamaulipas phases of the Classic period are clearly peripheral reflections of events to the south and southeast. Similarly, in southern Mesoamerica the characteristics of civilization, as here defined, do not extend south and east beyond the Motagua and Chamelcón drainages of eastern Guatemala and western Honduras.

The Postclassic Period

The Mesoamerican Postclassic period takes us beyond the scope of our survey of events leading up to the "threshold of civilization." Civilization persisted in this period, and the phenomenon of the urban zone or city-type settlement became even more common. It was a time of unrest and large-scale migrations that has been referred to as an era of militarism (Armillas, 1950). Certain cities of the period, such as Tenochtitlan of the Aztecs, became the centers of empires. In this, it is possible that Tenochtitlan may have been repeating an earlier pattern set by Classic period Teotihuacan. One major event of the Postclassic period was the spread of many of the criteria of civilization to parts of Mesoamerica that had not been so influenced previously. Such expansion marked western and northwestern Mexico, and in the far south influences penetrated into Central America to northwestern Costa Rica.

Mesoamerica and the New World

Cultural development in Mesoamerica did not remain isolated from the rest of the New World. We have referred to Mesoamerican territory as being a part of a larger geographical-cultural sphere in the preagricultural eras. This involvement with other areas of the New World continued in agricultural times. The village agricultural societies of Mesoamerica were interrelated with those of Peru, Ecuador, Colombia, and lower Central America; in fact, this whole vast zone of nuclear America, from northern Mexico to southern Peru and Bolivia, possessed food plants, ceramic technologies, and, almost certainly, religious and mythological concepts in common (Willey, 1955). Beyond the threshold of village agriculture, Mesoamerica and Peru took the lead in development of civilization. Diffusion and trade linked the areas of nuclear America during these developments. The spread of metallurgy from the Andes north into Mesoamerica is one of the best examples of such contact and interchange in later Precolumbian times. The cultural force of Mesoamerica was felt to the north, beyond the limits of the Mesoamerican area, in the North American Southwest and Southeast. Influences radiating out of Mesoamerica had first impinged on these areas as early as the incipient-cultivation period. They continued during the Preclassic period and after.

CONCLUSIONS

Let us summarize by turning to the questions proposed by this symposium.

1. *In the late glacial and early postglacial periods what major cultural events characterize your area? By what archeological traces are these expressed?*

In Mesoamerica these geological periods pertain to big-game hunters, whose artifactual remains have been found in the upland regions of central and north-eastern Mexico. These Early Hunters lived in a wetter and cooler climate than that of the present. The Early Hunters followed a nomadic or semisedentary life, and the only artifacts left behind are chipped-stone points, knives, and scrapers. Later the onset of aridity resulted in the disappearance of the great animals, such as the mammoth, on which they were dependent. In the early postglacial period, from 7000 to 5000 B.C., plant-collecting and small-game hunting replaced the earlier way of life, at least in the Mexican uplands. Even at this early time plant cultivation was probably a minor subsistence factor.

II. *Defining incipient cultivation (and/or animal domestication) as a minor or supplementary basis of total subsistence, when and how do such conditions appear?*

In the Mesoamerican uplands the conditions of incipient cultivation appear in the context of food-collecting societies of the early and later postglacial era— a span of from 7000 to 1500 B.C. Over these several millennia there is a steady increase in domestication and utilization of food plants. The actual plant remains (found in dry caves) and the grinding stones for seed preparation attest to this increase. Paralleling these events is a trend toward larger and more permanent settlements, and the earliest semipermanent architecture of Mesoamerica—houses of wattle-and-daub construction—date from late in this food-collector and incipient-cultivator era.

The food-collector and incipient-cultivator patterns are known from semiarid environments; almost nothing is reported of comparable cultures in the Mesoamerican lowland tropics.

III. *At what point in the cultural sequence of your area do you feel that you can identify effective food production (plant cultivation and/or animal domestication assuming a major subsistence role), and what are its artifactual expressions and social (directly inferred) consequences?*

At about 1500 B.C. the food-collecting and incipient-cultivating economies of Mesoamerica are replaced by those that are dependent to a major degree upon cultivation. Correlates of this change appear to be permanent village sites and pottery. At least, this is the course of events in certain regions of northern Mesoamerica where the transition from incipient cultivation to established cultivation is most clearly seen. It is possible—or even probable—that village-based agriculture was somewhat earlier than this in southern Mesoamerica. The geographical point of first cultivation of the most important Mesoamerican food plants—maize (*Zea mays*) and beans (*Phaseolus vulgaris*)—is uncertain, but probabilities favor southern Mexico and Guatemala. It is also likely that pottery appears first in the southern part of the Mesoamerican area.

Mesoamerican arts and crafts of this village-agricultural or early Preclassic period are household goods—pottery, figurines, and objects of personal adornment. They are all quite competently made.

Mound construction, for temples or other public buildings, has its inception at this time; but it is not clear as to whether or not an area-wide stage of simple farming villages without public architecture antedates mound construction.

From its beginnings, the early Preclassic period village-farming mode of life, with its effective food production, is found in both the upland and the tropical lowland regions of Mesoamerica.

IV. *Does effective food production appear as a part of an indigenous evolution, or does it (as revealed archeologically) suggest outside influence? To what extent does the appearance of effective food production (either indigenous or imported) seem explosive ("revolutionary")?*

Sequences in northern Mesoamerica (Tamaulipas) and also, now, farther south (southern Puebla) suggest an indigenous development of effective food production, through plant cultivation, within the Mesoamerican area. The several millennia of incipient cultivation, the indigenous nature of the plants, and the nuclear position within the Americas all support this interpretation. Importations of domesticated plants from the South American lowlands and from Peru seem to have been relatively late in Precolumbian times and of only secondary importance.

This revelation of the long incipient-cultivation history in Mesoamerica forces some revision in the concept of the agricultural threshold as a sudden "revolution." Nevertheless, our reading of the Mesoamerican archeological record is still too tentative to rule out completely "revolutionary" or "explosive" effects of a village-agricultural way of life. Even in Tamaulipas, where the transition from cultivation incipience to established farming appears most gradual and most complete, the final arrival of a Mesoamerican-type, full agricultural status effects something of a break with the past. For the time being we would surmise that, during the long millennia of incipient cultivation, plants were being exchanged among the various regions of Mesoamerica until, finally, in some one region, or regions, village agriculture emerged as a reality. From this place, or places—most probably the southern portion of the Mesoamerican area—the full agricultural complex and certain associated traits, such as pottery, were diffused to and accepted by the peoples of other regions rather rapidly. In this sense, then, the propagation of village agriculture could be described as sudden or "explosive."

V. *Could you, in your area, use the term "threshold of urbanization"? If so, what would you mean by it, and what is the evidence for its development?*

A concept of urbanization has been employed in Mesoamerica with particular reference to those large population agglomerations that once lived in upland basins, such as the Valley of Mexico. In addition to physical size of the community and archeological evidences for close-packed city living, other cultural and social characteristics of civilization obtain for such communities.

A related, but differing, concept of "civilization without cities" has also been suggested for lowland tropical forest environments of Mesoamerica, such as the Maya regions. Here the formal property of the densely settled urban zone seems lacking, but other achievements and criteria of civilization are present.

Both these patterns of civilization appear in ancient Mesoamerican life—at least in certain regions—by the time of the late Preclassic period, although both became more pronounced in the Classic period.

The trends leading from village farming to the threshold of urban life and/or to civilization are observed in the development of the ceremonial center. Such centers first appear, in a minor way, in the early Preclassic period. Presumably, they started as little more than tribal shrines. In the middle and late Preclassic they were elaborated, architecturally and artistically, into important temple and palace foci. It is assumed that their principal functions were political and religious. The degree to which, and the manner in which, such ceremonial centers may have become secularized is unknown; but one would suspect that secular and commercial functions were more important in a true urban zone, such as Teotihuacan, than in a Maya Classic period ceremonial center of the lowlands.

Insofar as we can tell, urban life, and other qualities of civilization, arose indigenously in southern and central Mesoamerica from antecedent patterns of village agriculture. Certain elements of urbanization and civilization then spread northward and westward in Mesoamerica in late Classic and Postclassic times.

BIBLIOGRAPHY

ARMILLAS, PEDRO
1948. "A Sequence of Cultural Development in Meso-America." In (W. C. Bennett ed.), *A Reappraisal of Peruvian Prehistory*. ("Mem. Soc. Amer. Archaeol.," No. 4, pp. 105–12.) Menasha, Wis.

1950. "Teotihucan, Tula, y los Toltecas: Las Culturas Post-Arcaicas, y Pre-Aztecas del Centro de Mexico: Excavaciones y Estudios, 1922–50, *Runa* (Buenos Aires), 3:37–70.

ARMILLAS, PEDRO, ANGEL
PALERM, and E. R. WOLF
1956. "A Small Irrigation System in the Valley of Teotihuacan," *Amer. Antiq.*, 21:396–99.

AVELEYRA ARROYO DE ANDA, LUIS
1950. *Prehistoria de Mexico*. Ediciones Mexicanas, Mexico, D.F.

1956. "The Second Mammoth and Associated Artifacts at Santa Isabel Iztapan, Mexico," *Amer. Antiq.*, 22:12–28.

AVELEYRA ARROYO DE ANDA, LUIS, and MANUEL MALDONADO-KOERDELL
1953. "Association of Artifacts with Mammoth in the Valley of Mexico," *Amer. Antiq.*, 18:332–40.

BARGHOORN, E. S., M. K. WOLFE, and K. H. CLISBY
1954. "Fossil Maize from the Valley of Mexico," *Bot. Mus. Leaflets* (Harvard University), Vol. 16, No. 9.

BOSCH-GIMPERA, PEDRO
1959. "La Prehistoria del Nuevo Mundo y Centro America," *Actas del 33d Congreso Internacional de Americanistas*, pp. 137–51. Costa Rica: San Jose.

BRAINERD, G. W.
1951. "Early Ceramic Horizons in Yucatan." In SOL TAX (ed.), *The Civilizations of Ancient America: Sel. Papers, 29th Internat. Cong. of Americanists*, 1:72–78. Chicago: University of Chicago Press.

1954. *The Maya Civilization*. Los Angeles: Southwest Museum.

1958. *The Archaeological Ceramics of Yucatan*. ("Anthrop. Records," No. 19.) Berkeley and Los Angeles: University of California Press.

CANBY, J. S.
1951. "Possible Chronological Implications of the Long Ceramic Sequence Recovered at Yarumela, Spanish Honduras." In SOL TAX (ed.), *The Civilizations of Ancient America: Sel. Papers, 29th Internat. Cong. Americanists*, 1:79–85. Chicago: University of Chicago Press.

CASO, ALFONSO
1938. *Exploraciones en Oaxaca, Quinta y Sexta Temporadas, 1936–37*. (Instituto Panamericano de Geografia e Historia, Publ. 34.) Mexico, D.F.

CHILDE, V. G.
1950. "The Urban Revolution," *Town Planning Review* (Liverpool), 21:3–17.

COE, M. D.
1959. "Una Investigación Arqueológica en la Costa del Pácifico de Guatemala," *IDEAH: Antropologia e Historia de Guatemala*, 11:5–11, Guatemala: Ministerio de Educación Publicas.

1960a. "A Fluted Point from Highland Guatemala," *Amer. Antiq.*, 25:412–13.

1960b. "Archaeological Linkages with North and South America at La Victoria, Guatemala," *Amer. Anthrop.*, 62:363–93.

COVARRUBIAS, MIGUEL
1957. *Indian Art of Mexico and Central America.* New York: Alfred Knopf.

CRANE, H. R., and J. B. GRIFFIN
1958a. "University of Michigan Radiocarbon Dates II," *Science*, 127:1098–1105.

1958b. "University of Michigan Radiocarbon Dates III," *ibid.*, 128:1117–23.

1959. "University of Michigan Radiocarbon Dates IV," *Amer. J. Sci., Radiocarbon Suppl.*, 1:173–98.

CUMMINGS, BYRON
1933. *Cuicuilco and the Archaic Culture of Mexico.* (Univ. Ariz. Bull., Vol. 4, No. 8; Soc. Sci. Bull., No. 4.) Tucson.

DEEVEY, E. S., L. J. GRALENSKI, and V. HOFFMAN
1959. "Yale Natural Radiocarbon Measurements IV," *Amer. J. Sci., Radiocarbon Suppl.*, 1:144–72.

DE TERRA, HELMUT, JAVIER ROMERO, and T. D. STEWART
1949. *Tepexpan Man.* ("Viking Fund Publs. in Anthrop.," No. 11.) New York.

DIXON, K. A.
Ceramics from Two Pre-Classic Periods at Chiapa de Corzo, Southern Mexico. ("Papers, New World Archaeological Foundation," No. 5, Publ. 4.) Orinda, Calif.

DRUCKER, PHILIP
1948. "Preliminary Notes on an Archaeological Survey of the Chiapas Coast," *Middle Amer. Res. Inst.*, Vol. 1, No. 1. New Orleans: Tulane University.

DRUCKER, PHILIP, R. F. HEIZER, and R. J. SQUIER
1957. "Radiocarbon Dates from La Venta, Tabasco," *Science*, 126:72–73.

1959. *Excavations at La Venta, Tabasco, 1955.* (Smithsonian Institution, Bur. Amer. Ethnol. Bull. 170.) Washington, D.C.

HEIZER, R. F., and J. A. BENNYHOFF
1958. "Archaeological Investigation of Cuicuilco, Valley of Mexico, 1957," *Science*, 127:232–33.

IRWIN, H. J. and C. C.
1959. "Excavations at the LoDaiska Site in the Denver, Colorado, Area," *Proc. Denver Mus. Nat. Hist.*, No. 8.

JENNINGS, J. D., and EDWARD NORBECK
1955. "Great Basin Prehistory: A Review," *Amer. Antiq.*, 21:1–11.

KIDDER, A. V., J. D. JENNINGS, and E. M. SHOOK
1946. *Excavations at Kaminaljuyu, Guatemala.* (Carnegie Inst., Publ. No. 561.) Washington, D.C.

KIRCHHOFF, PAUL
1943. "Mesoamerica," *Acta Americana*, 1:92–107. Mexico, D.F.

KRAELING, CARL H., and R. M. ADAMS
1960. *City Invincible: A Symposium on Urbanization and Cultural Development in the Ancient Near East.* (Oriental Inst. Spec. Publ.) Chicago: University of Chicago Press.

LIBBY, W. F.
1955. *Radiocarbon Dating.* 2d ed. Chicago: University of Chicago Press.

LORENZO, J. L.

1955. "Los Concheros de la Costa de Chiapas," *Anales Instituto Nacional de Antropologia e Historia,* 7:41–50. Mexico.

1958. *Un Sitio Preceramico en Yanhuitlan, Oaxaca.* (Instituto Nacional de Antropologia e Historia, Division Prehistorica, Publ. No. 6.) Mexico, D.F.

LOWE, G. W.

1959. "The Long Sequence of Preclassic Architectural Development at Chiapa de Corzo, Chiapas." In *Abstrs. of Papers, 24th Ann. Meeting, Soc. Amer. Archaeol., Univ. Utah,* p. 38.

MACNEISH, R. S.

1954. "An Early Archaeological Site near Panuco, Vera Cruz," *Trans., Amer. Phil. Soc.,* Vol. 44, Part 5.

1958. "Preliminary Archaeological Investigations in the Sierra de Tamaulipas, Mexico," *ibid.,* Vol. 48, Part 6.

1959(MS). "Origin and Spread of Some Domesticated Plants as Seen from Prehistoric Tamaulipas, Mexico." (Paper delivered at annual meeting Amer. Anthrop. Assoc. Mexico City, December, 1959.)

MANGELSDORF, P. C.

1958. "Ancestor of Corn," *Science,* 128: 1313–19.

MILLON, R. F.

1954. "Irrigation at Teotihuacan," *Amer. Antiq.,* 20:177–80.

1957a. "New Data on Teotihuacan 1 in Teotihuacan," *Boletin del Centro de Investigaciones Antropologicas de Mexico,* No. 4, pp. 12–17.

1957b. "Irrigation Systems in the Valley of Teotihuacan," *Amer. Antiq.,* 23:166–67.

MORLEY, S. G., and G. W. BRAINERD

1956. *The Ancient Maya.* 3d ed. Stanford, Calif.: Stanford University Press.

PORTER, M. N.

1953. *Tlatilco and the Pre-Classic Cultures of the New World.* ("Viking Fund Publs. in Anthrop.," No. 19.) New York.

RICKETSON, O. G., JR., E. B. RICKETSON, *et al.*

1937. *Uaxactun, Guatemala: Group E–1926–31.* (Carnegie Inst. Publ. No. 477.) Washington, D.C.

SANDERS, W. T.

1956. "The Central Mexican Symbiotic Region: A Study in Prehistoric Settlement Patterns." In G. R. WILLEY (ed.), *Prehistoric Settlement Patterns in the New World,* pp. 115–27. ("Viking Fund Publs. in Anthrop.," No. 23.) New York.

SHOOK, E. M.

1951. "The Present Status of Research on the Preclassic Horizon in Guatemala." In SOL TAX (ed.), *The Civilizations of Ancient America: Sel. Papers, 29th Internat. Cong. Americanists,* 1:93–100. Chicago: University of Chicago Press.

SHOOK, E. M., and A. V. KIDDER

1952. *Mound E–III–3, Kaminaljuyu, Guatemala.* (Carnegie Inst., "Contribs to Amer. Anthrop. and Hist.," Vol. 11, No. 53.) Washington.

SHOOK, E. M., and TATIANA PROSKOURIAKOFF

1956. "Settlement Patterns in Mesoamerica and the Sequence in the Guatemalan Highlands." In G. R. WILLEY (ed.), *Prehistoric Settlement Patterns in the New World,* pp. 93–100. ("Viking Fund Publs. in Anthrop.," No. 23.) New York.

Smith, A. L.
1950. *Uaxactun, Guatemala: Excavations of 1931–37.* (Carnegie Inst. Publ. 588.) Washington, D.C.

Smith, R. E.
1955. *Ceramic Sequence at Uaxactun, Guatemala.* 2 vols. (Middle Amer. Res. Inst., Tulane Univ. Publ. 20.) New Orleans, La.

Vaillant, G. C.
1930. *Excavations at Zacatenco.* ("Anthrop. Papers, Amer. Mus. Nat. Hist.," Vol. 32, Part 1.) New York.

Whitaker, T. W., H. C. Cutler, and R. S. MacNeish
1957. "Cucurbit Materials from Three Caves near Tamaulipas," *Amer. Antiq.,* 22:352–58.

Willey, Gordon R.
1955. "The Interrelated Rise of the Native Cultures of Middle and South America." In B. J. Meggers (ed.), *New Interpretations of Aboriginal American Culture History: 75th Anniv. Vol. of the Amer. Anthrop. Soc. of Washington,* pp. 28–45. Washington, D.C.

1960a. "New World Prehistory," *Science,* 131:73–83.

1960b. "Historical Patterns and Evolution in Native New World Cultures." In Sol Tax (ed.), *Evolution after Darwin,* 2:111–41. Chicago: University of Chicago Press.

Willey, Gordon R., Gordon F. Ekholm, and R. F. Millon
"The Patterns of Farming Life and Civilization." In R. Wauchope (ed.), *Handbook of Middle American Indians.* (In preparation.)

Willey, Gordon R., and Philip Phillips
1958. *Method and Theory in American Archaeology.* Chicago: University of Chicago Press.

Wolf, E. R., and Angel Palerm
1955. "Irrigation in the Old Acolhua Domain, Mexico," *Southwestern J. Anthro.* 11:265–81.

Wormington, H. M.
1957. *Ancient Man in North America.* 4th ed. ((Denver Mus. Nat. Hist., Pop. Ser.," No. 4.)

THE GREATER AMERICAN SOUTHWEST

EMIL W. HAURY

INTRODUCTION

B Y LONG-STANDING usage among archeologists, the Southwest of the United
States is defined as encompassing all the state of Arizona, all but the eastern
third of New Mexico, the southwestern and far-western margin of Colorado, the southern two-thirds of Utah, eastern and southern Nevada, and the
states of Sonora and Chihuahua in northern Mexico. As Kroeber has aptly pointed
out (1939, pp. 5–6), the geographical delineation of culture wholes is beset with
numerous problems, one of which is that sharply drawn boundaries convey the
impression of a cleavage that actually does not exist. Within the structure of
the culture-area concept, boundaries are intended to indicate only some notion
of the lateral spread of elements and through them our understanding of a way
of life reaching out from centers of cultural florescence. If we recognize this
limitation, the Southwest as noted above has some utility.

For our purposes, it is pointless to consider at length the history of the development of the culture area concept per se and how it has been applied to the
Southwest. Suffice it to say that the efforts of Mason (1896) focused on ethnic
environments and that Wissler's (1922) work depended upon natural-cultural
area relationships. Beals' studies (1932) represent essentially the analytical trait
approach for a small part of continental America, and Kroeber's important contribution (1939) looks—as does Wissler's, but far more perceptively—at the natural-cultural area correspondences. Kidder's (1924) analysis and, more recently,
the Seminars in Archeology: 1955 (Wauchope (ed.), 1956) have been motivated
by archeological considerations, the latter having concerned itself with areal and
focal shifts on a multichronological basis.

The foregoing delineations present us with an area too restricted for delving
into the problem that confronts this symposium. A larger unit of study will
provide us first with wider environmental and cultural ranges that, through comparison, will yield more rewarding results than if the area were kept smaller.
For this reason I wish to use as the basis for my remarks that portion of the
western United States and northern Mexico characterized as the greater Southwest by Kirchhoff (1954). Areally, this includes "Central, Southern, and Baja
California, the great Basin, Arizona, New Mexico, Southern Coastal Texas, and
Northern Mexico to the Sinaloa and Panuco River" (p. 533) (see Fig. 1). This
constitutes a region from one-half to one-third the size of the Near East as outlined by Braidwood (1958, p. 1419).

Whether this geographical subdivision of North America is a true cultural entity or not rests on one's taxonomic precepts, a problem that does not concern us here. It is important, however, to note that, in a broad sense, the greater Southwest is a natural area that locally harbors limited habitats. These differ sharply from the main pattern of aridity and maximum sunshine that characterizes the region as a whole.

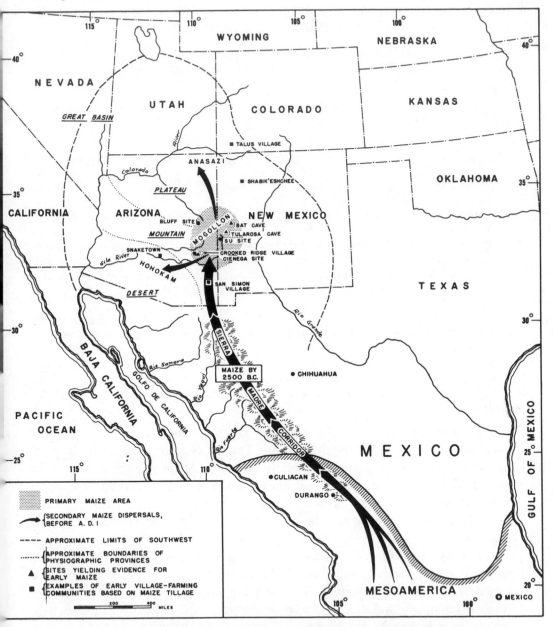

FIGURE 1. Map illustrating the probable route over which maize was diffused from Mesoamerica to the southwestern archeological zone and its subsequent dispersal to other cultural areas.

This large area supported varied culture types historically, and for some of these a long evolutionary record is demonstrable.

It is also evident that different groups of peoples, living in similar environments, followed divergent paths and at variable speeds in the progression of their ways of life from the simple to the more complex. It is these facts that make the region an especially attractive one for reviewing the core problem of this symposium.

ENVIRONMENTAL CONSIDERATIONS

Kroeber (1939) has done us a notable service in synthesizing the work of numerous botanists who have looked at the problem of vegetation areas. It is apparent immediately that the greater Southwest constitutes one of the most complex natural regions in all the New World, characterized by environmental ranges from extreme desert to high mountain forest.

For our purposes it will be sufficient to point out some of the broad distinctions by vegetation type (after Shelford, 1926) and to identify the areas:

1. *Broad-leafed Evergreen Semidesert:* south coast of California and north Pacific coast of Baja California.
2. *Extreme Desert:* south interior California, southern Nevada, western Arizona, Coahuila.
3. *Desert:* Great Basin, much of the Arizona plateau, most of Baja California, western Sonora, and Sinaloa.
4. *Succulent desert:* central and southern Arizona stretching south into Sonora, Rio Grande Valley from central New Mexico to the Pecos confluence with the Rio Grande, eastern Chihuahua, and Durango.
5. *Dry Grassland:* parts of western New Mexico, southeastern Arizona, northern Chihuahua, eastern New Mexico, isolates in eastern Durango, including a portion of western Coahuila and Zacatecas.
6. *Desert Coniferous Forest:* eastern Utah, much of north- and east-central Arizona, west and east flanks of Sierra Madre Occidental.
7. *Moist and High Mountain Coniferous Forest:* the backbone of the Sierra Madre Occidental.

It becomes apparent from the foregoing that no smooth transition from one environmental extreme to the other exists. On the contrary, the distribution of vegetation areas is spotty and dramatically changing. At the same time it is worth noting, as a possible favorable condition for south-to-north diffusion of cultural factors, that transits could have been made over long distances through either desertic or mountainous environments without radically departing from either of them.

More important, however, is the fact that these vegetation areas provide the range of climate, terrain, and plant resources on which man could work out a variety of subsistence activities. The adaptive process in a nearly universally harsh environment was eased because of the varied resources. And somewhere within the area agricultural stimuli, as a prelude to the development of a higher societal order, should have found fertile ground. One of our problems is to determine where and when this took place.

Except for coastal regions, diurnal temperature extremes are typical, and it is obvious that, as a function of the altitudinal extremes, mean temperatures also manifest a wide range. For most of the greater Southwest, rainfall comes in two seasons: the general storms of winter, bringing snow to the higher elevations and rain elsewhere, and the local intense thunderstorms of the summer. These are often separated by many months of intense heat and drought. In short, sharp variation in climate as between the dry and the wet season are the norm.

ETHNOGRAPHIC SYNOPSIS

We need to view the native peoples of historic times only in the most meager detail to give us some feeling for the spectrum of culture types. The range is as dramatic as was the ecological, from Seri fisherman to Zuñi farmer. Some of these differences are attributable to the responses of people to habitat, and the present may be taken to mirror the past.

For south coastal California, Baja California, and the coast of western Mexico, semimaritime cultures existed, drawing both upon the sea and the land for subsistence. They were non-agricultural, as were also some of the interior tribes. To exist under harsh living conditions and seasonal food sources, scattering and mobility were required. The nearest approach to sizable populations and permanent residences is met among the coastal groups, where the Gabrielino and Chumash reached a cultural climax (Kroeber, 1939, p. 44). Neither historically nor archeologically was food production a significant factor. These areas, thus, play no part in our problem except in helping to establish a primitive economic base over a wide geographical range.

Moving eastward from California, we encounter immediately the Colorado River, which, like the Nile, is flanked in its lower reaches by desert and mountains. It was a slender lifeline for the Yuman tribes who farmed the bottom lands without benefit of rain or irrigation, depending on the ever present ground moisture arising from a high water table.

East of the Yumans, the upper Pimas and Papagos, while living in villages, depended about evenly on natural resources and on farming. This is the giant cactus belt upon the fruits of which heavy reliance was placed.

In northwestern Arizona, other Yuman tribes—the Yavapai, Walapai, and Havasupai— had farming of sorts, but for at least half the year they were collectors, following the economy of other desert neighbors.

To the north, the Great Basin, the southern part of which concerns us, by climate and vegetation belongs to the Southwest (Kroeber, 1939, p. 50). Historically, its people, like the Paiutes, are characterized by a meagerness of culture and collecting subsistence habits.

Following the circuit clockwise, we next have the sedentary Pueblo farmers, whose towns contrast sharply with the mobile and scattered life of the adjacent Navajo and Apache. Here in the same environment we see two subsistence patterns that are poles apart.

Finally, in the northern Sierra Madre are the mountain-dwelling Tarahumara. By geography, they should have benefited by and perhaps retained the higher cultural attributes from Mesoamerica. But this seems not to have been the case as far as food dependence is concerned, for their economy is little above the level of subsistence farming. To the west of them the Cahitans and Pimans farmed the rich bottom lands of a series of rivers that rise in the Sierra Madre and empty into the Gulf of California.

The population density for the Southwest is given by Kroeber (1939, p. 143) as 10.7 per 100 square kilometers, exceeded only by the Northwest Coast and California in all North America north of Mexico. Yet, looking at the greater Southwest, the density range is from 2 to 5 in the Great Basin to more than 75 per 100 square kilometers in the Pueblo area, which, except for a small part of California, is the highest value for native populations north of Mexico. Kroeber also rates high the culture intensity of the Pueblos as a concomitant, in this case, of population density (1939, Map 28), and comparably low intensities where the population was thin. Human resources in historic times thus match the extremes already noted for the natural setting of the greater Southwest.

LATE QUATERNARY HISTORY

Geological studies in the greater Southwest bearing on terminal Pleistocene and Recent history have been late in getting started. It was the archeologists' interest in early human history and the perpetual need to develop water resources in an arid environment that stimulated much of the work that has been done. On the basis of this we conclude that within the last 15,000 years, in fact since mid-Pleistocene times, there have been no large-scale changes in surface relief. Although the region surely felt the fringe effects of the large ice masses far to the north, glaciation as such played no part in shaping the landscape save for a few isolated instances, such as the San Francisco Peaks. Stream terraces are discernible in many places, but these have not yet been convincingly correlated directly with the glacial and interglacial episodes. Climatic shifts from cool to warm and moist to dry, phenomena that do leave an imprint upon the land, have been attributed to the wide-ranging northern hemispheric climatic patterns. For our purposes it will be enough to note that within the time of the archeological record, conservatively 15,000 years, there has been progressive desiccation, intensified during the altithermal drought of about 4,500–7,000 years ago (Antevs, 1955). Since 5,000 years ago essentially modern conditions have prevailed.

The effects of vulcanism upon man were minimal because only localized activity is known. Sunset Crater, near Flagstaff, which erupted in the eleventh century A.D. is one, and its effects upon the region's residents have been studied (Colton, 1932). The Pinacate volcanic field in northwestern Sonora may have been active within the last 15,000 years, and some suspect that Capulin Mountain's eruptions were witnessed by Folsom man. I do not see vulcanism as a factor of any consequence.

The principal forces at work were the epicycles of erosion and sedimentation, evidences of which are best preserved in the inner valleys of the major drainage systems. This was fortunate, for it was along the main drainages that man congregated by reason of richer natural resources, upon which he was dependent. The locally changing landscape, by alternate scouring and filling, provided the opportunity for the preservation of human traces, fires, camps, and remains of animals killed, often in a decipherable geological context. The recent erosion cycle, starting some seventy-five years ago, is now providentially exposing these often deeply buried evidences, the location of which could never be predicted. It is obvious, too, that unless knowing eyes are present at the moment of exposure the traces may forever be lost by the destructive force of the next flood.

Detailed geochronological studies are only now well under way, and until these begin to produce meaningful results we must rest upon generalities in our efforts to relate man to nature on the incipient exploitative level.

PROGRESSION OF CULTURE PATTERNS

A hypothetical and simple approach to the problem of culture history is one in which a single pattern is recognized at the time of origin, or first appearance, out of which there emerged a complex of patterns, the product of diverse responses to various forces. The evidence for the New World begins to hint that no such simplified scheme is supportable. Taking the chronological short view of 10,000–12,000 years as the base line, at least two culture types are already in evidence. These show up in the greater Southwest, which invites our attention to them.

The readily identifiable elements of these two patterns are the stemmed and the lanceolate projectile point traditions. The former represents the Desert culture as seen in Danger Cave occurring as early as 9,000 years ago (Jennings, 1957, p. 265) and was associated with tools designed for seed-grinding and preparation of plant foods. This was a clear indication of an adaptation to wring the most out of an essentially arid environment. In all probability this pattern has a substantially greater antiquity than the dates presently indicate. It is predictable, on the basis of the Great Basin and western distribution of the Desert culture, that the oldest manifestations will be found in the West. Old World ties are not establishable on the data now available, but one may speculate that the complex was related somehow to the chopping-tool tradition of eastern Asia. Gidding's recent Alaskan studies of beach ridges and associated cultural remains may provide a much needed connection, for his oldest complexes consist of chopping tools and stemmed points.

The second pattern, that of the lanceolate blade, was used by the big-game hunter and was associated predominantly with meat and hide-dressing tools, as judged by the slim data now available. The distribution of this complex is wide, but chiefly east of the Rockies, with a southwesterly extension into the Southwest. At best, the age for lanceolate blades does not appear to extend much beyond 12,000 years ago, but, as with the Desert culture, a greater age would ease some of the problems related to the distribution of the type. And when older occurrences are found, they should be east of the Rockies. Old World connections for the lanceolate blade are not easily demonstrable, but, if there was a link, it doubtless arose from a quite different tradition than did the stemmed point of the Desert culture. The fluting technique, as has already been noted by others, was undoubtedly a New World invention.

The points relevant to our discussions are:

1. Within the last 15,000 years, two culture types seem to have entered the New World deriving from different Old World patterns, and distributionally they converged in the greater Southwest.
2. We see plant-food exploitation, on the one hand, and animal-food dependence, on the other, though obviously not to the complete exclusion of the opposite in either case.
3. Irrespective of the precise temporal relationship of these two patterns, they must have impinged on each other. The question here arises as to what the consequences were.
4. Central to our problem is an assessment of the survival potential of the two systems under conditions of increasing aridity.

Retracing our steps somewhat now, we find that Desert-culture remains are infrequently found in association with extinct fauna, the Sulphur Spring stage of the Cochise culture being an exception. Taking the Desert culture of Danger Cave in the Great Basin as the expression best suiting our needs, the Pleistocene fauna of 10,000 years ago was already gone, whereas it was still extant to the east. Thus, if the Desert culture ever depended on big game, it was forced early to rely heavily on plant resources and to develop the appropriate technologies. The long and intimate experience of a wide range of plant life undoubtedly saved them during adverse climatic shifts, for changing the dependency from desirable to less-desirable, and perhaps hardier, plants was made relatively easy. Under the conditions of marginal subsistence, with some fluctuations in the degree of impoverishment, florescence was unlikely, if not impossible. As a consequence, we see a truly phenomenal situation of a near-static way of life from a remote 10,000 years ago to the ethnological present, a classic example of man's tenacity in a little-changing and harsh environment. This is in specific reference to the Great Basin.

The big-game hunters on the fringes of the greater Southwest were faced with a distinct hazard. Extinction of the game, brought on by increasing aridity, loss of forage, and by man's own cutting-down of the herds, demanded a shift in economic dependence if life and residence were to be maintained. The temporal relationship of the collector and the hunter now becomes important in our speculative reconstruction, for if the collector was first, as has been held (Jennings, 1956, p. 72), then the hunter had a ready model to follow when he was forced to change his ways. The full transition from butchering to seed-grinding, as symbols of essential dependence, took time, and it is doubtful that the wrench was as severe as we would like to think. Hunters also collect, just as plant-collectors hunt, and the shift was therefore one of emphasis.

The urge to exploit vegetal resources possibly meant infiltration into previously unsettled or lightly populated areas, the higher altitudes, which may have been less desirable as haunts of big game and therefore had been bypassed by man. Extensions of habitat brought new challenges and gave societies experience in subsisting in environments ranging from desert to forest. This now established the broad base from which we must operate in assessing subsequent developments. The time is roughly 7000 B.C. and later.

Speaking of the Southwest proper, several points need to be noted: (1) On the local scene, the level of cultural achievement, a subsistence economy that required maximum energy from a maximum number of people, must have been receptive to the addition of any resource to the cultural inventory that would ease the quest for food. (2) The invention or acquisition of tools, the milling stones, and the mastery of their use in grinding native foods, certainly by 8000 B.C. (Jennings, 1957, p. 285), demanded no major overhauling of food-preparation practices when a new plant became available. (3) On the foreign scene Mesoamerican societies were flourishing and were already in possession of maize, whose durable influence was soon to be felt in the frontiers to the north.

The earliest appearance of maize in the greater Southwest, and here I assume—without detailing supporting arguments—that it came out of the south, has been determined in the order of 3000 B.C. by radiocarbon means. The places are Bat Cave (Mangelsdorf and Smith, 1949), Tularosa and Cordova caves (Martin et al., 1952) in New Mexico, all in altitudes over 6,000 feet; and at Point of Pines, Arizona (Ariz. W:10:112), in a valley floor geological context of first, possibly second, millennium B.C. age (Martin and Schoenwetter, 1960). The latter identification is based on pollen extracted from silts in a mountain valley at 6,000 feet above sea level. These stations are within a little more than a hundred miles of each other, a geographical clustering of the evidence that I believe to have significance.

Maize—whether cob, plant, or pollen—of comparable age has not yet been found in the subarid desert, though it was a staple by the beginning of the Christian Era. For most of the Great Basin, Southern California, and presumably Baja California, maize was not accepted. We are left, then, with the inference that the earliest maize, probably a variety adjusted for higher altitudes, spread along the cordilleran spine of the greater Southwest and found lodging in east-central Arizona and west-central New Mexico. Mangelsdorf and Lister (1956) conclude this to have been the case after a detailed review of the botanical evidence.

As an early cultigen companion to maize we must also add squash and, by 1000 B.C., the bean, thereby completing the conventional trinity of food plants that characterized so much of North America. We may think of this mountain region as nuclear in the sense that it represents the earliest seed-planting—

involving a grass in process of domestication—anywhere in the northern part of the greater Southwest. We assume that equally early and even earlier stations may be found stretching southward into Mesoamerica. Maize without pottery, possibly as early as that from the Arizona–New Mexico frontier, has been reported from caves in the Sierra Madre of Chihuahua (Mangelsdorf and Lister, 1956), but it has not been radiocarbon determined. For this area, then, incipient cultivation may be set at a time from 2500 to 3000 B.C.

The recipient people, the Cochise culture, a regional manifestation of the wider-spread Desert culture, are still imperfectly known. Their residence pattern and architectural forms, if any, have not been established, except that we know that caves were used for shelter where available and that, more commonly, settlements or camps in the open are deduced from implement and hearth concentrations in geological contexts exposed by recent erosion. The deep blanket of soil under which most of these remains occur has slowed the research on fuller definition of the culture. We know it chiefly through the stone implements that were geared to the collection and preparation of plant food, such as grinding stones and percussion-flaked choppers. These reflect typological stability over a long period of time.

For at least 2,000 years the advent of the new cereal grain that ultimately was to shape societies left no measurable effect upon the recipients, either in the complexity of the culture or upon the speed with which it progressed. It is evident that effective food production was long in coming, a subject to which we will return later.

Continuing now with our survey, some 2,000 years after the arrival of maize, a new craft reached the core of the greater Southwest, again a gift from nuclear Mesoamerica. This was the knowledge of pottery-making. The earliest dated pottery comes from within the area of oldest maize, from Tularosa Cave in west-central New Mexico (Martin *et al.*, 1952, p. 483) with a radiocarbon determination of about 150 B.C. Clearly here, as well as elsewhere in the world, pottery was not a direct concomitant of agriculture, but after A.D. 1 both flourished as correlates.

With this new trait, responsive in reflecting regional clay and mineral resources, susceptible to change through time, and a hallmark of cultural or tribal differences, the opportunity was enormously increased for eventual archeological analysis and identification. Before pottery, the relatively undifferentiated lithic typology of the far-flung Desert culture (Cochise) does not permit recognition of sharp or specific regional differences except over large areas and long stretches of time. After pottery, regional manifestations become evident not only in the pottery itself but in related attributes. As a consequence of this fact, the archeologist has recognized three main cultural streams: the Anasazi, centering in the plateau of the Four Corners area; the Hohokam of the Arizona desert; and the Mogollon of the mountain zone extending southward along the corridor far into Mexico. These are the so-called higher cultures of the Southwest. This is not the place to argue the ethnic separateness of these groups. We are interested, however, in cultural responses to the settling-down process in three strikingly different environments. These may be taken up as a series of problems.

Settling Down

As background for the cultural build-ups beginning roughly with the Christian Era, we need to dip deeply again into the time of food-collectors. It is axiomatic that in the New World, except for some maritime groups, the settling-down process was a correlate of maize tillage. This concept, I believe, needs some modification, at least for the Southwest. Because of their special attraction, caves cannot be used as a test of stationary living. The evidence must be found in open sites. The vast accumulations of grinding stones in stations of the Cochise culture, as exemplified in the Cave Creek site (Sayles and Antevs, 1941, p. 17), and the considerable accumulation of refuse strongly hint at localized and perhaps near-continuous residence. The extensive attrition of milling stones and the subsurface storage pits occasionally seen favor this idea. Some of these sites are datable to pre-maize times; others are within the first and second millennia B.C. after the advent of corn, but we have no knowledge that maize was grown in these sites.

It is not beyond probability that as early as 4000 B.C. the Cochise culture was engaged in deliberate plant cultivation of native species, as, for example, *chenopods* and *amaranths*. This experience with plants plus the possession of implements for processing plant foods, as noted earlier, predisposed the people to accept maize culture easily. For a long time maize did nothing to alter the mode of living beyond what was already known, though it must have supplied a greater measure of security achieved by the storage of surpluses.

We are still in the dark regarding the detailed nature of houses, their arrangement, or their number in a community during this period of incipient maize cultivation. Pit houses, with shallowly sunken floors, with dirt-covered beam and brush superstructures, and with entrance through the sides were probably the norm. This is predicated on architectural evidence of the first millennium B.C. (Sayles and Antevs, 1941, p. 27) and on the established architectural pattern observable in such villages as at Pine Lawn, the Vahki phase at Snaketown, and at Forestdale, dating near the time of Christ. All these are surely well up the ladder of architectural history.

The important point to reiterate, however, is that over much of the greater Southwest some experience had already been gained in settled living before the arrival of maize and other seed crops. At least two thousand years were to pass before formalized communities arose.

Which Subenvironment the Best for the Transformation?

The greater Southwest, as already indicated, provided a wide variety of ecological systems in which food-getting advances could have been made. It is also evident that the achievements were not uniform over the area but, instead, were spotty. Polar differences, as between the Great Basin collectors and the

Plateau planters, are found within the space of a few hundred miles. Is there anything to be learned by a closer inspection of this problem?

Jennings states (1957, p. 286) that "the Basin provides the semi-arid climate regarded by many as prerequisite to the beginnings of plant domestication." Prerequisites and antecedents, however, did not appear to be enough because the record does not support plant domestication as a Basin achievement or yet even tillage to any extent. This holds true also for the Succulent Desert, where, in modern times, tribes like the Papago depended upon native plants for 50–60 per cent of their food and agriculture at best was desultory (Castetter and Bell, 1942, p. 56). Sauer (1952, Pl. II) shows the Southwest as a recipient rather than a donor area.

Being on the receiving end of a diffusion pattern, three initial conditions were, I believe, primarily responsible in making the transition from collector to producer a reality. First was propinquity, the geographical closeness to the avenue through which elements were passing from nuclear Mesoamerica northward. The opportunity to acquire these had to be present. Second, the biogeographical setting needed to be similar in kind to that of the donor area, and, third, an optimum cultural environment was needed, a willingness to accept, to modify, and to build. These three requisites were met in the Sierra Madre corridor and, for our purposes, in the northern extension thereof—the higher regions and mountains of the Arizona–New Mexico border country.

For the most part, this was an open forested setting endowed with some natural clearings, with sufficient precipitation at the right times of the year for farming on a simple level without water-control devices. Both European and American scholars are holding the view that agriculture arose in wooded lands (Clark, 1946, pp. 57–71; Braidwood, 1948; Sauer, 1952, pp. 21–22), and it would seem logical that, during the initial dispersal of plant and technique, it would stick to this environment. At least the southwestern data support this view.

Not until agriculture was well established here did it flow out into the less favorable environments as a secondary expansion to the arid plateau and the desert (Fig. 1). The harshest part of the Southwest in terms of water scarcity was the desert. Farming, except in river bottoms, was impossible without water control, and measures to control water took some time in developing. But, once gained, the desert was ripe for full exploitation. Perhaps not until the beginning of the Christian Era did maize cultivation become significant among the Hohokam of the desert, as a result of simple canal development. It appears to have been no earlier on the Plateau among the Anasazi, whose planting was limited to small plots situated where ground moisture was concentrated and held after floods.

Kirchhoff's "Oasis America" (1954) centers in the "Great Sonoran Desert," a construct based on ethnology. But in a historical sense the desert appears to have been conquered late.

I conclude that the initial transformation took place in the uplands, that the truly great advances in agriculture came in some of the more arid regions but not until the techniques of canal irrigation were learned. Other arid sections, as the Great Basin, did not experience the same course. The road to stability was not obligatory.

Delayed Effects of Agriculture

The earlier observation with respect to the retarded effects of agriculture bears further discussion because it stands in sharp contrast to the usually accepted opinion that rapid cultural evolution followed as a consequence of food production. Childe's use of "revolution" (1952) has perhaps influenced our thinking, although he is careful to point out (1950, p. 3) that "revolution" denotes the "culmination of a progressive change." Redfield's "transformation" (1953, p. 5) is better suited, it seems to me, to describe what actually happened.

In any event, as previously noted, some two thousand years elapsed between the earliest record of maize in the Southwest and the appearance of village life and other concomitants signaling full sedentary living (Jennings, 1956, p. 76). A possible explanation for this may reside in the early knowledge and practice of seed-planting of non-domesticated forms. The addition of maize to the list of existing seed crops was valued as only one more. Early maize was also a primitive form—pod corn—and the yield was relatively small. Its introduction required no new tools for processing, thereby allowing the introduction to pass as a commonplace.

Another factor, perhaps even more important than the foregoing, was the later evolutionary change of maize. Left alone, changes in a single race were gradual, but the introduction of new races of maize produced striking evolutionary spurts. Mangelsdorf and Lister (1956, pp. 172–73) have demonstrated a rapid change in maize in northwestern Mexico at about A.D. 750 ± 250, when, in a few centuries at the most, a primitive race was almost completely transformed by the introduction of two new entities. The date above is too recent for our situation, but, given a similar circumstance in the core area of the Southwest shortly before the time of Christ, one begins to sense the possibility of explosive changes. Improved strains meant increased yields. Larger harvests spelled surpluses. The principle of storage, in underground pits or even in baskets, was already known, so now the economy was shifting from mere subsistence to one of relative abundance. When this happened, there was undoubtedly a real premium attached to the acceptance of maize as something new and prized. As a postulate, I would say that, with this event, new diffusion took place. The northern reaches of the greater Southwest and the Sonoran Desert now came under its influence. Basketmaker (Anasazi) and Hohokam farming was becoming a reality. It is significant that the oldest villages yet recognized, Falls Creek in southwestern Colorado (Morris and Burgh, 1954), the Pine Lawn villages (Martin, 1940, 1943; Martin et al., 1947, 1949), the Bluff Site (Haury and Sayles, 1947), and Snaketown (Gladwin et al., 1937), all date near the beginning of the Christian Era, following the postulated improvement in the races of maize. Furthermore, these villages represent the three main culture types—Anasazi,

Mogollon, and Hohokam—a strong indication that the factor operating to stimulate the formation of village life cut freely across cultural boundaries. Maize and its related domesticates stand as the logical candidates for bringing this about. I know of nothing in the climatic history of the region, another force operating without respect to culture, that might be called upon to help explain the rise of villages.

The full transformation, then, from collector to producer, was long in coming, attributable primarily to the primitive nature of maize. Its improvement, by introduction of new races, did produce the kind of revolutionary changes within a few centuries usually thought of as following the first farming.

ANIMAL DOMESTICATES

Unlike the Near East and other parts of the Old World, where domestication means both plant and animal, the North American problem is simple. Herd animals were never domesticated, and the only animal that clearly falls within this domesticated category was the dog. Archeological evidence indicates (Haury, 1950, p. 158) that the dog was already present several thousand years before Christ. The inference is indicated that the dog was not even domesticated here but was brought to the New World from the Old by its human masters.

Of uncertain status in the greater Southwest was the turkey. Some argue that it was domesticated, while others hold to the idea that it was kept. Whatever the outcome, it will have little bearing on our problem, for we must conclude that the people of the Southwest were seed-planters and that they could not count domesticated animals as having any real economic importance among their resources.

THE VILLAGE: PATTERN, SIZE, AND LONGEVITY

According to the previously stated postulate, the improvement in the race or races of maize, shortly before the time of Christ, greatly stimulated its planting in the core area and was responsible for its quick spread to all the greater Southwest except the Far West. Close upon the heels of this advance we see for the first time what Braidwood has aptly called (1958, p. 1428) "village-farming communities." I see these as distinct from the earlier long-occupied camps of the Cochise culture, whether in caves or in the open, because of formalized architecture, perhaps a closer clustering of the houses, usually the presence of a larger, apparently non-domestic structure, and a greater complexity of the material possessions. Of whatever cultural identity, that is, Hohokam, Mogollon, or Anasazi, the house pits remaining reflect a solidity of construction and an investment of labor that would arise only from a need for prolonged residence. These were not temporary camps, evidenced particularly by the Bluff Site (Haury and Sayles, 1947), where house pits were scooped out of solid sandstone. Although direct evidence of maize is not available for all, it does exist for some, and for the others the inference that maize was the dependent crop may be drawn from the types of metate or milling tools present.

In evaluating such factors as house distribution and size of community, we are seriously handicapped by the nature of the archeological digging. Few total villages have been cleared. Hence estimates must be based on what was dug and by extrapolation. A tacit assumption must also be made that, except where demonstrably different ages of houses can be established, all structures were simultaneously inhabited. Against these uncertainties let us examine a few test cases (Fig. 1).

I. MOGOLLON CULTURE

Bluff Site (Haury and Sayles, 1947).—Occupies the sloping top of a bluff; about 6,600 feet above sea level; 22 of a probable 30 domestic houses excavated; one large communal or (?) ceremonial structure, near village's center; house distribution random, separated from each other 5–25 meters; several structures date later than main occupation. Assuming 20 houses to have been simultaneously inhabited, and an average family-size factor of 4–5, the village population was 80–100 persons. Age of village: Mogollon I, *ca.* A.D. 300, by tree-ring dating. No direct evidence of domesticated plants, but maize cultivation is inferred.

Crooked Ridge Village (Wheat, 1954).— Situated on a long, well-drained ridge, 6,200 feet above sea level; 24 of a probable 100 rooms excavated; two large ceremonial structures are near apparent center of village; house distribution random, nearest about 5 meters apart. Some difference in age of houses is indicated, so, assuming that 50 houses were simultaneously occupied and applying the family-size factor of 4–5, the population was 200–250. Age of village, oldest horizon: Mogollon I, Circle Prairie phase, estimated pre–A.D. 400 (Wheat 1955, p. 213). Charred maize present (Wheat, 1954, p. 164).

SU Site (Martin, 1940, 1943; Martin and Rinaldo, 1947).—Located on low flat-topped ridge at 6,440 feet above sea level; 28 of a probable 34 houses were dug, randomly scattered in two groups each with nearly central ceremonial house. If 20 houses were occupied at once, probable population was 80–100. Age: Mogollon I, Pine Lawn phase, estimated pre–A.D. 500 (Martin *et al.*, 1949, p. 222). Maize inferred from presence in same time period at Tularosa Cave.

San Simon Village (Sayles, 1945).—On low terrace at 3,600 feet above sea level; 66 structures located, undetermined number remaining undug; no ceremonial structure. Architectural sequence greatly complicated by overbuilding during 6 phases. Oldest houses number about 12, yielding population of 48–60. Age: Mogollon I, Peñasco phase, estimated to be early centuries of Christian Era. No direct evidence of maize, but presence inferred.

II. ANASAZI

Talus Village (Morris and Burgh, 1954).—Houses terraced on 25° slope, Animas Valley, Colorado, at approximately 6,800 feet above sea level. A probable 9 houses, floors cleared, closely spaced; indeterminate number not excavated. No ceremonial structure recognized. Population estimate not valid, but at best community was probably small, 75–100. Age: Basketmaker II, pre–A.D. 400, by tree rings. Maize and pumpkin or squash inferred from presence of same in nearby shelter of same age.

Shabik'eshchee Village (Roberts, 1929).—On mesa top, about 6,600 feet above sea level; village completely dug, 18 houses and one ceremonial room; random distribution, 2–8 meters apart. Presumed population 75–90. Age: Basketmaker III, A.D. 400–700, dating by association. Maize culture inferred.

III. HOHOKAM

Snaketown (Gladwin et al., 1937).—Desert environment on terrace above Gila River at about 1,200 feet above sea level. A site of long occupation and only 2 houses recognized representing oldest horizon; initial village probably small, no population estimate possible; house size suggests extended family use. Age: near A.D. 1, dating by stratigraphy and association. Maize agriculture inferred.

In selecting the foregoing villages, I have concentrated on the earliest ones of which we have a record. It is evident that the data are woefully lacking and hardly comparable, especially for the Anasazi and Hohokam. Regardless, they may certainly be recognized as the Southwest's incipient villages, arising from the oldest architectural tradition for the whole of the area in late Cochise times (Sayles, 1945, pp. 1–3).

While these villages cut across cultural and environmental boundaries, they were all roughly of the same age. This synchronous build-up supports the idea that the time of village-founding under differing circumstances was the true threshold of settled living. Similarity in village plan is evident, a random scattering of units, with a centrally located ceremonial structure (temple?), especially early in Mogollon villages and somewhat later in those of the Anasazi. This feature remains to be identified among the Hohokam. Village population, by our gross estimates, seems to have been a hundred souls or fewer on the average, though Crooked Ridge village appears to be an exception. The evidence for maize culture in all is good, and we can accept it as the key factor in accounting for the new phenomenon in settlement history.

The volume of refuse and the lateral extent of it in late Cochise culture sites suggests a community size roughly comparable to that of the village-farming communities. One must agree, on our meager data, with Redfield (1953, p. 6) that the transition from food-collecting to food-producing was not accompanied by an immediate increase in community size.

It may be an accident of more intensive excavation that the Mogollon villages appear somewhat more solidly established than do those of the other groups, but these also coincide in distribution with the area from which the earliest maize data and the earliest pottery have come and which was ecologically similar to the donor area of maize. No sites comparable to these villages are known elsewhere in the greater Southwest, though they may well exist to the south in the Cordilleras. The advance from camp to farming village here lagged behind the Near East by at least 4,000 years.

The question of village longevity bids brief reference. Most of the afore-mentioned villages enjoyed a comparatively short life, at most through several developmental phases of the archeologist's time scale. The San Simon village, and especially Snaketown, had a demonstrably long life, 1,200 to 1,400 years for the latter, or 2,000 years if the historic Pima are admitted as the descendants of the Hohokam. Snaketown's is the outstanding stratigraphic record for a southwestern open site. I view village life span as the probable consequence of a particular advance in farming technology. This was water control by ditches. While our oldest readily supportable date for canalization at Snaketown is A.D. 700 (Haury, 1936), the sophistication of the canal of that date and the length of the ditch, more than 3 miles, presupposes a developmental period of considerable time. In view of the survival problem facing even a small com-munity in the desert without some form of water control, I do not find it difficult to believe that ditch irrigation in simple form was already known by A.D. 1. The enormous labor investment in canal construction rooted people to the spot. As the canals grew in length and complexity, bringing ever more acreage under cultivation, new villages would, as a matter of course, be estab-lished; but there would have been little reason to abandon the original settlement. So it grew, experiencing local shift in house sites, piling up ever deeper-layered deposits of refuse, and in the end giving the impression of maturity that only long occupancy supplies.

As for the San Simon village, initially of Mogollon identity and later carrying a Hohokam veneer, the reason for longevity is less readily explained. Neither terrain nor water resources were such as to permit canal irrigation, so the reason must rest on presently unrecognized advantages of the site. While other villages of the Mogollon and Anasazi were frequently overbuilt by later peoples, there were hiatuses in the occupational sequence. Canal irrigation was not employed by them, although simple forms of water control were known. In short, from the slim data we have for the Southwest, village longevity appears to be directly related to the level of hydraulic advances.

Subsequent histories of village and town development in the three areas took different paths. The Mogollon passed the scattered pit-house-living stage largely as the result of having come heavily under the Anasazi sphere of influence. Among the latter a new architectural form was emerging, rooms were joined to rooms, making a cellular structure, and rooms were built on top of one another, the ceiling of one becoming the floor of the next. The plaza or courtyard also puts in an appearance. Thus, Mogollon and Anasazi settle-ments of later times, certainly classifiable as towns, were essentially the same in composition.

The Hohokam, however, except for a short-lived intrusion of puebloid architecture into their domain in the fourteenth century, abided by the old tradition and lived in sprawling villages of shallow pit dwellings. This is all the more surprising because they had achieved a farming status not matched by the other societies. The reason obviously lies in cultural factors. One may guess that the security given by canal irrigation, a source of water for thirsty fields less capricious than rain, somehow must be taken into account. This dependability required fewer group efforts in formalized rain-making ceremonies and on religious structures per se. Also descent—patrilineal, if we may judge by the modern Pima analogy—and lack of emphasis on the extended family and clan may have been factors. Expertness in husbandry did not automatically determine the compactness or form of community development.

LAND USE AND IRRIGATION

The variety of environments in the greater Southwest into which agriculture eventually spread called for the adoption of various methods before effective farming could be established. These would have come only after long familiarity with the habitat. For the core area, the Mogollon, I would reason that there was ample time for this, in the order of 2,000 years. For the rest of the area it may be argued that some knowledge of method spread with material, so that adaptations dictated by the diverse environments were more quickly achieved. The flood-water farming described by Bryan (1929) undoubtedly mirrors the system employed literally from the beginning of planting in the plateau. For the mountains, where land was at a premium, some form of water run-off controls, such as low terraces and check dams, worked effectively to hold and spread the natural water that came as rain or snow (Woodbury, 1961). This system, too, must be old. Dating the tangible remains is notoriously difficult because the plots were in use into late prehistoric times. But, without these conjectures, I do not see how the oldest villages described could have reached the permanency indicated.

Irrigation by canal, however, is another matter. Here we must deal with a trait that, in developed form, required engineering skills and labor recruitment not demanded by the simpler systems. Since agriculture came out of the south, it is also tempting to attribute canal irrigation to the same source. I have been willing to accept this as probable, but recently serious doubts have arisen in my mind. Irrigation was only nominally practiced in Mesoamerica, with which most southwestern interconnections seem to have been established, and the antiquity has not yet been certainly determined beyond the Toltec era (Palerm, 1955, pp. 35–36). Only in the Rio Balsas does one find systems comparable to Hohokam and, beyond that, northern Peru. If the germinal idea did come with maize, it would appear that the Hohokam, by the early centuries of the Christian Era, had seized it and, spurred by their favorable topographical environment, achieved full mastery in quick order. The alternative is to entertain the thought that canals were spontaneous, inspired by the fingering-out of waters during flood stage in the Gila and Salt Rivers into numerous shallow channels on the flood plain. Nature's example would not have gone unnoticed, for before irrigation farming could have been only on flood plains.

A unique outcome of canal irrigation was the removal of restrictions that dictated village location (Haury, 1956, p. 9). For farming communities in the

Southwest two requirements ruled the place of residence: available water and land. Now with water control via ditch, naturally occurring water was no longer requisite, and, so long as the topography permitted it, canals could be made to reach out to farmlands far from rivers, with villages built adjacent. Actually, this emancipation of residence came late, not until the thirteenth or fourteenth century.

The chief significance for us in the foregoing discussion is that different systems of land utilization arose among the three subcultures, required by varied habitats, and that these systems were sufficient to engender subsequent florescences.

Elsewhere in the greater Southwest, especially in the northern and eastern perimeter, farming was little more than a subsistence activity. To the south, as one approaches Mesoamerica one infers intensification of planting where permitted by the environment. The irrigators of the lower Yaqui River in Sonora—because of the shallowness of archeological time and of what little is known of their historic relationships—may be presumed to have learned the art from the north.

OTHER CONSEQUENCES OF VILLAGE LIFE

The assessment of the kind and extent of cultural reorientation that followed full dependence on agriculture, beyond the more easily observed phenomena of architectural form and tool complexes, has not been undertaken. It is a difficult subject but one that begs attention, even though most of what can be said is still speculation.

Systematic efforts to note the influence of sedentary living on trade have not been made. It may be observed, however, that trade during most of prehistory in the Southwest was seldom more than a nominal exchange of goods, far below the level of commerce, as evident in the early settlements of the Old World. The liveliest exchange for the longest time of which we have any record appears to have been in marine shell from the west. This began even in the early-man horizon (Sayles and Antevs, 1941, p. 67; Haury, 1950, pp. 189–90), but it did not reach its peak until after A.D. 1000.

Exchange of pottery is the most readily identifiable evidence of trade, and this we know took place on the village-farming community level between neighboring tribes. Again, not until late in prehistory, however—in the fourteenth century—do we see this reaching significant proportions, that is, when the volume became large enough to make commerce in pottery appear as an institutionalized activity.

The initial appearance of maize, pottery, and the figurine complex from the south I regard as the product of diffusion. This continued through time, ultimately heavily affecting the Hohokam in particular. Direct importations of metal objects, notably copper bells, probably from Michoacan; the mosaic pyrites-encrusted plaques from still farther south; and the military macaw represent trade over the greatest distances. This long-range trade came, not as an antecedent to village and town development, but as a consequence of it. As far as the Southwest is concerned, it is my opinion that diffusion, principally of the stimulus category, was always more important in shaping the native societies than was direct commerce, the imposition of culture elements or patterns by minority immigrant groups or by large immigrant groups who initiated a life way *de novo*.

Coming now to a brief consideration of religion, our ideas clearly must be based on a few tangible remains, and they may be wide of the mark. Mural pictography, usually associated on the early level with the sacred rather than the secular, does not help us. No art of this kind has been surely identified to be as old as the incipient village level. The oldest mural paintings in the Southwest are probably those of Basketmaker II (Anasazi), and the subjects do not reveal to us any clear religious motivation.

Buildings are a somewhat surer base for making judgments. These are the "great houses" or "great kivas." They are major features in all Mogollon villages of pre-A.D. 400 age so far dug except the San Simon village (Wheat, 1955, p. 213), and they usually occupy a central spot in the village. The consistency of their appearance at this early time, the greater engineering skill required to build them over that required to build domestic structures, and the community of effort their construction demanded certainly means that the trait was not new even at this time level. While the origin of the kiva in space and time remains obscure, one may look to the south for its source, where religious systems were already crystallized. From Mogollon, the great kiva went to the Anasazi, where by A.D. 600 it was firmly established.

Curiously, the Hohokam, who were drawing on Mexico for cultural inspiration, especially by the end of the first millennium A.D., and who we know had also merged with the Mogollon in the overlapping frontier of the two groups, never seem to have acquired the great kiva. It is tempting at this point to re-evaluate the data from Snaketown (Gladwin *et al.*, 1937, pp. 74–77), referring to two large Vahki-phase houses by identifying them as great kivas. Typologically, this is supportable, but it would leave the Vahki phase without any domestic structures. If structures 1:7H and 8 were houses in fact, then the place of the great kiva may have been taken by the ballcourt, the idea having come out of the south perhaps as early as A.D. 500–700.

Reading backward in time from the modern pueblo analogy of the priesthood-kiva linkage, one may guess that a priesthood in its formative stages, or some kind of institutionalized religious leadership, was an associate of the oldest Mogollon kivas. Beyond this any assertions lose touch with reality.

The idea of a "kingship" appears to have been foreign in all the greater Southwest. At least there are no modern survivals among native peoples, and there is nothing in the archeological record to support it. Sociopolitical or socioreligious leadership, however, may be inferred. For Mogollon and Anasazi, the dispersal of houses around the great kiva hints the latter. For the Hohokam, no such distribution is observable. Here I would hold that the emphasis was on civil leadership, for this was more important in canal-building and maintenance than in organized ceremonialism oriented to producing rain.

A still further suggestion of effective political leadership is seen in the multi-village service given by one canal. The welfare of a number of villages depended upon co-operative efforts, and some form of centralized authority must have existed (Haury, 1956, p. 8). But these achievements, along with concepts of water and land rights, are already far beyond the beginnings of village-farming settlements in time. They are to be reckoned among the consequences of the technological advances of a hydraulic society.

FINAL CONSIDERATIONS

We have now passed in quick review some of the major aspects of the culture build-ups in the American Southwest (Fig. 2). On the collector level, from about 5000 to 3000 B.C., cultural uniformity characterized the region as a whole; but the subsequent routes were far from uniform. Progress was impressively unequal. Some tribes, as those in parts of Southern California, Baja California, and the Great Basin were essentially static, maintaining the old collector patterns for a probable 10,000 years. Others, starting from the same base, particularly the Hohokam, Mogollon, and Anasazi, reached the highest cultural evolution seen in the area. At any one time after A.D. 1 a cross section of economic patterns would have revealed a spectrum of all the variants ever present except the big-game hunter. In short, in only a part of the greater Southwest did the transition from food-collector to efficient food-producer become a reality (see map, Fig. 1).

The dictates of environment were partly responsible. The shortage of rain, the high evaporation rate, and the absence of live streams in most of the varieties of desert previously listed kept large parts of it uncultivable. Land tenure was possible only under a simple subsistence economy except in the Succulent Desert, where natural conditions favored a higher development. It is observable that a correlation existed between the better-endowed areas and the higher cultural achievements, but under these circumstances the environment was permissive and not compulsive. Cultural initiative and determination must also be reckoned with as dominant factors. Intensification of food-producing came as a happy combination of ecology, cultural outlook, and availability of outside stimuli.

In order of time, agricultural exploitation of the greater Southwest's sub-environments appears to have been oldest in the Desert Coniferous Forest, then spreading into the Dry Grassland, and the more favored parts of the Desert and the Succulent Desert as a nearly simultaneous expansion.

Viewed as a cultural process, the achievement of food production on a high level was far from explosive and not entirely indigenous in nature. Rather, it resulted from a combination of, first, several millennia of experience with and dependence upon native plants and, second, the introduction from the outside of new plants with nutritional and yield potentials higher than any of those

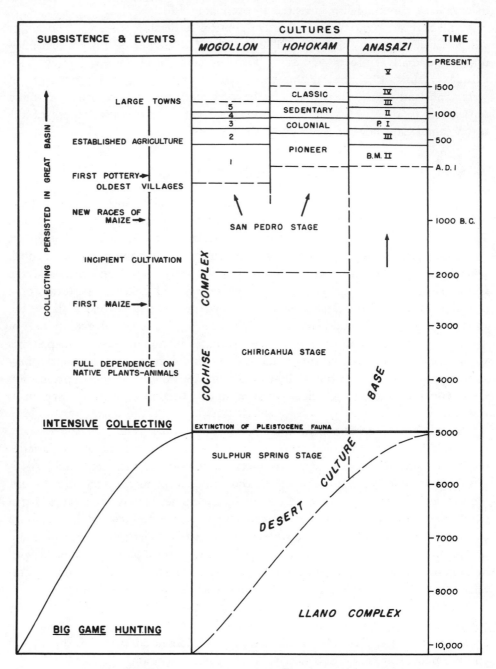

FIGURE 2. Synoptic chart of southwestern culture horizons and
approximate timetable of advances leading to urbanism.

in the local flora. Principal among these was maize from Mexico. Initially it was a primitive form, grown for perhaps 2,000 years by simple and desultory cultivation before its full capabilities were realized. In the Southwest, at least, the transition from incipient to advanced cultivation was a slow process.

The reconstruction that I have proposed, briefly summarized, holds that the northern Sierra Madre and the mountain country of Arizona and New Mexico were the core area of the Southwest so far as the transition from food collection to food production was concerned. This is predicated on the presence of the oldest maize, the oldest villages with "temple" structures, the oldest pottery, and a geographical setting favorable for simple agriculture at the end of the corridor along which elements of higher culture traveled from Mesoamerica. Improvement of the primitive maize in the first millennium B.C. by the arrival of new races, or perhaps by teosinte introgression, accounted for a second dispersal of the cereal to its ultimate limits in the greater Southwest. Then followed the development of agricultural techniques suited to differing eco-systems and the ultimate rise of the higher, more complex societies. It was not until these events occurred, at a time coinciding roughly with the beginning of the Christian Era, that we have reasons to consider effective food production a reality. Oddly, the climax areas, the riverine Hohokam of southern Arizona, and the plateau Anasazi of the Four Corners did not coincide with the original core area, where the mountain environment or cultural inertia seems to have had a suppressive effect in spite of having been congenial at the start. The Mogollon, although the initiators of what may be regarded as a good start toward the better life, lost their momentum and were eventually surpassed by their neighbors.

In late prehistory after A.D. 1000, we recognize the existence of large Hohokam villages—for example Snaketown, with perhaps a thousand inhabitants (14 houses excavated, an estimated 5 per cent of those present)—and the towns of the Anasazi, like Pueblo Bonito, with an estimated population of 1,000 (Judd, 1954, p. 1). Settlement expansion from the hundred or so inhabitants of the village-farming community to the large village or town of a thousand or more souls was ten centuries in coming. With this increase we see also, especially among the Anasazi, formalized architecture, religious concepts made real to us by kiva architecture, expanding arts and crafts, with perhaps some specialists, some increase in trade, and public works in the Hohokam canals. At the root of these advances were, first, the food surplus, which permitted concentrated populations, and, second, what Childe (1950) refers to as the "social surplus," members of the society who were not needed for food production. This level of attainment was maintained for 300–400 years, whence began a substantial reorientation of the societies, which took the form of shrinking boundaries accompanied by an increase in town populations. The Point of Pines ruin had a probable population of between 2,000 and 3,000 in the fourteenth century. This trend continued until the advent of the Spanish in the sixteenth century. Actually, the pueblos (Anasazi) of historic times added little to the pattern that was not already established long before. The Hohokam seem to have suffered almost complete eclipse after A.D. 1400, and the glory of their culture is but faintly echoed by the modern Pima Indians. The reasons for the decline are not readily apparent and do not concern us at present except in one aspect. Because the decline was already under way before the Spanish conquest, we can say that both Anasazi and Hohokam had reached their cultural climax before this disrupting influence arrived. It is thus pointless to speculate whether greater heights would have been reached by the native peoples if the Europeans had not come.

Turning to the final problem now, the evaluation of southwestern native cultural evolution against Childe's criteria for cities and civilized life (1950), the following brief observations may be made. The settlements of southwestern societies did not reach the status of cities, and their way of life fell short of civilization as defined, in spite of impressive accomplishments. Advances toward this state are seen in large aggregations of people, an increase by a factor of 10 or more over the early village-farming communities and a beginning of the development of public works, the canals of the Hohokam, to a limited extent canals among the Anasazi, and possibly the great kiva. But this is about all that can be said on the positive side. On the negative side, we have no data that would hint at centralized wealth arising from taxation, no writing, no developed foreign trade for raw materials controlled by segments of the population, no truly developed mercantile centers, no organized warfare, and no ruling class per se. Among the predictive sciences, only astronomy appears to lay claim to any recognition. The movements of the heavenly bodies and the equinoxes, important in modern Pueblo ceremonialism, undoubtedly stem from an old and deep-seated knowledge. But it was rudimentary at best and known principally by priests, who were the combined religious and political leaders. Archeology does not clearly tell us whether or not full-time specialists existed or what the rules of residence were.

The most we can say for the greater Southwest is that in a part of it, roughly the geographical core area, the necessary foundation for achieving urbanization was laid in the first millennium B.C. and that the ensuing centuries witnessed substantial advances. But innate cultural factors more than environmental restrictions set the boundaries of high accomplishments. Civilization as such, with its related cities and other attributes, was not to be. For the rest of the area the native people never rose above the level of a subsistence economy.

A significant sidelight on the greater Southwest is the fact that its archeological record of human progress is exceptionally complete up to the point of city achievement. We cannot yet say with certainty that all the historical processes of cultural evolution manifested in the region were experienced by one and the same people; but, at least until late prehistory, this appears to be a likely possibility.

BIBLIOGRAPHY

ANTEVS, ERNST
1955. "Geologic-Climatic Dating in the West," *Amer. Antiq.*, 20:317–35.

BEALS, RALPH
1932. *The Comparative Ethnology of Northern Mexico before 1750.* (Univ. Calif., "Ibero-Americana," No. 2.) Berkeley.

BRAIDWOOD, ROBERT J.
1948. *Prehistoric Men.* (Chicago Nat. Hist. Mus. Pop. Ser., "Anthropology," No. 37.) Chicago.

1958. "Near Eastern Prehistory," *Science*, 127:1419–30.

BRYAN, KIRK
1929. "Flood-Water Farming," *Geog. Rev.*, 19:444–56.

CASTETTER, EDWARD F., and WILLIS H. BELL
1942. *Pima and Papago Indian Agriculture.* Albuquerque: University of New Mexico Press.

CHILDE, V. GORDON
1950. "The Urban Revolution," *Town Planning Review* (Liverpool), 21:3–17.

1952. *New Light on the Most Ancient East.* 4th ed. London: Routledge and Kegan Paul.

CLARK, GRAHAME
1946. "Farmers and Forests in Neolithic Europe," *Antiquity* (London), 19:57–71.

COLTON, HAROLD S.
1932. "Sunset Crater: The Effect of a Volcanic Eruption on an Ancient Pueblo People," *Geog. Rev.*, 32:582–90.

GLADWIN, H. S., EMIL W. HAURY, EDWIN B. SAYLES, and NORA GLADWIN
1937. *Excavations at Snaketown: Material Culture.* ("Medallion Papers," No. 25.) Globe, Ariz.

HAURY, EMIL W.
1936. "The Snaketown Canal," *Univ. New Mexico Bull.*, Whole No. 296; Anthrop. Ser., (No. 5): 48–50. Albuquerque.

1956. "Speculations on Prehistoric Settlement Patterns in the Southwest." In G. R. WILLEY (ed.), *Prehistoric Settlement Patterns in the New World*, pp. 3–10. (Wenner-Gren Foundation for Anthropological Research.) New York.

HAURY, EMIL W., and E. B. SAYLES
1947. *An Early Pit House Village of the Mogollon Culture, Forestdale Valley, Arizona.* (Univ. Ariz. Bull., Vol. 18, No. 4; Soc. Sci. Bull., No. 16.) Tucson.

HAURY, EMIL W., et al.
1950. *The Stratigraphy and Archaeology of Ventana Cave, Arizona.* Albuquerque: University of Arizona Press and University of New Mexico Press.

JENNINGS, JESSE D.
1956. "The American Southwest: A Problem in Cultural Isolation." In ROBERT WAUCHOPE (ed.), *Seminars in Archaeology: 1955*, pp. 59–127. ("Mem. Soc. Amer. Archaeol.," No. 11.) Salt Lake City.

1957. *Danger Cave.* (*Ibid.*, No. 14.)

JUDD, N. M.
1954. *The Material Culture of Pueblo Bonito*. ("Smithsonian Misc. Coll.," Vol. 124.) Washington, D.C.

KIDDER, A. V.
1924. *An Introduction to the Study of Southwestern Archaeology*. (Department of Archaeology, Phillips Academy, Andover, Massachusetts.) New Haven.

KIRCHHOFF, PAUL
1954. "Gatherers and Farmers in the Greater Southwest: A Problem in Classification," *Amer. Anthrop.*, 56:529–50.

KROEBER, A. L.
1939. *Cultural and Natural Areas of Native North America*. Berkeley and Los Angeles: University of California Press.

MANGELSDORF, PAUL C., and ROBERT H. LISTER
1956. "Archaeological Evidence on the Evolution of Maize in Northwestern Mexico," *Bot. Mus. Leaflets* (Harvard University), 17:151–78.

MANGELSDORF, PAUL C., and C. EARLE SMITH, JR.
1949. "New Archaeological Evidence on Evolution in Maize," *Bot. Mus. Leaflets* (Harvard University), 13:213–47.

MARTIN, PAUL SCHULTZ, and JAMES SCHOENWETTER
1960. "Arizona's Oldest Cornfield," *Science*, 132:33–34.

MARTIN, PAUL SIDNEY
1940. *The SU Site: Excavations at a Mogollon Village, Western New Mexico, 1939*. ("Anthrop. Ser., Field Mus. Nat. Hist.," Vol. 32, No. 1.) Chicago.

1943. *The SU Site: Excavations at a Mogollon Village, Western New Mexico, Second Season, 1941. (Ibid., No. 2.)*

MARTIN, PAUL SIDNEY, and JOHN B. RINALDO
1947. *The SU Site: Excavations at a Mogollon Village, Western New Mexico, Third Season, 1946* ("Anthrop. Ser., Field Mus. Nat. Hist.," Vol. 32, No. 3.) Chicago.

MARTIN, PAUL SIDNEY, JOHN B. RINALDO, and ERNST ANTEVS
1949. *Cochise and Mogollon Sites, Pine Lawn Valley, Western New Mexico.* (Chicago Nat. Hist. Mus., "Fieldiana: Anthropolgy," Vol. 33, No. 1.) Chicago.

MARTIN, PAUL SIDNEY, JOHN B. RINALDO, ELAINE BLUHM, HUGH C. CUTLER, and ROGER GRANGE, JR.
1952. *Mogollon Cultural Continuity and Change: The Stratigraphic Analysis of Tularosa and Cordova Caves.* (Chicago Nat. Hist. Mus., "Fieldiana: Anthropology," Vol. 40.) Chicago.

MASON, OTIS T.
1896. "Influence of Environment upon Human Industries or Arts," *Smithsonian Institution, Annual Reports, 1895*, pp. 639–65. Washington.

MORRIS, EARL H., and ROBERT F. BURGH
1954. *Basket Maker II Sites near Durango, Colorado.* (Carnegie Inst. Publ. 604.) Washington, D.C.

PALERM, ANGEL
1955. "The Agricultural Basis of Urban Civilization in Mesoamerica." In J. H. STEWARD (ed.), *Irrigation Civilizations: A Comparative Study* pp. 28–42. (Soc. Sci. Monogs., No. 1.) Washington, D.C.: Pan American Union.

REDFIELD, ROBERT
1953. *The Primitive World and Its Transformations*. Ithaca: Cornell University Press.

ROBERTS, FRANK H. H. JR.
  1929. *Shabik'eshchee Village: A Lake Basket Maker Site in the Chaco Canyon, New Mexico.* (Smithsonian Institution, Bur. Amer. Ethnol. Bull. 92.) Washington.

SAUER, CARL O.
  1952. *Agricultural Origins and Dispersals.* (Bowman Memorial Lectures, Ser. 2.) New York: American Geographical Society.

SAYLES, E. B.
  1945. *The San Simon Branch, Excavations at Cave Creek and in the San Simon Valley.* ("Medallion Papers," No. 34.) Globe, Ariz.

SAYLES, E. B., and ERNST ANTEVS
  1941. *The Cochise Culture.* ("Medallion Papers," No. 29.) Globe, Ariz.

SHELFORD, VICTOR E. (ed.)
  1926. *Naturalist's Guide to the Americas.* (Ecological Society of America.) Baltimore: Williams & Wilkins.

WAUCHOPE, ROBERT (ed.)
  1956. *Seminars in Archaeology: 1955.* ("Mem. Soc. Amer. Archaeol.," No. 11.) Salt Lake City.

WHEAT, J. B.
  1954. *Crooked Ridge Village.* (Univ. Ariz. Bull., Vol. 25, No. 3; Soc. Sci. Bull., No. 24.) Tucson.

  1955. *Mogollon Culture Prior to A.D. 1000.* ("Mem. Soc. Amer. Archaeol.," No. 10.) Salt Lake City.

WISSLER, CLARK
  1922. *The American Indian.* (2d ed.) New York: Oxford University Press.

WOODBURY, RICHARD B.
  1961. *Prehistoric Agriculture at Point of Pines, Arizona.* ("Mem. Soc. Amer. Archaeol." No. 17.) Salt Lake City.

SOUTHWESTERN ASIA BEYOND THE LANDS
OF THE MEDITERRANEAN LITTORAL

ROBERT J. BRAIDWOOD AND BRUCE HOWE

I. THE REGION

THE GREAT BASIN made up of the drainage systems of such southwestern Asiatic rivers as the Euphrates, Tigris, Karun, and Karkheh lies beyond the coastal mountains of Palestine, Lebanon, and Syria. In fact, the Mediterranean coastal mountains form the western flank of a mountain crescent that arcs over the top of the basin (the Tauros range) and then runs in a southeasterly direction (the Zagros range) down beyond the head of the Persian Gulf (see map, Fig. 1). The major rivers spill into the Persian Gulf, while to the southwest the land rises gradually upward over the empty desert spaces of Arabia. North of the port town called Tripoli on the west, the mountains of the Syrian coast are very low, and over this "Syrian Saddle" flow the winter rain-bearing winds that water the Tauros and Zagros hill-flanks of the basin.

A number of environmental zones exist within the basin and along its higher flanks. To oversimplify the case, we might describe the zones as follows:

1. The alluvial Mesopotamian plain of the Tigris and Euphrates lies south of Baghdad and has its extensions into Iranian Khuzestan along the lower reaches of the Karun and Karkheh rivers. This is hot, dry country but very rewarding if water is brought to it. It does not appear to have had a role in the first development of food production, however.

2. North and west of Baghdad comes the sterile desert steppe of the Syrian "Jazireh," scarcely inhabited save immediately along the banks of the Euphrates and Tigris or as the desert merges into the following zone.

3. Bearing east and north of about the latitude of Kirkuk and passing west from about the latitude of Mosul along the Syro-Turkish border country to Aleppo, there is a rolling downland of grassy piedmont character that was the heartland of the Assyrian Empire.

4. Arcing along the inward-facing flanks of the Tauros and Zagros lies a somewhat higher zone, characterized by intermontane valley plains, well watered by the winter rain-winds that break through to it from the Mediterranean over the Syrian Saddle. This is open mixed-oak woodland and grassland country, perhaps most characteristically manifested at *ca.* 1,000 meters in elevation, and it extends southeastward about as far as the city of Shiraz. It may be worth noting that this environmental zone is not characteristic of the eastward slopes of the Mediterranean coastal ranges, these slopes being within a rain shadow: Perrot (this volume) considers one possible cultural adjustment to the submarginal environmental zone that lies behind the coastal range.

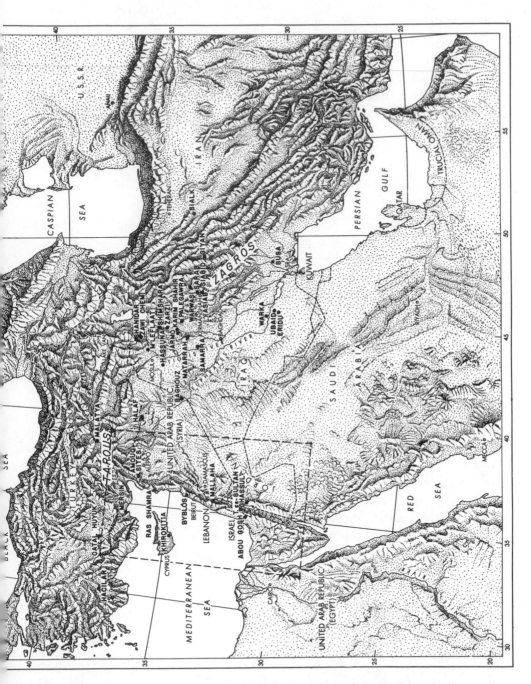

FIGURE 1. Map of southwestern Asia, showing location of the prehistoric sites considered. The position of Perrot's detailed map (p. 149) is indicated. (Base-map courtesy of the *Scientific American*.)

5. Above *ca.* 1,800 meters to the north and east of the basin the higher Kurdish alpine country, with precipitation that may go above 40 inches (or 1,000 millimeters) annually, is important in that it contains the headwaters of the rivers, but it is probably of no great significance for our present problem.

Above the rims of the Tauros and Zagros lie the plateaus of Anatolia and Iran, with their different climatic and vegetation patterns.

The "hilly-flanks of the Fertile Crescent" country par excellence is our zone 4 above. It appears to have been a natural habitat for that important constellation of plants and animals (wheat, barley; sheep, goat, pig, and cattle) which—in their domesticated forms—made up the important elements of the food-producing subsistence pattern of at least the westerly portions of the Old World. It is, however, also important to consider what may have been the role of the piedmont downlands of our zone 3 in the earlier phases of the village-farming community way of life. Further, it is still unclear as to whether the natural-habitat zone may not have extended some distance into the south central portions of the Anatolian plateau.

In recent years we have made a concentrated effort to encourage the work of natural scientists in southwestern Asia, especially in the hilly-flanks intermontane valley country of zone 4, and the downlands of zone 3; but vast tracts of this country (and of its adjoining zones) still await detailed study—both by prehistoric archeologists and by natural scientists.

II. GENERAL CULTURAL DEVELOPMENT

In its most completely oversimplified form, the general course of cultural development in prehistoric southwestern Asia runs—allowing for the incompleteness of our knowledge—about as follows.

A. *Food-gathering, with free-wandering hunting and earliest standardized tool-making traditions.*[1]—By at least about 75,000 years ago (consciously ignoring what may lie earlier), the middle elevations of the highlands, the upper Syrian steppe, and the coastal zones supported a population of food-gatherers who produced flint tools of Acheulean type. These show considerable typological uniformity over the whole area. In the cases in which a fauna has been found associated with these tools, such large forms as *elephas* and *rhinoceros* are evidenced, forms no longer at home in the area.

A naturally determined subsistence, involving food-gathering and the free-wandering hunting of the larger mammals, was beginning to be significantly determined culturally. Tools of the early standardized traditions of core bifaces, flakes, and the later pebble tools appear with broad distributions for given types.

Finds of this stage discovered in the Zagros flanks in both Iraq and Iran are

---

1. The subdivisions and suggested characterizations used in this outline are adapted from an exploratory attempt at the general classification of prehistoric subdivisions (Braidwood, 1960).

very limited as yet but do not contradict this picture, which is based largely on materials from the western portion of the region.

B. *Food-gathering, with elemental restricted wandering, hunting, and some variety in standardized tool forms within regions.*—What followed here, perhaps by *ca.* 60,000 years ago, is suggested by further traces of food-gatherers and hunters who made flint-flake tools of Mousterian and, especially to the west, Levalloiso-Mousterian type. By this time somewhat more regional variety is apparent (on a typological basis), and—in Iraqi and Iranian Kurdistan, at least— there was typological difference between the generally larger, coarser tools of the Mousterian of open-air sites and the smaller, more delicately made Mousterian of the caves, though perhaps this may be due to temporal or other factors. Caves were commonly occupied, where they existed, but there are also open-air scatters of artifacts. These last may be near water, or at commanding points on the landscape, or in various other localities of as yet undetermined significance.

Beginning with this sub-era and from then onward, the evidence available for fauna in Kurdistan, at least, suggests a completely modern type. Both large and small mammal forms comprise the great bulk of the faunal remains found.

C. *Food-collecting, with selective hunting and seasonal collecting patterns for restricted-wandering groups.*—This is marked by the appearance of the blade-tool tradition, for which a beginning date in this region of *ca.* 35,000 B.C. may at least be suggested by the C^{14} determinations of Shanidar C. By now the distinction between *gathering* and *collecting*, if it be valid (Braidwood, 1960) may begin to be noted as the blade-tool phases of Baradostian and Zarzian succeed one another. Certainly there is considerable typological variety, and there are "tools to make tools." One notes a rather marked regional restriction of any given industry, although the generalized blade-tool preparation tradition is widespread. The Baradostian of the Zagros flanks, now known from two localities, differs in a number of morphological and typological details from counterparts elsewhere in southwestern Asia and beyond. The same may be said, perhaps to an even greater degree, of the succeeding Zarzian. So far the generalized Zarzian industry is known only along the Zagros flanks, but blade tools do occur as well in hills north of Palmyra and near Adiyaman in the Turkish reaches of the Euphrates.

From these facts we suspect that the trend was toward increasingly intensified utilization of the resources of ever more localized situations. Such regional specialization may also, of course, have fluctuated seasonally, with shifts in locale in summer and winter. In Kurdistan, the generalized Zarzian blade-tool industry of the upper drainage areas of the two Zabs (e.g., Shanidar B, Palegawra, and Zarzi itself) and of the Kermanshah valley system (e.g., Warwasi) was a generically related affair but is different in details at individual sites located in each of these sub-areas.

We also strongly suspect that there may have been both cave and open-air aspects of each of these varieties of the generalized Zarzian industry. Although there is nothing approaching the impressive scale of settlement and specialization revealed by Klíma's excavations at the late upper paleolithic encampment of the mammoth killers at Doli Vistoniće in Central Europe (Klíma, this volume), there are, nevertheless, one or two small possible instances of open-air concentrations of Zarzian-type stone industry. Of course, the numerous clear-cut occupations of caves or rock shelters for the Zarzian stage indicate that these were still the living quarters of primary importance.

Based on the C^{14} determinations for Shanidar B, we suggest a possible end date for this generalized Zarzian phase of about 10,500 years ago.

D. *Suspected food-producing—incipient manipulation within the zone of potential plant and animal domesticates.*—The next fifteen hundred or two thousand years in all probability witnessed at least the culmination of, along the Zagros flanks in any case, events of considerable importance for what was to follow. The range includes the generalized Karim Shahirian industry, with its Zawi Chemi Shanidar, M'lefaat, and now possibly Asiab (near Kermanshah) variants, but may also include other industries not yet recovered or identified, perhaps preceding or following the Karim Shahirian. Typologically, the Karim Shahirian exhibits some sort of continuation and a certain recombination of the blade tools of the Zarzian tradition and a portion of its end-phase microlithic element, but a few ground-stone and even modeled-clay artifacts appear. The Karim Shahirian has not been noted in caves (with the possible exception of traces in the uppermost layer of Shanidar), and the open sites of its occurrence indicate the crude beginnings of architecture for this region. Largely through hindsight (from what follows next) we suggest that this range may represent a time of incipient manipulation, if not of cultivation and animal domestication. We also suggest that it may be the last aspect of the long trend toward regional specialization and intensified utilization of the resources in restricted locales within our generalized environmental zone 4 (above), the hilly flanks of the Fertile Crescent, which included the potential plant and animal manipulates.

Given the possibility of some sort of incipience of food production during the approximately 2,000 years of this sub-era—perhaps as one culmination of a long range of unconscious manipulation of the potential plant and animal domesticates —one still lacks any specific direct evidence for this manipulative development.[2] Such primitive architectural traces as there are (close-set stone scatters at Karim Shahir; small circular or ovid excavated basins, suggesting possible semisubterranean structures, at Zawi Chemi Shanidar and M'lefaat; and a larger shallow excavated ovoid basin at Asiab) would seem to have no critical bearing on a link between the start of food production and sedentary living in the light of the

2. In the spring of 1961, well after the above was written, we were informed by Dexter Perkins (personal communication), the zoölogist on Solecki's staff at Shanidar and Zawi Chemi Shanidar in the 1960 season on these sites, that the domestication of sheep is attested at Zawi Chemi. Although the details are not yet available, this evidence would certainly appear to validate the case for human manipulation of the potential domesticates. It would also, as things now stand, make the domestication of animals appear to have been earlier than that of plants along the Zagros flanks, thus paralleling the apparent situation at Tell es-Sultan (cf. Perrot, this volume).

late paleolithic clustering of hut remains at Dolní Vistonić̇e, so clearly demonstrated by Klíma's excavations (see his essay, this volume). The potential animal domesticates are present at these sites in Kurdistan.[3] Hunting is still very much a part of the order of the day at all these sites, while at Asiab there is added an intensive collecting of fresh-water clams. Data on plant manipulates may come from the extensive categories of clay lumps and "coprolites" recently recovered at Asiab and now awaiting study. On the other hand, the limited study so far made of materials from Karim Shahir, Zawi Chemi Shanidar, and M'lefaat have yielded no hints of plant manipulation.

Thus, one must at present depend entirely upon the indirect evidence to be drawn from the implements and other artifacts of stone or other materials at these sites for any indication of food production. Moreover, these would cast light only on the manipulation of plant foods, not of animals.

Artifacts found at this group of sites for which a reasonable interpretation (but certainly not the only possible interpretation) would point to manipulated plant foods include: (1) flint "sickles" with edge sheen; (2) milling stones, rubbers, mortars, pestles; and (3) chipped celts (hoes?). At present we see no reason to attempt—by a higher degree of abstraction—an interpretation of the clay figurines, ground-stone decorative objects, etc., from these sites, as hinting at a food supply from either animal or food-plant manipulation.

E. *Food-producing and the appearance of the primary village-farming community.*—By about the first quarter of the seventh millennium (e.g., *ca.* 6750 B.C.)—if our assessment of the conflicting C^{14} determinations for the site of Jarmo is valid (Braidwood, 1959)—the basic level of the effective village-farming community had already been achieved. But, while there is a degree of typological continuity within certain categories of artifacts (especially in the flints of both normal blade and microlithic size) between the Karim Shahirian phase and the Jarmoan phase, we suspect that a phase (or phases) will yet be found calling for intercalation between these two (Braidwood and Howe *et al.*, 1960).

Our in-the-field impression of the Asiab materials suggests a typological positioning of them somewhere between the Karim Shahirian and the Jarmoan phases. On the other hand, we are also sensitive to the fact that there is sufficient regional variation between the archeological materials of the Kermanshah and the Jarmo-Karim Shahir regions, so the matter may not be quite this simple. Our radioactive carbon samples from the sites of the Kermanshah region, of course, still await determination.

In the same sense, Tepe Sarab, another new site near Kermanshah, yields archeological materials that—on the basis of an in-the-field typological assessment—seem slightly more developed than do those of the Jarmoan phase proper, but also it need not follow directly that the Sarab assemblage is thus later than that of Jarmo.

3. As the study of the animal remains advances (May, 1961), there is the increasing suggestion that the frequencies of the different forms correspond roughly to the several sites. Thus, onager bones predominate in sites on or overlooking valley floors, goat bones in sites situated in the rocky ridges.

For our present purposes, the following observations would seem to be of significance for understanding an early phase of the sub-era of the primary village-farming community, as Jarmo exhibits this phase:

1. It does yield positive traces of a village-farming community way of life; several-roomed rectangular houses within villages of some degree of permanence; the remains of at least domesticated wheat, barley, probably the dog and the goat, and possibly even the sheep, with the pig appearing in the upper levels; the conventional artifactual traits of the "neolithic," with pottery appearing before the phase is completed. As they pertain—by reasonable but *not* absolutely guaranteed interpretations—to food production, these artifacts are querns and rubbing stones, mortars and pestles, flint sickle blades with sheen, occasional subfloor storage pits, a peculiar form of oven, possibly for the parching of grain, a few large celts (hoes?), and an occasional large pierced stone ball (digging stick weight?). Overwhelmingly, however, it is the demonstrated presence of the plant and animal domesticates and the apparent year-round permanence of a village of perhaps twenty-five well-built houses that make Jarmo impressive for our present purposes. It should remain clear, however, that a very significant portion of the Jarmo subsistence pattern still depended upon collected foods.

2. Jarmo does indicate firm traces of longer-range trade, especially evidenced by the great bulk of obsidian (closest natural flow near Lake Van in Anatolia) in its chipped-stone category. We suggest that this first indication of a bulk carrying trade—with its implications of attendant exchanges of ideas—may well presage a reversal of the above-mentioned trend toward regional specialization and localized intensification.

3. There is now some evidence (Braidwood and Howe *et al.*, 1960, p. 49) to suggest that the Jarmoan phase may not have been absolutely restricted to the intermontane valley zone of the Zagros but may also appear along the edge of the downlands of our zone 3 near Kirkuk. If our theoretical reasoning is correct, a pre-Jarmoan phase of this sub-era must still await discovery in the intermontane valley hilly-flanks zone of the natural habitat, and, in fact, we believe that it will have been restricted to this zone (cf. Haury's upland corridor, this volume).

Our in-the-field assessment of the yield from Tepe Sarab near Kermanshah calls for a bit more comment. In such categories as pottery and clay figurines, the Sarab assemblage would appear to be typologically advanced over that of Jarmo, while the flint and obsidian industry of Sarab is slightly less varied than is that of Jarmo. On the other hand, our exposures at Sarab did not yield traces of mud-walled houses. The Sarab settlement seems to have consisted of shallow pit-dwellings—perhaps with some sort of reed roofing—and has little of the appearance of architectural permanence of Jarmo. Detailed laboratory analysis of the Sarab plant and animal remains is only now beginning; there were no obvious caches of carbonized kernels of wheat or barley, although the presence of at least some of the animal domesticates does seem assured. The most significant evidence for the grains at Jarmo came as impressions in clay lumps; many clay lumps are available at Sarab, but their contents await laboratory study. Again, as at Jarmo, significant quantities of collected food (e.g., land snails, wild pistachio nuts) are evidenced at Sarab. Our minds are open to the proposition that Sarab *may* yet prove to have been a seasonally occupied site.

Unfortunately, we still know very little about the general broad distribution of assemblages of the Jarmo or Sarab type. The hilly-flanks zone in the upper Tigris and Euphrates basin regions of Turkey is, unfortunately, completely unknown for this range of time. This is the more exasperating since modern problem-oriented prehistoric research in this area could contribute much to our general understanding. We cannot, as yet, quite grasp how the preceramic village materials of Khirokitia on Cyprus (Dikaios, 1953) or of the Thessalian plain in Greece (Milojćić, 1956; Theocharis, 1958) fit into the general picture. Radioactive carbon determinations are available for the pertinent level of Khirokitia, that is, 5635 B.C. ± 100 (St–415/415, average). Also to be fitted into the general picture—although possibly in part with our next sub-era, F, below— are the early village materials excavated by Mellaart (1960) in the southwesterly portion of the Anatolian plateau. For one of the early levels of Mellaart's Haçilar site there is a determination of 5590 ± 180 years B.C. In our own opinion, none of these materials can be understood properly until the general developmental sequence in southern Turkey becomes known.[4]

F. *Food-producing and the developing village-farming community.*—It is now known (Braidwood and Howe *et al.*, 1960) that the Jarmoan materials are stratigraphically overlayed by those of Hassunan-Samarran type at Tell Shimshara in the higher Lesser Zab drainage. Otherwise, the Hassunan assemblage appears to characterize the Assyrian downlands of the Tigris about Mosul and perhaps stretches into the upper Syrian Jazireh (again we know nothing of Turkey save the possible pertinence of the lower levels of Haçilar [cf. above]). We do not yet know the antecedents of the Hassunan assemblage—it may share some simpler elements of its ceramic tradition with the Jarmoan, but the typologically wretched Hassunan flint industry is *not* derived from the Jarmoan. The Hassunan assemblage suggests a now well-stabilized village-farming community way of life (Braidwood, 1952) following *ca.* 6000 B.C., and it is probably significant that the domesticates were now certainly flourishing at altitudes lower than those of their natural habitat. We must also note a variety of doubtless approximately contemporary counterparts for the Hassunan, in our general area, most of which are assemblages with complexions of their own.

1. In the western portion of the upper Syrian Jazireh (e.g., from at least Ras al-Ain westward) there are hints that elements of the Hassunan assemblage may co-exist with elements of the Amouq A-B or Syro-Cilician dark-faced burnished-ware assemblage. This is underscored by the traces of exchange between Amouq B and Hassunan II-V themselves (cf. Perrot, this volume).

2. The Samarran painted pottery style need not occur only within the matrix of a

4. Toward the end of his last season at Haçilar in the late summer of 1960, Mellaart exposed preceramic levels of the site, well below that of the 5590 ± 180 years B.C. determination (Mellaart, 1961). As the details of assemblage of these early levels become known, either we *may* find evidence to suggest the extension of the native habitat zone to southwest-central Anatolia or we may discover that Haçilar represents a first step beyond this zone to the northwest.

Hassunan assemblage, as the sites of Baghouz, on the middle Euphrates, and Samarra, on the middle Tigris, show (Braidwood and Howe *et al.*, 1960, p. 37). Braidwood (1952) once suggested that these sites may hint at a first fingering of the village-farmers down on the mud-flats of the great rivers toward the alluvial plains of classic southern Mesopotamia.

3. The Sialk I assemblage of the Iranian plateau doubtless needs consideration here on grounds of its generalized typological similarity (although not in specific detail) to the Hassunan. Although the presence of metal in Sialk I may or may not be a disturbing element, it makes us somewhat diffident about suggesting very exact chronological contemporaneity for Sialk I with the basic Hassunan assemblage.

4. The probability of a counterpart for the Hassunan assemblage along the Zagros flanks of Iran was examined by the Iranian Prehistoric Project in early 1960. At least it is clear that we are not dealing here with anything strictly Hassunan or Samarran in character. We did not, in fact, satisfy ourselves that any of our sondages in the post-Sarab range yielded materials that might fit into the Hassunan block of time and can make this judgment solely on the basis of surface collections. Our earliest excavated post-Sarab materials, from a site called Tepe Siabid, probably were approximately contemporary with the Halafian and earliest Ubaidian phases.

It should not, however, be assumed that the old trend toward regional specialization and intensification has been revived. Men everywhere in the general area were achieving stable adjustments to the new food-producing economy, although significant portions of their diets were of course still derived from collection; the several assemblages noted above do suggest differences in cultural complexion, subarea by subarea, but there are also firm hints of exchange of raw materials, of habits in the preparation of certain artifacts (if not of the exact artifacts themselves), and of the exchange of ideas. The basic elements of the food-producing pattern were certainly held in common.

G. *Food-producing; further development and diffusion of the village-farming community way of life.*—It is downright difficult for us to compose a free-flowing picture of what happened next. The most familiarly known assemblage name in the phase following the Hassunan (and its generalized typological and roughly contemporaneous counterparts, as described above) is the Halafian. The Halafian certainly also had at least some generalized typological and roughly contemporary counterparts (e.g., see Tepe Siabid, above), but it has been our misfortune—east of the Euphrates—that all these assemblages included rather spectacular painted-pottery styles. In the milieu of archeological interest up to World War II little was taken to be of importance save these painted-pottery styles. To mix a metaphor, we often cannot see the woods for the motifs. Therefore we restrict our observations here to two suggestions:

1. It was probably at this time that an effective food-producing way of life was first established in classic southern Mesopotamia, although Adams (1960, p. 25) very reasonably suspects that there were riverine-oriented food-collectors there beforehand. The new start in the south is hinted at in the basal levels of Eridu, and was soon to crystallize into the Ubaidian achievement. We await with considerable interest detailed news of the new British excavations of David Stronach, which are reported to deal with a site of this immediately pre-Ubaidian range in the area south of Baghdad.

2. The countertrend away from regional specialization was now further accelerated, if we may follow certain hints (e.g., the Halafian painted style reaches the Mediterranean coast) and hindsight from what was to happen next.

H. *Food-producing; incipient urbanization as suggested by towns with temples and with ancillary smaller settlements.*—However misty the vista may still be, the Ubaidian "period" (*ca.* 4250–3750 ± ??) suggests the earliest of the great *oikoumenēs* of the ancient Near East. It is not improper to speak of painted pottery of Ubaidian type from highland Iran, or from parts of highland Turkey (Malatya), or along the Syrian coast, or even into the Dead Sea valley (Ghassul, cf. Perrot, this volume), but the focus of the Ubaidian achievement was in classic southern Mesopotamia. Here, proper towns of many acres in area are evidenced, with temple structures of some degree of monumentality. Surface surveys suggest that there may well have been smaller settlements ancillary to the large Ubaidian towns (although in fact this has not been tested by excavation).[5]

The Ubaidian is already up to, if not upon, the threshold of urban civilization and presents problems for the culture historian that have quite new dimensions (Adams, 1960). Once again, we resort to *post facto* judgment in our own assessment of the general cultural level that the Ubaidian must represent. Positive urban establishments do follow soon after the Ubaidian in the Mesopotamian record, and there are significant artifactual elements (especially in architecture) that were established in Ubaidian times and carry over into Protoliterate and Dynastic times.

The completely oversimplified picture given above of the cultural history of southwestern Asia east of the Euphrates (especially from *ca.* 15,000 to *ca.* 4000 B.C.) might suggest to us at least five generalizations of particular relevance to the interests of this symposium.

1. There was from the beginning, throughout the late glacial and earliest postglacial period,[6] an increasing trend toward regionality and intensified extraction of food

5. It is probably worth saying—for those readers who normally see only secondary sources on Near Eastern archeology—that the number of excavated Ubaidian sites from the southern Mesopotamia area reaches hardly a dozen. The actual excavated exposures that have been made on these sites are startlingly small in most cases. The assessment of the original size of a settlement is usually by extrapolation from a very restricted exposure of the material *in situ* to the impressive stretches on the surfaces of the great mounds over which Ubaidian pottery may be scattered. But in most cases these mounds had later occupations as well, and area of surface scatter may be an uncertain guarantee of subsurface architecture and positive settlement.

If the words "Hassunan," "Samarran," or "Halafian" are substituted for the word "Ubaidian" in the generalization made above, the warning is just as valid—or more so!

6. If one relies on the extensive and largely consistent structure of absolute dating now provided by C[14] age determinations from different latitudes and geographical regions of Europe and Asia, one may lessen the dilemma of comparing data from glaciated areas with those from essentially non-comparable unglaciated ones.

resources from ever more localized environments. This appears to have been entirely on hunting, gathering, and collecting levels and at no point to have reached the degree of sedentism recorded, for instance, for Central Europe at Dolni Vistonice by Klíma (this volume). The shift away from the bigger game animals, as the result of as yet undetermined natural or cultural factors, seems to run very broadly parallel to a shift toward smaller, more specialized tools and, ultimately, even composite tools (some of which were geometric in form and microlithic in size).

2. Over some undetermined period, ten or twelve thousand or more years ago, this trend also came to involve the manipulation of certain plants and animals within their natural habitats, a process that culminated eventually in domestication. There is as yet no direct evidence for such tentative or advanced manipulation, but the pre-requisite forms, albeit still equivocal, occur in both artifactual and non-artifactual categories at a number of open-air sites. Thus it is strongly suspected that, in view of what is already well under way in the succeeding known archeological horizon, the foundations for the food-producing economy and the village-farming community way of life were already being laid.

3. As the village-farming community way of life became effective, and moved out of the natural habitat zone, the old trend toward regional specialization and intensification was—in general terms—reversed, one result being the spread of the boundaries of the known world and an increasing commonality in the new ways of life.

4. While it may seem to us quite probable—with the occurrence of such necessarily postulated mutations or introgressive hydridizations as would have allowed the domesticates to (a) be utilized more effectively as food sources and (b) be moved outside the bounds of their natural-habitat zone—that there would have been a rather explosive acceleration in cultural activity, we do not yet have evidence to quantify this acceleration in any detail. It is a thing about which we must keep our eyes open as field research proceeds.

5. The way to urban life did not lie within exactly the same environmental zone as that in which the village-farming community made its first appearance.

III. COMMENTS

We may now turn to consideration of what might be *suggested*—from the evidence we now have—concerning how all this came about.

In the first place, we do not believe that the answers will lie within the realms of environmental determinism in any direct or strict sense. In an interim report on the work of the Iraq Jarmo Project (Braidwood and Howe *et al.*, 1960) we and our natural-science colleagues reviewed the evidence for possibly pertinent fluctuations of climate and of plant and animal distributions or morphologies and convinced ourselves that there is *no* such evidence now available. At a recent seminar in the Institute of Archeology of the University of Tehran (Braidwood, Howe, and Negahban, 1960), with an essentially different cast of natural scientists, there was again agreement that no evidence exists for such changes in the natural environment (in the *pertinent parts* of southwestern Asia of *ca.* 12,000–8,000 years ago) as might be of sufficient impact to have predetermined the shift to food production.

Examination of the two sources cited above will underscore the point. Ganji sees no evidence for significant climatic change, and Wright—as an experienced

Pleistocene geologist in the area—hands the problem directly back to the archeologists. Helbaek (cf. also 1959) and Pabot agree on the general distribution of the wild wheats and barleys, on the nature of wheat as a plant of the uplands (Pabot claims never to have seen it below *ca.* 1,000 meters, from Iran to Palestine) and of disturbed soil conditions; both agree on the break in the distribution of wheats in the country of the Syrian Saddle and south to the Beirut-Damascus road. Reed (cf. also 1959) remarks that the patterns of social behavior of the potential animal domesticates had pre-adapted them for domestication some hundreds of thousands (if not millions) of years ago. Reed also rejects any idea of climatic change as of pertinence and looks for the development of a necessary but unspecified level of cultural achievement as the requisite for domestication. Interestingly, both Pabot and Reed independently suggest that the transition to effective domestication may have taken about two thousand years (and it is perhaps of some further interest that both Chang and Haury (see their essays, this volume) independently suggest the same approximate duration). It is far from clear in our area, however, whether this two thousand years (from *ca.* 11,000 to *ca.* 9,000 years ago) was the entire time span of man's manipulation of the potential plant and animal domesticates.

The only environmental determinative our natural-science advisers will allow us is the presence, within the hilly-flanks intermontane valley environmental zone, of the classic constellation of the potential plant and animal domesticates at the pertinent time. This includes specific rejection of the lush and low-lying coastal strips of the eastern Mediterranean, Black Sea, and Caspian. At the same time, our natural-science advisers frankly admit ignorance of much of the Anatolian plateau and of the north and east of Iran and beyond into Turkmania and the Afghan-Pakistan area. A final interesting observation is our botanical and zoölogical colleagues' convictions that the plant and animal domesticates are *artifacts*—that they did not domesticate themselves.

This then does appear to force primarily back upon the culture historian the problem of how food production and the village-farming community way of life was achieved. There are possibly one or two points calling for comment in this connection. We grow increasingly disinclined to countenance Carleton Coon's (1954) suggestions for an incipience of food production on the Caspian coastal plain. With the possibility of an incipience of food production in Palestine, the case is more complicated. While traces of domesticated grain have not yet been reported from the earlier levels of Tell es-Sultan (Jericho), and Zeuner's (1958) claim for wild wheat in the lower elevations of the Jordan valley would appear to need rechecking, he seems reticent (in the same paper) to claim a fully effective agriculture at Tell es-Sultan. Perrot (this volume), although realizing that grain itself has not yet been reported from Tell es-Sultan, finds it impossible to conceive of the cultural complexity of the site without an effective cereal agriculture (cf. Caldwell, this volume) and makes the very interesting point that here we may be seeing the first moment of impact of cereals now freed from their native habitat by permissive mutations or introgressive hybridizations. Reed (1959) agrees that the evidence for domesticated dogs and goats does seem acceptable at Tell es-Sultan. However, none of our own advisers in the natural sciences will subscribe to "the oasis theory" of agricultural origins. They (as does Perrot) would look to the Judean Hill country as being more a part of the natural habitat, in considering any role that Tell es-Sultan may have had in the general story.

If the case for an incipience of *effective* food production and the appearance of a village-farming community way of life is to be made in Palestine, we believe that the evidence is much more likely to come from more upland sites of the type of Perrot's Abou Gosh. And in Palestine, as in our own area, the distinction between what is evidence of food production proper and of a highly intensified level of food collection must be examined with great care. Ambiguously labeling the Palestinian materials as "mesolithic," "protoneolithic," and "prepottery neolithic" will not lead to clarity in understanding.

On the whole—as regards all southwestern Asia—our own inclination is *not* to look for only one "center" as the scene either for the incipience of cultivation or for the appearance of effective food production. We are convinced that the scene was the natural zone of the hilly flanks of the Fertile Crescent of perhaps some 2,000 kilometers in extent! We have made the point that we believe in a natural zone—not a restricted "center"—often, but there still seems to be some tendency to overlook it. Even granting the gap in the known distribution of wild wheats between the Syrian Saddle and the Beirut-Damascus road, we dislike the idea of two entirely separated "centers." For lack of better evidence we might reluctantly grant that such completely generalized traits as the start of the domestication of some one plant or animal species, the use of flint blades as sickles, the invention of mud-walled houses and, eventually, pottery, etc., occurred twice within one general area. But, to our minds, such a thing as the broad distribution of obsidian over the whole area at the pertinent time would remain to plague a double-origin theory. We cannot conceive of the wide distribution of obsidian—to consider only this one clue—without an attendant distribution of ideas in general as well.

We ourselves strongly incline toward the implications of our point 3 on page 142. Given an incipience of food production during the *ca.* two thousand years of our sub-era D—perhaps as the culmination of a longer range of unconscious manipulations of the potential domesticates—we suspect that the trend toward regional intensification and regional specialization began then to reverse itself. The entire constellation of elements of this incipience, we believe, need not have been achieved at only one spot along the natural-habitat zone on the hilly flanks—in fact we hardly conceive of a "center" at all.

Since the Jarmo versus Jericho discussion has mainly simmered down to who has faith in which radioactive carbon counter, or the best personal judgment in matters of comparative artifactual stratigraphy (Kenyon, 1959, and cf. Perrot, this volume) we have little else to say as to which segment of the whole arc of the hilly-flanks zone we believe to be most fruitful for examining the first phases of agricultural incipience. Our first draft of this paper was written in a further promising segment, the valley system of Kermanshah, on the western flanks of the Zagros, in Iran. If the interpretation of the Turkish antiquities law ever makes modern prehistoric research rewarding in that country, we should be just as anxious to see work done there.

Whatever the case may have been for the locale of the first village-farming communities, we believe that the incipience of towns (in any meaningful sense of that word) was achieved in classic southern Mesopotamia in the Ubaidian "period." This happened following a series of developing phases of village-farming community life, for each of which the web of diffusionary interactions appears to have become more complicated and more widespread.

Thus we very consciously end this paper on a note of diffusion and spread. What were the cultural mechanics that assured this diffusion and spread of a new way of life over vast areas of the Old World, areas that were already populated by successful food-collectors who might either reject or accept as they pleased any element of this mode of life? We are certain that the word "diffusion" alone has too heavy a load of meanings for the time with which we are dealing; we are not even sure how aptly the notation of "stimulus diffusion" may apply. Indeed, a very great deal of evidence, both artifactual and chronological, must be in hand before even a very modest diffusionist stance may be maintained; but we think that the prospects are not hopeless and that they hold much of interest for the general culture historian. In the consideration of even very low levels of diffusionary influence from the Near East to Europe, for example, we would maintain that two factors must be borne clearly in mind:

1. There was a succession of sub-eras of development in the Near East, and it is important that thought be given to which of these is under discussion in any consideration of diffusion.

2. ". . . the peoples of the west were not slavish imitators; they adopted the gifts of the East . . . into a new and organic whole capable of developing on its own original lines" (Childe, 1925, p. xiii).

BIBLIOGRAPHY

ADAMS, ROBERT, M.
    1960. "Factors Influencing the Rise of Civilization in the Alluvium: Illustrated by Mesopotamia," and "Early Civilizations, Subsistence, and Environment." In KRAELING, CARL H., and ROBERT M. ADAMS (eds.), *City Invincible*, pp. 24–34, 269–95. Chicago.

BRAIDWOOD, ROBERT J.
    1952. *The Near East and the Foundations for Civilization*. Eugene, Ore.

    1959. "Über die Anwendung der Radiokarbon-Chronologie für das Verständnis der ersten Dorfkultur-Gemeinschaften in Sudwestasien," *Österreichische Akademie der Wissenschaften, phil.-hist. Klasse, Anzeiger, Jahrgang 1958*, 95:249–59.

1960. "Levels in Prehistory: A Model for the Consideration of the Evidence." In SOL TAX (ed.), *Evolution after Darwin: The Evolution of Man*, 2:143–51. Chicago.

BRAIDWOOD, ROBERT J., BRUCE HOWE, *et al.*
1960. *Prehistoric Investigations in Iraqi Kurdistan.* (Oriental Institute "Studies in Ancient Oriental Civilizations," No. 31.) Chicago.

BRAIDWOOD, ROBERT J., BRUCE HOWE, and EZAT O. NEGAHBAN
1960. "Near Eastern Prehistory," *Science*, 131:1536–41.

CHILDE, V. GORDON
1925. *The Dawn of European Civilization.* London.

COON, CARLETON S.
1954. *The Story of Man.* New York.

DIKAIOS, PORPHYRIOS
1953. *Khirokitia.* London.

HELBAEK, HANS
1959. "Domestication of Food Plants in the Old World," *Science*, 130:365–72.

KENYON, KATHLEEN M.
1959. "Some Observations on the Beginnings of Settlement in the Near East," *J. Roy. Anthrop. Inst. Great Britain and Ireland* (London), 89:35–43.

MELLAART, JAMES
1960. "Excavations at Haçilar: Third Preliminary Report, 1959," *Anatolian Studies* (London), 10: 83–104.

1961. "Two Thousand Years of Haçilar—Starting from Over Nine Thousand Years Ago: Excavations in Turkey which Throw Light on the Earliest Anatolia," *Illustrated London News*, 238:588–91.

MILOJČIĆ, VLADIMIR
1956. "Die erste präkeramische bäuerliche Siedlung der Jungsteinzeit in Europa," *Germania*, 34:208–10.

REED, CHARLES A.
1959. "Animal Domestication in the Prehistoric Near East," *Science*, 130:1629–39.

THEOCHARIS, D.
1958. "Pre-ceramic Thessaly," *Thessalika* (Volo), 1:70–86. (In Greek.)

ZEUNER, F. E.
1958. "Dog and Cat in the Neolithic of Jericho," *Palestine Explor. Quart.*, (London), pp. 52–55.

PALESTINE—SYRIA—CILICIA

JEAN PERROT

I. GEOGRAPHICAL SETTING

THIS STUDY[1] is confined to Palestine on the two sides of the Jordan, to the Lebanese-Syrian littoral, and to Cilicia. This area is bounded on the south by a natural barrier, the desert, stretching from the Sinai Peninsula through southern Palestine into the heart of southwestern Asia. On the north we are limited not by nature itself but by the scarcity of evidence. While in Palestine the archeological sequence is nearly uninterrupted, in Syria and Cilicia we still have everything to learn about the periods preceding the appearance of pottery. This deficiency is particularly regrettable since the sequence present in Palestine shows a general similarity to that observed in the Kurdistan-Zagros region (Braidwood and Howe, this volume). Investigations in the hills of southern Turkey could help to establish a relationship between the two areas.

Unaffected by any appreciable climatic changes, at least from the end of Pleistocene times, the region under study, in spite of its limited area, presents a great diversity of ecological conditions. The principal natural zones of most of southwestern Asia (Mediterranean, semiarid, arid) are represented here in the west on a smaller scale, and, in addition, the general picture is complicated by accidents of topography (e.g., the Jordan Rift).

1. *The Mediterranean zone* is represented here by the western slopes of the Judean and Samarian hills, Mount Carmel, the Galilean mountains and the upper Jordan Valley, the lower slopes of the Lebanon range, the hills of the Syrian littoral, and the Hatay region up to the foot of the Taurus and the Kurdistan

1. I am very much indebted for criticisms and suggestions to the colleagues with whom I was able to discuss questions connected with this paper after the symposium; in particular, to Miss K. Kenyon and to Mr. J. d'A. Waechter, who kindly gave me the opportunity to look again at the Jericho and Ksâr Akil materials; to Professor F. E. Zeuner; to Dr. G. Kurth and to Mlle. D. Ferembach, who communicated to me the latest results of their studies of the Palestinian anthropological material; and to Professor M. Stekelis, who gave me essential data on the unpublished Wadi Fallah material and helped me with his wide knowledge of the Palestinian evidence. I am very grateful to Miss D. Kirkbride for communicating unpublished documentation on the Beida excavations, and to Mr. J. Cauvin for his *exposé* of the extremely important results of his and Mr. M. Dunand's work in the neolithic level of Byblos. In Paris, Mr. Claude Schaeffer gave me access to the earliest Ras Shamra material. Dr. J. Kaplan and Mr. M. Prausnitz kindly showed me the material from their excavations at Teluliot Batashi and Sheikh Ali. For all this aid, I am most grateful.

foothills. Certain hot and humid sections of the narrow coastal plain, especially where interruptions by dunes and marshes occur, never offered favorable conditions for settlement, even in historic times. On the other hand, the hills and the mountains above them offered the shelter of their caves and Mediterranean-type vegetation; wild wheat and barley are found today in this area, which was also rich in potentially domesticable animals.

2. *The semiarid zone.* East of the Syro-Palestinian mountains, stretching parallel to the coast, one finds a semiarid region with a steppe vegetation that becomes increasingly desert-like toward the south and the east (i.e., toward the Syro-Arabian desert, southern Negev, and Sinai).

3. *The arid zone.* The deserts noted above seal the passage to Africa. From Middle Pleistocene times (as evidenced by the stone industries) until the third millennium B.C., Palestine was a cul-de-sac open only to Eurasian influences.

The semiarid zone of the Middle East extends mainly to the north and east of the Syro-Arabian desert to the upper Tigris and Euphrates basin. It is represented in Palestine only by a very narrow strip extending from Gaza, on the Mediterranean coast, and the northern Negev, to the Transjordanian and Syrian plateaus (see map, Fig. I, where the three natural zones—Mediterranean, semiarid, and arid—are delineated). Moreover, the semiarid zone contains topographical accidents such as the Dead Sea and Jordan Rift, where near-desert conditions give way to subtropical conditions, as in the case of the Jericho oasis and on the river banks. The Jordan valley never presented an obstacle to communication between the two sides. The western edge of the Transjordan plateau is well watered, presenting as far south as the Red Sea general conditions of life similar to those of the Mediterranean zone of central Palestine: cultural development in Cisjordan has always been paralleled in Transjordan.

This ecological diversity is reflected in the history of human development. A high degree of particularism is frequent, and we cannot, therefore, expect the Palestinian sequence to be always typical of the human development of southwestern Asia as a whole.

II. TOWARD FOOD PRODUCTION

1. From Food-Collecting to Incipient Cultivation

a) If the middle upper paleolithic is relatively well known in Palestine and Syria, with Aurignacian-like industries in the caves of Mount Carmel, the Judean desert, or the Lebanon range, we cannot say the same of the following period, just before the appearance of the Natufian.

At el-Wad, Kebara, and el-Khiam, intermediate layers have yielded poorly represented industries (Atlithian [Garrod, 1937], Kebaran [Turville Petre, 1932], el-Khiam layers D-E [Neuville, 1951, p. 134]) characterized by the appearance of some microliths (obliquely truncated backed bladelets). That the complete stratigraphical and typological sequence must be more complex is suggested by

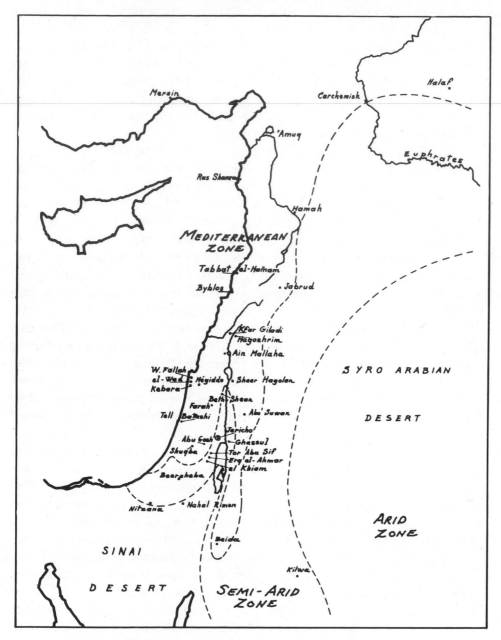

FIGURE 1. Map of the coastal portions of southwestern Asia, west
of the Euphrates River. Note three general climatic zones:
Mediterranean, semiarid, and arid.

the six layers in the 2.5-meter thickness of deposits at Jabrud (Rust, 1950) from
Aurignacian to Natufian, and the more than 3.0-meter thickness of deposits at
Ksar Akil (Ewing, 1947) from middle Aurignacian (Antelian) to Kebarian. No
C^{14} determination is available for these post-Aurignacian horizons, although a

single determination, on shells in the Aurignacian range of Ksar Akil (7.5–6.0 meters yields 28,500 B.P. ±380 (GRO 2195).

From an increase in the number of known sites, most of them open-air sites— in the coastal plain (Kfar Vitkin, Umm el Khalid [Stekelis, 1938]) and on the Transjordan plateau (Wadi Dhobai [Waechter, 1938], Petra [Kirkbride, 1960, p. 239])—we may surmise a slight increase in the population of the country. From the appearance of microliths, we may infer a first use of composite weapons indicating perhaps an intensification of hunting.

b) The late or epipaleolithic industries are succeeded (at el-Wad, Kebara, el-Khiam, Jabrud) by a typologically new industry, the Natufian. The Natufian, like the preceding industries, makes its first appearance in all parts of Palestine, in particular in the caves and terraces of el-Wad (Garrod, 1937), Wadi Fallah, that is, Nahal Oren (Stekelis, 1960), Kebara (Turville Petre, 1932), Shuqba (Garrod, 1932), Erq el Ahmar, Abu Sif, el-Khiam (Neuville, 1934, 1951), etc., in the Judean and Carmel mountains. It also occurs in the open at Ain Mallaha or Eynan (Perrot, 1960), Jericho (Kenyon, 1959), Beida (Kirkbride, 1960), and Nahal Rimon (Stekelis, personal communication). These sites are shown on our map (Fig. 1).

The Natufian layer of Jericho has a C^{14} determination of 7800 B.C. This date is perhaps too high but is not unacceptable in view of the determinations for the Kurdistan-Zarzian sequence (10,000 B.C. [Shanidar B2] and 8650 B.C. [Shanidar B1]), which is not unlike the Kebaran industries. The total duration of the Natufian is unknown; it could be estimated from one to two thousand years and its beginning put somewhere around 9000 B.C., but this date cannot be considered as well established.

A subdivision of the Natufian will have to await the completion of the new evidence coming from Wadi Fallah and Ain Mallaha. The typological classifications proposed by Garrod and Neuville will perhaps give way to regional differentiations and new subdivisions that aim at expressing the increasing trend toward specialization and adaptation to the various environmental conditions.

The most significant flint tools of the Natufian assemblage are geometric microliths (but probably not in a proportion as high as found at el-Wad), sickle blades with sheen (sometimes found still mounted on bone hafts with ornamented handles) and a few heavy bifacial core tools, such as those called "picks." Other stone implements include basalt pestles, grinding and polishing stones, net weights, hammer stones of various sizes, and a few querns. Bone tools comprise skewers, needles, awls, harpoons, and fishhooks.

This assemblage conveys the impression of an economy still essentially based on hunting and fishing and, by comparison with the preceding assemblages, on the intensified collection and consumption of seeds (including probably wild wheat and barley). We have no clear evidence of cultivation, but, from the subsequent development in Jericho, it is not unreasonable to infer that the economy of late Natufian times was already oriented toward the cultivation of cereals in the zone of their natural habitat.

The Natufian settlements seem to correspond to numerically more important groups: the Ain Mallaha settlement extends over more than 2,000 square meters. A certain continuity in settlement had also been achieved, as is suggested by the cemeteries discovered on the terraces of the el-Wad and Shuqba caves and at Ain Mallaha. Since Ain Mallaha is situated in what must have been exceptionally favorable conditions on the shores of the Huleh lake, fishing could have permitted even a complete stability of settlement.

The appearance and development in the Natufian of a crude architecture may be interpreted as another indication in the same direction of settlement stability. Impressive walls were built in Wadi Fallah to support a graded succession of occupational floors on the terrace. In Ain Mallaha, where no good natural shelter was available, circular stone houses, seven meters in diameter, were built surrounding an area into which plastered bell-shaped pits had been dug.

Natufian art, the first to appear in Palestine, includes naturalistic representations of animals, sometimes reminiscent of the Magdalenian IV of France. But in some of its manifestation it shows also a tendency to more schematic or geometric expression.

2. Trends to Specialization and Adaptation to a Particular Environment

The trends that can already be traced near the end of the Natufian express themselves more clearly in the following phase. At Wadi Fallah, at Jericho, and at el-Khiam, the Natufian is followed stratigraphically, typologically, and culturally by what is sometimes called the "Tahunian." It would be better, however, to discard this appellation altogether, or to reserve it to the development of the Natufian in the semiarid zone *only*. It might be confusing to continue its use in designating the different developments of the Natufian, in each of the different natural zones of Palestine. Hence I propose to restrict the use of "Tahunian" to post-Natufian developments in the semiarid zone alone.

a) On the Wadi Fallah terrace (Mount Carmel), above the Natufian layers, round stone houses were built, similar to, although smaller (2–5 meters in diameter) than, the Ain Mallaha structures and also featuring a central stone-lined fireplace. Sickle blades, tranchets, picks, flaked-stone axes, rare arrowheads, limestone vessels and polishing stones, etc., seem to suggest a mixed economy in lightly wooded country, in continuation of the development of the preceding phase in the Mediterranean zone. The Abu Suwan industry near Jerash (Kirkbride, 1958) on the Transjordan plateau, seems to belong to the same stage and type of development.

b) The broad terrace of el-Khiam in the Judean mountains was probably occupied by a settlement of some importance, but the evidence from a few trenches is too scanty to allow a definition of the material culture. Nevertheless, we are struck by the relative importance of the typical arrowhead group (Perrot, 1952*b*) and by the rarity of the sickle blades, as if the emphasis were more on hunting. Domestication of animals is still not clearly evidenced at el-Khiam—no more so than in the rest of the country (Reed, 1959).

c) The most spectacular development is certainly the one we may observe in the Jericho oasis with the sudden appearance of a settlement (Prepottery Neolithic A, abbreviated "PPNA") extending over more than 36,000 square meters (Kenyon, 1959). A C^{14} count for charcoal found on the floor of a building of the third stratum (in a long succession of houses built one on top of the other) gave a determination of *ca.* 6840 B.C.; the beginning of the settlement is reckoned as "going back at least to 7000 B.C." The settlement was surrounded by a stone wall 1.75 meters wide, surviving at some points to a height of 3.60 meters and flanked on the inner side by a circular tower, still standing, 8.15 meters high, with an inner staircase giving access to its top. The houses are of brick, of the same circular plan as those of the Wadi Fallah terrace, the origin of which can be traced to Ain Mallaha in the preceding phase. The flint industry includes sickle blades, typical tranchets, borers, rare arrowheads, and rare scrapers.[2] The stone industry includes pestles and basalt axes (round in section), rubbers, polishing stones, bowls, etc. Bone tools consist principally of picks.

To understand this development and its particular significance, it is first necessary to recall the extraordinary conditions of Jericho, in a well-watered oasis, isolated on an arid and desolate high terrace of the lower Jordan, 200 meters under sea level, at the foot of the 1,000-meter wall formed by the eastern slopes of the Judean hills. No other oasis of the lower Jordan valley or around the Dead Sea can be compared to the Jericho oasis. Direct evidence of wheat and barley has not been reported from the PPNA settlement. On the other hand, it is difficult to conceive of a settlement of such extent and importance without a reasonable level of food production having been attained, either through the domestication of animals—which is not yet evidenced—or also, and principally, through the cultivation of cereals.[3]

Cultivation did not originate in the oasis. Even if the presence of contemporary wild wheat can in the future be demonstrated in the lower elevations of the Jordan valley, the archeological evidence of the Jericho "nucleus tell" does not give any indication of early attempts at cultivation or even consumption of seeds or cereals, such as those we may observe at the same time on the Natufian sites of the Mediterranean zone.

The sudden modification in the type and extent of the Jericho settlement reflects a marked change in the history of the site's economic development. This

---

2. The flint industry of the PPNA could have been called Tahunian in the old sense, although not the industry of the PPNB settlement. But Miss Kenyon and Dr. Waechter now agree with the author (conversations in London, 1960) that it would be better to drop this appellation altogether.

3. In Professor Zeuner's opinion, the economy of the PPNA settlement is only an intensified form of food collection in the oasis and its periphery, with agriculture and domestication of animals having been introduced only by the PPNB settlers. If such had been the case, we would expect more marked differences between the PPNA and PPNB settlements and a softer transition between the Natufian or "nucleus tell"—the primitive stage of which corresponds well to the natural resources of the oasis—and the PPNA settlement.

change can be better interpreted as the result of external influence, that is, the introduction into the oasis of cultivation techniques. There is no break in the Natufian tradition between the underlying "nucleus tell" and Jericho PPNA. There is no essential difference between Jericho PPNA and the sites of the Mediterranean zone: Jericho PPNA is closely linked to the post-Natufian (round-house layer) of Wadi Fallah. But, whereas the Wadi Fallah settlement may be considered as a continuation of the Natufian tradition in a Mediterranean type of environment, it is in Jericho PPNA, under its exceptional conditions, that we witness an exceptional development. Here we see the first economic and social results of the preceding attempts at cultivation in the Mediterranean zone. In our opinion, the foundation of the PPNA settlement can be interpreted as the first evidence in Palestine that domestication of cereals is an accomplished fact, as it is most probably also at the same time in the hilly zone of the entire Middle East.

III. EFFECTIVE FOOD PRODUCTION

From this time, around 7000–6500 B.C., cereals could be introduced by cultivation from the zone of their natural habitat into new areas, including the coastal plain and parts of the semiarid area. The cultural horizon of Palestine opened up; the appearance of obsidian is the first evidence of contacts as far north as Anatolia.

We know nothing of Syria and Syro-Cilicia in the period of time we have just reviewed in Palestine, and we know almost nothing until a still later time when pottery makes its first appearance. But we may expect to find in northern Syria a development parallel to that of the Natufian in Palestine. First indication of such a Syrian co-tradition is already found in the prepottery layers at Ras Shamra (Schaeffer, 1960) and also in the material from some Syrian surface sites that may be attributed on typological grounds to phases of development contemporary to the Natufian. The Syrian tradition is characterized by a particular blade technique, by particular types of arrowheads, blades, sickle blades, polished adzes, querns, stone bowls, and, in architecture, rectangular houses with plastered floors.

The Syrian tradition ultimately overrides the Natufian tradition in Palestine. The new assemblage of the Jericho Prepottery Neolithic B (abbreviated "PPNB") settlement appears to be of Syrian origin. True, we need more comparative material from Syria on the same horizon, but in the next phase of development (with pottery) the same assemblage appears well at home in Syro-Cilicia (Braidwood, 1959, p. 501).

An explanation for the two parallel archeological traditions in Syria and Palestine in Natufian times could be found in the break observed by Helbaek and Pabot in the distribution of wild wheats in central Syria and south to the Beirut-Damascus road (Braidwood and Howe, this volume). The Natufian tradition would appear to have been a particular development linked to the southern area of distribution, while the Syrian one (necessarily still largely a postulate until more field work is done) would appear to have been linked to the northern-northeastern area. The contact between the two traditions would perhaps have been established only at the time of the first extension of cultivation beyond the limits of the two natural zones of distribution of the cereals. The Syrian tradition appears to have been the stronger. Palestine, which may have seen its general progress slowed down by its natural poverty, will have assumed from this time onward a more modest role; it seems no longer to have been a center of development but rather became marginal to the new centers of northern Syria and Mesopotamia.

The Syrian tradition was not, I believe, essentially different from the Palestinian one. The two probably had the same origin and may have been less differentiated in very early Natufian times. At Jericho, even if we see some spectacular changes in architecture and to a lesser degree in the stone industries of the PPNA and the PPNB settlements, there is no break or even significant change in the economic development.

1. The architecture of the Jericho PPNB settlement is characterized by "well built houses, with large rectangular rooms, rectilinear and vertical walls and wide doorways. . . . Walls and floors are covered by a continuous coat of fine plaster, cream or pinkish in colour, and burnished to a high finish" (Kenyon, 1959b, p. 38). A partially excavated building, 6x4 meters, with curious curved annexes, is interpreted as a temple.

The extent of the settlement is approximately equivalent to the preceding one of PPNA. Its duration was even more considerable. In some places, as many as twenty-six superimposed floors were distinguished. At a stage midway in the life of the settlement (ca. 5850 B.C.) "a massive defensive wall was built . . . but it cannot be said if it is a tower wall or a citadel wall." In the ruins of this settlement, ten skulls were found "with the features restored in plaster. . . . Fragments of painted plaster statues portraying the human form have also been recovered from the highest surviving level." In the upper levels appears a new type of burial in extended position (Kurth, personal communication), the anthropological type being more évolué than the typical Natufian type found in crouched burials of the PPNA settlement.[4]

2. In the Mediterranean zone a more normal development is found at Abu Ghosh (Perrot, 1952), on the west slope of the Judean hills near Jerusalem. The settlement may extend over about 1,000–1,500 square meters; traces of plastered floors have been found with a stone industry that shows—accidentally ?—a mixing of Syrian and Palestinian types. Animal figurines in unbaked clay appear. At the Wadi Fallah an upper level with a rectangular house probably belongs to the

---

4. The extended skeletons are often without skulls. Crouched burials do not disappear completely, but their frequency diminishes in the upper layers of the PPNB settlement. They are found still later in one of the "Proto-Urban" tombs. Dr. Kurth's study covers about 350 individuals for the prepottery levels and hundreds for the "Proto-Urban" period.

same phase. At Beida, near Petra, on the western Transjordan plateau, Miss D. Kirkbride (1960, p. 236, and personal communication) has excavated "a most curious building, well built, dry stone walling . . . composed so far of two parallel corridors with small rooms opening off each side of them" and "little absidal rooms at the end of the corridors." Building and associated finds constitute for Miss Kirkbride "a definite link with Jericho PPNB" and "a near relation to Abu Ghosh. The flint artifacts . . . the ground stone tools, rubbers and querns are very close to Jericho."

Since all these sites are known only by soundings, we do not have indications of the extent of the settlements or precise information on the character of their economy; from the general picture, however, we may reasonably assume that by that time the stage of an effective village-farming community had been reached in the area as a whole. New settlements were founded, such as Sheikh Ali or Tell Eli (Prausnitz, 1959) on the low terrace of the Jordan south of the Tiberias Lake, and Hagoshrim north of Lake Huleh, at the foot of Mount Hermon. Numerous surface stations can also be attributed to this phase.

From Syria, comparative material is available at Ras Shamra, at the base of the 1955 sounding by Dr. Kushke (Schaeffer, 1960). Plastered-floor houses are found associated with a flint industry similar to that of Jericho PPNB and Abu Ghosh. Pottery was still unknown to the inhabitants of these basal levels of Ras Shamra. The availability of three new C^{14} determinations from the preceramic levels of Khirokitia on Cyprus (St. 414, 415, 416; average *ca.* 7600 *B.P.* $\pm 150, = ca.$ 5650 B.C.) poses further problems for consideration in this general connection, although it is not yet clear how the Khirokitia materials bear, comparatively, on the preceramic materials of mainland southwestern Asia.

The prepottery layers of Jarmo in Iraqi Kurdistan (Braidwood and Howe, this volume) seem to offer an upland equivalent of the "Mediterranean" type of settlement of this general stage rather than of the particular "oasis" type. In my opinion, a comparison between prepottery Jarmo and sites of the Abu Ghosh, Hagoshrim, and Beida type would be more promising than that between Jarmo and Jericho. This does not exclude the possibility of finding some Jericho-like pre-Hassunan assemblage in the Mesopotamian lowlands near the river banks.

3. There is practically no information on what one must suppose to have been the nomadic or seminomadic population of the semiarid area of Palestine in this general range of time. Hunting was probably still the basis of the economy of the population of southern Negev (surface stations of the Nitzana area), but the domestication of animals seems in progress at Kilwa in southern Transjordan (Rhotert, 1938, where rock drawings depict scenes of trapped animals or early domestication), and the cultivation of cereals could from this time onward assume at least a minor subsistence role.

IV. THE APPEARANCE OF POTTERY AND DEVELOPED
VILLAGE LIFE IN THE MEDITERRANEAN AREA

The use of pottery characterizes the beginning of a new phase of development of the early village-farming communities. Numerous new settlements appear in the record, seeming to indicate a growing population. Unfortunately, however, the archeological evidence is scanty, most of these settlements being known only from surface collection or limited soundings.

A dark-faced burnished ware is the familiar hallmark of the Syro-Cilician assemblage, which also includes, as in prepottery times (Ras Shamra), rectilinear structures with plastered and burnished walls and floors, a chipped- and flaked-stone industry, fully ground celts, and stone bowls. It has been recognized (Braidwood, 1959) in the basal level (Phase A) of the Amuq sites, of Yümük Tépé (Mersin), Gözlu Kule (Tarsus), Ras Shamra V, Hama, and, somewhat later (= Amuq B), at Tabbat el-Hammam (Hole, 1959) and Byblos "Néolithique Ancien." The flint industry of the south-Syrian sites shows more specific connections with Palestine.

The dark-faced burnished ware also appears in Palestine, but only a few sherds have been found, mixed with the painted pottery of the Jericho AB horizon (i.e., the post-PPNB levels; cf. Amuq Phase D), at Kfar Giladi (Kaplan, 1959) near the Lebanese border, at Sheikh Ali (Prausnitz, 1959), and at Tell Batashi (Kaplan, 1958) near Tel-Aviv. These occurrences are a good illustration of the slow diffusion of the ware from its Syro-Cilician center. This dark-faced burnished ware, however, is not the first to appear in Palestine; it is preceded at Shaar Hagolan (Stekelis, 1950) by a pottery with incised decoration also found with other classes of impressed or combed ware in basal Byblos— *Néolithique Ancien* (Dunand, 1950)—where it is associated with the dark-faced burnished ware. Although more evidence is needed, particularly from Palestine on the Shaar Hagolan horizon, we feel that the "cardial" wares could be part of a Palestinian and south-Syrian assemblage parallel to the Syro-Cilician assemblage of the dark-faced burnished ware.

No general impression of settlement size or complexity is yet available at this stage for Syro-Cilicia or Palestine. Byblos is the only settlement excavated to any extent (about 1000 square meters). Small (4x2.5 meters) rectangular houses with plastered floors, of the prepottery Jericho and Ras Shamra type, rebuilt five to six times one on top of the other, are a reasonable indication of the permanence of the settlement; C^{14} determinations of *ca.* 5000 B.C. for the earliest houses and *ca.* 4600 B.C. for the upper stratum are available. Hints of a similar duration and permanence of settlement are also given by the study of the stratigraphy of other Syro-Cilician sites, such as Mersin or Ras Shamra. Wheat and barley were cultivated; animal bones indicate pig, sheep, and cattle. Although a solid base is still lacking for a general cultural interpretation, we may consider that a stage of development has been generally attained permitting the establishment of permanent villages of some size.

The sudden appearance of pottery at this stage is surprising. In the present state of our knowledge, its first use cannot be linked to sedentary living or to a particular level of food production or to a higher degree of technological knowledge.

V. FROM PASTORAL NOMADISM TO VILLAGE LIFE IN THE SEMIARID REGION

In post-Natufian and later times up to the end of the fifth millennium B.C., we have almost no traces of the nomadic populations of the semiarid area. The Kilwa rock drawings in south Transjordan are doubtful evidence of first attempts by nomads at the domestication of animals. But from subsequent evidence we may infer that the peoples of the semiarid zone had made some progress on the road to pastoralism and to a more settled way of life. Cereals were probably known to them and cultivated in certain areas, constituting at least a small complement to their diet.

Wandering with their flocks on the periphery of the Syro-Arabian desert, these nomadic or seminomadic populations may have been in contact to the east and north with Mesopotamia and the Anatolian plateau, and to the south with the Arabian coast and Africa. We can consider them as even having taken some part in the diffusion of cultivated cereals and their introduction into Egypt and the Nile Valley in the first part of the fifth millennium. Their mobility made them the best instrument of diffusion of Mesopotamian and eastern influences into the Syrian and Palestinian provinces to the west. Perhaps it is not too rash to attribute to them the introduction of the eastern tradition of pot-painting to the Mediterranean littoral region and also some of the new cultural traits that one finds appearing simultaneously in the Amuq (D), at Ras Shamra (IV), at Byblos (*Néo. Moyen*), and at Jericho AB.

Jericho, abandoned after PPNB, was indeed resettled by the newcomers (in A and B, the first pottery-bearing layers),[5] who introduce a new architecture— bun-shaped bricks on stone foundations—and a new pattern of settlement. The dwellings, some of them subterranean, extend freely down the slopes of the pre-pottery neolithic tell and around it.

Further penetration in Palestine during the fourth millennium B.C. is best evidenced in those parts of the country around the Dead Sea, in the northern Negev and along the coast in regions that were not settled at that time and had never before known a sedentary occupation.

Although evidence is still scanty, we have to look to the Transjordan plateau

---

5. According to Miss Kenyon, the distinction between A and B is based for the time being on typological grounds only. The pottery of A and B was found together in the same pits. The pottery of A and B types also appears similarly associated at Batashi and Sheikh Ali and thus may well be of the same age. In any case, it will be difficult to distinguish between local tradition and "foreign" influence.

for the immediate origin of the newcomers and also for the formative phase of their culture, the Ghassulian.[6]

The Ghassulian (from Teleilat el-Ghassul, northeast of the Dead Sea), (Mallon, 1934; Perrot, 1955a) presents a mixed economy, with stock-breeding making up the better part of it, and cultivation of wheat, barley, and lentils serving only as a complement but being sufficient to permit an almost sedentary life. In fact, the Ghassulian may be described as an attempt by an originally seminomad population at a more permanent settlement.

By the time they appear in Palestine, these people had reached a very high level of food production. In Beersheba, in north-central Negev, bones of hunted animals account for less than 5 per cent of the animal bones—65 per cent sheep and goat; ox, dog, and rare pig accounting for the rest (Josien, 1955). There are no arrowheads.

Metallurgy, in pure copper, is fully developed, with casting of axes, chisels, hammers, points, and hollow maceheads, implying a high degree of technological skill. The metallurgical activities were concentrated in one of the small settlements of the Beersheba group (Abu Matar), the copper ore—malachite—having been extracted 100 kilometers to the east, in Transjordan.

Hard stones like basalt, hematite, and volcanic rocks were imported from the same region, east of the Dead Sea, for the manufacture of maceheads, palettes, and hollow-footed vessels. The drill was known. Local limestone was used for mortars, loom-weights, figurines, etc. The flint industry includes a high proportion of tools made on pebbles (chopping tools, picks, scrapers, knives); also tranchets (in continuation of the post-Natufian el-Khiam type tradition?), sickle blades, borers, and gravers. Bone tools include skewers and needles, wool-combs, picks, and sickles.

Pottery was handmade, the only exception being certain small bowls that exhibit wheel marks and string-cut bases. Characteristic forms of pottery vessels include imitations of skin containers, common among nomads. Painted decoration in red (bands, arcs, lattices) is usual.

Taste for personal ornament (beads, pendants, pins) is developed; artistic and religious feeling finds its expression in ivory male or female figurines and statuettes, probably in relation with some fertility cult.

In the Beersheba group dwellings are completely subterranean at first and are sometimes dug 5 meters deep into the sandy deposits of the terraces. At Safadi they are distributed around a 10×3 meter hall, which could have been some sort of ceremonial or communal center. The settlement comprises 15–20 dwellings; the population probably did not exceed 200. The total population of the six settlements of the Beersheba group, extending over a few kilometers on the two banks of the wadi, could have been from 500 to 1,000. Each agglomeration shows a certain degree of industrial specialization (metallurgy at Abu Matar, soft stone and ivory carving at Safadi); the group as a whole apparently formed an independent economic and social unit.

6. The appellation used here in its *sensu lato* meaning.

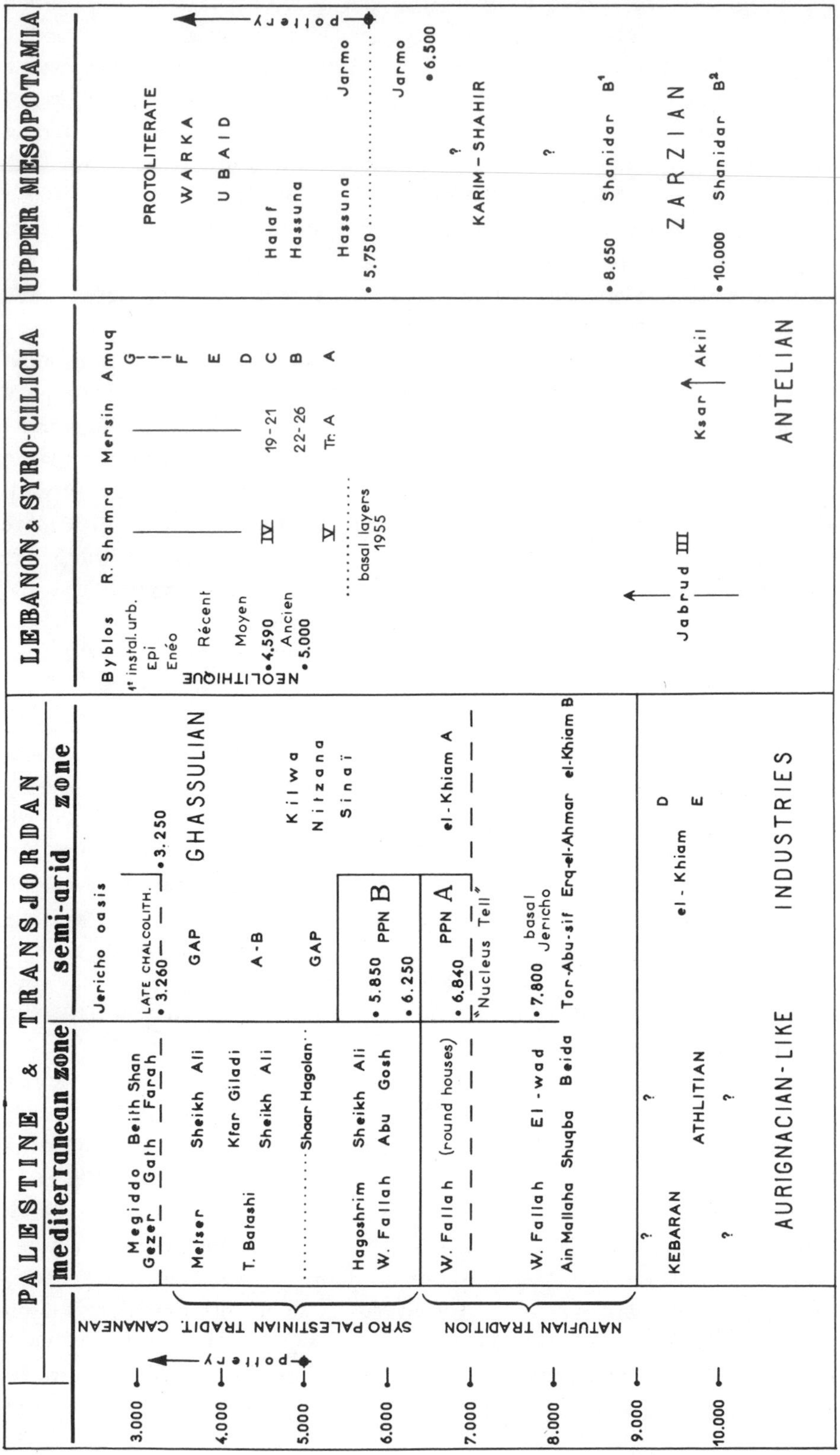

FIGURE 2. Comparative chronological chart of southwestern Asia, particularly of the regions west of the Euphrates River.

The same general disposition lasted to the end of the short-lived occupation (about 200–300 years; the middle layer has C^{14} determinations of 3460 ± 350 [M 864a] and 3310 ± 300 [M 864b] B.C.). The subterranean dwellings were then replaced by rectangular houses built of wood and mud brick on stone foundations. This same architectural technique, first seen at Jericho AB, also characterizes the village of Ghassul, where the plastered walls of the houses were sometimes covered with frescoes (schematic figures of animals and geometrical motives). Some idea of the houses of that period may be obtained from the house-shaped ossuaries of pottery found on a number of contemporary sites along the coast.

At this stage of development, the Ghassulian culture came to an abrupt end. The Ghassul and Beersheba villages were abandoned, and all traces of sedentary life disappear in the semiarid zone. One explanation could be the deterioration of the security situation in Syria and Palestine, compelling the populations to choose naturally protected sites in the proximity of an adequate water supply. This is the time when Gezer, Megiddo, Beth Shan, Farah, etc., were founded in the hills. As for the population of the semiarid regions, we may suppose that, unable to adapt themselves to the new conditions, they turned back to a more fully pastoral seminomadic type of subsistence pattern, perhaps something like the type we can see later evidenced in historic times by the Amorites.

VI. TOWARD URBAN LIFE

The Palestinian archeological sequence from the Natufian caves or open-air sites to the upper strata of prepottery Jericho, as incomplete and unsatisfactory as it may seem, nevertheless gives an idea of the general evolution from the food-collecting stage to the threshold of food production and village life. For later times, however, the incompleteness of the archeological record does not permit such a comparable general evolutionary interpretation. We can say only that the development from village to urban life took a much longer time in Palestine than in some other parts of southwestern Asia, and that the marginal character of Palestine becomes more and more apparent in contrast (for example) with the lowlands of Mesopotamia.

The phase following the appearance of pottery at Shaar Hagolan is represented, other than in Jericho AB, only by the material of a few soundings at Tell Batashi and at Kfar Giladi (Kaplan, 1959) and at Sheikh Ali (Prausnitz, 1959). On this last site burnished red pottery (including bow-rim jars) and red painted pottery with reserved spaces covered with incised or combed motifs, characteristic of this horizon, are associated with a rectangular building of considerable dimensions with a pebble-paved courtyard and plastered-floor rooms. The same pottery occurs also in the *Néolithique Moyen* of Byblos (Cauvin, personal communication).

We could consider this pottery as a continuation of the Syro-Palestinian tradition of the preceding phase, now marked by the first influence of the eastern

(Ubaidian) painted techniques and repertoire upon the Mediterranean coastal zone. This same influence manifests itself in the Syro-Cilician sites (Amuq Phase D) where the repertoire includes the bow rims and hole-mouth jars, the small triangular-sectioned jar handles, the pierced pedestal bases, the red wash, etc. (Braidwood, 1960, p. 510).

We still lack clear stratigraphical sequence in Palestine between this phase and the following one represented by the basal layers of such Mediterranean zone hill-country sites as, for example, Megiddo, Beth Shan, Farah, and Gezer. No information is available on the extent or organization of these settlements. The impact of the contemporary Ghassulian culture of the semiarid zone is felt on their pottery, sometimes as imports, more often as imitations (e.g., a gray burnished ware imitates the basalt vessels), but the Ghassulian ceramic does not seem to affect the essentially indigenous Mediterranean tradition. The influence of the eastern nomads is evidenced in the *Néolithique Récent* of Byblos, lessening in the following *Enéolithique*, which also corresponds to the basal layers of the Palestinian settlements mentioned above.

Byblos (Dunand, 1950) is at this time the only site that can give evidence toward urbanization. The *Enéolithique* settlement (*ca.* 3500–3200 B.C.) covers the entire acropolis; rectangular, round, then apsidal houses were sometimes connected by paved paths inside the settlement. Copper, gold, and silver were in use. Pottery was still handmade.

The following stage (*ca.* 3200–3050 B.C.) is represented by long houses internally divided, grouped sometimes in enclosures. Metal was by now commonly used. Burials were made outside the agglomeration.

Then, around 3000 B.C., appeared what is called a *"première installation urbaine"*; multiroomed rectangular houses, sanctuaries, paved streets, and sewers; pottery was mass produced; cylinder seals of Jemdet Nasr type were in use, implying long-distance contacts with Mesopotamia. Trade relations by sea also existed with Egypt.

We are probably nearer the "threshold of urbanization" with the next phase of Byblos settlement two centuries later; rectangular houses were built on well-dressed stone foundations; monumental temples (Baalat Gebal temple, oval temple) appeared, and the agglomeration was surrounded by a huge rampart. A parallel development may be expected in Syro-Cilicia.

In Palestine, from the scanty evidence from Megiddo, Beth Yerah, Beth Shan, Farah-Gezer, Jericho, etc., we can say only that with the beginning of the third millennium we certainly enter into a phase of cultural and social acceleration pointing toward urbanization. Whether they were walled or not, we see the appearance of permanent settlements of some considerable size and density; there was the building of communal granaries (Beth Yerah), craft specialization was by now assured, and industrialization was in progress. The first temples and monumental buildings are another indication that the swing toward the social order of the urban type was under way. We have no assurance, however, that a stage of urban life similar to that of early dynastic times in lower Mesopotamia was really achieved in Palestine proper at the beginning of the third millennium or even before the second millennium B.C.

VII. SUMMARY

In post-Pleistocene times, we can observe in the Syrian and Palestinian regions two parallel cultural developments.

The first development, originating in the Mediterranean zone, leads us, through a still insufficiently documented phase of incipient cultivation (the Natufian), to a point at which it had become possible to cultivate cereals beyond the limits of their natural zone, thus making effective food production possible, at least as a supplementary basis of total subsistence. We see the first clear social and economic results of this achievement in the Jericho oasis around 7000 B.C.

The second development, which took place in the semiarid zone, is not archeologically evidenced before 3500 B.C. (i.e., the Ghassulian). By then, however, produced food (from sheep- and cattle-breeding, supplemented by the cultivation of cereals) represented such a large proportion of the diet that we feel justified in pushing back the beginnings of this development (the first attempts at the domestication of animals) by at least one thousand years. This does not exclude earlier attempts at domestication in the Mediterranean zone and in the Jericho oasis.

The nature of the archeological record and the existence in Palestine and southern Syria of a natural-habitat zone for cereals and potentially domesticable animals give reason for considering that food production in its two aspects (plant cultivation and animal domestication) appeared there, as in Syro-Cilicia and in the Kurdistan-Zagros foothills, as an indigenous evolution. This slow but regular progress can be opposed to what we can see in the Nile Valley, where the sudden and late (around 4500 B.C.) appearance of the first villages seems to give to the emergence there of food production an explosive, "revolutionary," character.

Pottery makes an independent appearance along the Mediterranean coastal zone around 5000 B.C. with two apparent foci: "cardial" wares in Palestine and southern Syria and dark-faced burnished ware in Syro-Cilicia and the region immediately to the east.

From that moment and for some time thereafter, the incompleteness of archeological evidence makes general cultural interpretation extremely difficult. We can recognize during the fourth millennium in the semiarid area the short-lived attempt by the pastoral populations at a more sedentary life—as seen in the Ghassulian. Their settlements stopped short, however, of any urban character.

Incipient urbanization can be detected around 3000 B.C. in Palestine and Syria, but the process appears to have been slowed down, particularly in Palestine, by limited natural resources, an increasingly restrictive factor for a growing population. The "threshold of urbanization" was reached later in Palestine than in lower Mesopotamia.

BIBLIOGRAPHY

BRAIDWOOD, R. J., and BRAIDWOOD, L.
1959. *Excavations in the Plain of Antioch.* (Oriental Inst. Publs., No. 61.) Chicago: University of Chicago Press.

DOTHAN, M.
1957. Excavations at Meser, 1956," *Israel Explor. J.,* Vol. 7, No. 4.

DUNAND, M.
1950. "Chronologie des plus anciennes installations de Byblos," *Revue biblique,* 57:583–603.

1955. "Rapport préliminaire sur les fouilles de Byblos," *Bull. Musée Beyrouth,* 12:7–23.

EWING, F. J.
1947. "Preliminary Note on the Excavations at the Palaeolithic Site of Ksar Akil, Republic of Lebanon," *Antiquity,* 84:186–95.

GARROD, D. A. E.
1932. "A New Mesolithic Industry: The Natufian of Palestine," *J. Roy. Anthrop. Inst.,* 62:257–69.

1937. *The Stone Age of Mount Carmel, I.* Oxford: Clarendon Press.

1957. "The Natufian Culture: The Life and Economy of a Mesolithic People in the Near East: Albert Reckitt Archaeological Lecture, British Academy," *Proc. Brit. Acad.,* Vol. 43.

HOLE, F.
1959. "A Reanalysis of Basal Tabbat al-Hammam, Syria," *Syria,* 36:149–83.

JOSIEN, TH.
1955. "La faune chalcolithique des gisements palestiniens de Bir Es-Safadi et Bir Abou Matar," *Israel Explor. J.,* 5:246–57.

KAPLAN, J.
1958. "The Excavations at Telulyot Batashi in the Vale of Sorek," *Eretz Israel,* 5:9–24, 83–84.

1959. "The Neolithic Pottery of Palestine," *Bull. Amer. Sch. Oriental Res.,* 156:15–21.

KENYON, K. M.
1959*a.* "Earliest Jericho," *Antiquity,* 33:5–9.

1959*b.* "Some Observations on the Beginnings of Settlement in the Near East," *J. Roy. Anthrop. Inst.,* 89:35–43.

KIRKBRIDE, D. V. W.
1958. "Notes on a Survey of the Pre-Roman Archaeological Sites near Jerash," *Bull. Inst. Archaeol.* (Univ. London), 1:9–20.

1959. "Short Notes on Some Hitherto Unrecorded Prehistoric Sites in Transjordan," *Palestine Explor. Quart.,* 91:52–54.

1960. "Chronique archéologique," *Revue biblique,* 67:230–39.

MALLON, A.
1934. *Teleilat Ghassul I.* Rome: Pontifical Biblical Institute.

NEUVILLE, R.
1934. "Le préhistorique de Palestine," *Revue biblique,* 43:237–59.

1951. *Le paléolithique et le mésolithique du Désert de Judée.* ("Arch. Inst. Paléontol. Humaine," Mém. 24). Paris.

PERROT, J.

1952a. "Le néolithique d'Abou Gosh," *Syria*, 29:120–45.

1952b. "Têtes de flèches du Natoufien et du Tahounien (Palestine)," *Bull. Soc. Préhist. Franç.*, 49:439–49.

1955a. "The Excavations at Tell Abu Matar, near Beersheba," *Israel Explor. J.*, 5:17–189.

1955b. "Les fouilles d'Abou Matar," *Syria*, 34:1–38.

1957. "Le mésolithique de Palestine et les récentes découvertes à Eynan (Ain Mallaha)," *Antiquity and Survival*, 2:91–110.

1960. "Excavations at 'Eynan (Ain Mallaha), 1959 Season: Preliminary Report," *Israel Explor. J.*, 10:14–22.

PRAUSNITZ, M. W.

1958. "Khirbet Sheikh 'Ali," *Revue biblique*, 65:414.

1959. "The First Agricultural Settlements in Galilee," *Israel Explor. J.*, 9:166–74.

REED, C. A.

1959. "Animal Domestication in the Prehistoric Near East," *Science*, 130:1629–39.

RHOTERT, H.

1938. *Transjordanien-Vorgeschichtliche Forschungen*. Stuttgart.

RUST, A.

1950. *Die Höhlenfunde von Jabrud (Syrien)*. Neumünster: Karl Wacholtz.

SCHAEFFER, C. F. A.

1960. *Ugaritica 4*. Paris: Geuthner.

STEKELIS, M.

1938. "Contribution to the Study of the Premesolithic Age in Palestine." In *Magnes Anniversary Book*, pp. 461–64. (In Hebrew.) Jerusalem.

1950–51. "A New Neolithic Industry: The Yarmukian of Palestine." *Israel Explor. J.*, 1:3–20.

1960. "Wadi Fallah (Nahal Oren)," *ibid.*, Vol. 10, notes.

TURVILLE-PETRE, F.

1932. "Excavations in the Mugharet el-Kebarah," *J. Roy. Anthrop. Inst.*, 62:271–76.

WAECHTER, J. D'A., *et al.*

1938. "The Excavations at Wadi Dhobai, 1937–38, and the Dhobaian Industry," *J. Palestine Oriental Soc.*, 18:172–86, 292–98.

THE CENTRAL ANDES

DONALD COLLIER

INTRODUCTION

THE AREA under consideration includes the coast and highland of Peru and the adjoining Titicaca basin in Bolivia (Fig. 1). This stretch of the Andes contained a major native areal culture with time depth, which Bennett has called the "Peruvian Co-tradition" (Kroeber, 1944, p. 111; Bennett, 1948).

The narrow coastal region is an extremely arid but temperate desert cut transversely at intervals by mountain-fed rivers that form oasis valleys. The highland consists of intermontane valleys and basins separated by lofty plateaus and high mountain passes. In the coastal valleys intensive agriculture is dependent on irrigation, although small-scale cultivation is possible without irrigation in the moist areas at valley mouths close to the sea. In the mountain valleys irrigation is less vital, but everywhere it increases crop yields. In spite of differences between coast and highland, there are certain major uniformities. Both regions have large cultivable areas with rich soils not covered with resistant grasses or forest and with water available for irrigation. Temperature and other contrasts due to differences in altitude are minimized by the cold Peru current and proximity to the equator. The Peru current also accounts for an exceptionally rich marine fauna, which amply compensates for the barrenness of the coastal desert. Both coastal and highland valleys are geographically isolated but close enough to other valleys for trade and cultural interchange.

Native history in the Central Andes may be divided into three major stages of subsistence. These are a largely inferred early hunting stage (about 8000 B.C. until an unknown date), a stage of food-collecting and incipient cultivation (2500–750 B.C.), and a stage of agriculture (750 B.C.–A.D. 1532). The incipient cultivation stage includes two major periods: the earlier Preceramic, which lacked both ceramics and maize, and the later Initial Ceramic, which included pottery-making and the cultivation of maize (Fig. 2). The agricultural stage is divisible into an earlier substage of established agriculture[1] (Formative period) and a later substage of intensive agriculture (Classic and Postclassic periods).

In a previous paper on the development of agriculture in Peru (Collier, n.d.) the Initial Ceramic was included as the first subperiod of the Formative, but I

---

1. The term "established agriculture" was introduced by Willey (1960).

FIGURE 1. The Central Andes

pointed out that in terms of subsistence patterns it should be grouped with the Preceramic in a stage of incipient agriculture. The Initial Ceramic could well be set apart as a transitional stage between the stages of incipient cultivation and established agriculture.

	Subsistence Stages	Periods	North Coast	North Highland	Central Coast	Central Highland	South Coast	South Highland
1532			Inca	Inca	Inca	Inca	Inca	Inca
	INTENSIVE AGRICULTURE	POSTCLASSIC	Chimu	Late Huamachuco	Late Chancay / Late Ancón	Early Inca	Late Ica Poroma	Callao
800			B-W-R Geom Coast Tiahuanaco	Middle Huamachuco Wilcawaín	B-W-R Geom Coast Tiahuanaco	Huari Lucre	Middle Ica Huari Pacheco	Decadent Tiahuanaco
		CLASSIC	Mochica Galli-nazo	Recuay B / Recuay A	Nievería / Maranga	Waru / Derived Chanapata	Nazca	Pucara / Classic Tiahuan-aco
A.D. B.C.	ESTABLISHED AGRICULTURE	FORMATIVE	Gallinazo / Salinar	Huaraz W-on-R	Playa Grande / Baños de Boza	Classic Chanapata	Paracas Paracas	Pucara / Early Tiahuanaco Chiripa
400 750			Cupisnique Cupisnique	Kuntur Wasi Chavín de Huantar	Colinas Curayacu 2 (Early Ancón)	Marcavalle	Paracas Cerillos	
1200	INCIPIENT CULTIVATION	INITIAL CERAMIC	Middle Guañape / Early Aldas Guañape		Curayacu 1 Aldas			
2500		PRECERAMIC	Huaca Cerro Prieta Prieto		Aspero Río Seco		Asia Otuma	

FIGURE 2. Cultural periods in the Central Andes

EARLY HUNTERS

As yet, evidence of the early hunting stage in the Central Andes is minimal. Heavy, pressure-flaked, stemmed and/or lanceolate projectile points have been found on the coast in Chicama Valley, at San Nicolás south of Nazca, in the highland in caves near Huancayo, and in a surface deposit at Viscachani south of La Paz, Bolivia (Bird, 1948, p. 27; Larco Hoyle, 1948, pp. 11–12; Strong, 1957, pp. 8–11; Tschopik, 1946; Menghin, 1953–54). Although typologically these finds appear early, there is no evidence linking them with extinct Pleistocene mammals, and both geological and absolute dates are lacking. But the presence of early hunting cultures at the southern tip of the continent shortly after 7000 B.C. (Bird, 1938; 1946; 1951, pp. 44–46), and the recent discovery of an apparently early lithic assemblage near Quito, Ecuador (Bell and Mayer-Oakes, 1960), strengthen the probability that the Central Andean finds pertain to the early hunters. Until additional geological and archeological investigations are made, nothing reliable can be said about the environment and the ecological adaptations of these post-Pleistocene hunters.[1a]

1a. Since this was written, Kardich (1960, pp. 107–14) has published a brief description of an early lithic sequence in caves at Lauricocha, Department of Huánuco, Peru. The earliest of three preceramic horizons (Lauricocha I) contained crude flake tools (scrapers and perforators but no projectile points), animal bones, and human skeletons. Carbon samples from this horizon have yielded a date of 7566 ± 250 B.C.

COLLECTORS AND INCIPIENT CULTIVATORS

At present there is a hiatus between the inferential early hunting stage in the Central Andes and the beginning of incipient cultivation about 2500 B.C. This gap may have been occupied by a food-collecting stage, during which a culture similar to the shell fishhook culture of northern Chile (Bird, 1943) existed along the Peruvian coast, but as yet no remains of this hypothetical fishing culture have been recognized.

More than forty habitation sites of the incipient cultivation stage, called the Preceramic in Peruvian archeology, are known from the Peruvian coast (Bird, 1948; Engel, 1957a, b, 1958). The earliest of these seems not to have been occupied before 2500 B.C. These sites are located near the sea at the mouths of rivers or on the shores of coastal lagoons. Subsistence of these people, as revealed by plant and animal remains recovered from refuse deposits, was based on collecting wild fruits and tubers, gathering shellfish, catching fish by net and line, taking sea lion and porpoise by unknown methods, and cultivating squash, chili peppers, jack beans (*Canavalia*), lima beans,[2] and achira tubers. They also cultivated gourds, which were used for containers and net floats, and cotton, which they made into cordage, nets, twined and looped textiles, and, rarely, woven textiles. This first cultivation was carried out without irrigation in the moist areas at the mouths of valleys, which were the natural habitat of some of the wild plants gathered for food.

The surprisingly crude stone tools of these people were roughly chipped flakes, cores, and hammerstones. Pressure flaking was absent on the north coast but seems to have been practiced by the Preceramic peoples on the central and south coasts. Fishhooks were of shell. Stone projectile points were not made except on the south coast. Cooking was done with heated stones, thousands of burned fragments of which are found mixed with the shells in the refuse deposits. Houses were small rectangular or oval structures of beach cobbles, rough stone, adobe, or wattle-and-daub construction, with roofs supported by beams of wood or whalebone. Settlements consisted of a few to a dozen houses scattered at random on the refuse deposits. At two of the sites there are specialized structures that may be the first shrines or community buildings.

Toward the end of the Preceramic, woven textiles appear at most sites, and at the very end of the period, probably between 1400 and 1200 B.C., the first maize is found. The evidence consists of a few maize cobs in the upper levels of four Preceramic sites (Lanning, 1959, p. 48; personal communication, 1959). The first pottery appears about 1200 B.C., marking the beginning of the Initial Ceramic period (Bird, 1948; Strong and Evans, 1952; Lanning, 1959). The first pottery was simple in form and undecorated; color was variable because of lack of control in firing. Later, burnishing and incising were added. These early pottery-makers cultivated peanuts and maize in addition to the plants of the

2. Lima beans (*Phaseolus lunatus*) occurred in the earliest levels at Huaca Prieta (M. A. Towle, personal communication, 1960).

Preceramic period. In spite of the use of these new food plants, there was no immediate shift in subsistence pattern, and settlements were still close to the sea. Probably there was a progressive increase in dependence on cultivated plants, but evidence for this is lacking. There was a gradual shift from twined to woven textiles, and jet mirrors, which may have had ritual uses, were made for the first time. Some of the Initial Ceramic settlements were larger than those of the Preceramic and contained small temple centers. The most impressive of these is the terrace–pyramid–sunken–court complex built of rough basalt blocks at the Aldas site on the north-central coast (Engel, 1957*b*; Lanning, 1959).

In contrast to the coastal region, there is no evidence bearing on the presence and nature of human occupation of the highland during the Preceramic and Initial Ceramic periods.

AGRICULTURALISTS

FORMATIVE PERIOD

During the Formative period full-time agriculture was achieved and many of the basic traditions or trends were established in Central Andean technology, religion, and art.

The Formative began with the appearance of loom weaving,[3] the Chavín style of ceramics and stone carving, the use of gold for ornaments, and at least three new plants—warty squash, sweet manioc, and avocados. Although there is no direct evidence of canal irrigation at this time, the shift from seaside to inland settlements, the size of some settlements, and the magnitude of some of the ceremonial centers they supported suggest that water control had advanced beyond simple flood-water irrigation.

The community consisted of several villages of stone or adobe houses clustered about a ceremonial nucleus. In some valleys the ceremonial centers were small, simple platform structures of stone or adobe. In others they were large stepped platforms of stone or adobe with sculptured, incised, or painted decorations. The most elaborate center, at Chavín de Huantar in the north highland, was composed of a sunken court flanked by stone-faced platforms and a terrace surmounted by a massive temple of dressed stone containing a honeycomb of interior galleries. The temple and other buildings were ornamented with stone sculpture and low-relief carving on stelae and flat slabs.

The Chavín style and associated religious cult, which was centered around jaguar and serpent deities, spread widely and rapidly over much but not all of the Central Andes. But there is no evidence of wide political control or organized warfare. Probably the villages supporting a ceremonial center were integrated by priestly leadership.

The later Formative was a time of regional development and experimentation. It was characterized by the following important new traits and developments: expanding canal irrigation; agricultural terracing; kidney beans, pepino fruits, and

3. It is not clear whether the loom was already in use in the initial ceramic period.

quinoa; domesticated llama,[4] alpaca, and guinea pig; coca-chewing; positive and negative painting on pottery; and ornaments of copper and copper-gold alloy. Wool was used in textiles, and weaving techniques were elaborated. Weavers produced turbans, headbands, shirts, shawls, breechcloths, and girdles, which together comprised the basic Peruvian clothing pattern from this time onward.

The number of villages greatly increased, but they remained small. Groups of villages were clustered around pyramid mounds of stone or adobe. Elaborate hilltop fortifications of stone were constructed, probably for defense against intervalley raids. Variations in the richness of burial offerings suggest differences in wealth and social status.

CLASSIC PERIOD

The full utilization in the Classic period of the Formative technologies emphasized the geographical differences of size and fertility of regions, and these differences played a part in the development of marked regional specialization. Of particular significance are the following Classic traits and complexes: intensive agriculture based on transvalley irrigation systems and use of fertilizer; marked population increase; craft specialization and production of luxury goods; the construction of enormous temple mounds of adobe bricks; ornaments of gold, copper, silver, and their alloys; copper tools and weapons; class-structured societies; state control under the leadership of priest kings; and organized warfare. Villages became larger, and a few towns, clustered around the temple pyramids, grew by accretion until they contained a thousand or more closely packed dwellings.

POSTCLASSIC PERIOD

The Postclassic period is characterized by increased warfare, progressive urbanization, mass production of goods, and final political unification of the Central Andes under the Inca empire. Planned urban centers laid out on a rectangular grid and enclosed by defense walls appeared at the beginning of the period and reached a climax in Chanchan, the Chimu capital, which had a population estimated at 50,000. The growth of cities coincided with the development of intervalley irrigation systems. Mold-made domestic pottery was mass produced, and bronze was used for the first time.

DISCUSSION

Owing to a gap in our knowledge of Andean prehistory, it is not possible to assess the degree and nature of the intensification of food-collecting prior to the emergence of incipient cultivation in the area. When initially observable, about 2500 B.C., the first cultivated plants, playing together a minor subsistence role, fitted neatly into a well-diversified system of exploitation of wild food

---

4. The llama may have been domesticated in the early Formative or toward the end of the Initial Ceramic.

plants and marine fauna. The moist areas at valley mouths that were most favorable for initial cultivation were also the habitat of the most useful wild food plants, and these places were convenient to the marine food supply. This congruence of the loci of food resources accounts for the concentration of settlements in such locations throughout the stage of incipient cultivation in the coastal zone. It is noteworthy that two of the cultivated plants, the gourd and cotton, were of no immediate food value but were important in net fishing.

The first maize, which probably appeared about 1400 B.C., one or two centuries before pottery, was a primitive and not very productive variety. It seems to have been of minor importance in subsistence throughout the Initial Ceramic period. Only in the early Formative (Chavín) subperiod, five or six hundred years after the first maize, did this plant assume a major role. At this time an improved form of maize was introduced, and warty squash, sweet manioc, and avocados were added to the earlier cultivated plants. Effective food production (established agriculture) can be said to have begun (Fig. 2). But even before this, in the Initial Ceramic period, plant cultivation seems to have had a cumulative effect, for it was already possible for small ceremonial centers to develop. Thus, in the Central Andes, in contrast with Mesoamerica, the ceremonial center had its beginning before full food production.

It is not at present possible to identify the effects of expanded cultivation in terms of changes in the tools of food production and preparation, but the inventory of food remains in refuse, and the location and size of settlements do reflect the new pattern. There was a progressive shift of settlements away from the sea, marine foods diminished in importance, and villages became larger. These shifts seem to have resulted from the increasing productivity of plant cultivation and the inadequacy of the valley mouths for the expanding agriculture. The ability to build and maintain large ceremonial centers at this time and the development of elaborate stone architecture and sculpture also suggest the effectiveness of food production. The extent of canal irrigation, which was well developed in the following subperiod (late Formative), is still uncertain.

The problem of the origin of the patterns of incipient cultivation and of effective food production in the Central Andes is extremely complex, and it is not possible to review here the revelant botanical and cultural evidence. It is probable that both patterns were stimulated at least in part by diffusion of plants and ideas from Mesoamerica. Specimens of maize in both the Preceramic and the Chavín period include varieties that are related to Mexican races that have greater antiquity in the north (Mangelsdorf, 1959; personal communication, 1960). Effective agriculture, including improved varieties of maize, began spreading southward from Mesoamerica shortly before 1000 B.C. (Mangelsdorf, MacNeish, and Willey, n.d.), and the beginning of established agriculture in Peru about 750 B.C. at the start of the Chavín period appears to be a reflection of this diffusion. This conclusion is strengthened by other cultural evidence. For example, a number of ceramic traits of Chavín are found in various pottery complexes of the middle Formative period in Mesoamerica (Porter, 1953; Coe, 1960), and a connecting link is found in the ceramics of the Chorrera period on the coast of Ecuador (Meggers and Evans, 1957). There seems little doubt that these traits diffused from north to south.

On the other hand, the presence in Peru of non-Mesoamerican maize and bean varieties of considerable antiquity suggests the possibility that there were primary or secondary centers of plant domestication in the Central Andes (or neighboring areas), as well as in Mesoamerica. Furthermore, the highland complex of Central Andean root crops, which appears to be very old and to have been largely independent of maize cultivation until the Postclassic period (Sauer, 1950, pp. 513–19; Murra, 1956, pp. 13–31), may well have developed quite independently of Mesoamerican influence. The connection between this complex and Sauer's suggested center of root-crop domestication in northeastern South America (Sauer, 1953, pp. 40–73) is an important but, at the moment, completely speculative question.

In the Central Andes the establishment of effective food production had a markedly explosive effective. In the brief span of 750 years, which comprised the Formative period as used in this paper, the culture of the coast of Peru developed from a simple, relatively uniform level to the complexity of the regionally differentiated Classic cultures, which were on the threshold of civilization. This rapid evolution contrasts sharply with the slow development in the preceding stage of incipient cultivation, during which culture changed relatively little, in spite of the introduction of maize and ceramics. If, as it appears, Formative development was more rapid in the Central Andes than in Mesoamerica, the explanation probably lies in the fact that Peruvian village-farming culture was initially established at a more complex level than in Mesoamerica as a result of strong cultural influence from the latter area.

I have shown in Figure 3 the general time of appearance in the Central Andes of various aspects of urban life. The first ten characteristics are Childe's criteria of the city (Childe, 1950), arranged in the order of their appearance. Two of these—large settlements and writing—have been subdivided to bring out the special situation in Peru. Highways have been added as an additional important characteristic of urbanization.

It is seen that half these urban characteristics were developed during the Formative period and that by the early part of the Classic the only essential traits lacking were really large settlements and some form of notation. In the Postclassic, large, planned cities were built, state control was vastly extended, a highway system was developed, and there was a system of numerical notation (the quipu); but writing was completely absent. There was a notable lack of development in mathematics, astronomy, and calendrics; undoubtedly these lacks were related to the absence of writing. And yet the Incas were able to maintain a governmental bureaucracy, to construct elaborate public works (roads, bridges, canals, and terrace systems), and to carry out social and economic planning (city planning, "valley authorities," and resettlement projects). The quipu was evidently adequate for keeping track of statistical and fiscal matters—census figures,

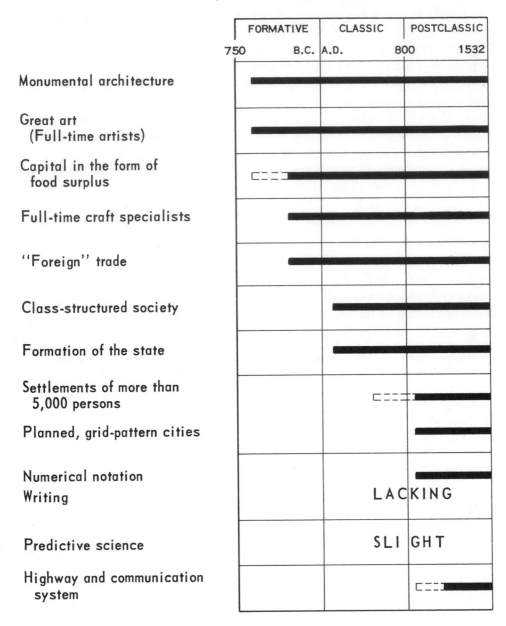

	FORMATIVE	CLASSIC	POSTCLASSIC
	750 B.C.	A.D. 800	1532

FIGURE 3. The time of appearance of aspects of urbanism in the Central Andes.

army statistics, stocks in government storehouses, the size of llama herds, and the like. But it could not be extended beyond these functions, and the valuable economic and demographic data recorded on the Inca quipus were lost to us with the passing of their professional keepers, the *quipu-camayoc*, after the Spanish conquest.[5]

5. It was asserted by a few chroniclers that the quipu was used to record history, but there is no evidence to confirm this and it seems improbable.

In terms of Central Andean data the most essential preconditions of urbanization appear to be (*a*) an intensified food production capable of producing substantial surpluses, (*b*) a high population density, and (*c*) an economically and socially differentiated society. All these were found in Peru by the end of the Formative. Of the three, a dense population seems to be the most essential. On the Peruvian coast maximum density was on the order of twenty-five times that of the density during the Chavín (early Formative).[6] This maximum was achieved by the Middle Classic in some valleys (e.g., Virú, Chicama) but not until the Postclassic in others (Lambayeque, Casma, Rimac).[7] The situation in these coastal valleys suggests a correlation, which needs much more substantiation, between the first really large settlements and near-maximum population density.

In the Central Andes, as apparently in other areas that developed cities, urbanization tended to intensify further the characteristics mentioned above as preconditions. For this reason it is extremely difficult to distinguish cause from effect in the process of urbanization. The more precise determination, both qualitative and quantitative, of these preconditions and investigation of the varieties of urbanization itself appear to be the two most fruitful approaches to an understanding of the urbanization process.

6. This estimate is based on Virú valley data (Willey, 1953).

7. Available data (Collier, n.d.; Kosok, 1959; Schaedel, 1951; Stumer, 1954; Willey, 1953) point to this conclusion, but much more supporting evidence is needed.

BIBLIOGRAPHY

BELL, ROBERT E., and W. J. MAYER-OAKES

1960. "An Early Lithic Site near Quito, Ecuador." (Paper delivered at the 25th Ann. Meeting, Soc. Amer. Archaeol., New Haven, May 5, 1960.)

BENNETT, WENDELL C.

1948. "The Peruvian Co-tradition." In W. C. BENNETT (ed.), *A Reappraisal of Peruvian Archaeology*, pp. 1–7. ("Mem. Soc. Amer. Archaeol.," No. 4.) Menasha, Wis.

BIRD, JUNIUS B.

1938. "Antiquity and Migrations of the Early Inhabitants of Patagonia," *Geo. Rev.*, 28:250–75.

1943. *Excavations in Northern Chile.* ("Amer. Mus. Nat. Hist. Anthrop. Papers," Vol. 38, Part 4.) New York.

1946. "The Archeology of Patagonia." In J. H. STEWARD (ed.), *Handbook of South American Indians*, pp. 17–24. (Smithsonian Inst., Bur. Amer. Ethnol., Bull. 143, Vol. 1.) Washington, D.C.

1948. "Preceramic Cultures in Chicama and Virú." In W. C. Bennett (ed.), *A Reappraisal of Peruvian Archaeology*, pp. 21–28. ("Mem. Soc. Amer. Archaeol.," No. 4.) Menasha. Wis.

1951. "South American Radiocarbon Dates." In F. Johnson (ed.), *Radiocarbon Dating*, pp. 37–49. ("Mem. Soc. Amer. Archaeol.," No. 8.) Salt Lake City.

Childe, V. Gordon
1950. "The Urban Revolution," *Town Planning Review* (Liverpool), 21:3–17.

Coe, Michael D.
1960. "Archeological Linkages with North and South America at La Victoria, Guatemala," *Amer. Anthrop.* 62:363–93.

Collier, Donald
1955a. *Cultural Chronology and Change as Reflected in the Ceramics of the Virú Valley, Peru.* (Chicago Nat. Hist. Mus., Fieldiana: "Anthropology," Vol. 43.) Chicago.

1955b. "Development of Civilization on the Coast of Peru." In J. H. Steward (ed.), *Irrigation Civilizations: A Comparative Study.* (Pan American Union Soc. Sci. Monogs., 1:19–27.) Washington, D.C.

1958. "El Desarollo de la Civilización Peruana," *Revista Colombiana de Anthropología*, 7:271–87. Bogotá

n.d. "Agriculture and Civilization on the Coast of Peru." (Paper given in the Symposium on the Evolution of Native Horticultural Systems in South America, Ann. Meeting A.A.A., Mexico, December 28, 1959.) (In press.)

n.d. "Archaeological Investigations in the Casma Valley, Peru." (Paper presented at the 34th Internat. Cong. of Americanists, Vienna, July 20, 1960.) (In press.)

Engel, Frederic
1957a. "Early Sites on the Peruvian Coast," *Southwestern J. Anthrop.*, 13:54–68.

1957b. "Sites et Établissments sans Céramique dans le Côte Peruvienne," *J. Soc. des Américanistes* (Paris), 46:67–155.

1958. "Algunos Datos con Referencia a los Sitios Precerámicos de la Costa Peruana," *Arqueológicas.* (Museo Nacional de Antropolgía y Arqueología, Lima), Vol. 1, No. 3.

Kardich, Augusto
1960. Investigaciones Prehistóricas en los Andes Peruanas. In *Antiguo Peru: Espacio y Tiempo* (Trabajos Presentados a la Semana de Arqueología Peruana, 9–14 Noviembre de 1959), pp. 89–118. Lima.

Kosok, Paul
1959. " El Valle de Lambayeque." In *Actas del II Congreso Nacional de Historia del Peru, 1958*, pp. 49–67. Lima.

Kroeber, A. L.
1944. *Peruvian Archeology in 1942.* ("Viking Fund Publs. in Anthrop.," No. 4.) New York.

Lanning, Edward P.
1959. "Early Ceramic Chronologies of the Peruvian Coast." Berkeley. (Mimeographed.)

Larco Hoyle, Rafael
1948. *Cronología Arqueológica del Norte del Perú.* Buenos Aires.

Mangelsdorf, Paul C., Richard S. MacNeish, and Gordon R. Willey
n.d. "Origins of Agriculture in Mesoamerica." In Robert Wauchope (ed.), *Handbook of Middle American Indians*, Vol. 1. (In preparation.)

MANGELSDORF, PAUL C., and ROBERT C. REEVES

1959. "The Origin of Corn IV: Place and Time of Origin," *Bot. Mus. Leaflets* (Harvard Univ.), 18:413–27.

MEGGERS, BETTY J., and CLIFFORD EVANS

1957. "Formative Period Cultures in the Guayas Basin, Coastal Ecuador," *Amer. Antiq.*, 22:235–47.

MENGHIN, O. F. A.

1953–54. "Culturas Precerámicas en Bolivia," *Runa* (Buenos Aires), 6:125–32.

MURRA, JOHN V.

1956. "The Economic Organization of the Inca State." (Unpubl. Ph.D. diss., Univ. Chicago.)

PORTER, MURIEL N.

1953. *Tlatilco and the Pre-Classic Cultures of the New World.* ("Viking Fund Publs. in Anthrop.," No. 19.) New York.

ROWE, JOHN H.

1956. "Archaeological Explorations in Southern Peru," *Amer. Antiq.*, 22:135–50.

SAUER, CARL O.

1950. "Cultivated Plants of South and Central America." In J. H. STEWARD (ed.), *Handbook of South American Indians*, pp. 487–543. (Smithsonian Inst., Amer. Ethnol., Bull. 143, Vol. 6.) Washington, D.C.

1952. *Agricultural Origins and Dispersals.* New York: American Geographical Society.

SCHAEDEL, RICHARD P.

1951. "Major Ceremonial and Population Centers in Northern Peru." In SOL TAX (ed.), *The Civilizations of Ancient America*, pp. 232–43. Sel. Papers 29th Internat. Cong. Americanists. Chicago.

STRONG, WILLIAM DUNCAN

1957. *Paracas, Nazca, and Tiahuanacoid Cultural Relationships in South Coastal Peru.* ("Mem. Soc. Amer. Archaeol.," No. 13.) Salt Lake City.

STRONG, WILLIAM DUNCAN, and CLIFFORD EVANS, JR.

1952. *Cultural Stratigraphy in the Virú Valley, Peru: The Formative and Florescent Epochs.* ("Columbia Studies in Archael. and Ethnol.," Vol. 4.) New York.

STUMER, LOUIS M.

1954. "Population Centers of the Rimac Valley, Peru," *Amer. Antiq.*, 20:130–48.

TSCHOPIK, HARRY, JR.

1946. "Some Notes on Rock Shelter Sites near Huancayo, Peru," *Amer. Antiq.*, 12: 73–80.

WILLEY, GORDON R.

1953. *Prehistoric Settlement Patterns in the Virú Valley, Peru* (Smithsonian Inst., Bur. Amer. Ethnol., Bull. 155.) Washington, D.C.

1960. "Historical Patterns and Evolution in Native New World Cultures." In SOL TAX (ed.), *Evolution after Darwin*, Vol. 2: *The Evolution of Man*, pp. 89–118. Chicago.

WILLEY, GORDON R., and JOHN M. CORBETT

1954. *Early Ancón and Early Supe Culture.* ("Columbia Studies in Archaeol. and Ethnol.," Vol. 3.) New York.

CHINA

KWANG-CHIH CHANG

IN CHINA, prehistoric archeology is only just beginning. It may be said to have started in 1920 with the discovery of a neolithic site at Yang-shao-ts'un, in Mien-ch'ih Hsien, Honan Province, by J. G. Andersson, and a paleolithic implement near Chao-chia-chai, in Ch'ing-yang Hsien, Kansu, by Pére Émile Licent. During the subsequent decade and a half, through the efforts of Chinese and Western scientists, information concerning the stone ages and the initial bronze age began to accumulate at a moderate rate, until 1937, when the outbreak of the Sino-Japanese War put a stop to the scientific field researches in China. Systematic archeological field work in this part of the world was not resumed until 1949, when Communist archeologists began to unearth materials with bewildering rapidity. Thus, what scientific information we have on the formative stage of Chinese civilization was gathered during a mere twenty-seven years (1920–37, 1949–59). The brevity of this period of work, the shifting personal, national, and ideological biases of the Chinese, Western, and Communist workers during its various stages, and the complete absence (with a handful of exceptions) of collaboration with natural scientists, all help to explain the tentativeness of the interpretation of the formation of the Chinese civilization that is to follow.

It is apparent that a complete areal coverage of China, as large in area as the whole of Europe or most of either of the Americas, with ecological zones no less varying, is next to impossible to achieve in a short essay. We shall therefore focus our attention here upon the area where Chinese cultural tradition emerged and developed, the area of the middle and lower Huangho (or the Yellow River). The northern peripheries of the area in Mongolia and Manchuria and, to the south, the part of the Huaiho, the Yangtze, and the Pearl River valleys into which the Chinese civilization and its formative phases radiated will also be briefly treated.

The temporal coverage of our subject matter is, on the other hand, not difficult to define. Since our interest, in this symposium, lies mainly in the process and mechanism of cultural and social development, suffice it here to delineate our time range, simply on the basis of developmental concepts, as stretching from the terminal stage of the paleolithic food-gathering cultures to the emergence of urban life in China. This time span, furthermore, can be pinned down in absolute dates. In spite of the fact that in China none of the modern techniques of dating have so far been utilized, we can date the termination of our developmental sequence in the nuclear area of Chinese culture to the middle part of the second millennium B.C., when historic records began with the emergence of urban life, and place its commencement at the late glacial period, which probably is synchronous with the Würm glacial in Europe in geological terms.

THE TERMINAL FOOD-GATHERERS

After the stage of Choukoutien sedimentation, on the eroded surface of the reddish clay (*terra rossa*) in north China (Chingshui erosion of Barbour), a variety of zonal loessic facies accumulated during the climatic interval that has been correlated with the fourth Glaciation of the Himalayas (Movius, 1944) and the Würm glacial in Europe (W. C. Pei, 1939). The climate over north China during the loessic stage was cool and dry—continental—with a prevailing wind from the northwest, though neither cooling nor desiccation is regarded as having then reached a higher peak than now exists in northeastern Asia (Teilhard de Chardin, 1941, pp. 35–36). The various regional facies of the loess in north China have been grouped by Pére Teilhard de Chardin into two distinct subcycles: A, the true Malan loess with slope deposits dominant; and B, the Mongolian-Manchurian Sands with lake or *nor* deposits dominant (Teilhard de Chardin, 1941, p. 37).

The human industry of subcycle A is represented by the paleolithic assemblage at the site of *Shui-tung-kou* in northwest Ordos in the province of Ninghsia, and that of subcycle B by the finds at *Sjara-osso-gol* in the southernmost part of Suiyuan (Boule, Breuil, Licent, and Teilhard de Chardin, 1928). "The geological and palaeontological evidence shows that broadly speaking the two sites are contemporary, although Shui-tung-kou may be slightly older than Sjara-osso-gol" (Movius, 1955, p. 279). Both assemblages are characterized by a blade-and-flake tradition and were presumably hunting cultures, as judged from the associated fauna (wild ass, rhinoceros, bison, ostrich, elephants, antelope, horse) and the presence of projectile points. But unlike Shui-tung-kou, which is a blade industry par excellence (blade cores, blades, burins, end scrapers) with a high percentage of "Mousterian" flakes (perforators, points, side scrapers), the Sjara-osso-gol assemblage is, above all, characterized by the predominance of a microblade tradition,[1] which, together with the abundance of bone and antler implements and the apparent increase of the microfauna (insect-eaters, rodents, birds), seems to indicate that, on the one hand, in addition to the hunting of big game the small-game collecting pattern also played an important role and, on the other, the importance of the composite tools apparently increased.

Subsequent to the loessic facies in north China began the recent period, which started with a land movement (and *Panchiao* erosion) and a climatic amelioration that intensified the lacustrine-riverine facies of the loessic stage and extended it to all north China. In other words, the post-Pleistocene started off there with the extinction of the Pleistocene fauna, a rise in temperature and precipitation, an

---

1. This, however, may in part be due to the paucity of raw materials for stone manufacture (cf. Movius, 1955, p. 279).

increase of vegetation cover, and a gradual continental uplift and stage of general erosion. This was a moist and warm period, well covered by forests in the loessic highlands in western north China and Manchuria ("the Black Earth stratum") and by *nors*, swamps, marshes, and lakes in the eastern alluvial plains. The woods were inhabited by a variety of animals (including many southern and warm-climate species), but deer were the predominant inhabitants.

If the beginning of the Recent period intensified the lacustrine-riverine facies of the loessic landscape and witnessed its distribution all over north China, it did the same thing with the culture of this interval—the mesolithic stage of north China in general witnessed a general spread and upsurge of the microblade tradition[2] and of composite tool manufacture. But the stage did not spread all over north China. Remains of the early post-Pleistocene hunter-fishers are found only in Mongolia (along the oases where they primarily fished) and in Manchuria and the eastern fringes of the western north China highlands (in the woods and by the water where they hunted and fished; e.g., the Upper Cave of Choukoutien and the Sha-yüan assemblages in central Shensi and northern Shansi). Such remains are not noted in the eastern plains, which may possibly have been too wet to be habitable at that time. The environment chosen by the post-Pleistocene hunter-fishers was a favorable one, and their culture was fairly intensified, specialized, and elaborated. Aside from these broad generalizations, we are ill-informed concerning these terminal food-gatherers as regards the other aspects of their life.

EMERGENCE OF FOOD PRODUCTION IN THE HUANGHO BASIN

We have little evidence on which to base a conclusion about the earliest dates of food production in China. Speculation is rife in the matter, but the paucity of reliable data forces us to refrain from commenting on the origin of food production in this part of the Old World in any positive manner. We do not even know whether it was spontaneously invented or introduced from the outside as the result of stimulus diffusion. The available archeological record, furthermore, is regrettably lacking in evidence on the transitional stage from food-gathering to food-producing, and as yet we are substantially ignorant of the when, the where, and the how of this important event in China.

We can, however, legitimately make some well-grounded guesses. If the important event that Gordon Childe has termed the "neolithic revolution" took place in China at all, it probably did so in the region that I have tentatively called the "north China nuclear area," that is, the region around the confluences of the three great rivers, Huangho, Fenho, and Weishui, or the joining place of the three provinces Honan, Shansi, and Shensi (K. C. Chang, 1959a). The north China

2. The microblade tradition in China, also known as the Chinese microlithic culture, is characterized, above all, by small blade cores; retouched or unretouched small bladelets; and the technique of pressure-flaking. It lacks the geometric forms of the microliths, made by the so-called microburin technique, which characterize many microlithic assemblages in western and northern Europe.

nuclear area is in fact a small basin encircled on the north, west, and south by the Shansi plateau, the Shensi-Kansu loessic plateau, and the Tsinling Mountains, but open to the eastern plains. The speculative role of this region as a cradle for the food-producing cultures of north China has been based on a number of considerations. In the first place, as described above, during the "climatic optimum," the nuclear area was located on the border between the wooded western highlands and the swampy eastern lowlands, and thus it had both the "hilly flanks" and the habitat for the sedentary waterside fishermen that Robert Braidwood (1952) and Carl Sauer (1948) consider, respectively, as the birthplace of farmers and herders. It had, first, rain and warmth enough to be comfortably off and herds of game and fish shoals enough to sustain its inhabitants. It was also conveniently located at the intersection of natural avenues of communication. Second, it is in the nuclear area that the only Huangho basin mesolithic assemblage was found in the Sha-yüan (sand-dune) region in Chao-i and Ta-li Counties in eastern Shensi of the lower Wei-shui valley (K. C. Chang, 1958, pp. 51–55). Third, the only stratigraphically suggested pre-Yangshao neolithic evidence was found in Pao-chi Hsien in the middle Wei-shui valley, peripheral to the nuclear area (T. K. Cheng, 1959, p. 68). In the fourth place, the importance of fishing, as shown during the subsequent Yangshao stage in this area, is highly suggestive (N. Hsia, 1957). In the fifth place, archeological evidence is ample to demonstrate that the nuclear area played a leading role in the transition from the Yangshao to the Lungshan (K. C. Chang, 1959a; C. M. An, 1959). Finally, during most of the four thousand years of historic China, the nuclear area had always been one of the strategically vital regions that have controlled the destiny of the entire Empire to a considerable extent (c. f. Lattimore, 1951, pp. 27–33).

It is thus conceivable that at a few millennia B.C. the terminal food-gatherers in the nuclear area, having possibly already settled down and having a well-developed culture, switched to food production by inventing or adopting plant cultivation and animal domestication. Although in the subsequent neolithic stages there were still a handful of items of a mesolithic woodland heritage (e.g., pressure-flaked projectile points and arrowheads, chipped-stone discs, microblades, prismatic arrowheads, semisubterranean dwellings, and semilunar and rectangular stone knives), and the possibility cannot yet be entirely ruled out that the first idea of food production was introduced rather than invented, yet—from what we know of it—Chinese neolithic culture assumed a distinctive pattern from the very beginning that shows independence and originality. The following traits, considered either singly or totally, have been enumerated as being characteristic of the Chinese neolithic culture tradition (K. C. Chang, 1959a).

1. The cultivation of millet, rice, and kaoliang (and possibly the soybean)
2. The domestication of pig, cattle, sheep, dog, chicken, and possibly horse
3. The *hang-t'u* (stamped earth) structures and the lime-plastered house floors
4. The domestication of silkworms and the loom (?)-weaving of silk and hemp
5. Possible use of tailored garments
6. Pottery with cord-mat-basket designs
7. Pottery tripods (especially *ting* and *li*) and pottery steamers (*tseng* and *yen*) and the possible use of chopsticks

8. Semilunar and rectangular stone knives
9. The great development of ceremonial vessels
10. The elaborate complex of jade artifacts; a possible wood-carving complex
11. Scapulimancy

In addition to these, the Chinese language presumably had a neolithic basis. Such a cultural tradition was not accumulated overnight, but of its initial stages there is as yet scarcely any evidence in the archeological record. That the earliest ceramic phases in north China were probably characterized by the cord-mat-basket-marked wares (Shengwen horizon; see K. C. Chang, 1959a) has been speculated upon, on the ground of geographic distribution (Ward, 1954), and is meagerly substantiated by some stratigraphical evidence (T. K. Cheng, 1959, p. 68). But of the general cultural configuration of the earliest ceramic phases we know next to nothing. An era of incipient cultivation has been assumed on the ground of necessity (K. C. Chang, 1959a); whether this era can be equated with the Shengwen horizon is a big question.

From this point on we are on surer ground (cf. K. C. Chang, 1959a, T. K. Cheng, 1959; G. D. Wu, 1938; Andersson, 1943; Teilhard de Chardin and Pei, 1944). From a small part of north China, the part with the nuclear area as a center and including northern and western Honan, southern and central Shansi, southwestern Hopei, central Shensi, and eastern Kansu, still largely confined within the drainages of the middle Huangho, Fenho, and Wei-shui, there have been found hundreds of prehistoric sites that are grouped together by their similar stratigraphic position and by the presence of a number of common distinctive horizon markers —painted pottery, some pottery forms (pointed-bottomed jars, flat- and round-based cups and bowls, thin-necked and big-belly jars, and possibly li-tripods), and some characteristic stone forms (rectangular knives and round axes, mostly symmetrically edged). In terms of cultural style this was the Yangshao horizon —which as a horizon had a solid functional basis, as will be presently seen—and in terms of ecosocial development this was the stage of the establishment of the farming villages and effective food production.

Archeological remains of the Yangshao horizon indicate the appearance of moderate-sized (200–300 meters to a side) nucleated villages. Approximately a dozen round or rectangular semisubterranean dwellings, or sometimes a few long, partitioned communal houses, comprised the village, which, according to the community patterning, might have sheltered one or several lineages or clans. The inhabitants engaged in farming, cultivating millet (*Setaria* and *Panicum*), kaoliang (*Andropogon*), and rice (*Oryza*), and in animal husbandry (dog, pig, and possibly sheep-goat and cattle). The cultivating implements included the hoe, spade, digging stick, and weeding knife. According to the shifting and repetitive pattern of settlement—indicated by the multiple components of the sites and the brevity of occupation of each component—it seems reasonable to assume that these early farmers engaged in slash-and-burn cultivation. Stone axes with a round or lentoid cross section and a symmetrical edge were manufactured, presumably for clearing fields in the woods. Stone implements were chipped, pecked, or ground, and pottery of a variety of paste was manufactured, by hand (often coiled) or with the aid of a mold. Most of the ceramic wares were of a domestic nature, cooking pots, water jars, storage jars, and bowls and cups; some of them (especially the cooking pots) were impressed with cord-mat-basket patterns, and others were beautifully painted in monochromic or bichromic decorations. Hunting and fishing took place, sometimes on a considerable scale, but these activities remained of a supplementary nature. The bow and arrow, harpoons, spears, and fishhooks were among the principal implements. Silkworms were raised, and hemp was possibly cultivated; the fabrics were spun (spindle-whorls), woven (loom?), and sewed (eyed needles).

Each village of Yangshao farmers was apparently a self-contained "little community," consisting of a dwelling area, an incorporated or separate quarter with kilns, and a village cemetery. Considering that the decorative art was focused upon domestic activities, that the evidence of a religious nature points to a fecundity cult and a fertility ritual that was presumably performed on behalf of the whole community rather than for a selected portion of the inhabitants, and that the community pattern shows no symbolic orientation of outstandingly privileged personnel, one tends to conclude that the internal status-and-role differentiation of the village inhabitants was not significantly developed; presumably, such distinctions as existed were based on age, sex, and personal achievement. The tenor of life seems to have been peaceful in the main, since evidence of both defensive measures and offensive weapons is scanty.

Presumably during this stage the Yangshao farmers were only beginning to become established, and the process of their expansion, within the limited region of the nuclear area and its peripheral surroundings, was largely confined to the gradual reclamation of immediately accessible and cultivable land by the descendant villages, which had split from their relatively overpopulated parent villages. Evidence from the Pan-shan hills in eastern Kansu and from a group of settlements in Hua Hsien in eastern Shensi shows that several neighboring villages shared a common cemetery, and this can best be interpreted in terms of the split-village situation rather than in terms of the formation of alliances of many discrete villages. The argument for this kind of expansion is also supported by the uniformity of style over the entire area of distribution of the Yangshao horizon. Though there were minor regional variations and two possible micro-horizons (Honan and Kansu), the stage shows striking stylistic uniformity over a wide area, as compared with the stage that was to follow.

EXPANSION OF THE HUANGHO FARMING VILLAGES AND THE FORMATION OF REGIONAL TRADITIONS

Since the transition from food-gathering to food-producing is not documented in the archeological record of north China, the consequences of the emergence of food production in the Huangho basin are not directly observable in the brief account we have presented so far; but from what followed, one is able to extrapolate and examine certain highly probable consequences.

The rate of growth of productivity brought about by the introduction of agriculture and animal husbandry can hardly be exaggerated. Two immediate consequences were the growth of population density and the potentiality for the elaboration of culture owing to the reserve energy released by surplus. Further consequences consisted of the fixity of settlements, the internal status-and-role specialization of communities, the frequency of warfare, the general spread of farming villages into the hitherto unexplored and underexplored areas, and the formation of a number of regional traditions that were synchronized in a wide-spread Lungshanoid horizon. Let us examine each of these phenomena in turn (cf. K. C. Chang, 1959a, b; T. K. Cheng, 1959; S. Y. Liang, 1939; C. Li *et al.*, 1934; Andersson, 1943, 1947).

The Lungshanoid settlements were spread over most of China proper, but they can be grouped together on the basis of stratigraphy and a horizon style that was distinctive of this stage. These horizon-markers include the following:

1. A great variety of pottery forms, particularly tripods (*li, ting, chia, kui*) and ring-footed vessels (*tsun, p'o,* and *tou* or fruit-stand). These forms characterize not only the Lungshanoid of north China but also areas far beyond it, and they may, together with scapulimancy, reflect the complexity of rituals in this stage.

2. A distinctive ceramic style. One of the most striking features of the pottery of this horizon is the sharpness of the curves on every part of the body, in great contrast to the "roundness" of the pottery shapes of the Yangshao horizon.

3. The perforated-ring feet of fruit-stands and other forms of vessels.

4. The decline of the art of ceramic painting, the increase of incisions and combed marks and the appearance of checker impressions.

5. Certain edged tools of stone, which are often square or rectangular in cross section and which have assymmetrical edges.

The ecosocial basis of these stylistic expressions is not hard to find. The Lungshanoid settlements were considerably larger than the Yangshao ones in areal dimensions and were often of longer duration. The repetitive settlement occupation pattern had given way to settled, permanent villages, as indicated by the conditions of continuous deposition, the permanent earthen village walls, the predominance of adzes and chisels (woodworking complex) over axes (for forest-clearance primarily), and the general configuration of the settlement culture, among other things. Besides noting some basis in ecology (the wet and fertile land provided by the eastern low countries into which the farmers had expanded), we are still uncertain as to the basic factors that brought about the tendency toward permanent settlement in north China as a whole. Irrigation, the use of fertilizer, the fallowing of fields, and the improvement of cultivating implements and techniques are all possible innovations of this stage, but we have no substantial evidence of any one of them. Metals might have been used to a small extent (a few metal objects have been found from a Lungshan-stage site in Kansu and from one in Hopei, and the sharp curves of pottery are suggestive of a metallic fashion), but it seems extremely unlikely that metal was used for making agricultural implements at this time. In fact, metal does not seem to have been widely employed for this purpose in ancient China until iron came into use in the middle first millennium B.C. From the little we do know about status-and-role differentiation and the presence of public works (the village wall), it is not altogether unreasonable to assume that the fixity of settlements during this stage resulted, to a certain extent, from a kind of organized management of manpower that could have achieved a greater efficiency than heretofore. But there is a good deal of speculation in this statement.

In the Huaiho valley, remains of rice and wheat grains were found in a Lungshanoid context, but it seems proper to assume that millet remained a leading staple in the north. Hoes, spades, digging-sticks, and sickles are the principal farming tools that are known archeologically; and stone, clay, bone and antler, shell and presumably wood constituted the raw materials of artifact manufacture. Livestock varieties remained unchanged, but cattle and sheep-goats may have gained in importance, and the horse may have been added at this time. Hunting and fishing were locally important. In a word, the basic technology does not seem to have undergone any considerable improvement during this stage, and the growing productivity can be accounted for only in terms of social organization and management. The significant novelty of this stage seems to lie in its increasing population density and the growth of internal specialization and differentiation among the populace.

The internal specialization and differentiation of the villages are shown by a number of indications. In several of the Lungshan traditions the potter's wheel was now in use. This, plus the fact that some of the black pottery was extremely finely and delicately manufactured, points to the fact that by this time pottery-making was already a full-time job. Metallurgy, as was suggested above, may have begun in this stage; what metallurgy implies in terms of craft specialization is common knowledge.

There is also some evidence of a differentiation of personnel in other terms at this stage. At the Liang-ch'eng-chen site in Jih-chao on the coastal Shantung, there was one spot where finely made jade objects were concentrated. Also at this settlement and at a site at Ta-ch'eng-shan near T'ang-shan in Hopei, the burials were both face up and prone, a sure indication of status differentiation, according to the Yin-Shang mode of interment. Furthermore, during this stage the art of scapulimancy appeared, seen all over north and central China in Hopei, Shantung, Honan, Shansi, Shensi, Kansu, Anhwei, and Kiangsu, which was presumably handled by a specialized class of shamans or priests. In this regard, the prevalence and variety of ceremonial vessels is highly suggestive. Taken together, such indications support the conclusion that in the Lungshanoid settlements there were specialized craftsmen, full-time administrators, and priest-shamans, and that there were also a theocratic art and a theocratically vested ceremonial pattern, which, no longer the common property of the entire village, was focused upon a selected portion of the villagers. From what we know of the later (Yin-Shang) practices, the basis of selection might have been founded on kinship.

Each of the Lungshanoid villages, however, seems to remain self-contained in the basic ecosocial and religious affairs, as indicated by the completeness of the functional network of the settlement culture. Relationships among settlements might have been more frequent than previously, but not infrequently the relationship was rather hostile and took the form of warfare. The earth walls of the Lungshanoid settlements at Hou-kang in northern Honan and at Ch'eng-tzu-yai in central Shantung appear too high and too thick to have served as decorations or boundary markers in time of peace. Arrowheads, daggers, spears, halberds, and clubs were among the offensive weapons. Skeletons were found at a site near Han-tan, Hopei, that show evidence of violent death, some having even been beheaded or scalped. This is hardly unexpected, for as population grew, taxing the land's capacity, people either reclaimed more land or fought for the field that was already available.

The transition from the Yangshao stage to the Lungshan stage seems to have started somewhere in the nuclear area (K. C. Chang, 1959a.) There are some two dozen sites now where the Lungshan-over-Yangshao-with-a-break-in-between stratigraphy has been observed, sites distributed all over the middle Huangho valley, from Kansu to northern Honan. On the other hand, in the nuclear area, in western Honan, southern Shansi, and eastern central Shensi, there are a number of sites of the transitional stage that show a mixture of the markers of both horizons, although the Yangshao markers predominate in quantity in the lower portions of the deposit, as the Lungshanoid ones do in the upper. The famed site at Yang-shao-ts'un itself, for instance, belongs to this transitional category, though for the sake of convenience the name Yangshao has been temporarily maintained for the horizon stage that preceded the Lungshan. Moreover, it is in the nuclear area that an early form of the Lungshan-stage horizon has been found (C. M. An, 1959) that seems to be the prototype from which the other peripheral Lungshanoid traditions radiated.

Following the lead of the nuclear area, the Lungshan settlers gradually developed upon the basis of the Yankshao shifting-farmer level into the entire area on the western highlands of north China. Population pressure, among other factors, might have been responsible for causing the north China farmers to spread into the formerly unexplored or underexplored riverine, lacustrine, wooded and hilly regions in the east, north, and south. The distribution of Yangshao sites indicates that the eastern plains, the Huaiho valley, and the Shantung uplands were not at this time significantly occupied by the farmers, if at all, possibly owing to the swampy environment. The Lungshan settlers, however, began to penetrate into this area and build earth mounds on which village sites were located. To the north, agricultural settlements began to appear in the southern fringes of the Jehol mountains, the Liao-Sungari plains, and the southeastern Manchurian uplands. Remains of these settlements show a clear mixture of the Lungshanoid elements and the woodland and maritime mesolithic and sub-neolithic hunting-fishing inventories.

South of the Tsinling mountains and the Huaiho valley, insofar as we know at present, evidence of agriculture and animal husbandry begins with the wide-spread appearance of the Lungshanoid horizon (K. C. Chang, 1959b). Prior to this horizon, the evidence indicates that only the southwestern portion of south China was inhabited by mesolithic food-collectors, whom some scholars have labeled the "Hoabinhian" because of the similarity of their cultural inventory to that of their Indochinese contemporaries. Subsequent to the nonceramic phase of this sheet of culture and prior to the appearance of the Lungshanoid farmers there was probably an intermediate ceramic stage, characterized by the appearance of cord-marked pottery and some polished-stone implements. These remains have been located in scatters in the southwest, on the coasts of Kwangtung, and on the island of Formosa. But evidence of both agriculture and its cultural affinities is still wanting. At any rate, the extensive exploration—at an early agricultural level—of the central and south China jungles, hills, and swampy valleys was the achievement of the Lungshanoid farmers spreading from the north. When these farmers had moved into a new ecological zone, they were forced to perform a series of important adaptive changes, which led to the predominance of rice and presumably fruit-and-root crops over millet, and the abandonment of stamped-earth structures and of lime-plastered floors. Mounds or pile-dwellings were built along the eastern coasts, and there is a generally pioneer aspect to their settlement and culture. These southern Lungshanoid farmers then began to settle down and, after receiving considerable stimulation (primarily in connection with metallurgy and decorative patterns) from the urban civilization subsequently developed in the north, a southern geometric horizon developed that was assimilated shortly before the time of Christ by the Ch'in and Han empires.

On account of the wide expanse of the area; the great environmental differences that the settlers encountered in moving into it; the hostility between settlements, with a resultant semi-isolation; and the different groups of hunter-fishers assimilated by the settlers in the new environment, the Lungshanoid horizon—although unified by its constituents' common heritage, by their similar developmental situation, and by far-reaching trade—was divided into a number of regional stylistic traditions. The most easily distinguished of these are the Honan, the Shansi-Shensi, the Kansu, the Shantung, the southern Manchurian, the Huaiho, the Hanshui, and the southeastern coastal traditions. It was with one of these regional Lungshanoid traditions (Honan, Shensi-Shansi, or Hanshui, according to different advocates) as a base that the first Chinese civilization eventually came into being.

EMERGENCE OF CIVILIZATION IN THE HUANGHO BASIN

The Lungshan horizon of the formative stage of ancient Chinese culture in the alluvial plains of the lower and middle Huangho valley and in the Huaiho valley, in the provinces of Honan, western Shantung, southwestern Hopei, eastern Shensi, northern Anhwei, and northern Kiangsu, was followed by the first civilization in Chinese history that has been amply substantiated by archeology, the Yin-Shang Dynasty (cf. C. Li, 1957; T. K. Cheng, 1957). The Yin-Shang civilization has all the essential ingredients that a civilization is supposed to contain—writing, a fully developed bronze metallurgy, palaces and temples, science and the calendar, chariots and squads of warriors, a political and religious hierarchy of a royal house, class differentiation, far-reaching trade, a centralized management and redistribution of agricultural produce and other scarce goods, and a great artistic tradition. There are two settlement groups of this period that are relatively well known archeologically, Anyang and Chengchow, both in northern Honan. Each was composed of a number of small farming and handicrafting communities, whose close ties are indicated by their clustering within eye-sight distances and their sharing of a common administrative and ceremonial center. This was Hsiao-t'un in the case of Anyang and an earth-walled town in the case of Chengchow.

The emergence of such a highly developed civilization in the Huangho basin appears to have been in itself relatively sudden and new, and most archeologists believe that there must have been a transitional period between the Lungshan and the Yin-Shang horizons. It must be stressed, however, that from the neolithic Lungshan to the bronze-age Yin-Shang there was a developmental continuation rather than a cultural break. The accompanying chart shows in a preliminary manner the neolithic heritage of the Yin-Shang bronze-age culture and its innovations (cf. S. Y. Liang, 1939; C. Li, 1957).

Continuities	Discontinuities
A. Formation of village aggregates	a) Mature urbanism and related institutions (especially the formation of differentiated groups)
B. Raids and warfare	
C. Status differentiation and prone burials	
D. The elaborate ceremonial complex (more lineage-ancestral than community-agricultural)	b) Class differentiation
	c) New government and economic patterns (conquest, tribute, redistribution)
E. Cultivation of millet, rice, kaoliang, wheat, hemp	d) Wider trade, currency
F. Use of domesticated dog, pig, cattle, sheep, horse, chicken	e) New war patterns (capture of slaves and use of the chariot)
G. Stamped-earth structures	f) Chamber burials and human sacrifice
H. Semisubterranean houses and lime-plastered floors	g) Domestication of water buffalo; possible use of wooden plow
I. Industrial specialization	h) Highly developed bronze metallurgy
J. Scapulimancy	i) Writing
K. Some pottery forms (especially ritual forms with ring-feet and lids)	j) Advanced stone carvings
L. The Shengwen (corded ware) tradition	k) New pottery forms
M. Some decorative motifs	
N. Some stone implements and weapons	
O. Shell and bone craft	
P. Silk	
Q. The jade complex	
R. Language (?)	

From the mere enumeration given in the chart it becomes apparent that in the past the "suddenness" of the emergence of the Yin-Shang civilization has been unduly exaggerated. Even the new items in the right-hand column mostly indicate a process of intensification and a change in degree. It is apparent, however, that civilization in China started with the Yin-Shang and not, as is sometimes asserted, with the Lungshan stage and that these two are decisively different. First of all, the Yin-Shang witnessed the intensifications of all aspects of Chinese culture—more advanced technology, greater population density, more intensified status-and-role differentiation, greater centralization of government and economy, more frequent warfare, and more institutionalized communication in the form of writing and trade.

The developmental change of society culture during the Yin-Shang is, furthermore, most distinctively marked off by the formation of the differentiated settlement groups and the specialization of the various settlements in a settlement group in ecosocial functions. The Lungshan communities, as previously stated, were self-contained "little communities," in spite of their sometimes large size and some degree of internal specialization and differentiation. But the Yin-Shang settlements had become specialized externally in ecosocial functions. Each community no longer worked only for its own survival and wealth, but worked for other communities and was worked for by others as well. The new horizon was marked by the appearance of centers of administration, redistribution, and ceremony, which one may call towns or cities, where officials and priests managed rather than labored. There were also farming and handicrafting hamlets, the inhabitants of which engaged in organized labor co-ordinated under a central control. This phenomenon, the ecosocial interdependence among specialized communities, is to this author one of the most decisive criteria of urbanization, which in turn was brought about by a change of the total social-cultural structure. Insofar as one can see from the archeological record of this part of the world, no single factor alone makes a civilization appear.

COMMENT

The foregoing discussion can be summarized, in a simplified fashion (Figs. 1 and 2), in stratigraphical-typological profiles cutting through most of China longitudinally and perpendicularly, respectively.

The tentative nature of the foregoing synthesis is most readily admitted. Indeed, it will be astonishing if, within a decade, new information that is now accumulating does not force an amplification and amendment of our scheme—perhaps even its drastic alteration. At the present time the scheme given above is the most we can do, but this is an attempt that has to be made if a world-wide consideration of cultural alternatives is to be made. Alfred Whitehead once observed that China "forms the largest volume of civilisation which the world has seen." Any consideration of the nature of civilization's growth in general cannot afford to leave China out, and China must be dealt with in the theoretical terms that

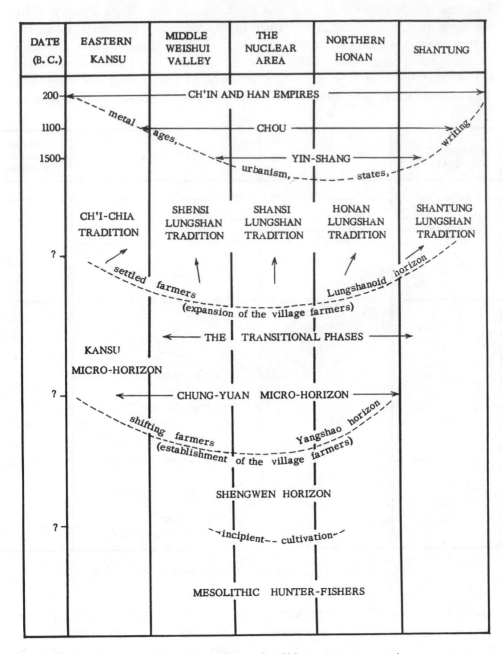

FIGURE 1. Formative cultures in China: west-east section

anthropologists all over the globe are at home with. These theoretical terms are not those of the traditional doctrine in Chinese archeology. It is the traditional viewpoint that in neolithic China (and, for some obscure reason, only in a late aspect of it) there were two (or possibly three) distinctive cultural strains. The

Yangshao (or "Painted Pottery") and the Lungshan (or "Black Pottery") are the main suggested strains, the former in the west and the latter along the eastern coast. Yin-Shang civilization was derived—the traditional viewpoint holds —from a third strain, which came to China fully developed from some source not yet fully specified. It is only now that, equipped with a good deal more data, we can begin to consider some of the major premises afresh and adopt a holistic,

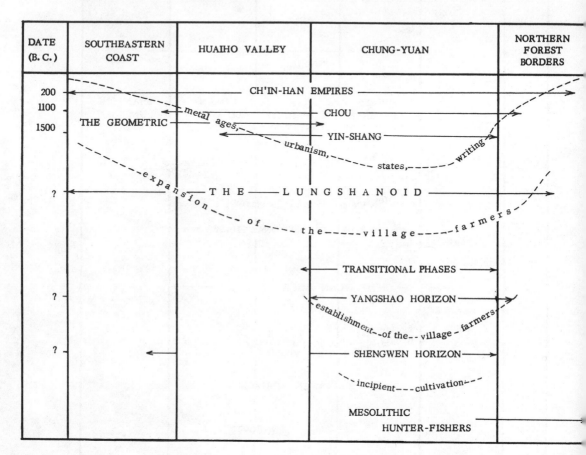

FIGURE 2. Formative cultures in China: north-south section

configurational, and functional approach that a new and probably truer picture has emerged. The prehistoric cultures in China are no longer regarded as a conglomeration of indigenous and exotic traits each of which had a separate history of development. Rather, the structural covariations and efficient causes are being stressed in terms of social mechanism and cultural pattern.

In the same manner, the problems regarding the "origins" of cultural elements in ancient China, which were the focusing point of many archeologists and sinologues, have also received some basically fresh reappraisal. The origin and history of the development of various and sundry objects are highly interesting and instructive matters, no doubt; but it is becoming clear that the basic issues of cultural and social growth do not necessarily rely upon their solutions. It is this writer's profound conviction that ancient China owed much of her riches to loans from the outside, just as many outsiders owed their riches to loans from her. But, to the writer, the important issue lies primarily in the functional context of the development sequence itself, without an understanding of which one will never understand how and why China received outside help at a certain point of time and how and why she had such things to offer in return.

BIBLIOGRAPHY

Note: For the sake of readers who do not read Chinese, the writer has given mainly references in Western languages, even though many of them are second- or thirdhand. Original sources can be located through the bibliographies of these works, particularly Loehr, Beardsley, and Chang, 1959.

AN, CHIH-MIN
1959. "Shih lun Huang-ho Liu-yü Hsin-shih-ch'i-shih-tai wen-hua" ("On the Neolithic Cultures of the Huangho Valley"). *K'ao-ku*, 1959:10:559–65. Peiping.

ANDERSSON, J. G.
1943. *"Researches into the Prehistory of the Chinese,"* Bull. Mus. Far Eastern Antiquities, No. 15. Stockholm.
1947. "Prehistoric Sites in Honan," *ibid.*, No. 19.

BOULE, M., H. BREUIL, E. LICENT, and P. TEILHARD DE CHARDIN
1928. *Le paléolithique de la Chine.* (Arch. Inst. Paléontol. Humain, Mém. 4.) Paris.

BRAIDWOOD, ROBERT J.
1952. *The Near East and the Foundation for Civilization.* Eugene, Ore.

CHANG, KWANG-CHIH
1958. "New Light on Early Man in China," *Asian Perspectives*, 2:41–61. Hong Kong.
1959a. "Chung-kuo Hsin-shih-ch'i-shih-tai wen-hua tuan-tai" ("Dating the Neolithic Cultures in China"), *Bull. Inst. Hist. and Philol., Acad. Sinica*, 30:259–309. Taipei.
1959b. "A Working Hypothesis for the Early Cultural History of South China," *Bull. Inst. Ethnol., Acad. Sinica*, 7:43–103. Taipei.

CHENG, TE-KUN
1957. "The Origin and Development of Shang Culture," *Asia Major*, n.s., 6:80–98.
1959. *Archaeology in China*, I: *Prehistoric China*. Cambridge: W. Heffer & Sons.

HSIA, NAI
1957. Our Neolithic Ancestors, *Archaeology*, 10:181–87.

LATTIMORE, OWEN
1951. *Inner Asian Frontiers of China.* ("Amer. Geog. Soc., Res. Ser.," No. 21.) 2d ed. New York.

LI, CHI
1957. *The Beginnings of Chinese Civilization.* Seattle: Washington University Press.

LI, CHI, et al.

1934. Ch'eng-tzu-yai. KENNETH STARR (trans.). ("Yale Univ. Publs. in Anthrop.," No. 52.) New Haven.

LIANG, SSU-YUNG

1939. "The Lungshan Culture: A Prehistoric Phase of Chinese Civilization," Proc. 6th Pacific Sci. Cong., 4:69–79.

LOEHR, MAX, RICHARD K. BEARDSLEY, and KWANG-CHIH CHANG

1959. COWA Bibliography, Area 17—Far East, No. 1. Cambridge: Council for Old World Archaeology.

MOVIUS, HALLAM L., JR.

1944. Early Man and Pleistocene Stratigraphy in Southern and Eastern Asia. (Papers Peabody Mus., Harvard Univ., No. 19.) Cambridge.

1955. "Palaeolithic Archaeology in Southern and Eastern Asia, Exclusive of India," Cahiers d'Histoire Mondiale, 2:257–82, 520–53. Neuchâtel.

PEI, WEN-CHUNG

1939. An Attempted Correlation of Quarternary Geology, Palaeontology and Pre-history in Europe and China. ("Inst. Archaeol., Univ. London, Occ. Papers," No. 2.) Geochronological Table No. 1, pp. 3–16.

SAUER, CARL O.

1948. "Environment and Culture during the Last Deglaciation," Proc. Amer. Phil. Soc., 92:65-77.

TEILHARD DE CHARDIN, P.

1941. Early Man in China. (Inst. Géo-Biol., Pékin, Publ. 7.)

TEILHARD DE CHARDIN, P., and WEN-CHUNG PEI

1944. Le Néolithique de la Chine. (Inst. Géo-Biol., Pékin, Publ. 10.)

WARD, LAURISTAN

1954. The Relative Chronology of China through the Han Period. In R. W. EHRICH (ed.), Relative Chronologies in Old World Archaeology. Chicago: University of Chicago Press.

WU, G. D.

1938. Prehistoric Pottery in China. London: Kegan Paul.

THE FIRST GROUND-PLAN OF AN UPPER PALEOLITHIC
LOESS SETTLEMENT IN MIDDLE EUROPE
AND ITS MEANING

BOHUSLAV KLÍMA

T HE PROBLEMS chosen for discussion by the 1960 symposium sponsored by the Wenner-Gren Foundation for Anthropological Research are of great concern for many investigators interested in the remotest history of man and human society. These problems may be subsumed under the single question: What is prehistoric archeology able to tell us about the origin and genesis of urban civilizations? The specialized literature actually only hints at such considerations, although new finds and many excavations of recent years would seem to present deeper understanding and perhaps broader generalizations concerning some part of the problem. These hints are only partial because they stem, on the one hand, from the hesitation of some investigators to publish such evaluations, though new material is at their disposal; or, on the other hand, from the fact that other authors feel the need to answer such questions, even on the basis of preliminary and fragmentary publications, but are not able to utilize such sources to the necessary extent without the direct and thorough knowledge that proved evidence would offer. We may assume with justification that these were the considerations that not only urged taking into account the latest discoveries and opinions, so that a new general historical idea of the period under study might be formed, but, further, made apparent the need for direct and open exchange of ideas as well as general discussion. In view of these facts, we must express our gratitude to the originators and organizers of this symposium.

The archeologists of the Czechoslovak Socialist Republic have been dealing with these questions for a considerable length of time. Up to now, the investigations have been performed less along theoretical lines than by excavations. Excavations constitute the major part of the first task in the long-range scientific planning of investigations by the Archeological Institute of the Czechoslovak Academy of Sciences in its search for the "transition from the non-productive to the productive form of economy" as laid down by Jaroslav Böhm. We propose to concentrate on the deeper understanding of the highest non-productive forms of economy in order to elicit the motivations and conditions that initiated the transitions from hunting and gathering economies in the upper paleolithic to the oldest forms of agricultural production during the neolithic, that is, to productive economy. For some years now, our field surveys have been oriented toward these problems, and we may point to a certain amount of success in this area. Credit for this success must go especially to the proper directives and assumptions of

Böhm, who foresaw the future development of a specialized profession, attesting not only its useful possibilities but also the actual demand and need for planned excavation and scientific effort. It is, however, necessary to provide an exact and theoretical evaluation of the results of the sites studied so far, and this contribution will attempt to give an outline for such considerations.

This paper differs from the other essays to a certain extent, especially since it does not offer a survey of social development in the Czechoslovakian region. In that respect, it will be restricted to a few observations and to a table of changes of settlement patterns. Basically, it will not differ very much from the paper that Pittioni has prepared for this occasion. As far as Pittioni deals with the questions of the neolithic in Central Europe, he agrees basically with conclusions drawn by Tichý from his most recent excavations at Mohelnice and Žopy in Moravia showing spiral-meander and Moravian-style painted pottery. Pittioni also agrees with the insights gained by Soudsky from the extensive excavations at Bylany near Prague and, to a degree, with the ideas of Neústupný. The latter studies assume an earlier date for the beginning of the neolithic and have the support of radiocarbon determinations. The genetic interconnections and the many gaps in the development have, however, not yet been explained. With regard to the origin of our oldest spiral-meander pottery, most of our scientists tend to assume a southeastern European provenance. To date, however, they lack sufficient indications to prove a graded development from a mesolithic base. Only a few indications point toward autochthonous development in our area, such as, for instance, the flint industry of Žopy, which was found with spiral-meander pottery in one of the oldest phases.

Also connected with the earliest spiral-meander ware is the appearance of productive economy, that is, agriculture and animal husbandry. Nevertheless, we may observe in the late paleolithic assemblages that greater attention was already given to the vegetal portion of the environment, and we may assume a large proportion of vegetal food in the nutrition of man. Neolithic settlements, supervening in considerable density over the sporadic ones of the mesolithic, must be considered revolutionary.

Quite remarkable insight has been gained during the last few years in Czechoslovakia concerning the mesolithic period. Even shortly after World War II we possessed no reliable evidence of mesolithic settlements. Only through extensive exploration of the terrain have we recovered finds of microlithic industries of this mesolithic level. Those known up to now are, however, mere hints as to the actual incidence of settlement and cannot, therefore, be made a base for broad conclusions as yet. Some facts, however, as indicated by Mazálek and Žebera, as well as by Pittioni(this volume), make it apparent that it will be possible to trace a development from a magdalenoid Gravettian milieu and to demonstrate contemporaneity—in the late phase—of geometric microlithic industries with the earliest phases of the ceramic neolithic.

It will certainly be relevant to the solution of problems concerning the origins of urban civilization if we direct our attention to the upper paleolithic, that is, as much as 10,000 years before the major time focus of this symposium. The reason is that in settlements of this period we can already find traces and first indications of certain settlement plans, their total configuration, and—in favorable cases—even the *in situ* connection and relationship between the artifacts themselves and the surrounding settlement setting.

There are in Czechoslovakia some exceedingly important stations of the late paleolithic, which—by their geographical location alone—occupy a key position for the geological-stratigraphic, anthropogeographical, and archeological synchronism between western and eastern Europe. Thus these sites have become objects of systematic excavation and concentrated attention. Their contribution to the given theme lies chiefly in showing the forms, manner of construction, and interior arrangement of houses and huts, as well as the over-all arrangement of the settlement. We shall occupy ourselves primarily with considerations of this order.

The earliest discovery of a paleolithic settlement in the foregoing sense in central Europe was reported by Zotz in 1942, at Moravany near Piešťany; but as early as 1932 Böhm had investigated a distinct hut outline on the Gravettian station of Lubná near Rakovník—for which there is a detailed report in the archives of the Archeological Institute of the Czechoslovak Academy of Sciences in Prague. Finally, a few remaining traces of the cultural layers at Dolní Věstonice, as well as dispersed finds, hearths, and other circumstances, all attest to the fact that at this site, in the 1920's, Absolon was actually investigating the remnants and contents of such a hut settlement. However, since the residue of the roofs of these huts was destroyed and the whole situation poorly preserved, he was unable to distinguish reliably their foundations.

Extensive excavations have been carried on at different sites since 1948 within the framework of the general plan. The plan itself had immediately led to some notable discoveries of habitation sites at several locations. Besides fixed encampments, such as Ražice and Děravá jeskyně in Bohemia, as well as Tibava, Barca, and Seňa in Slovakia, there were the localities of Petřkovice, Gottwaldov, and, especially, Pavlov and Dolní Věstonice. The results of the latest work at the well-known encampment of late paleolithic mammoth-hunters in the Pollau Mountains at Dolní Věstonice in southern Moravia have already been so thoroughly studied that we may discuss them in some detail.

Systematic excavations at this important late paleolithic station enable us especially to solve the problems of the total configuration of the settlement, which formerly in great measure was attributed to one unified cultural level. Intensive study of a sizable number of profiles at various locations within the investigated area resulted in the establishment of three main phases of slippage, when larger or smaller sections of the ground shifted on the slope within the station. In connection with these earth movements, four characteristic main settlement phases could be defined. These settlements seemed to be gradually moved upward along the hillside, apparently because of changed locations of the water supply.

Within the loess layers of the station at Dolní Věstonice there are, then, several encampments to be found—that is, at least four separate settlements, which are connected by common development. To this may be added other encampments in the Pollau Mountains, of which only the settlements at Milovice in the brickyard near Dolní Věstonice and, more particularly, the notable settlement at Pavlov could be verified and explored by excavation. The occupation of

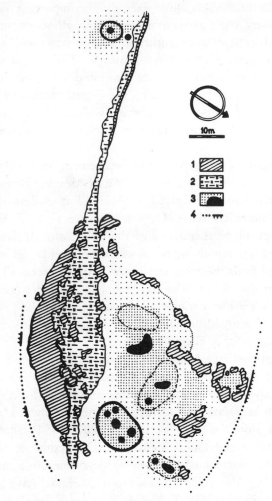

FIGURE 1. Plan of the upper paleolithic settlement in the upper part of the station at Dolní Věstonice. *1*, Bone deposits; *2*, water course; *3*, remains of the living settlement with hearths (black) and lines of the hut-plan borders; *4*, edge of the solifluxed soil layer.

the hillsides of the Pollau Mountains thus was of considerable duration, as proved also by stratigraphic evidence: it extended from the beginning of the Interstadial W 2–3 into the period of turbulent solifluction at the base of the youngest loess (Würm 3). Recently, the duration of the settlement has also been expressed in an absolute number of years—29,000–24,000 years, as determined by radiocarbon.

Gro 2598 Dolní Věstonice—western wall of brickyard   28,900 ± 350
Gro 2092 Dolní Věstonice—eastern wall of brickyard   28,000 ± 380
Gro 1286 Dolní Věstonice upper part of station   25,600 ± 170
Gro 1325 Pavlov paleolithic station   24,800 ± 150

Geological and economic conditions obviously enforced a change of camp location upon the inhabitants after a given length of time. It is likely that this change of location took place within relatively short distances and remained within the same natural setting; although this does not preclude the idea that the matrilinial kin groups may have left the flanks of the Pollau Mountains for grave reasons (unknown to us), only to return after a given time to light their hearths once again. The character of the settlement strata excludes the possibility of seasonal nomadism in connection with game migration.

Settlement was, then, basically continuous. Within its enclosed geographical boundaries this development constitutes a localized Gravettian grouping that in certain traits and individual and characteristic elements differs from the nearby eastern Gravettian, although the local Gravettian must be counted within the generalized eastern sphere. For these reasons it would be possible to propose a separate designation for this independent group. The auxiliary working term "Pavlovian" may be suggested, since the essential development in all its manifold expressions may be traced particularly in the Pollau Mountain settlements and, especially, at the station of Pavlov.

The material culture of the Pavlovian is characterized by a rich, highly developed lithic industry tending in the direction of the microlithic and having geometrically regular forms and composite tools. The industry is uncommonly rich and principally derived from narrow blades. It shows a marked florescence of Gravettian elements, especially in various blades with blunted backs, as well as in notched and denticulated blades; in addition, there are small triangles, numerous sickles of different kinds, chisels, points, and other tools, rarely also with surface retouch at the base; besides this, there is a rich, coarse industry. Tools and hunting implements of bone or mammoth ivory also attain remarkable perfection. These appear in the form of awls, needles, punches, knives, smaller or larger points or javelin heads, pointed mammoth ribs for lances, powerful mace heads, and shovel-shaped tools and hoes of reindeer antler. This brief inventory of working implements is complemented by numerous finds that may be classified as ornamental but that also have deeper significance in connection with primitive religious concepts. Among these are a number of pendants and composite necklaces (animal teeth, shells, pebbles, etc.), clasps and headbands of mammoth ivory with incised ornamental patterns, and, finally, artistic expressions—especially in the form of animal figures, among which relief carvings in mammoth-ivory and small figurines of baked clay are particularly noteworthy.

In the most recent excavations the greatest attention was devoted to the higher portions, that is, the latest settlement phases within the area of the Dolní Věstonice site. This is precisely the portion pictured by Absolon in three reports concerning the results of the first excavations in 1924–26, which up to now have conveyed the idea of a basically uniform paleolithic settlement.

The new excavations were executed by the surface removal method, and this made possible, as early as 1947–49, the discovery and investigation of the first hut plan of the settlement. Its remarkably large ground plan (9 × 15 meters), the modest remains of the structure that were to be found within the limits of the excavation, and numerous pieces of limestone indicate that we are dealing with a tent-like, roofless summer hut. We assume that the base was of post-and-rubble construction. The walls were formed of animal skins, which in places may have continued on up to form a roof. The ground plan of the hut contained five hearths in regular distribution. This also speaks against a continuous roof structure. The enclosed lenticular cultural layer was restricted to the interior area of the hut plan and faded out beyond its confines. Since this area contained a significant quantity of implements of production, tools and weapons of stone, bone, and mammoth ivory, as well as ornamental objects, one may view these remains as truly those of an actual habitation and working site.

An extensive deposit of mammoth bones extended in close to the hut. Probes and a series of drillings established this to be a shallow, moist depression in the open terrain where discarded, unutilized bones were swallowed up by the mud A stream flowed through the center of the space. At their densest, the bones were packed and piled up to the extent of 12 × 45 meters. The contents of this assemblage, judged by the quantity of bone found over the excavated area, has been estimated to represent the remains of about one hundred, mostly young, mammoths. From this concentration we gain a certain idea of the extent and duration of the settlement. At the same time, we may accept it as eloquent evidence of the productivity of collective, well-organized hunting, as well as of the fact that the inhabitants of this encampment must have formed an economic entity, an organization for collective production.

Close scrutiny of the bone deposits proved that similar aggregations of animal bones accumulated as large waste heaps in direct relationship with and proximity to habitations. Smaller deposits of selected kinds of bones within the settlement area proper constitute building materials and fuel or are remnants of separate habitations. They may also be the remains of protective walls at the outer margin of the settlement. More often, we find, entirely within the bone heaps, remains of fires not contained by the prepared hearths but lit at ground level and fed chiefly by bone fuel. It seems likely that they had a purely defensive function against the predatory animals that were certain to have scavenged discarded food remnants on the bone heaps. Most of the bones were piled up within the swampy bottom of a depression in the terrain, which was readily filled up by flooding and solifluction. In higher locations, at the rim of the depression, bone is found that has been broken into small fragments and splinters. This was certainly done for the purpose of extracting marrow. But it is very probable that many more of the bones were broken open in connection with various magical customs—

seemingly to assure success in the hunt—than were broken for the removal of marrow.

In 1951 we investigated a second hut, located up higher on the slope. The well-preserved remains and grading of the circular ground plan, 6 meters in diameter, permitted us to form a very exact conception of the complete room construction. The floor was dug into the slope at one side, where it was re-tained by means of a wall of large pieces of limestone, especially selected and laid in regular courses. In this wall stones also formed the sheathing of vertical post holes; the roof structure spanned the distance from the slope to the posts. This habitation may be regarded as a well-built earth lodge with a sunken en-tranceway, belonging to the category of so-called "winter houses." It differs from similar ones particularly by the complete and well-preserved construction, as well as by the unique assemblage found within. In the interior of the hut we located only a minor quantity of the usual artifacts and hunting weapons or other means of production, which—in considerable quantity—occurred only out-side this space and even then in smaller quantity than was usual at Věstonice. In the interior we discovered some transversely cut, hollow bones—possibly musical instruments. Furthermore, in the center of the hut a most unusual bake oven appeared. This oven was made of hard, marly soil mixed with ground lime-stone (similar to the wall-like ring around the hut) in such a way that the raised body of the oven reached around the dug-out hearth, even overhanging it like a dome on one side. Its sooty deposit, which attests complete combustion, con-tained more than 2,300 small fired lumps of clay, which could be sorted into groups of numerous small heads, feet, and other fragments of animal figurines, small lumps of various shapes, and even some that retained the imprint of the papillary ridges of the fingers and hands of their creators. Their state of preserva-tion did not, however, permit a more precise classification. Thus was discovered in the paleolithic stratum a bake-oven-like shape, a predecessor of later potters' kilns, which served for the hardening and firing of the oldest known ceramic productions of man. This is a distinctive feature of the settlements of mammoth-hunters at the foot of the Pollau Mountains. One cannot deny the impression that this second unit within the settlement has a special significance.

While in recent years we uncovered some isolated huts and considered these finds and their conscientious study a great success, Soviet scientists have out-distanced us by far. At the same time that we were receiving sporadic reports about the habitation sites at Fourneau-du-Diable and that the earth lodge of Lang-mannersdorf was being discovered, Soviet scientists surprised us with the dis-covery of huts at the stations of Gagarino, Kostjenki, and Buret, while at the same time they were also engaged in the excavation and investigation of whole settlement sites. They were, indeed, able to offer the first complete picture of entire hunting encampments at Kostjenki I (upper stratum) and Avdějevo, be-sides other complete houses from the lower stratum of Kostjenki IV. And recently even very numerous remnants of separate huts with almost entirely preserved and quite unmistakable remains of roof construction have appeared (Mezin). All this is available not only from the upper paleolithic but even from the far older Molodovo V–Mousterian.

We should not like to let this opportunity go by without attempting the reconstruction of such a settlement in our milieu. The knowledge that we gained at our most recent excavations in the Pollau Mountains, and more specifically at the settlement of Pavlov, explains in a reliable manner circumstances obtaining at earlier investigations near Dolní Věstonice. When we combine these elements as they are reconstructed from Absolon's published reports with the results of our excavations in the upper portions of the paleolithic site at Dolní Věstonice, we achieve a well-rounded and vivid impression of an "urgemeinschaftlichen" settlement with many accompanying articles and manifestations.

The upper part of the site of Dolní Věstonice constitutes an independent unit of settlement, which is situated on a projecting tongue of land. Its boundary utilizes the morphology of the terrain, which was notably unaffected by secondary movements, such as short-range slippage. The axis of the settlement is formed by a stream bed that widens out into an elongated depression with quiet water in a very swampy environment. This also forms one margin of the settled area; the second boundary is formed by a rise that also extends in the longitudinal direction of the slope, separating this settlement unit from the earlier locations and settled places at the lower portion of the site. In the lower portion, also, a broader valley and fan-shaped earth movements are indicated, which had destroyed and dispersed the extinguished hearths and ruined habitations. The upper part of the station lies on a ridge that gives a good view over the valley and the entire scene, which in that climatically cold period may have resembled a tundra and cold steppe.

On the basis of published documentary material we may make the serious assumption that the massive remains of the cultural layers and, at times, the gentle depressions with two hearths in the sectors investigated by Absolon indicate the tent-huts of the settlements of matrilineal kin groups of the Puškari type. The great fire in the space between the two perhaps constitutes a common central fire maintained in an open place by the primal community. The ashes of this fireplace attain a depth of 100 centimeters. In these ashes was found the well-known female figurine, the Venus of Wisternitz (Věstonice), the symbol of the "urmutter," preserver of the kin group and protectress of the common economic existence.

The winter huts seemed to be complemented by and alternated with larger ones—that is, summer habitations with several hearths—which were, however, not provided with roofs. The first settlement, uncovered in 1947–49, belongs in this category. However, one cannot suppose that reconstruction took place with seasonal regularity; rather, the roof constructions collapsed and were replaced by new ones. In their collapse the hut remains were covered over, the cultural layer grew, and the superseding horizon disturbed the lower layers in the foundation. Hence it has previously been impossible to ascertain and circumscribe the exact ground plan.

The margin of the settled area is covered by mammoth bones, which are spread over a considerable area. Groups of sorted bones constitute building materials; others store fuel. In places mammoth tusks were rammed into the ground to form—in conjunction with brush fill—simple defensive walls, beyond which all signs of habitation are absent. The circular deposit that encircles the cultural layer diverges from the margin line of the western part of the settlement area and seems to be built up of the remains of a collapsed and abandoned hut. Smaller concentrations of bones and a coarse industry by the edge of the stream suggest places where game was dissected into large pieces and where the skins were worked. In the swampy basin the primal community of hunters gradually built up over the duration of the long settlement the extensive accumulation mentioned above.

Such observations, even if they be in part reconstruction, lead inevitably to reflections concerning the social order and its structure. Through convincing arguments and especially on the basis of ethnographic material, we may assume that one of our hut types was the habitation of a consanguineally interrelated social-territorial unit: the matrilineal kin group. Five or six such related matrilineal kin groups formed the primal community of the settlement. With this in mind, we might consider that the mass grave at Předmostí may represent the members of such a matrilineal kin group. Second, considering ethnographic parallels and the quantity of game represented in our settlement, we arrive at the conclusion that a hut housed 20–25 persons and that the primal community numbered about 100–120 members.

All the members of the primal community formed a single indivisible economic unit, a common production organization. Only this type of formation would have been capable of assembling a group sufficiently numerous and strong, given the then available means of production, to secure the enormous hunting yield attested by the vast bone accumulation. The formation is also attested by the very fact that a mighty pachyderm like the mammoth could be conquered at all and that its dissected parts could be transported to the settlement. This explanation, derived from an interpretation of the upper portions of the station at Dolní Věstonice, essentially agrees with the generally accepted image of the life in the permanent settlements of the upper paleolithic.

The interpretation of our particular site is, however, somewhat complicated by the existence of the second hut type, mentioned above. This is so not only because of its advanced type of construction or its cultural contents but, especially, because of its unusual and strange location in the settlement complex. The single example of the second hut type was completely isolated from the remainder of the settled area and had been erected 80 meters higher up the slope, adjacent to the inlet at the upper end of the flooded depression. In view of the previous description of the finds (see above), this habitation cannot be considered as the usual settlement unit or residential building. It must rather be regarded as a place where small animal figurines were manufactured of baked clay, that is, a workshop for the production of objects for magical practices and the home of a specialized craftsman and his kin group.

But, whose hut was this that was so differentiated from all the other huts? Who produced the religious objects that bespeak a well-developed sense of observation, dexterity in the working of clay, and artistic expression? Who was this person, and why did he withdraw into solitude and seclusion? An answer would be very simple if such a situation were discovered in a much more recent settlement, where under certain socioeconomic conditions the existence of a shaman or other specialized manipulator of primitive religious rites might be demonstrated within an advanced productive system and on a higher developmental step of religious concepts. In earlier phases of kin-group communities such a function could, apparently—according to some authors—be exercised by the chief of a maternal kin group, although only on the occasion of the most important ceremonies and feasts that were communally celebrated. Normal activities and everyday magical customs and sorcery were practiced by each for himself.

Conclusions of this kind come to us most usually from ethnography. Occasionally, however, we encounter archeological material in which human forms are depicted garbed in animal skins and in masks—thus in such garments as are used by shamans and sorcerers of backward peoples. It is customary to interpret such archeological material along ethnographic lines. Possibly we can interpret our own finds in such a way that our second hut type in the settlement of Věstonice would be the dwelling of the older selected members of the kin group or of the chief of the primal community. Or perhaps it was, rather, the home of the predecessor of later sorcerers—a person who possessed the power to perform certain actions and had attained considerable dexterity in the course of their execution. In the course of magical practices he threw broken animal figurines and the results of abortive attempts at clay sculpture into the bake-oven-like structure at the center of the hut. The more successful figurines served religious purposes for an extended time. At dry, raised locations within the area of the deposits, he, jointly with other members of the community, performed magical ceremonies for the benefit of the hunt, as they were also performed, according to the opinion of Boriskovskij, at a similar deposit of bones of the European aurochs at the site of Amvrosievka. These ceremonies were probably not too different from those performed before the animal pictures and other artistic forms in the caves of western Europe. Single bones representing entire animals seem to have been intentionally broken at these ceremonies.

The latest excavations produced some problematical evidence about a certain practice at the primitive religious ceremonies. In 1948 we discovered in the first hut a human face engraved on a small tablet of mammoth ivory that was totally different in technique of production as well as in representational expression from the small female head (sculptured in perfect three-dimensional form) found by Absolon in 1936 at Dolní Věstonice. Our find follows a simple scheme and gives the impression of a caricature or mask as it might be used at cultic ceremonies. Both objects have, however, one thing in common. The asymmetrical left facial halves, reminiscent of slack features, may be thought to be indications of total debility of the menetic muscles and a clear evidence of a peripheral paralysis of the left facial nerve. This had already been pointed out by Keith (1937) when he described Absolon's find.

It is therefore quite remarkable that the female whose strongly flexed gracile skeleton we found in 1949 under two mammoth scapulae, below the level of the cultural stratum near the edge of the first settlement unit, also showed a defect of the left half of the face. Her head and chest had been sprinkled with red ocher; in her fist she held canines of a polar fox and a skeletal portion of the same animal; and near her head was a flint point—a typical example of funerary rites of religious character in the upper paleolithic. Physical anthropologists agree that pathological processes that involve the left maxillary joint could cause peripheral paralysis of the nerves of the cheek, thereby producing deformation of the entire left half of the skull and apparently also of the facial morphology.

Could these three seemingly disconnected finds be connected with an actual person? Three such expressive and quite explicit elements tend, to a certain extent, to rule out coincidence. On the other hand, it is possible and necessary to engage in deeper considerations. It seems that in both representations the artist was endeavoring to capture the physiognomy of an actual person. For fuller understanding we strengthen this explanation by comparison with a similar burial at Brno noted by Francouzská in 1891, where only a caricaturized male figurine was added. Both instances apparently constitute graves of important members of a society who engaged in magical rituals. In any event, the woman interred in the grave at Dolní Věstonice (DV-III-1949) was of small stature, and her delicate appearance was certainly in contrast with the representation of the pregnant female and "urmutter." On the other hand, however, the disfigured face of the woman in the grave marked her for ritual practices as if she had been "born" for them.

If the woman in the grave filled an important role in the cultic activities of the community, she was a direct participant in religious practices. We may also suppose that she would be symbolically represented, as were the protagonists in the woman-cult of the female leaders of the kin group. Her faithful depiction was achieved by one of her contemporaries of the settlement represented by the lower portion of the site (which includes the burial below the spot where we encountered the first hut). Some generations later, in the upper part of the settlement, she was depicted a second time but now in an entirely different manner (as she was now known only in traditional memory) as a ritual mask for ceremonies. She might also (in life) have functioned as a ceremonial practitioner or assistant, who gave explanations of everyday occurrences through mimicry, gestures, or vocal utterances.

We may therefore assume that in the open sites of the upper paleolithic there took place the same complex religious ceremonials that were performed before the excellent paintings, engravings, and animal sculptures of the western European caves. Selected individuals of the primal communities seem to have dedicated themselves to such ceremonials. Some of the established facts, furthermore, raise the question whether or not the finds at Dolní Věstonice represent a first indication of social differentiation that in later times led to the specialization of independent sorcerers, who lived at the expense of other members of the settlement. It is, of course, possible that, as with the Chukchi—where women were better acquainted with all ceremonial concerns and cults than were men—women assumed as "guardians of the fire" the care for sanctified objects. Furthermore, the domestic magic of women was credited with greater power and force than were the hunting efforts of the men on the tundra. At the lower phases of economic and social development, cultic concerns were also women's tasks.

It is natural that we should be able to discern, in the optimal conditions of this natural setting of prehistoric development, an ever accelerating expansion and perfection of the implements of production. This trend is also quite regularly reflected in finds representing the spiritual plane. These generally valid facts attain special significance in the upper paleolithic. In certain regions there always arises a concentration of settlement, whether at one specific locality or within an entire area of settlement, where developments outdistance their surroundings. Quantitative elements accrue and predispose toward a qualitative jump. But even this cannot occur so rapidly that it would prevent tracing the gradual changes, which are surely accompanied by a series of contradictions. And is it not exactly the coherent settlement on the slopes of the Pollau Mountains that allows one to recognize direct manifestations and primitive beginnings of such a gradual qualitative transformation. A variety of important experiences may be observed here. Among these are sedentism; evidence of the construction and arrangement of well-built semisubterranean habitations; certain very effective weapons and tools, as well as implements for working the ground, which tell of increasing contributions to the diet through collecting activities; and the knowledge of modeling and of firing clay, as well as the grinding of stone. All these were important experiences and conditions, which we were here able to observe at a very early time. However, they showed little further development and only much later pointed directly toward the cultivation of grain, and so signified the way to the transition to productive agriculture. Under the conditions of the cold period that accompanied the end of the last glaciation these forces were not capable of gaining the ascendancy and became effective only when climatic circumstances had become much more favorable, and so made possible the earliest cultivation.

As early as the upper paleolithic we meet with open-air sites in the loess regions, where life had been governed and directed by regularized custom and strict organization of a highly developed hunting and collecting economy and where are shown some economic and social traits foreshadowing later forms of existence in the settlements of the early agriculturalists. Larger settlements, with more

numerous inhabitants, could grow, however, only under conditions of further
increased productivity and yield, at which time more explicit and defined tribal
organizations resulted. We can perhaps take the indications and early origins
of the latter as the attributes that could have led to the delimitation of independent
cultural entities in the late paleolithic.

Southern Moravia is, without doubt, one of the important regions where such
a rapid advance and progress in the culture of the primal community took place.
We thus assign to it a characteristic position and, for this reason, evoke the

FIGURE 2. Engraving of a plant
on a small rod of mammoth ivory,
Pekarna cave near Brno, Scale 1:1.

special designation "Pavlovian." It cannot be doubted that this advanced cultural
grouping played an important role in the great historical transformation from a
non-productive to a productive economy as well as in the shaping of further developments of man in Europe.

We have attempted to offer some findings and ideas as a Czechoslovakian contribution to the open discussion of the seminar concerning what prehistoric archeology can, at this juncture, say about the development and origins of urban
civilization, in the sense that constitutes the subject matter of the symposium. If
we considered this on a broader basis, we might be able to move away from some
of the, up to now, rather rigid views and interpretations. We shall, however,
have to await further results; our later work at the sites, especially those at the
foot of the Pollau Mountains, gives cause for expectation and will, it is hoped,
prove productive.

RÉSUMÉ

This contribution is restricted, as a survey of social development in the area of the ČSSR, to a listing of changes in the forms of settlements. Otherwise it would not be very different from Pittioni's paper. To the extent that Pittioni deals with questions of the neolithic in central Europe, his conclusions agree with those of the Czechoslovakian investigators who, in their most recent work, have assumed an earlier dating for the beginnings of the neolithic on the basis of radiocarbon determinations. However, many genetic relationships and gaps in development are not yet clarified. Regarding the origin of the oldest spiral-meander pottery, most of the Czechoslovakian scientists prefer to assume a southeast European provenance. To date, specific evidence is lacking that would indicate a continuous development on a mesolithic basis. The appearance of food production, agriculture, and animal husbandry is tied to the oldest spiral-meander pottery. Nevertheless, even in the late paleolithic we may observe that increased attention was being paid to the flora and may assume a greater share of vegetal food in the diet of man. Since neolithic settlements appear in considerable density, in comparison with the sporadic distribution of mesolithic ones, we may regard the change as revolutionary. Only in recent years has reliable evidence been gathered for the mesolithic period. These finds of microlithic industries constitute, however, no more than the faint traces of the actual sites of settlement and hence cannot yet be made the foundation for broader conclusions. Some facts show, nevertheless, that it will apparently be possible to trace their development from a Magdalenian-Gravettian milieu and, in later phases, to demonstrate the simultaneity of geometric microlithic industries with the earliest phases of the ceramic neolithic.

Besides isolated remnants of older hut constructions, excavations of paleolithic sites during recent years have produced the first ground plans of complete settlements. These, in conjunction with recognized connections and relationships between various living units, can certainly lead to understanding important for the reconstruction of economic situations and the structured organization of the primal community. In some especially favorable cases, they may lead even to the understanding of specific magical ceremonies. Thus, it would be of interest, for the solution of problems concerning the beginnings of urban civilization, if we would direct our attention more closely to this time period.

In this respect the most recent investigations at Dolní Věstonice have led to very important understandings. Through extensive study of the stratigraphic situation, the character of the over-all layout of the site could be established. Solifluction caused here a gradual relocation of the settlements upslope. Four clearly defined phases were outlined here, representing independent settlements, which, however, were related by common development, although differing somewhat in time and stratigraphic content. Together with other known encampments of this period, these exemplify continuous and permanent settlement and constitute a locally characteristic group of the eastern Gravettian-Pavlovian.

During our latest work the greatest attention has been given to the most recent phases in the upper portion of the site. Here, on the basis of newer understandings, we were able to interpret findings of Absolon's earlier excavations. The upper portion of the station is situated on solifluxed ground, the axis of which forms a watercourse. On the left flank of this shallow depression were erected tent-like huts of oval ground plan with two hearths built along the longitudinal axis. These huts were complemented by summer huts when necessary. In the center of the settlement was the large central hearth in which, in 1925, the well-known female statuette of the Venus of Věstonice was discovered. Since, during the span of the settlement, the habitations had been rebuilt many times and their traces as well as the ground plan had been disturbed, it had formerly been impossible to differentiate between them.

The swampy depression (12 × 45 meters) was filled with extensive accumulations of mammoth bones, coming from more than one hundred predominantly young animals. This dump heap indicates great productivity, by means of well-organized collective hunting, and also shows that the inhabitants of the settlement must have formed a communal production organization—the primal community. Smaller groupings of arranged bones represent structural remains of huts and fuel stores. The extensive deposits at the periphery of the settled area represent the remnants of simple ramparts, which apparently served the same protective function as the simple fire locations at the edge of the large dumps—that is, defense against wild animals.

Such findings also force us, with the aid of ethnographic materials, to give some thought to the organization and composition of the society. It may be assumed that each hut was the home of a social unit, a matrilineal kin group of about 20–25 members. If 5–6 huts were built in the settlement at one given time, the primal community may have reached a population of 100–120. This picture agrees essentially with the generally accepted views concerning life in the hunting encampments of the upper paleolithic.

In 1951 and 1952 we studied the well-preserved remains of a circular hut, about 6 meters in diameter. Its floor was sunk into the hillside and bounded on the opposite side by a stone retaining wall. By its advanced construction, by its contents, as well as by its isolated position—that is, 80 meters from the main settlement area—it differed materially from the other units. It yielded only a few implements of production, but in a bake-oven-like structure in the center of the hut a great quantity of baked lumps of clay was found. Among these there were several small modeled lumps, heads, numerous feet, and other fragments of animal figurines and even some that showed the impression of the fingers and hands of the artist. The hut seemed to be a workshop for the devising of magical articles. It was doubtless also the quarters of their producer, who was perhaps even the protagonist of common religious rites of the primal community and some sort of precursor of the later shamans. The magical ceremonies, which were centered in the hunting cult, were probably performed on raised portions of the massive deposits in a manner similar to that at the station of Amvrosievka. At these ceremonies separate bones, representing entire animals, were broken into small fragments.

The problem of primitive religious rites presents itself in the form of artifacts. From the first hut came a small tablet of mammoth ivory bearing an engraved human face. It created the impression of a ceremonial mask and was essentially quite different from the small female head of 1936. Both objects, however, have asymmetrical left facial halves, reminiscent of slack features and indicative of peripheral paralysis of the left facial nerve. It is therefore definitely worth noting that the strongly flexed and remarkably gracile female skeleton that we discovered in 1949 under two mammoth scapulae showed the defective left half of the skull as well as, apparently, the deformed soft portions of the face consequent upon a pathological process. This agreement of the three finds almost necessitates the conclusion that all referred to the same person: a delicate woman with a deformed face, an immediate participant at ritual ceremonies.

This sketch of the integrated unity of the paleolithic station at Dolní Věstonice clearly shows that as early as this period we find an advanced hunting and collecting life, with economic and social features that remind us of life so much later in the settlements of the earliest agriculturalists. The Pavlovian, as a developed cultural group, certainly played an important role in the later phases of

		SETTLEMENT TYPES	DATES	PERIODS	SITES
Urban Conformations	C	EARLY FEUDAL FORTIFIED CITIES	850	GREATER MORAVIAN STATE	Mikulčice
	B	PRODUCTIVE AND MERCHANTILE CITIES WITH FULLY DEVELOPED FORTIFICATIONS	−100	LATE LA TÈNE	Stradonice Malé Hradisko u Plumlova
	A	FORTIFIED MERCHANTILE CENTERS OF URBAN CHARACTER	1500	Lausitz Umfield culture BRONZE AGE Aunjetitz culture	Obřany u Brna Biskupin in Poland Barca u Košic
Primitive Settlement Types	c	FORTIFIED VILLAGES OF AGRICULTURALISTS AND CATTLE BREEDERS	3500	ENEOLITHIC	Homolka
	b	PEASANT SETTLEMENTS OF RATHER LONG DURATION, LATER ALSO SURROUNDED BY FENCES	5000	Moravian painted pottery NEOLITHIC Spiral-meander pottery	Hluboké Mašůvky Bylana u Prahy
	a	ENCAMPMENTS OF SPECIALIZED HUNTERS, PERMANENT SETTLEMENT	25000	UPPER PALEOLITHIC Gravettian	Dolní Věstonice

FIGURE 3. Steps in the development of settlement types within the ČSSR

the upper paleolithic as well as in the incipient transformation from non-productive to productive forms of economy and, beyond this, in the further development of European man. Perhaps further excavation at the settlement of Pavlov—which promises to give us additional undisturbed and complete ground plans of the entire settlement of this primal hunting community—will allow us to say more on the validity of this presentation.

BIBLIOGRAPHY

ABSOLON, K.
1945. "Die Erforschung der diluvialen Mammutjäger-station von Unter-Wisternitz an den Pollauer Bergen in Mähren," *Arbeitsbericht über das dritte Jahr* 1926. Brno.

BAYER, J.
1921. Der Mammutjägerhalt der Aurignaczeit bei Lang-Mannersdorf an der Perschling, Nieder-Österreich. Mannus XIII.

BÖHM, J.
1946. *Naše nejstarší města.* Praha.

BORISKOVSKIJ, P. J.
1953. "Paleolit Ukraijny," *Materialy i issledovanija po archeologii SSSR*, 15:40.

ČERNYŠ, A. P.
1959. "Paleolit srednevo Pridněstrovja," *Trudy Komissii po izučeniju četvertičnovo perioda*, Moskva.

GERASIMOV, M. M.
1935. "Raskopki paleolitičeskoj stojanki v sele Malta," *Paleolit SSSR.* Moskva.

JEFIMENKO, P. P.
1953. *Pervobytnoje obščestvo.* Kiev.
1958. *Kostjenki I. Izdatelstvo AN SSSR.* Moskva-Leningrad.

JELNEK, J.
1954. "Nález fosilního člověka Dolní Věstonice III." *Anthropozoikum*, 3. Praha.

KEITH, A.
1937. *New Discoveries Relating to the Antiquity of Man*, 3:24. London.

KLÍMA, B.
1954. "Palaeolithic Huts at Dolní Věstonice, Czechoslovakia," *Antiquity*, 109:4–14.

1955. "Beitrag der neuen paläolithischen Station in Pavlov zur Problematik der ältesten landwirtschaftlichen Geräte," *Památky archeologické*, Vol. 46. Praha.

1957. "Übersicht über die jüngsten paläolithischen Forschungen in Mähren," *Quartär*, 9:85–130.

1959. "Zur Problematik des Aurignacien und Gravettien in Mittel-Europa," *Archeol. Austriaca*, 26. Wien.

MAKOWSKY, A.
1892. "Der diluviale Mensch im Löss von Brünn," *MAG* Vol. 22. Wien.

MAZÁLEK, M.
1953. "Třetí rok výzkumu paleo-mesolitické oblasti u Ražic," *Archeol. rozhledy*, 5. Praha.

NAHODIL, O.
1954. *O původu náboženství*. Orbis-Praha.

NEUSTUPNÝ, J.
1951. "Neolitická opevněná osada v Hlubokých Mašuůkách," *Časopis Národního musea*, 117–19. Praha.

NEUSTUPNÝ, E. F.
1956. "The Linear Pottery and Vinca," *Chronol. préh. de la Tchécoslovaquie*, pp. 40–43. Praha.

NOVOTNÝ, B.
1956. "Beitrag zu den chronologischen Beziehungen des Frühneolithikums in der Tschechoslowakei," *Chronol. préh. de la Tchécoslovaquie*. Praha.

PROŠEK, F
1961. "Mladopaleolitická obydlí v Československu," *Anthropozoikum*, 10. Praha.

ROGAČEV, A. N.
1953. "Issledovanije ostatkov pervobytno-obščinovo poselenija verchněpaleoličeskovo vremeni u s. Avdějevo na r. Sejm v 1949 g," *Materialy i issledovanija po archeologii SSSR*, 39.

1955. "Kostjenki IV—poselenije drevněkamennovo věka na Donu," *Materialy i issledovanija po archeologii SSSR*, 45.

SOUDSKÝ, B.
1960. "Station néolithique de Bylany," *Historica II*. Praha.

ŠOVKOPLJAS, I. G.
1957. "Nekotoryje itogi issledovanija Mezinskoj pozdněpaleolitičeskoj stojanki v 1954–1956 gg," *Sovětskaja archeologija*, 4. Moskva.

TICHÝ, R.
1961. "Einige Bemerkungen zum Neolithikum in der Tschechoslowakei," *Forschungsberichte zur Ur- und Frühgeschichte*. Wien.

VLČEK, E.
1952. "Otisky papilárních linií mladopaleolitického člověka z D. Věstonic," *Zprávy Anthropolog. společnosti*, 4. Brno.

ZOTZ, L. F.
1942. "Der erste altsteinzeitliche Hausgrundriss in Mitteleuropa," *Quartär*, 4.

ŽEBERA, K.
1958. *Československo ve starší době kamenné*. Praha.

SOUTHERN MIDDLE EUROPE
AND SOUTHEASTERN EUROPE

RICHARD PITTIONI

GENERAL REMARKS

THE TITLE of our symposium is interesting and promising. In choosing it, our two colleagues evidently started from a geographical core-area concept that permitted such wording, for example, from the zone that, years ago, Braidwood (1957, p. 125) had designated as the flanks of the "Fertile Crescent" and which I augmented (1950) by extension to the so-called "neural zone" of Syria and Palestine as well as North Africa. These regions offer special conditions, primarily related to the environmental configuration provided by the natural setting. This made possible the further steps of transformation by man.

The question now arises whether the point of view derived from the Fertile Crescent of Mesopotamia and its Kurdistani margin, or the secondarily derived questions and basic orientations expressed in the title of the symposium, possess general validity. Is it factually possible to generalize this regionally oriented point of view, and the problems connected with it, so that a common overview of different cultural areas may be gained from it? For this reason, I shall begin with some general remarks of a basic nature.

The period indicated by the title begins with an absolute date and ends with a relative one. What was it like in the Old World about 15,000 B.C.?

Considering Europe, this was—drawing on the applicable radiocarbon determinations as a basis of judgment—the late phase of Würm III, to name a chronological concept of some currency. We cannot enter here into the detailed problems that are connected with the Würm chronology. Relating the date of 15,000 B.C. with late Würm III is the result of C^{14} determinations that permit us to fix the Alleröd fluctuation from about 10,000 to 8500 or 8000 B.C.

This term of absolute chronology may therefore be used for comparisons within the various *Lebensräume*. However, the fixed time point is juxtaposed to a concept of relative chronology, the beginning of urban civilization. This latter is a beginning that differs for the several cultural regions. For this reason, it is impossible to make comparisons among them.

Since a term of absolute chronology and one of relative chronology cannot be brought into relationship with each other, it would seem desirable to revise our working title. It is easy to make such a proposal if we start from Mesopotamia and from Egypt. Here, urban civilization set in about 3000 B.C. Our working

211

title could then have the following formulation: "Between 15,000 and 3000 B.C.: A world-wide Survey of the Cultural Texture of This Period."

Thus, one may ask what occurred during these 12,000 years in the various cultural regions and how their inhabitants related to each other.

The following sectors stand out:

a) The historical events from 15,000 to about 8000 B.C., i.e., from late Würm III to the younger Dryas, inclusive

b) The historical events from about 8000 to about 5000 B.C., i.e., during the Pre-boreal and the Boreal

c) The historical events from about 5000 to 2500 B.C., i.e., during the Atlantic

and these, generally speaking, span the above-mentioned absolute boundary dates.

Viewed from the standpoint of cultural morphology, the indicated time span of roughly 12,000 years subsumes the historical contrasts between hunters and gatherers, on the one hand, and farmers, on the other.

In this connection I should like to say a few words concerning the idea of a "neolithic revolution," which has enjoyed some popularity in recent years.[1] This phrase means to underscore, in contrast to the hunting and gathering way of life of the paleolithic, the newly arisen form of economy and the general cultural changes connected with it. Without a doubt this is justified. But there is the question of whether it is justifiable to designate the so-called "progress of neo-lithization" as a revolution. Usually, we think of a revolution as a spontaneous event, an action or a chain of actions tending to cause basic changes in the historical situation within a very brief span of time. The idea of revolution is customarily associated with politico-historical events, so application of the term to other sectors of human action submerges its original meaning. If we retain it, however, in connection with the "neolithic revolution," the question arises whether or not this contrast between food-gatherers and food-producers (in Braidwood's understanding of the village-farming community way of life) did indeed occur so suddenly, so dynamically, that there was a distinct break in historical tradition and continuity. In advancing this question, I have no intention of speaking in favor of any evolutionistic tendencies, of which, as a historian, I do not generally think very highly, since they only too often seek support in a priori-isms. As a historian, however, I must ask myself about the manner in which this contrast developed, analyzing the heuristic burden of the situation that is conducive to such understanding. And this must be done, not only at one location or in one zone, but quite generally for the historical events in all the known investigated cultural regions.

Here then—if I have correctly understood the goals of our symposium—is the

1. Coined by Childe (1936) and elaborated in 1958; Cole (1959) has recently given a lucid exposition of the events connected with the process of neolithization. She advocates the idea of a primary farming culture in the Near East and its gradual expansion from there over Europe, without taking the results of the most recent research projects into account. Not enough stress, therefore, is given to the historical aspects of the neolithic (cf. Pittioni, 1953, pp. 105 ff., in which the considerations and directions regarding method are still valid today).

center of gravity of our discussion, which, in all likelihood, will elicit very widely divergent opinions.

If I may briefly define at this point my own attitude toward the notion of a "neolithic revolution," I should say that, in my opinion, it is inapplicable to the main problem that we propose to treat here. There are several essentials to the form of economy of agriculturalists and cattle-raisers: these are their sedentism, their striving to remove themselves from the conditioning factors of nature by interference with its web, and their efforts to support this striving by the utilization of new tools, which are the visible evidence of their intention. The well-known pairs of opposed-couple concepts; paleolithic-neolithic, periods of chipped-stone versus polished-stone tools, and food-gatherers versus food-producers, attempt to circumscribe this heuristically attested contrast with greater or less success.

If these contrasts are subjected to closer scrutiny, it will be found that they can, at best, be called upon for rough and ready characterization of the paleolithic and the neolithic. Actually, the situations during both periods are far more complex. The criteria adduced for the neolithic have rudimentary antecedents in the paleolithic and mesolithic. In recent times, investigations of the paleolithic have demonstrated with increasing clarity the existence of settlement forms tied to specific locations, which thus endured for extended periods of time. Our colleague Klíma, the excavator of Pollau near Nikolsburg, can give a far better account of this than I can. The contrast between chipped- and polished-stone artifacts loses significance. The polishing of stone has already been shown for Würm II in the middle Gravettian of eastern and Central Europe, as is proved by Kostjenki and Willendorf. When, at that time, slate and plates of marl were utilized for the purpose, this was only showing a preference for a relatively easily worked mineral. The flat maces of Předmost, however, attest the use of harder stones, not to speak of the Maglemosian stone maces. We see that this type of raw material for ground or polished tools had been known even before 15,000 B.C. Though it is true that silicious minerals (i.e., chipped flint) were then preferred, it is likewise true that this preference was never generally discarded during the neolithic. Wherever flinty materials constituted the essential source of raw material, they were utilized to a significant extent during the neolithic and, in some areas, even during the bronze age. The "period of chipped stone" is not a specific term identifying the paleolithic but is, at best, a most general designation, without value as a historical marker. Finally, it is sufficiently well known that the domestication of wild animals must be placed in the mesolithic, after which it undergoes an intensification that takes its character entirely from regionally differentiated conditions.

Thus, as early as the paleolithic and mesolithic periods, certain potentials are realized within human activity whose intensification is determined by the physical factors of nature and the physical factors of man as the possessor of these potentials. This reciprocity contains the historical dynamism that constitutes the essence of the neolithic, in its nascence, its florescence, and its metamorphis into new historical manifestations. Whether the realization of the potential is associated with individuals or with complex structures is in itself immaterial where its effectiveness as a historical agent is concerned. But the realized potentials must find responses. First, within the community in which they originate, but then also in the physical prerequisites of nature. *Time* and *space* are therefore the primary determining factors for the reciprocal relationship of forces and their achievements during the neolithic within the various cultural regions.

In connection with these general remarks, I shall now embark upon a brief characterization of the cultural conditions in southern Central and southeastern Europe between 15,000 and 3000 B.C.

HISTORICAL EVENTS BETWEEN 15,000 AND 8000 B.C.

The culture type associated with Würm III is the central-European Gravettian. The basis for its recognition is the material found at Pollau in Czechoslovakia,[2] to which we may probably add Kamegg in lower Austria (Brandtner, 1954–55, pp. 1 ff.). Pollau is a settlement of considerable permanence, while the character of the Kamegg establishment is less clearly recognizable. For Hungary, we may mention here the settlement at Pilismarót (Gabori, 1960, pp. 57 ff.), while Ságvár can be connected with Pollau only in a very general sense. Observations to the same effect come from Romania (Nicolaescu-Plopşor, 1958, pp. 383 ff.). On the strength of recovered material, Klíma has established the Pavlovian as a comprehensive designation for the late Gravettian of Würm III. The eastern expansion of the Magdalenian falls in the same period, although it has left no traces in the Danubian regions or in southeastern Europe. In this area all cultural configurations are rooted in the late Gravettian. The late Gravettian contains two elements that are decisive for its later modification: acquaintance with combustible synthetics (baked-clay figurines, etc.) and the production of flint microimplements. We do not know yet whether this synthetic has been used at stations other than Pollau. Kamegg, however—just as Pollau—has produced evidence of microimplements. The tendency toward geometric forms, which becomes apparent herein, points toward a future, fundamental orientation.

We cannot demonstrate for our area anything comparable to the metamorphosis of the late Magdalenian base into the Federmesser groups (in the sense of Schwabedissen) characteristic of the Alleröd fluctuation in northwestern Europe, with its regional variants of Tjonger, Rissen, and Wehlen. There is, as yet, no possibility in this area of dating sites by palynological methods. Also, we have too little information concerning the Alleröd period to have much light shed on its forest history. A clue is offered in the peat marsh at Roggendorf near Melk in Lower Austria[3] (Brandtner, 1949, pp. 5 ff.); another comes from

2. Cf., for this as well as for the general cultural situation in Central Europe, Klíma, 1959, pp. 35 ff.

3. Giving a radiocarbon determination of 9450 ± 90 B.C. (Gro-1198).

Bad Tatzmannsdorf in Burgenland. The Roggendorf marsh has shown that the forest conditions of the Alleröd resembled those of the Atlantic to a certain extent. To be able to study how the climatic improvement of this period has expressed itself in the various latitudes upon the forest inventory, it would, however, be necessary to correlate all the Alleröd profiles known to date according to their regional order. Stress would need to be given here to the *various latitudes*. For, just as the entire Quarternary phenomenon must be considered world-wide and fundamentally simultaneous, we must also apply this latitudinal consideration to the Alleröd fluctuation that is linked with the Quarternary cycle. Taken in terms of absolute chronology, the Alleröd fluctuation may have begun somewhat earlier in the southern latitudes. The mutual interinfluencing among the various latitudes, which has recently been made clear by Wundt (1958–59, pp. 15 ff.)—for the phenomenon of the Quarternary in general—may be taken into account to show this. The Kebaran and the early Natufian are culture-historically associated with this period in the Mediterranean area.

Kamegg accentuates an orientation in the heuristic inventory of Central Europe, which later on emerges more clearly in the Hamburgian of northwest Germany; it is the use of reindeer antler in the manufacture of points. On the basis of its radiocarbon determinations (Pittioni, 1957, pp. 357 ff.; 1959, pp. 200 ff.), the Hamburgian is related to the latest Würm III and to the late Magdalenian associated with it, which—in its own right—has produced evidence for this method of manufacturing points. The Hamburgian, however, is marked by certain flint implements. Its *Stielspitze* shows a certain relationship to the east-European Swiderian, which may be regarded as probably belonging to the Alleröd period. It might not be completely wrong to see the cultural foundations of the Swiderian in the late Gravettian. The Swiderian reaches from Poland into Romania. A lack of pertinent archeological data makes it nearly impossible to give a detailed account of events in this area. The brief younger Dryas should, however, hardly have caused major changes.

We might enumerate the following as giving a general characterization of the late Gravettian: settlement at preferred and favorable locations; systematic hunting of large mammals; knowledge of how to polish flint, marble, slate, and marl; the first indications of microlithic tool-making; and, during the Swiderian, further transformation in the direction of *Stielspitzen* (as specialized weapons?).[4]

There is a clear regional differentiation between the Azilian of western Europe and the typical Capsian of northern Africa.

HISTORICAL EVENTS BETWEEN 8000 AND 5000 B.C.

As the previous paragraphs have indicated, certain potentials begin to be outlined during the period from 15,000 to 8000 B.C. to which we can hardly deny the attributes of fundamental innovations. These potentials rest upon the

---

4. This already anticipates the answer to the first question asked at the symposium: In the late glacial and early postglacial periods what major cultural events characterize your area?

experience of the Gravettian. The next epoch, which encompasses about 3,000 years, is a consequence of the indicated new orientation, supported and augmented by the reaction of these liberated potentials with the physical factors of nature then obtaining.

With respect to the forest and climatic history, the natural factors are subsumed under the Preboreal and Boreal, that is, in pollen zones IV and V (Firbas, 1949). Their transliteration into absolute chronology by means of radiocarbon determinations applies, with its corresponding evidence, to Central Europe. The confinement of these factors to certain latitudinal zones must, however, be stressed. In this respect the Mediterranean lands and the Near East offer nothing, since the natural prerequisites for the formation of such palynological elements is lacking. This is not to say that the climatological events necessary for their formation have occurred only in Central Europe. The basic uniformity of the Quarternary also presupposes that—similar to the Alleröd fluctuation—these early postglacial manifestations have shaped the conditions of the ecological environment in the Mediterranean region as in the Near East, in northern Africa, or on the high plateau of Iran. Corresponding to the different latitudes (and altitudes), the Preboreal will, in all likelihood, have begun somewhat earlier in the lower latitudes than in the higher ones. A morphology—shaped by Würm III, the Alleröd period, and the younger Dryas—is decisive for its ultimate effectiveness. This morphological state is one of the most important preconditions for the vegetal cover of these soils. Only climatological history and the related paleoecology can provide factual information concerning such problems. Representatives of these specializations would therefore be most welcome. If prehistorians now declare that the mesolithic, which sets in with the Preboreal, was determined by the changes in floral and faunal inventory of the early postglacial, they can be supported with some references to their own source materials (Pittioni, 1954b, pp. 367 ff.). Understanding of the total structural change over this span of time will probably be gained only by way of climatology, which illuminates the preconditions of the *bios* of plants and animals. Such questions are, of course, neither simple nor easily answered. A comparison with today's climatic conditions would be deceptive, since terminal Quarternary factors were still operative during the Preboreal and Boreal. Consideration of the earliest neolithic cultural remains in the Sahara and of the inventory of large mammals and aquatic animals (crocodile, water buffalo) shows clearly enough how long the over-all climatic situation may have been codetermined by late Quarternary formations.

If we go along with the radiocarbon determinations (in conformity with the most recent arguments of our colleague Waterbolk [this volume]), we will not be surprised, after what has been said above, if the oldest evidence in the Near East of a cultural constellation—which can only be called neolithic—proves to be contemporary with the transitional period between the central-European Preboreal and Boreal. In this connection I should like to point to Braidwood's (1958, pp. 249 ff.) interesting discussion concerning the absolute chronological ordering of his Jarmo material. From the viewpoint of climatological history it signifies an early active growth of the flora/faunal changes through the Preboreal and Boreal.

Returning to our Central European region, we have to draw attention to a disagreeable hiatus in the investigative record. It consists, in the first place, of the lack of even a single stratigraphic cultural clue; second, in the absence of palynologically related information (a great deficiency when compared with Star Carr and northwestern Europe); and finally in the paucity of the entire heuristic inventory.

Evaluation of the cultural situation during this period is therefore possible only through the typological changes within the stone tools. From this standpoint, three phases may be distinguished within the 3,000-year time span. The first may possibly be correlated with the western-European Sauveterrean, the second is characterized by semilunar and triangular microliths, and the third is clearly defined by semilunar, triangular, and trapezoidal microliths (Pittioni, 1954a, pp. 111 ff.; 1956, pp. 370 ff.; Table 4, col. 5).

For the first phase—which I designated years ago as the Gratkorn group (after Gratkorn in Styria)—there is an evident but not yet clearly expressed tendency toward microliths. The stone implements show a certain imbalance; among the geometric forms is the lunate, which we already know from the Pavlovian. The bone industry, which has harpoons and fishhooks of designs characteristic of the Maglemosian, is important. Although it is demonstrated in Styria, we do not yet know how wide a distribution we may assign to this oldest mesolithic. Whether it occurs in the Balkans, in Romania, and in Hungary in the same form or whether it is replaced by a continuation of the Swiderian remains to be discovered. Here, therefore, is a regrettable gap in our knowledge.

I have given the name of "Limberg group" to the second phase. The generally mesolithic tendency toward microlithic forms appears strengthened in this phase. Lunates and triangles (isosceles as well as scalene) exist here parallel to western Europe. Dispersed finds in Slovakia, Hungary, and Romania (Nicolaescu-Plopşor, 1959, pp. 221 ff.) possess a more or less general uniformity. A more exact characterization is, however, not yet possible.

That material that in western Europe is subsumed under the name Tardenoisian belongs to the third phase. I do, however, have misgivings in applying this name to our material. Tardenoisian should, perhaps, cover only that typological entity which is built upon the Sauveterrean and which therefore permits us to discern regional ties. The trapeze—demonstrable, along with lunates and triangles, in this third phase—would by itself hardly be enough to justify transferring to Central and southeastern Europe a term that is associated with western Europe. It is to be regretted that the tendency toward modification that becomes apparent here is not yet clear enough to formulate. There are as yet no systematic investigations of settlement forms, although special work of this sort would especially in richly stratified caves, produce a foundation. We can create an approximation of the true picture only by connecting occasional pieces of the mosaic. It shows that the then colonizable terrain was occupied and that, as good evidence for this third phase, distribution of the trapeze from lower Austria to Romania had been established.

Thus it is hardly possible at this time to compile a set of general characteristics for this second epoch between 8000 and 5000 B.C. We may, however, adhere to the assumption that the Gravettian-Swiderian constituted the basis for the new configurations. A definite genetic-historical orientation of our mesolithic— quite different from those in other cultural regions—becomes visible in it. Regional peculiarities assert themselves despite a general mesolithic tendency toward geometric microliths.

The present state of discovery in the regions of the middle and lower Danube (the very center of the European loess zone) hinders discussion of questions concerning the faunal inventory that was at the disposal of the hunters of that period. This inventory constituted, at the same time, the natural reservoir from which motivation for domestication could arise. It is probably only a gap in investigations that demonstrates the occurrence of the dog only in the north and in the Near East. Because we lack appropriate palynological investigations, we know hardly anything about the distribution of the floral pattern, although the loess zone does have fundamental significance in relation to a question concerning the inventory of wild grasses—the basis for future agriculture. We thus arrive at very concrete formulations of questions to be asked of paleontology and paleobotany; the answers will be decisive for a deeper treatment of problems germane to the third epoch.[5]

HISTORICAL EVENTS BETWEEN 5000 AND 3000 B.C.

The determination of the beginning of this epoch comes as a result of radiocarbon determinations for the onset of the main Atlantic phase and of the heuristically demonstrated connection of the neolithic with this climatic period on the strength of palynological tests. A further indication for this beginning is offered by radiocarbon determinations for the Danubian neolithic (*Linearkeramik*) from eastern Belgium by way of southern Germany to central Germany. None are as yet available for the middle and lower reaches of the Danube; Vinča A (late), with an inventory comparable to the *Linearkeramik* has, according to Waterbolk, a determination of 4010 ± 85 B.C. and thus agrees with the dates for the *Linearkeramik*. The lack of determinations for the Hungarian-Romanian Körös-Cris culture (Petrescu-Dimbovitsa, 1958, pp. 53 ff.; Dumitrescu, 1960, pp. 116 ff.) is regrettable, for it impresses one as the oldest neolithic culture in the Danubian region. However, the process of internal integration of the Körös culture is still too little known completely to justify its often claimed equating

5. This is the answer to the second question asked at the Symposium: Defining incipient cultivation and/or animal domestication as a minor or supplementary basis of total subsistence, when and how do such conditions appear?

with that of Starčevo in Yugoslavia. One has the impression that Starčevo is a
late Körös. This also accords with a radiocarbon determination of 4440 ± 75 B.C.
for Starčevo material from Gonja Tuzla in northeastern Bosnia, if one keeps
in mind that in the middle and lower Danubian region Körös is older than the
Linearkeramik. From this we gather that the formation of the Körös complex
is to be moved back to the beginning of the fifth millennium B.C. and that the
Linearkeramik was formed simultaneously alongside it.

Both were preceded by a very early neolithic, about which we are rudi-
mentarily informed through Crvena Stijena in Bosnia (Benac) and the Thessalian
tell disclosures (Milojčić and Theokaris) (Berciu, 1958, pp. 99 ff.; 1960, pp. 15 ff.).
Thessaly produced a very old neolithic without pottery (as well as a prepottery
phase such as Jericho) and in addition a coarse ware with fingernail impressions,
which formed the starting point for the Sesklo sequence. As yet, no radiocarbon
determination exists for this, although one would anticipate the end of the sixth
millennium for it. Such a conclusion derives from the Crvena stijena, where—
as in the Arene Candide (Liguria)—the fingernail-ornamented ware rests upon
a late mesolithic stratum and where we can perceive this tradition in the inventory of stone implements. In Thessaly also we may note the microlithic
tendency, and the same may be said for the *Linearkeramik* (from Belgium to
Hungary). Here we are supposedly dealing with internal, genetic relationships
between the late mesolithic and the early neolithic. But the last word concerning
this has not yet been spoken. We shall require many more radiocarbon determinations for the Körös and *Linearkeramik* cultures. The border regions between
Austria, Czechoslovakia, and Hungary will be of great significance, for it is here
that we expect to find the origins of the *Linearkeramik*.[6] From this area it
spread along the northern slopes of the Carpathian Mountains by way of
southern Poland as far as Romania (Walachia) and formed there the basis for
Cucuteni A. The C[14] determinations for Habaeşti (Cucuteni A) of 3130 ± 80
B.C. corroborate the findings of Romanian investigations that were founded on
cultural-stratigraphic studies.

In this manner, the notion—which, even without the aid of radiocarbon determinations, I had maintained as early as 1954—of a relatively great age for the
neolithic in the middle and lower reaches of the Danube is now attested more
and more clearly. I shall allude only briefly here to the important questions
connected with its genesis.

In his report on the Radiocarbon Meeting at Groningen Waterbolk raised

6. Quitta, 1960, pp. 1 ff. Since there is no culture-stratigraphic evidence in central Europe
for a closed sequence from mesolithic through an early neolithic to *Linearkeramik*, the oldest
Linearkeramik can be described only with the aid of typological criteria, especially those referring to the system of decorations. This offers too large a source of error to permit definitive statements. However, Quitta shows a distinct component trait, characterized by the use
of fingernail indentation, in the material that he ascribes to central Germany and that has
been regarded as the oldest *Bandkeramik*. Perhaps we have here a certain relationship with
manifestations indicated by proto-Sesklo and Körös-Cris.

the question whether we may have faith in the determinations pertaining to the neolithic. For a fruitful discussion we must start from a common reference point; in what follows I shall therefore utilize radiocarbon determinations known to me at this time.

The subject of this discussion is the question whether the European neolithic should be regarded as an offshoot of the Near Eastern neolithic—thus being of a relatively young age.

To assume an opposing point of view was formerly—in the absence of radiocarbon determinations—rather difficult. One could only advance a general line of reasoning and point to the Atlantic as an instigating factor in the economic transformation. Today, however, radiocarbon determinations demonstrate that the *Linearkeramik* had already reached the loess zone of eastern Holland by the end of the fifth millennium (Sittard 4250, 4150; Geleen 4180). The pottery found at these sites cannot be assigned to the earliest *Linearkeramik* since it is somewhat younger—such, at least, is the preliminary opinion concerning these finds. The same applies to Wittislingen in Bavaria and to Westeregeln near Magdeburg (4080, 4250). Neither of these sites has produced the classic spiral-meander pottery that is agreed to stand at the beginning of this range of decoration. If this agreed-to proposition is correct, this would also result in moving back the *Linearkeramik* to at least the middle of the fifth millennium. In any event, the later *Notenkopfkeramik* (note-headed pottery) bears such a characteristic stamp that it is recognizable on even the smallest fragment. It thereby establishes a very close union.

The same may be said about the Körös-Starčevo material. Crvena stijena has indicated its roots, so the C[14] determination of Gonja Tuzla comes as no surprise. This is also true for Vinča A, whose unique character will be discussed later.

So far, there are no radiocarbon determinations from Thessaly or Greece; one for Khirokitia on Cyprus yields 5685 ± 100 B.C. and confirms the asumptions made for Thessaly and the Balkans.[7]

If we compare these chronological data with those from the Near East, we arrive at the first third of the seventh millennium for Jarmo, and at the first half and end of the sixth millennium for Hassuna. I know of no radiocarbon determination for the Halafian period; but, on the basis of its stratigraphic position, it should be assigned to 5000–4500 or 4300 B.C., especially when compared to the early Obaid of 4120 B.C.

It is well known that the advocates of diffusion credit especially the Halafian forms with great significance in the transmission of cultural values from the Near East to southeastern Europe and thence to Central Europe. This is possible theoretically because the Halafian was certainly sufficiently integrated internally that it could share its cultural substance (potential) with its surroundings. Since

7. This date offers corroboration, having been published only after the conclusion of this symposium (*Radiocarbon Supplement* 2 [1960], pp. 193 ff.) Khirokitia is a very early neolithic, perhaps best compared with the prepottery neolithic B of Jericho.

there is no plausible reason to deny a diffusionary tendency to the Halaf style a priori and since we cannot yet say with which neighboring cultures Halaf maintained actual contact, it might be possible to derive from it certain manifestations of the southeastern European neolithic, above all for Thessaly. But, was central and southeastern Europe actually free of neolithic manifestations at that time? The answer is provided by the radiocarbon determinations cited above, which show that at the same time as Matarrah VI/4 and Hassuna V (i.e., during the sixth millennium) new types had their beginning that seem indicated by Crvena stijena and preceramic Thessaly. If Starčevo-Körös is to be assigned to the middle of the fifth millennium, then it is probably also contemporary with the Halafian and is—no less than the Halafian—a thoroughly integrated cultural form.

It should now be possible to see the intention of my remarks. They seek only to point out that the present state of the discipline hardly permits us to think of a transmittal of the neolithic from the Near East to Europe. It is much easier to assume indigenous, local origins for southeastern Europe and the Danubian region. (For radiocarbon determinations cited, see Fig. 1).

To this we must add a theoretical reflection. It deals with this question: At what stage of cultural development does contact with nearby or distant neighboring areas become possible? If I am correctly informed, we know nothing of contacts between Mesopotamia, or Palestine, on the one hand, and Egypt, on the other, during predynastic times. I am thinking of the discussions about the wavy-handled jars of the Maadi period and their connection with those of the Ghassulian, as well as of the contacts between Egypt and the Near East that have been stressed by Kantor. They closely precede the unification of Egypt. Such relationships, then, occur relatively late between two regions of vigorous cultural potential. I have no knowledge that there was any contact at the time of the Fayum-Merimdian, in the middle of the fifth millennium, with any contemporary cultures (apparently not even with Upper Egypt). From this we must apparently learn that only an integrated cultural form that has command over a sufficient reservoir of capacities can move outside its own proper region to share these capacities with its nearer or farther surroundings. One could maintain a different opinion if it became possible to document the expansion of the *Linearkeramik* into the Padana or even into western France. As far as my knowledge of Europe goes, I consider such a possibility too utopian for serious consideration. A culture requires a certain amount of time in order to gather and consolidate itself, for—being the product of man—it can be fully realized only through a process of integration in which time acts as a formative factor. I therefore see little promise in assuming far-reaching contacts of any kind for so early a period as the sixth and fifth millennia B.C. It is not even permissible to speak of stimulus diffusion, for even the transmittal of ideas presupposes close relationships between consolidated communities.

Thus I arrive at the conclusion that the neolithic in the lands of the middle and lower Danube, as well as in southeastern Europe, must be viewed as sets

Time	Forest–Climate Periods	Cultural Sequence	Radio–Active Carbon Determinations			
			Middle Danube	Lower Danube	Cyprus	Mespot.–Syria–Palestine
3000	ATLANTIC	LINEARKERAMIK / Late KÖRÖS / Early STARCEVO / Early VINCA	3890±120 Zwenkau-H (K555) 3985±60 Geleen (Gro.996) 4080±110 Witteslingen (Gro.265) 4180±60 Geleen (Gro.995) 4250±150 Sittard (Gro.423)	3130±80 Habaşeşti (Cucuteni A) (Gro.1985) 3645±160 Vinča D (Gro.1537) 4010±85 Vinča A, "late" (Gro.1546) 4440±75 Gonja Tuzla (Gro.2059)	3190±100 Kalavassos B (St.419) 3200±130 Sotira (St.357) 3510±110 Sotira (St.350)	3450±325 Gawra 17/18 (C.817) 3510±160 Pisdeli (O.157)
4000						4120±160 Warka (H138/123) 4600±200 Byblos A (W.627)
5000		KÖRÖS-CRIŞ				5090±200 Hassuna V (W.660)
6000	BOREAL	PRE-CERAMIC NEOLITHIC			5685±100 Khirokitia (St.414–415)	5620±250 Matarrah II.4 (W.623) 6000±200 Mersin (W.617) 6720±200 Jericho (F.41) 6750 Jarmo-average 6885±210 Jericho (F.40) (Pre-Ceramic Neolithic)
7000	PRE-BOREAL	MESOLITHIC				
8000	YOUNGER DRYAS					7950±70 Jericho (Gro.942) (Mesolithic)
9000	ALLERÖD	LATE – GRAVETTIEN and LATE – SWIDERIEN				
10,000	OLDER DRYAS					
11,000	BÖLLING / OLDEST DRYAS (Würm III)					
12,000						

FIGURE 1. General chronological table for Central Europe, with some southwestern Asiatic comparisons.

of manifestations that arose indigenously within the several cultural regions not merely in their general but also in their particular characteristics.[8] They may be considered equivalent to—and, in part, also contemporary with—all others in the Near East or Egypt. I would rather think of the process as one of historical convergences than as one of diffusion.[9]

If I adhere to the *terminus ad quem* that I proposed in the introduction, I have actually reached the end of my observations. However, two remarks by our colleague Braidwood contained in a letter to me cause me to add a few words. One of his remarks refers to the reciprocal interinfluencing of neolithic village cultures; the other asks whether it was merely an accident that both Childe and Hawkes conclude their presentation of the prehistory of Europe at about 1500 B.C.

About the first point I should like to say that, keeping in mind the *terminus ad quem* that I have proposed, the neolithic cultures of the middle and lower Danube regions and of southeastern Europe have produced hardly anything that would point to such interinfluencing. Could it be that one might interpret the sequence Körös-*Linearkeramik*-Cucuteni, which has been demonstrated for Romanian Wallachia, in this sense, and could it be that one might also intend to stress that the *Linearkeramik* appears to have been stronger than the Körös, which, in Hungary too, was replaced by the *Linearkeramik?* I do not know which reasons were operative here. However, these discernible changes and reciprocal influences in the region discussed by me occur only in the third millennium, thus being later than my self-imposed temporal boundaries.

Concerning the second point, I can only stress that, in my opinion, this is an arbitrary limitation, seemingly formed under the impression that Mycenae actually represents an urban culture. However, the Mycenae of the shaft and tholoi graves can hardly be classified as an urban culture and therefore is structured differently from Crete. Anything resembling an urban culture was not formed on the Greek mainland before the Mycenean *Koiné*. If we accept

8. This opinion also takes in an answer to the third question asked during the course of the symposium: At what point in the cultural sequence of your area do you feel that you can identify effective food production (plant cultivation and/or animal domestication assuming a major subsistence role), and what are the artifactual expressions and social (directly inferred) consequences? For heuristic evidence of effective food production we may point to the generally known inventory of objects; the respective material for the stone implements of Danubian culture has recently been assembled by Vencl (1960, pp. 1 ff.). The arguments of Waterbolk presented before the symposium regarding settlement forms should be mentioned here; likewise, in complementation, those of Felgenhauer (1960, pp. 1 ff.).

9. This also answers the fourth question with respect to our region: Does effective food production appear as part of an indigenous evolution, or does it (as revealed archeologically) suggest outside influences? To what extent does the appearance of effective food production (either indigenous or imported) seem explosive ("revolutionary")? Regarding the German version of the question, it should be noted that "explosive" is not the same as *umwälzend*, but serves to indicate rapid change. The changes in structure that occurred between mesolithic and neolithic were, without doubt, *umwälzend*, since they formed the foundations for the neolithic.

the palaces of this period and the Linear B writing that was encountered here as pertinent indications, they may also be interpreted in this sense—as may the far-flung commercial relations that prevailed at that time. Childe had, if I judge correctly, a most subjective attitude when he spoke of Mycenean capitalism, making it responsible for the florescence of Central-European copper-mining—heuristically this is not provable.

All Europe during the second and first millennia (except Greece, beginning about 900, and Italy from 700 to 400 B.C.) has a village-culture orientation and offers no signs of any process that would lead to the threshold of urban culture. Urbanism can scarcely be proved conclusively for the Celtic *oppida*. I cannot even conceive that the urban cultures had impressed themselves at all intensively on the village cultures of Europe. Not even classical Greece of the sixth century B.C. initiated the formation of cities in the Thracian hinterland; neither could the Etruscan cities cause a transportation of their farming environment. There is no need to adduce further negative examples.[10]

10. The fifth question asked during the symposium was: Could you in your area use the term "threshold of urbanization"? If so, what would you mean by it, and what is the evidence of its development? We have already indicated that for our area the answer must be negative. But it must be stressed that the definition of the constituent elements of an urban culture is the task of the historian and that a final decision can come only from an evaluation of his arguments concerning prehistory. For this reason I should like to add some remarks about the arguments of Childe (1950, pp. 3 ff.). Using examples drawn from the Near East, he attempted to define ten elements of urban culture (i.e., civilization) without considering that here—as in Egypt or Mesoamerica—we are always dealing with discrete, unique manifestations. Hardly a single one of his constituent elements is decisive. The first one (i.e., the earliest cities must have been more extensive and more densely settled than any prior settlements) is contradicted by bronze-age Biskupin and the large settlements of the late Latène period. The second element (differentiation between rural and urban population according to composition and function) is likewise untenable in view of the occupational specialization within populations that have been demonstrated for bronze-age Europe. The third element (relinquishing the surplus of farm produce to a deity or a divine king) cannot, in this particular form, be documented for Europe, although this need not mean that such tributes did not exist merely because they cannot be archeologically proved. Element four (truly monumental structures as symbols of the concentration of society's surplus) is attested for Europe by Stonehenge, Avebury, Karnak, the Nuraghen, and others, to the extent that they were built of stone and managed to survive. The existence of monumental timber structures cannot be demonstrated because of the lack of telling remains. It can scarcely be doubted, however, that the named examples have come about only through an institution that Childe has called "social surplus." Element five (the maintenance of all people not engaged in agriculture by means of the agrarian surplus) is sensibly applicable in Europe in the context of industrial facilities for mining. Otherwise, it would hardly have been possible to support the large labor forces that can be calculated for the Alpine copper-mining establishments. Elements six and seven (invention of writing and the exact sciences by individuals excluded from subsistence production) are not criteria for urban culture, since this observation holds true equally well for the comprehensive chemical (i.e., also exact) knowledge of the earliest metallurgists. Furthermore, it must be mentioned that the miners of the *Urnen* period had developed a system of signs, which probably served for communication, although it cannot be called writing. Here, in the area of mining technology, knowledge in the exact sciences developed sooner than writing, so writing does not constitute a prerequisite for such knowledge. Element eight (a particular art style practiced by specialists)

I think, then, that it is best to conclude with a date of 3000 B.C. and thereby make clear the process of formation that produced the rise of closed village cultures in the middle and lower Danubian regions and the Balkans. I am, of course, aware that this will make a difficult situation for those colleagues who are to discuss north Germany and Scandinavia; but such an absolute date may be especially suited for bringing to the fore the historical contrasts between the various cultural regions, thus gaining a point of reference for questions concerning the temporal and genetic relationship between northern, western, and southern Europe and the ecological area that we have here considered.

---

is largely vitiated by a reference to the Nordic bronze-age art or to that of the Latène culture. At best, it might be said that an urban culture has monumental art of individual character; but even here caution is indicated, considering the art of the paleolithic. Element nine (purchase of imported objects with the agrarian surpluses and other interchange through far-reaching commerce) loses significance in view of the neolithic long-distance trade in obsidian, amber, and spondylus, or the bronze-age trade in copper. From this, it finally follows that element ten (supplying of raw materials to the specialists and security within a state organization) cannot be a criterion of urban culture either. What Childe thought possible of enumeration found manifold expression in late neolithic and bronze-age Europe without permitting us to think of urban culture. It does not happen to be possible for one sociological-economical mechanism to contain such complex and variegated historical events as those leading here and there to urban culture.

BIBLIOGRAPHY

BERCIU, D.

1958. "Néolithique préceramique dans les Balkans," *Studi și cercetari di istorie veche*, 9:99 ff.

1960. "Asupra protoneoliticului europei sud-estice," *Omagiu Daicoviciu*, pp. 15 ff.

BRAIDWOOD, R. J.

1952. *The Near East and the Foundations for Civilization*. Eugene: University of Oregon Press.

1957. *Prehistoric Men*. Chicago: Chicago Natural History Museum.

1958. "Über die Anwendung der Radiokarbon-Chronologie für das Verständnis der ersten Dorfkulturgemeinschaften in Südwestasien," *Anzeiger der österreichischen Akademie der Wissenschaften, phil.-hist. Klasse*, 95:249 ff.

BRANDTNER, F.

1949. "Die bisherigen Ergebnisse der stratigraphisch-pollenanalytischen Untersuchung eines jungeiszeitlichen Moores von interstadialem Charakter aus der Umgebung von Melk a.d. Donau, NÖ," *Archaeol. Austriaca*, 2:5 ff.

1954–55. "Kamegg, eine Freilandstation des späteren Paläolithikums in Niederösterreich," *Mitteilungen der Prähistorischen Kommission*, 7:1 ff.

CHILDE, V. G.

1936. *Man Makes Himself*. London: Watts.

1950, "The Urban Revolution," *Town Planning Review*, 21:3 ff.

1958. *The Prehistory of European Society*. (Pelican Books, A415.)

COLE, S.
1959. *The Neolithic Revolution.* London.

DUMITRESCU, W.
1960. "O descoperire en ceramica criş şi en ceramica Liniara in Transilvania de Sud-Est," *Omagiu Daicoviciu,* p. 161 ff.

FELGENHAUER, F.
1960. "Bandkeramische Groszbauten aus Mannswörth bei Wien," *Archaeol. Austriaca,* 27:1 ff.

FIRBAS, F.
1949. *Spät- und nacheiszeitliche Waldgeschichte Mitteleuropas nördlich der Alpen,* Vol. I.

GABORI, M.
1960. "Der heutige Stand der Paläolithforschung in Ungarn," *Archeol. Austraica,* 27:57 ff.

KLIMA, B.
1959. "Zur Problematik des Aurignacien und Gravettien in Mitteleuropa," *Archaeol. Austriaca,* 26:35 ff.
1957. "Übersicht über die jüngsten paläolithischen Forschungen in Mähren," *Quartär,* 26:35 ff.

NICOLAESCU-PLOPŞOR, C. S.
1958. "Les phénomènes périglaciaires et la géochronologie du paléolithique supérieur de terrasse en Roumanie," *Dacia,* n.s., 2:383 ff.
1959. "Discussions autour du paléolithique finissant et du néolithique en Roumanie," *Studi şi cercetari di istorie veche.* 10:221 ff.

PETRESCU-DIMBOVITSA, M.
1958. "Contributions au problème de la culture Criş en Moldavie," *Acta Archaeol. Acad. Hung. Scient.,* 9:53 ff.

PITTIONI, R.
1950. "Beiträge zur Geschichte des Keramikums in Afrika und im Nahen Osten," *Prähist. Forschungen,* Vol. 2.
1953. "Altweltliches Keramikum als historisches Problem," *Archaeol. Austriaca,* 13:105 ff.
1954a. *Urgeschichte des österreichischen Raumes.* Wien.
1954b. "Späteste Steinzeit und Lebensraum," *Anz. Österr. Akad. Wissenschaften, phil.-hist. Klasse,* 91:367 ff.
1956. "Zur Chronologie des Lithikums," *Forschungen und Fortschritte,* 30:370 ff.
1957, 1959. (Ed. and comp. *Der Beitrag der Radiokarbon-Methode zur absoluten Datierung urzeitlicher Quellen.* Parts I and II, *Forschungen und Fortschritte* (1957), 31:357 ff.; (1959) 33: 200 ff.

QUITTA, H.
1960. "Zur Frage der ältesten Bandkeramik in Mitteleuropa," *Prähistor. Zeitschr.,* 38:1 ff.

VENCL, S.
1960. "Kamenné nástroje prvnich zemědělcu ve stredni Evropě," *Sbornik Narodniho Musea v Praze,* Ser. A, 14:1 ff.

WUNDT, W.
1958–59. "Die Penck'sche Eiszeitgliederung und die Strahlungskurve," *Quartär,* 10–11:15 ff.

THE LOWER RHINE BASIN

H. T. WATERBOLK

INTRODUCTION

EARLY DEVELOPMENTS in food production took place in such river valleys as the Nile, the Tigris-Euphrates, and the Indus. These rivers may have played an important if not decisive part in the cultural development that is the theme of this conference. It may therefore be useful to consider the prehistory of other river valleys of the same order of magnitude in different climatic regions. Of European rivers, the Danube and the Rhine would serve this purpose.

The Rhine, with its main course flowing northward, would seem to be an especially suitable instance for study. By way of its tributaries, the Neckar and Main, there are easy connections with the Danube, and by way of the Porta Burgondica with the Rhône. The Rhine valley was thus directly open to influences from both the eastern and the western Mediterranean.

At present the lower Rhine valley is rather short. From Bonn to the Dutch coast the distance is only 300 kilometers. During the last ice age, however, its mouth lay at least 500 kilometers farther to the north. At that time, the river Thames was a left tributary of the Rhine. This situation persisted throughout the greater part of the period with which we are now concerned. After the separation of the British Isles from the Continent (roughly 5000 B.C.), the Rhine delta in its present position remained an important starting point for cultural influences into Britain, just as it was a bridgehead for reflected currents of influence (de Laet and Glasbergen, 1959).

Traffic along the Atlantic coasts appears to have been important for thousands of years. The Rhine delta was thus also open to influence from Iberia and Brittany on one side, and from the western Baltic on the other.

Finally, we may note that the valleys of the Maas and Scheldt connected the delta with the French mainland, including the Paris basin, and that to the east the way to the great European plain north of the German Mittelgebirge, was not seriously barred by the rivers Weser, Elbe, Oder, and Vistula.

Besides the Rhine, a few other rivers contribute to the same delta: the Scheldt, the Maas, the Ijssel, the Vecht, and the Ems.

More closely defined, the area under consideration corresponds to the present Dutch territory, adjacent parts of Germany, including parts of the Rhineland,

Westphalia, and Lower Saxony, Belgium (north of the Maas and Sambre), and France (north of the Artois downs).

The area can roughly be divided into three zones: (*a*) the loess-covered hills, (*b*) the sandy plain, dissected by river and brook valleys and covered at places by large raised bogs, and (*c*) the alluvial area, partly lying below sea level. As a fourth zone, the now submerged parts of the late-glacial landscape in the North Sea can be considered.

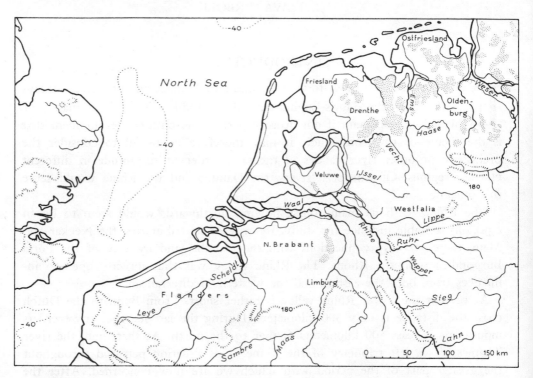

FIGURE 1. General geography, rivers, raised bog areas (stippled), and 180 m. contour, lower Rhine basin.

The Riss glaciation left a more or less continuous sheet of boulder clay in the subsoil north of the river Vecht. The outer limit of this glaciation coincides more or less with the course of the Rhine and of the Lippe.

Having geographicallly defined the lower Rhine basin, we may now proceed to a short survey of the prehistory of this area (de Laet and Glasbergen, 1959), against the background of the sequence of climatic periods (Waterbolk, 1954). For another special feature of the Rhine delta area is the great change in climate, both in temperature and degree of oceanity, that took place during the last 15,000 years as a direct or indirect result of the last ice age. We shall try to discover how man behaved under these varying circumstances of cultural influences and climatic changes, and to determine the type of food economy in the different periods. Emphasis will be laid on evidence obtained in the area itself.

THE PALEOLITHIC

Around 15,000 B.C. the Low Countries were still strongly influenced by the ice age. Snow storms swept the barren tundras. No organic remains have so far been found from this early period; vegetation must have been poor (van der Hammen, 1952). In the plain, the Riss and early Würm topography was flattened out by the deposition of the older cover-sand, and on the hills the fine material from the same sources was deposited as loess; *pingos* (frost mounds) were a common local feature (Maarleveld and van den Toorn, 1955). No human life was possible in this pleniglacial period.

But soon the climate improved. Sand deposition ceased. The ice cores of the *pingos* melted away, leaving round, deep depressions as their trace, in which lakes formed. The pollen content of the sediments of these lakes gives a clear and vivid picture of plant life.

In the beginning, trees were still completely lacking, but the herbaceous cover was luxurious and rich in species. The late-glacial vegetation contained not only arctic-alpine plants but also steppe elements, showing that the summer temperature was fairly high (Iversen, 1954). Among these plants were some that reappeared as weeds in cultivated fields (e.g., *Centaurea cyanus*, *Plantago* spec.).

Steppe elements have also been recognized in the rich fauna, which of course had in general a distinctly arctic character.

The first clear climatic improvement is called the Bölling oscillation, in which birch trees became rather frequent. In the Rhine delta a C^{14} age of 10,500 B.C. is found, but earlier determinations are obtained more to the south.

A short-lived deterioration of the climate (around 10,000 B.C.), in which tundra conditions again prevailed must be contemporaneous throughout the area. The next improvement of climate is the well-known Alleröd oscillation, which in our area can be neatly divided into two parts, a birch and a birch-pine stage. Especially in the latter, the forest must have been fairly dense, since, in the pollen diagram herb percentages show only very low values.

Then the Würm ice age produced its last, very cold stage (the *upper Dryas* period). Over a period of some 1,000 years, the forest dwindled again. The pine trees died; and, although the birches continued to grow locally, they did not prevent the sand from starting to blow again. The younger cover-sand was deposited often at the expense of the older cover-sand. New topographical features were added, for the younger cover-sand was often deposited in the form of ridges. Locally, even actual dunes were formed.

The enormous expanses of dead pinewood that remained were easily set on fire. A single lightning bolt or a careless human act or volcanic activity in the Eifel might have caused enormous forest fires. What we find in the cover-sand region is that the buried soil profile of the Alleröd period ("Usselo layer"), is everywhere rich in charcoal, dating from the transition of the Alleröd period to the upper Dryas period at *ca.* 9000 B.C. (de Vries, Barendsen, and Waterbolk, 1958).

Through all these different stages the plant and animal life was relatively rich compared with what may be observed in the present-day circumpolar region. This fact is essential for the understanding of the human activity of this period.

The Hamburgian reindeer-hunters were probably the first to enter the delta. Their beautiful flint industries have been found only in the northeastern part of the area (Bohmers, 1956). A few radiocarbon determinations suggest an age of about 11,000 B.C. On typological grounds, two stages may be distinguished. The well-known investigations of Rust and his co-workers at the classic sites of Meiendorf and Stellmoor near Hamburg are our main source of information about the way of life of these specialized reindeer-hunter communities (Schwantes, 1958).

On pollen-analytical grounds, the sites near Hamburg seem to have been occupied well before the optimum of the Bölling oscillation. So far, no finds can be attributed with certainty to the Bölling oscillation proper or to the cold phase following it. There are present in the area, however, a few upper paleolithic flint assemblages of a different type that might fall into these periods; i.e., the *Cheddarian* and the *Creswellian*. The first term has recently been coined for a small group of surface sites in the Netherlands with flint industries identical to those of some caves in the Cheddar Gorge near Bristol in England. Both cultures illustrate the existence of a land bridge between Britain and the Continent. It should be repeated, however, that the geological age is still uncertain.

Scattered all over the sandy eastern and southern parts of the area are sites belonging to the Tjongerian culture (Bohmers, 1956). Together with the Creswellian, this culture can be considered as part of the "Federmesserzivilisation" of Schwabedissen (1944b). At a few places the culture layer is situated in the Alleröd soil-profile. A recent excavation of a site on the shore of a former lake has shown that the site dates from the birch phase of the Alleröd period (Bohmers and van Zeist, unpublished). A number of varieties of the Tjongerian culture can be distinguished on the basis of flint typology, but it is not yet certain whether they reflect chronological stages or different hunting groups.

Gravette points are characteristic for the Tjongerians. That they were actually points was recently nicely illustrated by the finding of a jawbone of a giant Irish deer in which the top part of a Gravettian point was found embedded.

The Tjongerians must have been hunters. They lived in an environment in which the forest already played an important part. Animals of a different kind had now appeared (e.g., elk, beaver, and bear), and the large herds of reindeer had probably moved northward. But our knowledge of the Tjongerian food economy is still insufficient. We need a site like Meiendorf or Stellmoor really to illustrate the Tjongerian culture, but on the dry and acid cover-sands, conditions for the preservation of bone and antler materials are very poor.

Sites of the type of the Tjongerian and related cultures do not occur north of Hamburg. This may have been due to a climatic factor or to a limit of some

essential food factor, but, also, it may have been due to the presence farther
north of the Bromme-Lyngby people. The southern limit of the Lyngby points
coincides with the northern limit of the Tjongerian culture. The now submerged
parts of the North Sea may have been inhabited by the Bromme-Lyngby people.
The single find of a Lyngby point in the northern Netherlands might be taken
to point in this direction.

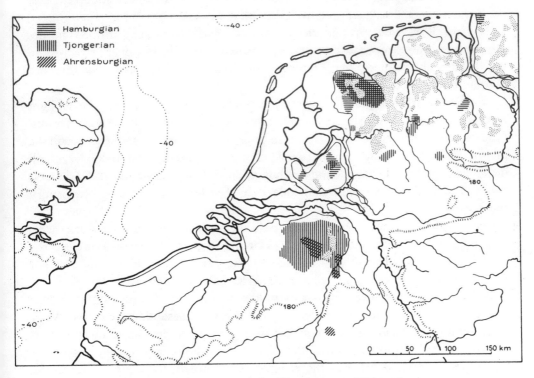

FIGURE 2. Distribution of the Hamburgian, Tjongerian,
and Ahrensburgian materials, lower Rhine basin.

We do not know what happened to the Tjongerians in the following cold
period, the upper Dryas time. The forest fires and climatic deterioriation suddenly caused a great change in the environment for man.

Finds from the upper Dryas period are restricted to the southern part of the
area. At the foot of the loess-covered hills on both sides of the river Maas a
fair number of sites have been found that pertain to the Ahrensburg reindeer-
hunter culture, again described so well by Rust in the Hamburg area. Possibly
the reindeer herds, for unknown reasons, followed a more southerly course on
their annual wanderings through the plain. At one site, a habitation layer of
Ahrensburgian type was found within the younger cover-sand.

A few typical Ahrensburgian bone implements have been dug up from the
beds of the Maas by suction dredgers. So far, however, no bone industries have
been found *in situ*.

THE MESOLITHIC

About 8000 B.C. the climate again improved suddenly. The glaciers quickly withdrew northward. Birchwoods grew dense again (the *Preboreal*), and in not more than a few centuries pine reached dominance (the *Boreal*). For some 3,000 years this tree characterized the vegetation in the lower Rhine basin. During the course of the Boreal period, warmth-loving trees successively appeared, first hazel, then elm and oak, and finally lime, alder, and ash.

The sea level rose, precipitation increased, and lakes were formed in depressions in the cover-sand topography. Britain was still, however, attached to the Continent. Summer temperatures soon rose to present-day heights, but winters remained cold.

Northern European pine woods are not normally very dense, and the sunlight reaching the soil will always be more abundant than in deciduous forests. Grasses and other herbs may thrive in such circumstances, and there will be plenty of food for game of different kinds. If we consider that there were still many lakes present in this period (although small and shallow ones), with their fish and waterfowl, we must conclude that the Boreal environment was very suitable for man.

Once again, we must rely in great part on evidence obtained in other areas to get full insight into the circumstances of life in those days. Nevertheless, the mesolithic has been intensively studied in the Low Countries during the last ten years, and interesting facts have come to light (Bohmers, 1956).

Wherever the younger cover-sand in the sandy zone forms ridges or hills a few meters high, one finds at least a few flints of mesolithic character. Very often sand dunes have formed on such places in more recent times, and the flints are then found at the bottom of the blown-out valleys, where they may have taken on a secondary luster as the result of wind polish. Such is the case in the Hulshorst dunes in the Veluwe and in many other inland dune areas. During the last few years some sites have been excavated where flints were found more or less *in situ*, affected only by soil formation and the activity of animals and roots.

At Haule, Siegerswoude, and other places, Bohmers (unpublished) found— apart from numerous flints—dwelling pits with circular or oval outline (diameters, 2.0–3.0 meters) and small pits (diameters, 0.5 meters) full of charcoal, sometimes with a few burned flints and broken stones of fist size. These fireplaces occur both inside and outside the larger pits.

Fireplaces of this type are frequently met with, and a number of C^{14} determinations have been obtained from them. The surprising result is that all of them fall within the late Boreal period (de Vries and Waterbolk, 1958), even though the flint industries show fairly broad differences—for example, in the presence of such items as trapezoidal arrowheads and surface-retouch. Whether these differences represent minor differences in age, or different hunting groups, or both remains uncertain for the time being.

Only one group of sites is probably exceptional. Because of their typological affinities to the Ahrensburgian culture, these sites are probably somewhat older than the others (Preboreal or early Boreal).

There is, however, other evidence pointing to the presence of hunting groups in this early period. First, the dugout canoe of Pesse (early Boreal; C^{14} age, 6500 B.C.) can be mentioned (van Zeist, 1957). This canoe (length 3.0 meters) was made from a pine trunk and hollowed out by fire. Its prow and stern ends could be distinguished. It was found near the center of a small peat-filled depression at a depth of 2.0 meters, in layers containing pollen of such plants as water lily and *Potamogeton*, indicating a last stage of open water.

Second, a curious phenomenon should be mentioned. At a neolithic site near Anlo, some thirteen horseshoe-shaped depressions (length, 3.0 meters; breadth, 2.5 meters) were found (Waterbolk, 1960, and in press), without characteristic identifying finds but so vaguely outlined that a high age was probable. Radiocarbon determinations for the site, including one pit with neo-lithic finds, gave ages of more than 6000 B.C., showing the presence of early mesolithic charcoal at the site. Although hardly any mesolithic flints were found, it seems probable that these horseshoe-shaped depressions were dug by mesolithic people, probably for some types of hut. The depressions remind us of some structures found by Rust (1958) on the Pinnberg.

Pits of this type seem to occur fairly regularly. At another site such a pit was found to be cut through by a mesolithic fire-place of the ordinary type.

All the mesolithic sites can be assigned to the western group of Schwabedissen (1944), occurring west of the Elbe. They are found on both sides of the Rhine. True microliths of many different types occur in large numbers, but there are no core and flake axes, so characteristic for Schwabedissen's northern group.

A number of bone and antler harpoons with one row of barbs, found along the Scheldt and its tributaries, are generally attributed to the *Maglemosian* culture. Other harpoons have been dredged up by fishermen from the bottom of the North Sea. It is clear that the now submerged parts of the North Sea were inhabited in Boreal times, and the people living in these swampy regions may well have belonged to the Duvensee or Maglemosian cultures of the northern group.

The hunting of game of different kinds (red deer, roe deer, pig, oxen), as well as fishing, must have played an important part in the economy of these cultures, and one may assume that the collecting of plant food was important as well. But there is no direct evidence for this or for any cultivation. Pollen analysis has so far only shown a slight increase of Chenopodiaceae, but these plants may have settled spontaneously on the organic refuse of the settlements. There are no mortars, pestles, or any stone implements other than such items as flint points and scrapers to suggest the exploitation of plants.

It is a curious feature that no bog sites are known comparable to such as those of Maglemose, Star Carr (Clark, 1954), and Pinnberg. Perhaps the in-habitants of the sandy plain relied less on fish and waterfowl than did their northern neighbors, who always kept to the lake and river sides. Even on the Veluwe, where lakes have always been very rare, mesolithic sites are common.

Although sites are numerous, the actual population was probably very small. Large quantities of flint artifacts are seldom found. Most sites yield only a few worked objects. The absence of lakes of any importance compared with the "Jungmoraine" landscape of northern Germany may have caused a more intensive wandering than was necessary for the northern mesolithic groups.

The Boreal was followed about 5500 B.C. by the *Atlantic* period. The sea invaded the greater part of the Rhine delta and the climate acquired a definitely oceanic character. Pine lost its dominance, and varied types of deciduous woods covered the area. On wet places alder and ash played an important part. Elsewhere the oak dominated, with birch on poorer soils and elm and lime on better soils.

The increasing precipitation led to raised bog formation wherever lakes had become full or water stagnated in the woods in broad river valleys. Pollen analysis has shown that the greater part of the late-glacial and Boreal lakes changed into raised bogs. Some remaining ponds lost their eutrophic character and became oligotrophic. It is clear that this new environment of dense woods and huge raised bogs was much less suitable for man. It cannot be an accident that in this period no finds have been made in those areas that were generally inhabitable in Boreal times.

One site must be singled out. It is situated on a sandy promontory at the shore of a relatively large depression, de Leijen, in Friesland, which, according to pollen analysis, was still a lake in early Atlantic times (van Zeist, unpublished). As a result of recent peat digging, it is now again a lake. In the culture layers, quantities of charcoal were found, including the remains of hazelnuts and spikes of Trapa fruits. The flint industry must be attributed to the northern mesolithic (Bohmers, unpublished). No bone or antler remains came to light. The radiocarbon determinations suggest an early Atlantic age (5000 B.C.).

A site with a related flint inventory was found along the Maas in Dutch Limburg, but no date is available so far. It may also fall within the Atlantic period, but this would hardly affect our observation that there is a great contrast in habitation density between the Boreal and the Atlantic periods.

THE NEOLITHIC

When neolithic men appeared in the area, they thus found a practically uninhabited landscape, covered by dense woods, interrupted only by raised bogs (varying in size from a few acres to many square miles) and by stream valleys with their marshy winter beds. The coastal area showed a complicated and ever changing pattern of open water, salt marshes, sand banks, creeks, and raised bogs on poorly drained areas (Pons and Wiggers, 1959–60).

One feature in the coastal area soon became fairly constant, a system of parallel ridges or sand banks, on which dunes were formed. It was behind these dunes that the Rhine delta gradually acquired its present shape, but the continuous sedimentation, the rising of the sea level, and the subsidence of the land remained to cause great changes in the delta pattern.

Neither these newly formed alluvial areas nor the sandy plains witnessed the first neolithic settlers, however, but rather the loess-covered middle terraces of the Rhine and the Maas in the southeastern part of our area. Here a vegetation formed in which lime and elm played an important role and which was just as dense as all other oak woods in the area and certainly was not attractive for neolithic man through inherent openness, as has often been thought.

In recent years the *Bandkeramik* in the Netherlands has been the subject of intensive investigation, as a glance at the journal *Palaeohistoria* (e.g., 1959) will indicate. At three sites, areas of more than three acres each were excavated (Sittard, Geleen, Elslo) with the result that as many as six stages can now be distinguished, on the basis both of house typology and pottery development. A cemetery was also found. The sites of Sittard and Elslo were permanently inhabited. This is clear from consideration of the gradual changes in house types and pottery styles. There is no reason at all to assume breaks in the habitation. Reconsideration of the evidence obtained at the classical site of Köln-Lindenthal (Buttler and Haberey, 1936), in the light of the new facts, also does not support the old theory of a *Wanderbauerntum*.

The houses of Sittard and Elslo were always built of wood. A kind of floor may have been made of loam dug out of irregular pits alongside the houses, but these were not burnt as in the Tripolye settlements. Nor, apparently, were the wattle-and-daub walls burnt. The climate would not permit the utilization of mud bricks. This, in combination with the dissolving and oxydizing effects of the high precipitation in this area, may be the main reason that no tells were formed, as is the case in southeastern Europe and beyond.

The houses of the older phase were all equally large (28.0–36.0 meters long) and show a familiar subdivision into three different parts, each of which probably had its own function. In the younger phases, however, houses with the same sub-division were present, but besides these "complete" houses we find houses in which one or two functional parts are reduced or lacking. This points to a certain differentiation within the settlement, and in this respect a distinct step toward urbanization can be observed. Near one of the "reduced" houses so much flint was found that one might assume the house to have been the flintworker's house. In the very youngest stage the obvious threefold division of the buildings seems to be lost. The central part of the houses is always present. When occurring alone, it has a plan resembling the megaron type.

Throughout all the phases, contacts with other parts of the Bandkeramik area persisted. At first no difference at all can be observed between the Dutch and the Moravian sites, but gradually local styles were developed. Nevertheless, in the shapes of the pots, in the occurrence of *Notenköpfe* (or punctate decoration on the pottery) in various familiar ways, and in a few imports, among other things, features common to the whole of the Bandkeramik manifestation can be observed.

A striking feature is the fact that the flint industry was well developed in the Netherlands, while flint artifacts are less common in middle Europe. In that area, however, shoe-last celts and their fragments are far more frequently found than in the west. The rocks from which shoe-last celts were made are alien to our area. Was there an exchange of flint for the celt adzes? If so, we may reckon with the possibility that exploitation of the Maastrichtian flint at Ryckholt (see below) could go back to this period.

A remarkable fact is that every settlement contains one house that is somewhat larger than the rest, built according to the same principles of internal subdivision, but with a much heavier wall. There is one example at Geleen, two at Sittard (one of the earlier type and one of a later type), one at Elslo, one at Arnsbach, two at Köln-Lindenthal Nordring, and one at Köln-Lindenthal Südring. The wall construction of these houses conforms everywhere to the type of that of the northwestern part of the ordinary houses (i.e., the foundation trench with posts, no parallel loam pits).

It looks as if these buildings had a special function, perhaps a ritual one, and in that case one might assume that the similarly built part of the ordinary buildings had a function of the same kind. Since soil conditions do not permit us to find floors with hearths, altars, etc., no proof of this assumption can be given.

Dutch Bandkeramik settlements occur in a circle along the edge of a loess plateau of fifteen square miles at such short distances that it seems rather improbable that we should find all six stages everywhere, if the old *Wanderbauerntum* theory were the correct one. One does observe a gradual displacement of the settlement at Sittard and Elslo. At Geleen the shift seems to have amounted to one mile. In this respect Köln-Lindenthal shows the opposite: here the settlement seems always to have been at the same place. But not even here was a building intersected by a later one more than once. Apparently, in general, new houses were built between existing buildings.

At Sittard traces of a fence belonging, as in Köln-Lindenthal, to the middle phase of the settlement have been found. Inside the fences there was room for about fifteen houses.

Radiocarbon determinations do not yet allow an estimation of the duration of the settlements, but one might assume some 300 years (for example 4200–3900 B.C.). The Belgian sites west of the Maas have a predominantly young character.

Although typically continental and bound to the loess soils, the distribution pattern of the Bandkeramik shows the great importance of such rivers as the Rhine, Danube, and Elbe for the diffusion of the culture and for its internal connections. Often a predilection for riverside sites can be observed within a broad expanse of loess.

It is regrettable that the deeply decalcified loess of the area has only rarely preserved bones and other organic material. Some Belgian sites have yielded remains of cow, sheep, goat, and pig, as well as deer, boar, birds, and fish. Our picture of the ecology of the Bandkeramik settlements thus remains incomplete.

Still, I believe that sufficient evidence is being brought forward to ask for a reappraisal of the Bandkeramik manifestation.

The permanent character of the settlements, the long-range trade, the flint exploitation and industry, the functional differentiation of the buildings, and the presence of one large building per settlement are important features, which show that the Bandkeramik peasants were well on the way toward urbanism. In the opinion of the author the Bandkeramik settlements in the Low Countries exhibit a level of barbarism higher than that which followed it. This higher level was only regained late in the iron age.

At first glance it seems surprising that the very oldest phase of the Bandkeramik (i.e., the *ältere Linienbandkeramik*, without *Notenköpfe*) is present at the extreme northwest of its area of distribution. This fact does not agree with the commonly accepted theory that Bandkeramik farmers spread from a center in southeastern Europe. A better explanation would be the assumption of a pre-Bandkeramik phase in middle Europe (Quitta, 1960). Radiocarbon determinations for the Starčevo culture in Yugoslavia give us at least 700 years for the establishment of such a phase (Waterbolk, 1960). In the Starčevo culture those elements of plastic decoration occur that we find in the Bandkeramik, besides the dominant incised linear motifs so uniquely characteristic of this culture.

An essential precondition of the explosive expansion of the Bandkeramik must have been the culture's adaptation to a forest environment. If we realize that the forest-adapted Bandkeramik and the tell-building culture of Vinča both developed on the same or at least a related substratum (the Starčevo-Körös complex), it seems reasonable to suppose that this adaptation to the forest took place somewhere in the area of the Starčevo-Körös complex. It may have happened early in the fifth millennium B.C. or even before.

This cultural complex occurs far to the southeast. A direct influence from the other side of the Dardanelles would even seem possible. However, Milojčić's (1959) recent excavation of a prepottery neolithic culture in Thessaly suggests other interesting possibilities for the origins of food production in Europe.

Nothing of the Bandkeramik culture survived directly in our loess area. Whether the climate, the soil, or the technique of agriculture prevented the establishment here of an equilibrium between man and his environment such as was achieved in the Balkans is a problem common to large parts of the area of the Bandkeramik, and no solution is so far evident.

Quite unexpectedly, the Bandkeramik does not seem to have been of much direct importance for the neolithization of the lowlands north of the loess belt. A northward spread could not have happened in our area, since the sandy plain seems to have been completely depopulated by 4000 B.C. But even in Schleswig-Holstein and Denmark, where the early Atlantic Oldesloe-Gudenaa culture preceded the Ellerbek-Ertebölle culture, Bandkeramik influences were restricted to a few doubtful shoe-last celts. Schwabedissen (this volume) has been able to show that incipient cultivation and stock-breeding in these areas were accompanied by pottery types with convincingly clear western affinities. Schwabedissen shares Troels-Smith's (1953) view that the classical Ertebölle culture was semi-agricultural.

Of special interest for us are Schwabedissen's finds from Bad Zwischenahn and the Dümmer in Oldenburg, at the eastern boundary of our area. So far, only one Dutch pottery find can probably be added; a vessel from Eibergen, already referred to by Lüüdik-Kaelas (1955).

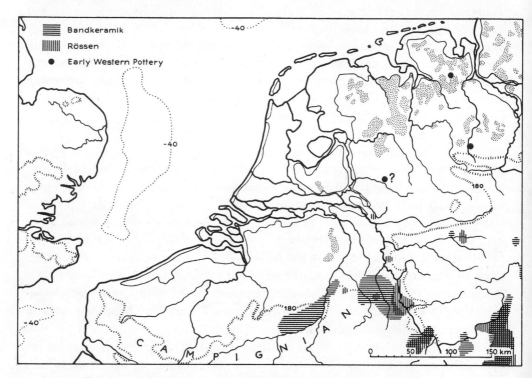

FIGURE 3. Distribution of the Bandkeramik and Rössen materials, and of early western pottery, lower Rhine basin.

At the southern border of our area, on the hills just south of the loess area, remnants have been found of the *Campignian* (Nougier, 1950), including the *Precampignian*. This culture occupies large parts of France and Belgium. The flint industry has many traits in common with that of the Ellerbek-Ertebölle culture (e.g., flake axes, triangular tools). Sometimes potsherds are found, but the association is never certain. Radiocarbon determinations are not available, so until now the chronological position of the Campignian may be determined only by referring to the Ertebölle resemblances.

Although many things have still to be cleared up by new excavations, it now seems probable that the Campignian played an important role in the transmission of new ideas, derived probably from the Cardium culture of southern France.

Whether the gap between the Campignian and the Ellerbek-Ertebölle culture will ever be bridged in the well-investigated sandy plain seems doubtful. One could think either of the hills along the edges of the Mittelgebirge or of the submerged parts of the coastal area as holding the answer to this problem.

Many Bandkeramik traditions were continued by the Rössen culture. No certain finds of this culture have so far been recognized in the Netherlands and Belgium, but they do occur sporadically in the adjacent parts of Germany.

The flint and stone industry, so uniform in the Danube area, connects the Rössen culture with the Bandkeramik, but the pottery has a distinct character of its own—in fabric, shape, and decoration. Characteristic are the trapeze-shaped houses, which have many features in common with the later Bandkeramik houses. A single radiocarbon determination supports the assumption that the Rössen culture is a younger derivative of the Bandkeramik.

The Rössen culture has played an important part in the development of advanced neolithic groups in the plains (Behrens, 1959). Its pottery has many traits in common with the northwest German-Dutch province of the funnel-beaker culture (see below).

For the period between 3200 and 2400 B.C. there is a great difference between the area north of the Rhine and that south of it. The *funnel-beaker culture* occupied the area north of the Rhine, with only a single outpost in the Dutch province of North Brabant. Concentrations can be noted in the Hümling, just over the river Ems, and in eastern Drenthe. Characteristic of this culture are its megalithic grave monuments.

This culture occupies large parts of northern and eastern Germany and the Baltic. It must have originated, according to Schwabedissen, locally in northern Germany and Denmark under influences from the east. Within this culture the Drenthe-Emsland group occupies a special position. Recently evidence has been brought forward (Lüüdik-Kaelas, 1955) that suggests that this group might not be as late as has hitherto been generally assumed. The beginning would fall within the Scandinavian early neolithic C group.

As early as 3200 B.C. distinct traces of cultivation of cereals can be observed in the pollen diagrams (van Zeist, 1959), but a radiocarbon determination for a flat grave below the mound of a megalithic monument of the ordinary type yielded only 2700 B.C.

There is thus an interesting pre-megalithic period at 3200–2700 B.C., in which incipient cultivation may have taken place but which cannot yet be illustrated by corresponding archeological material. In any case, it starts much later than in northern Germany, and this would suggest that a slow diffusion took place from that area. In this respect it is interesting to note also that the Dutch megaliths are of later age than are those in the apparently more nuclear northern Germany.

The variety of pottery styles found in the megalithic tombs points to a long use of these monuments. At first glance one might suppose that the settlements, too, should have had a permanent character, but this does not seem to have been the case. For, at the few known settlement sites in our area, the pottery belongs to one style only. The megalithic tombs, therefore, seem to have been the ritual centers for communities that might have shifted their actual settlements just as often as their presumed slash-and-burn economy made necessary. A site at Anlo (Waterbolk, 1960) was stripped off carefully over an area of three acres. Many pits were found, but no traces of post holes could be observed. Houses cannot, therefore, have been of the same type as those of the Bandkeramik settlements. Perhaps they were of the same small size as the huts found at Dümmerlohausen in Oldenburg (*ca.* 4.0 × 5.0 meters) and were not founded deeply (Reinerth, 1939).

Besides agriculture (emmer, wheat, and barley) and cattle-raising, hunting, fishing, and fruit-collecting were of great importance, as is shown by the Dümmer finds. According to pollen analysis of the old surface below the megalithic mounds (Waterbolk, 1956), the surrounding landscape had an open character, with many herbs of different kinds, bracken, and heather—in short, a vegetation that might be expected on deserted fields. Locally, a heather podsol profile was developed. No indications were found for permanent cattle-grazing as with later cultures (see below).

In the pollen diagrams of the bogs in the inhabited area, human influence can be detected only by counting large numbers of pollen grains. This means that the funnel-beaker people made only few and small clearings in the forest.

An interesting point is the decline of elm, which can be observed at the same pollen level at which the first traces of agriculture appear. In the discussion on the interpretation of this phenomenon, Van Zeist (1959) was able to endorse Troels-Smith's anthropogenic explanation. Elm leaves must have been the main fodder for the cattle.

Trade is attested by a few copper spirals from Silesia, amber beads, British jet beads, and probably also Baltic flint axes.

Meager though this evidence is, it tends to suggest that the funnel-beaker culture did not surpass the cultural level of that of the Bandkeramik. The megalithic monuments and the pottery attest a great skill in many respects, but so far nothing points to a labor differentiation within the communities.

Around 2400 B.C., when new peoples invaded the area, the funnel-beaker culture suddenly came to an end. Hardly any of its many distinctive features seem to have survived into the later periods.

In the southern part of the Rhine delta we meet a completely different situation. Mainly along the Middle Rhine, but also along the Saale, Weser, and Elbe, as far as they flow through the Mittelgebirge, the *Michelsberg* culture of undisputed Western origin is present. A number of regional groups can be distinguished (Scollar, 1959). The Belgian sites form one of these groups.

A remarkable feature in the Belgian Michelsberg culture is the flint mines, as at Spiennes. Exported pieces have been found as far away as Coblenz. It is very probable that the flint mines at Ryckholt in the Netherlands were also exploited by the Michelsberg people, but so far only little pottery has been found. A reinvestigation of this important site will take place in the coming years.

The finds of Lommel, occuring on the cover-sand plain, show that at least the Belgian group did leave the main river valleys and the Mittelgebirge. The peoples of this group might have occupied the Campine, which in the middle neolithic elsewhere would seem to be unoccupied. In brook valleys in this area, finds of antler or bone artifacts have been made fairly often, and in the older literature these have been attributed to the Robenhausian. In reality, it is quite possible that the artifacts were made by the Michelsberg people.

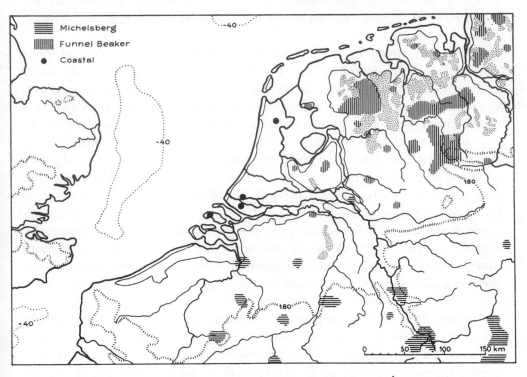

FIGURE 4. Distribution of Michelsberg, funnel-beaker, and coastal materials, lower Rhine basin.

The absolute age of the Michelsberg culture would, on the basis of existing radiocarbon determinations, seem to be at the beginning of the third millennium B.C., but Schwabedissen (1960) assumes that the manifestation started a few centuries earlier.

The fact is interesting that Campignian influences have been seen in the Michelsberg flint industry. This, too, points to the importance of the Campignian as a substratum for the neolithization of western Europe.

Recent finds have shown the presence of a third culture in the Rhine delta around the middle of the third millennium B.C. These finds occur not in the actual dune district but on sand flats or sandy creek banks in the lee of the dunes. The finds are often covered by younger sediments and lie below present-day sea level. They consist of the habitation places of a people who until recently were difficult to place in a European context. The number of sites is small, distinctive pottery types are scarce, and there seem to be fairly large differences among them. Relationships have been sought in both a northern and a southern direction, but recently, at Vlaardingen, Glasbergen was able to point to distinct

Chassey B affinities on the basis of rich pottery finds. Ecologically, this provisionally named *coastal culture* (de Laet and Glasbergen, 1959) is certainly related to the Ellerbek-Ertebölle culture. Though it is much younger, the coastal culture somehow bridges the gap between the Ellerbek-Ertebölle culture and the Campignian. It suggests the possibility of earlier contacts along the Atlantic coasts.

Leaving the origin of this coastal culture aside, we can state that these communities were adapted to delta life. They lived on temporarily dry banks and relied mainly on hunting and fishing. Shell mounds including fish remains were found at two places; numerous remains of sturgeon were identified at a third. The fragments of a net were found as well. Bones of the domesticated cow occur. That the people tilled even small plots seems to be improbable on environmental considerations. Querns have been found, however. Possibly they provided themselves with cereals by trading some of their products to their relatives on the sandy uplands, although the distances were at least some 50 kilometers as the crow flies. From two of the sites there is proof of direct connections with the sandy uplands, as we shall see in one of the following paragraphs. Further interesting facts about the coastal culture are being brought forward by Glasbergen's still-continuing excavations at Vlaardingen, where conditions for preservation of organic material are extremely good.

At about 2400 B.C. the area north of the Rhine was invaded by a new people, easily recognizable both by their material equipment and by the effects they produced on the landscape. Their settlements are scarcely known, but their graves are common, both as flat graves and as tumuli (van der Waals and Glasbergen, 1955). These may contain a cord-decorated *protruding-foot beaker*, a long flint dagger blade, a small flint axe, and, rarely, a stone battle axe or a second axe or second pot. Often only one of these objects is present. These groups doubtless belong to the well-known complex of the *corded-ware* or *battle-axe* cultures that really originated on the south-Russian plains. They entered our area through the plains north of the German Mittelgebirge.

From the distribution of these corded beakers it seems clear that the newcomers at first avoided the areas of dense funnel-beaker settlements. Their makers penetrated far to the west, and eventually reached the coastal site of Zandwerven. This is important, since, in general, the distribution of the corded ware is very continental; unlike the bell beakers, it does not cross the North Sea. If anything, this shows that the coastal culture, mentioned above, had connections with the sandy uplands. Typologically later beakers—with herringbone and zig-zag ornamentation—are also found in areas with dense megalithic habitation and on the eastern bank of the river Maas.

Stray finds of battle axes are fairly common. In Lower Saxony it has been found that the typologically earliest types of battle axes strictly avoid the areas of dense megalithic habitation. This nicely confirms the Dutch observations that are based on pottery distribution. Early protruding-foot beakers (abbreviated "p.-f. beakers") have not been found south of the Maas.

The influence of these immigrants on the landscape was enormous (Waterbolk, 1956). In a short time such large openings had been made in the forests that these are reflected in every pollen diagram in the area, even in those from the center of large raised bogs, miles away from inhabited country (van Zeist, 1959). Everywhere an increase of the lanceolate plantain weed is the most conspicuous feature, but it is accompanied by an increase of sorrel, grasses, and other herbs. The same pollen types show extremely high values in the spectra of barrows belonging to this culture. Furthermore, radiocarbon measurements on peat samples from this pollen level yield the same result—2400 B.C.—as those of charcoal from the graves.

Following Iversen's (1949) reasoning, there can be no doubt that the p.-f.-beaker culture had large herds, which grazed freely over the landscape that had been opened by the clearance-fire method. Grain imprints in pottery and pollen finds below barrows suggest that the people had some grain fields as well, but a heavy accent doubtless lay on cattle-raising.

At Anlo a cattle *kraal* was excavated (Waterbolk, 1960). It consisted of a deep foundation trench with heavy posts, enlarged twice, enclosing an area of about one acre, in which not a single post hole was observed. Near two of the three entrances typical cattle sluices were found. The *kraal* was stratigraphically older than some pits that were dug in the earliest part of the bronze age and most probably belongs to the p.-f.-beaker culture. It extended partially over a settlement site of the Havelte stage of the funnel-beaker culture. It seems likely that the invaders deliberately chose this site. Perhaps they caused the departure of the former inhabitants. Outside the kraal a few flat graves with p.-f. beakers were found.

From the foregoing emerges a picture agreeing well with the current views of the battle-axe cultures, of groups of warlike herdsmen migrating quickly along existing continental pathways. Although at first they occupied only the unsettled areas, they soon brought distress to the more sedentary people of the funnel-beaker culture, whose independent existence cannot subsequently be traced.

Less than two centuries later, new groups of invaders arrived in the delta, characterized by corded beakers of a different shape; in fact, these are *bell beakers*, as is clearly shown by the presence of internal rim decoration, by the external decoration being present from rim to base, by the associated finds (wrist protectors, etc.), and by the barrow types. The pots are considered to be bell beakers influenced by the p.-f. beakers (van der Waals and Glasbergen, 1955). At the site of Anlo they occurred in the same flat-grave cemetery as did typical p.-f. beakers.

The over-all distribution pattern of these all-over-corded bell beakers is, however, quite different from that of the p.-f. beakers. They occur mainly along the

Rhine below Coblenz, but their distribution extends to the west, on both sides of the river Maas. They occur also in Britain, which definitely proves that their makers were familiar with water transport. Pollen analysis has not yet given us a clear picture of the economy of these peoples, but we may assume that they followed the example of their immediate forerunners.

The group mentioned above has brought us into contact with the bell-beaker world as a whole. So far, there are no radiocarbon determinations that tell us definitely when the bell-beaker people arrived. It may have been a little later than the corded-beaker people, but one would expect that they would be earlier than the makers of all-over-corded beakers, who were present as early as 2100 B.C.

The earliest bell beakers in the Rhine delta belong to the pan-European type. It is probable that the bell-beaker people arrived in the delta by ship along the Atlantic coasts. Indeed, their seaborne character makes a strong contrast with the continental corded-beaker groups. On the other hand, even more than these groups, the bell-beaker people sought the old places of habitation. In Drenthe, the earliest bell beakers are found within the area of dense megalithic habitation. Not infrequently bell-beaker sherds are met with in the contents of megalithic monuments. A like situation exists in Spain and Brittany. Bell beakers have been found in at least three places in the coastal area.

So far, little pollen data is available from the grave monuments. It shows a vegetation much more like that around megaliths than around the monuments of the corded-beaker people. Apparently bell-beaker people were not specialized herdsmen like the latter. On the other hand, trade certainly was important; such things as amber, gold, and copper daggers were transported over large distances. But perhaps the most important trade stuff was salt, as has been recently suggested.

Apart from these three different beaker groups (the protruding-foot-beaker group, the all-over-corded-beaker group, and the true bell-beaker group), a fourth manifestation must be mentioned, the Seine-Oise-Marne culture (abbreviated "S.O.M. culture"). The S.O.M. people entered our area through the valleys of the Sambre and Maas but scarcely penetrated into the actual plain. Thus in this period, too, the area between the Scheldt and the Maas seems to have been less densely inhabited than the region north of the Rhine. Future investigations, however, may change the picture. The Michelsberg, Chassey B Beaker, and S.O.M. cultures may all have been more common in this area than would appear from the extant finds.

After these first immigrations in the centuries around 2000 B.C., local developments began taking place. Although no definite archeological proof can be given, one might suppose that the old population of the funnel-beaker culture was incorporated into the local bell-beaker groups. In the pottery and grave inventories, influences of both p.-f.- and bell-beaker groups can often be distinguished. Such high plantain values are found in the pollen spectra that cattle-grazing seems to have played an important part in the economy.

One local group must be mentioned especially—the makers of the beautiful bell beakers of *Veluwe* type, which occur in great number on the Veluwe but only sporadically in the surrounding areas. It is to be regretted that, so far, no settlement sites of this group have been excavated.

At about 2000 B.C. two timber trackways were built in a large raised bog in Drenthe. On one of these trackways a wheel was found. Perhaps the main purpose of the tracks was to bridge the wet zone between the sandy uplands and the rivers. In this way they would have served the long-distance contacts already suggested. That these contacts were maintained throughout the late beaker period is well attested by the grave finds. A highly characteristic group of imports in late beaker times is formed by daggers of Grand Pressigny flint. Their main distribution runs up to the river Weser.

Very often there are finds of beaker sherds pointing to a settlement, but excavation has so far provided only a few pits at most. Nothing points to the existence of permanent settlements. Wandering groups of various characters and origins, practicing both grain-growing and cattle-grazing, characterize the last stage of the neolithic in the Rhine delta.

In fact, it is clear that no local straightforward progressive development of food production can be observed. After the sudden appearance of the Bandkeramik, a period of incipient cultivation and domestication seems to have been present in the northern part of the area, but archeological evidence is scanty. It was followed by a period in which both the funnel-beaker and the Michelsberg cultures seem to have realized effective food production to a considerable degree. But, in the coastal area, hunting-fishing communities persisted. Then, after the partial clearing of the forest, herdsmen entered the sandy plain, soon to be followed by other immigrants.

The landscape had been opened by human activity to a considerable extent by the end of this general period, and *Calluna* heaths were formed locally. But, since men did not stay long in one place, an actual heather podzol profile was not yet formed and reforestation was always possible. Megalithic monuments are often built on a fairly strongly podzolized surface, while beaker barrows show this feature only seldom. The difference has been explained climatologically, but it seems more probable that the formation of a podzol profile depended also on the duration of occupation at a given place.

So far, we have not mentioned the *Subboreal* period, starting at about 3000 B.C A gradual decline of summer temperature can be observed in the record. In the forest, beeches appeared at the expense of lime and elm.

THE BRONZE AGE

Not until 1500 B.C. did the Rhine delta come under the influence of bronze-age cultures. Imports from the Unĕtice culture area to the east are extremely rare. But Irish bronzesmiths were active in the delta at about 1500 B.C., and a little later the Sögel bronze industry sent its exports all over our area. After about 1400 B.C., a strong influence from England can be noticed, and, still later, imports came also from northern France and southern Germany. The traveling bronze-smith was a new feature in the communities of our delta (Butler, 1959).

But there are more changes to be noted in the record for the beginning of the bronze age. Recent observations in Drenthe strongly favor the theory that, at about this same time, settlements again acquired a more permanent character. Cemeteries remained continuously in use from this time on; plough soil can be recognized, which means prolonged cultivation on one place; and strong pod-solization suggests permanent grazing grounds. Although direct evidence in the form of food remains is lacking, it is highly probable that not until now may we speak of a fully effective food production.

At Deventer a middle-bronze-age settlement was excavated (Modderman, 1955); one typical ground plan of a house was obtained (15.5 × 3.0 meters). Early-bronze-age pottery of the so-called "barbed-wire" decorated type was present at the same site.

In the southwestern part of the area and up to the sandy districts of Utrecht and Noord Brabant, direct influences from Britain are clearly indicated in middle-bronze-age pottery types (Hilversum urns) and barrow types (Glasbergen, 1954).

Long-distance trade is attested by the famous necklace of Odoorn, containing beads of Nordic amber, Cornish tin, and Egyptian segmented fayence beads. But in general the early and middle bronze ages in the Rhine delta have a poor character. Bronze objects are only rarely found in graves, and no such dramatic bog finds occur as in Denmark. Nevertheless, the contacts with the surrounding areas are clear. We can visualize a sedentary rural economy, relying on agri-culture and cattle-raising and with trade and the bronze industry playing a fairly important role.

Funeral rituals were complicated, as is attested by the temporary mortuary houses and the elaborate circumstructures of the barrows: ring-ditches, stone circles, berms, and at least five different types of post circles. Some of these wooden structures are clearly related to the famous British henge monuments. Special mention may be made of a bog "temple" recently found in a large raised bog.

During the late bronze age strong influences from the south can be noted in the record. Probably actual immigrations took place. The burial ritual changed and ring-ditch urn fields are, from now on, a conspicuous feature on the sandy soils. Often the total number of burials must have amounted to many hundreds.

On the basis of the pottery and the ring-ditch types, at least two main groups can be distinguished: a northern group occupied Drenthe, Twente, and parts of Westfalia and a southern group occurred on both sides of the Rhine. For the southern group, the *Kerbschnitt* ware is quite typical. Our knowledge of settlements from this period is restricted, but grain imprints on the pottery suggest that a variety of crops were grown, including wheat, barley, and millet.

The bronze objects from this period show trade connections with many different areas, including Britain, Brittany, and southern Germany. Although in the northern part of our area a local bronze industry seems to have existed, the Rhine delta in general was very poor compared to Brittany or Switzerland or Denmark.

A few bronze-age finds are known from the dune district, and one alluvial area (West Friesland) had, at about 1000 B.C., a bronze-age population that left a great number of barrows, mostly built upon a plough soil that shows beautiful markings of cross-ploughing. However, no settlement site has so far been excavated in this region.

But, in general, throughout the greater part of the bronze age, habitation was restricted to the sandy uplands. It was not until the end of this period that large-scale colonization of the sea marshes took place and that the perennial struggle between man and sea started, which then characterized all subsequent human development in the Rhine delta.

THE IRON AGE (from about 500 B.C.)

In the southern urn-field area the iron age started with the appearance of Hallstatt warriors, who left richly furnished graves with such things as chariots, horse trappings, and swords, the products of Italian bronze industry. These warriors may have been either immigrants or local rulers who took over the customs of their southern neighbors and who could afford to buy costly Mediterranean wares.

Recent investigations in the northern provinces of the Netherlands (Waterbolk, 1959) have thrown more light upon the causes and circumstances of the colonization of the sea marshes. The series of successive immigrations and cultural impulses, to which we have briefly referred, were probably accompanied by improved methods of land cultivation. This led, about 500 B.C., to a dense population, at least in Drenthe. Synchronous cemeteries and cultivated fields ("Celtic fields") occur at intervals of only one mile, and, since completely excavated urn fields make possible an estimate of the population involved, one may conclude that the population of Drenthe was of the same order of magnitude as it was in, say, the eighteenth century. Hamlets were probably very small; they consisted of only three to five families.

The increase in population and number of settlements was at first possible at the expense of the forest, but, as the last remnants of the forest vanished, the fields became exposed to the wind. Sand dunes originated, and detailed profile studies show that this process was more or less synchronous over large areas.

Exactly the same archeological material as that of the blown-over settlements occurs also in the sea marshes of Frisia. It is found in the deepest layers of the so-called "terpen," the artificial mounds that are so characteristic for the tidal flats behind the southeastern shore dunes of the North Sea. These mounds grew in height (up to 6 meters) as a combined result of the accumulation of organic debris and the deliberate enlarging of the settlement. Once in many years the sea might invade the area, and people would never forget an event of this kind. In fact, the development of the terpen did not end until the building of the dykes began, about 1000 A.D.

While the sandy uplands were practically depopulated for a couple of centuries, the clay marshes witnessed an enormous increase of population. Excavations have shown large farms, with places for many cattle. Grain cultivation was also possible. And, when the Roman conquerors arrived in the Rhine delta, they were astonished by the activities of these Frisians, as they called them. Their reputation was "clarum inter Germanorum." A relative richness can be observed in their material equipment, and the Frisians provided themselves very soon with what they could get of Roman luxury.

It was not only the sea marshes of Groningen and Friesland that were inhabited. Settlements were established during the centuries around A.D. 1 on the creek banks along the Rhine and the other rivers, on bog surfaces, on the dunes—in short everywhere that circumstances were at least temporarily propitious, although by no means safe forever. Although there is as yet little archeological proof of the point, the assumption is justified that these other settlers came from adjacent sandy regions, just as had the Frisians. In the early iron age the area south of the Rhine was just as densely inhabited locally as was Drenthe, and here, too, sand dunes destroyed the fields.

Apparently the rural economy was of a high standard. The resulting increase in the population led to colonization of hitherto uninhabited land but not to the founding of towns or other centers of importance. For neither the archeological evidence nor the written records of the Romans suggest the presence of these. Every farm and every village was self-supporting. Even iron-smelting was probably a home craft. Surplus food, skins, and textiles were goods that the farmers could trade for various necessary imports, such as basalt-lava grinding stones or luxury wares.

Cemeteries are known only on the sandy uplands. They consist of the remnants of a funeral pyre, covered by a low barrow, or only surrounded by a ditch, often square in form.

After having tried to establish a more northern frontier, the Romans soon made the Rhine the limes of their empire. A row of castella was built to protect the limes, and the area south of the Rhine was soon Romanized, with the result that for the first time in the history of the Rhine delta, actual towns originated. Thus such places as Nijmegen, Cologne, and Xanten became such centers of military and civil activity that they may well have deserved to be named towns, at least temporarily.

But their origin was possible only within the Roman empire, and after its collapse these towns probably lost much of their essential urban features. They were certainly not the result of an independent development in the Rhine delta. Some again attained importance in medieval times as religious or political centers.

Actual towns, in Childe's sense, did not start until the eighth century A.D. Dorestad, Tiel, Deventer, and Utrecht all were trade centers situated along the main waterways. With these towns began the expansion of sea-bound trade and commerce, which, in the following centuries, led to the originating of other new and flourishing towns and ultimately to the present independence of the Low Countries. But the elucidation of these historic developments cannot be the task of a prehistorian.

CONCLUSIONS

Summarizing the immediate considerations given above, we may conclude that real urbanization, as the result of a more or less independent development, was realized only relatively late in historic times. It was based on fishery and long-distance trade, and the favorable geographic position certainly was also an important factor.

This period was preceded by one of some thousand years, in which a peasant society attained great skill in the cultivation of the fertile but often dangerously flooding delta sediments. A thorough knowledge of the water in every respect was gradually obtained, as was also knowledge of such things as shipbuilding and the building of canals and dykes. From Roman times onward a few towns were important as political and religious centers, but they depended on foreign political or religious powers.

The decisive impulse to the colonization of the delta seems to have been an agricultural catastrophe on the sandy plain, where improved agricultural methods and successive immigrations had led to overpopulation. This emigration came at the end of the bronze age, which had a duration of some 1,000 years and in which sedentary groups practiced a probably fully effective mixed farming. Bronzes were traded over long distances; in the late bronze age the northern part of the area had a small bronze industry of its own.

In the neolithic a number of highly divergent cultures can be distinguished, from the specialized fishing and hunting communities in the coastal area to the highly developed Bandkeramik farmers, whose degree of barbarism has been underestimated in the past. Their settlements were permanent, and a certain labor differentiation can be deduced. For some centuries they maintained an economy so well adapted to the loess environment that comparison is only possible with the terpen population in the iron age.

Throughout the neolithic and bronze ages, outside influences were of paramount

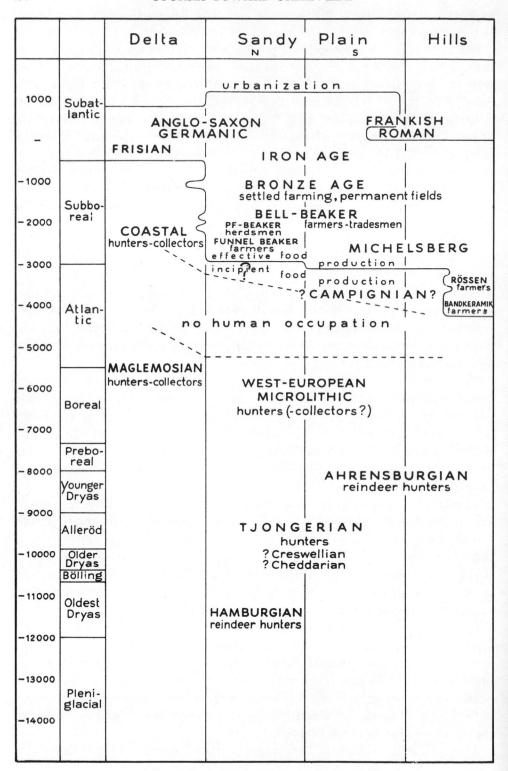

FIGURE 5. Chronological sequence in the lower Rhine basin.

importance. Local developments can be traced only for durations of at most a few hundred years; they were broken off as a result of an agricultural catastrophe, or the immigration of new peoples, or for unknown reasons.

A stage of incipient cultivation and animal domestication can be assumed on good grounds, but this too seems to have been connected with diffusion of allochthonous peoples rather than with a development out of a local mesolithic tradition. For it seems that raised bog formation and the closing of the forest had already made the area uninhabitable for mesolithic man. This happened long before any stimulus to food-producing could come from the outside world.

The influence of the Rhine and the other rivers has always been important, albeit in many different ways. Very often the Rhine was the border between two contemporaneous cultures or a geographic barrier. But in other cases the Rhine directed the diffusion of cultures, either because actual water transport took place (bell-beaker culture) or because the valleys were the binding element (Bandkeramik, Michelsberg). The delta itself, with its rich plant and animal life and fertile but unstable soils, was exploited by the mesolithic Maglemosians and in the neolithic by the coastal culture. From the iron age onward it served as the settlement area for a well-adapted peasant society that had mastered its environmental difficulties. The experience of these peasants may well have been a prerequisite for the successful unfolding of trade and commerce that led to the final urbanization of the lower Rhine basin.

BIBLIOGRAPHY

BEHRENS, H.
1959. "Die Rössener Kultur und ihre Bedeutung für die Herausbildung der Tiefstich-keramik aus der Trichterbecherkultur," *Die Kunde*, n.s., 10:44–50.

BOHMERS, A.
1956. "Statistics and Graphs in the Study of Flint Assemblages I–III," *Palaeohistoria*, 5:1–38.

BUTLER, J. J.
1959. "Vergeten schatvondsten uit de bronstijd." In W. A. RUYSCH (ed.), *Honderd eeuwen Nederland*, pp. 125–42, 's Gravenhage: Luctor et Emergo.

BUTTLER, W., and W. HABEREY
1936. *Die bandkeramische Ansiedlung bei Köln-Lindenthal.* Berlin: Walter de Gruyter & Co.

CLARK, J. G. D.
1954. *Excavations at Star Carr.* Cambridge: Cambridge University Press.

GLASBERGEN, W.
1954. "Barrow Excavations in the Eight Beatitudes," *Palaeohistoria*, 2:1–134 (Part 1); 3:1–204 (Part 2).

HAMMEN, T. VAN DER
1952. "Dating and Correlation of Periglacial Deposits in Middle and Western Europe," *Geologie en Mijnbouw*, n.s., 14:328–36.

IVERSEN, J.

1954. "The Late-Glacial Flora of Denmark and Its Relation to Climate and Soil: Studies in Vegetational History in Honor of Knud Jessen," *Danmarks Geologiske Undersøgelse*, II, Raekke 80:87–119.

1949. "The Influence of Prehistoric Man on Vegetation," *Danmarks Geologiske Undersøgelse*, IV, Raekke 3, No. 6.

LÜÜDIK-KAELAS, L.

1955. "Wann sind die ersten Megalithgräber in Holland entstanden?" *Palaeohistoria*, 4:47–79.

LAET, S. J. DE, and W. GLASBERGEN

1959. *De voorgeschiedenis der Lage Landen*. Groningen: J. B. Wolters.

MAARLEVELD, G. C., and J. C. VAN DEN TOORN

1955. "Pseudosölle in Noord-Nederland," *Tijdschr. Kon. Nederl. Aardrijkskundig Genootschap*, 72:344–360.

MILOJČIĆ, V.

1959. "Zur Chronologie der jüngeren Stein- und Bronzezeit Südost- und Mitteleuropas," *Germania*, 37:65–84.

MODDERMAN, P. J. R.

1955. "Woonsporen uit de bronstijd en de ijzertijd op de Margijnen Enk onder Deventer (Overtijssel)," *Berichten van de Rijksdienst voor het Oudheidkundig Bodemonderzoek*, 6:22–31. (English summary, p. 31.)

NOUGIER, L. R.

1950. *Les civilisations campigniennes en Europe occidentale*. Le Mans: Imprimerie Ch. Monnoyer.

PONS, L. J., and A. J. WIGGERS

1959–60. "De holocene wordingsgeschiedenis van Noord-Holland en Zuiderzeegebied," *Tijdsch. Kon. Nederl. Aardrijkskundig Genootschap*, 76:104–52 (Part 1); 77:2–57 (Part 2). (English summary of Part 1 on pp. 104–5; of Part 2 on pp. 3–4.)

QUITTA, H.

1960. "Zur Frage der ältesten Bandkeramik in Mitteleuropa," *Praehist. Zeitschr.*, 38:1–38.

REINERTH, H.

1939. "Ein Dorf der Grossteingräberleute," *Germanen-Erbe*, 4:225–42.

RUST, A.

1958. *Die Funde von Pinnberg*. Offa Bücher 14. Neumünster: Karl Wachholz Verlag.

SCHWABEDISSEN, H.

1944a. *Die mittlere Steinzeit im westlichen Norddeutschland*. Offa Bücher 7. Neumünster: Karl Wachholz Verlag.

1944b. *Die Federmesser Gruppen des nordwesteuropäischen Flachlandes*. Offa Bücher 9. Neumünster: Karl Wachholz Verlag.

1960. "Die Ausgrabungen im Satruper Moor," *Offa*, 16:5–28.

SCHWANTES, G.

1958. *Die Urgeschichte* (Part 1). Neumünster: Karl Wachholz Verlag.

SCOLLAR, I.

1959. "Regional Groups in the Michelsberg Culture," *Proc. Prehist. Soc.*, n.s., 25:52–134.

TROELS-SMITH, J.
1953. "Ertebøllekultur-Bondekultur," *Aarbøger for Nordisk Oldkyndighed og Historie*, pp. 5–62. (English summary, pp. 47–62.)

VRIES, H. DE, W. BARENDSEN, and H. T. WATERBOLK
1958. "Groningen Radiocarbon Dates II," *Science*, 127:129–37.

VRIES, H. DE, and H. T. WATERBOLK
1958. "Groningen Radiocarbon Dates III," *Science*, 128:1550–56.

WAALS, J. D. VAN DER, and W. GLASBERGEN
1955. "Beaker Types and Their Distribution in the Netherlands," *Palaeohistoria*, 4:5–46.

WATERBOLK, H. T.
1954. "De Praehistorische mens en zijn milieu." (Thesis, Groningen.) (English summary, pp. 141–146.)

1956. "Pollen Spectra from Neolithic Grave Monuments in the Northern Netherlands," *Palaeohistoria*, 5:39–51.

1959. "Nieuwe gegevens over de herkomst van de oudste bewoners der kleistreken," *Akademiedagen*, 11:16–37.

1960. "The 1959 Carbon-14 Symposium at Groningen," *Antiquity*, 34:14–18.

1960. "Preliminary Report on the Excavations at Anlo," *Palaeohistoria*, Vol. 8:59–90.

ZEIST, W. VAN
1957. "De mesolithische boot van Pesse," *Nieuwe Drentse Volksalmanak*, 75:4–11.

1959. "Studies on the Post-Boreal Vegetational History of South-Eastern Drenthe (Netherlands)," *Acta Botanica Neerlandica*, 8:156–84.

NORTHERN CONTINENTAL EUROPE

HERMANN SCHWABEDISSEN

A. LANDSCAPE, MAN, AND THE MOVEMENT OF CULTURES

LOWLAND PLAINS extend over the greater part of northern continental Europe. The ice ages formed their essential features. To the south they border on a mountainous zone that is shaped by pre-Pleistocene formations. This Central European mountain shield extends rather far north, pointing in the general direction of the Cimbric Peninsula.

The mountainous shield is enclosed by lowlands that broaden out toward the southeast and southwest. Rivers in the northern European lowlands tend to flow in a southeast-northwest direction; those of the westerly plains flow from the south to the north or from the east to the west. The geographical situation is of significance for the history of permanent settlement. (*a*) It provided man with the environment of a specific lowland-plains vegetation and a landscape of lakes, rivers, and bogs. (*b*) It channeled the movement of cultures and peoples either from the southeast and southwest into northern Continental Europe or in the opposite direction.

Another fact to be considered in our culture-historical reflections is the different distribution of land and water. Investigations dealing with the history of culture and the occupation of new territory in times past cannot proceed from the geographical situation as it is now, but only from the geohistorical situation of the various epochs. We need only recall the existence of extensive dry-land areas in the North Sea and Baltic areas during the late- and postglacial period. From several examples we shall see that these changes did indeed play significant parts.

B. CULTURES

I. The Upper Paleolithic

At the outset we find the Hamburgian culture. Its early and late phases both belong to the older Dryas (terminating, according to C^{14} determinations, about 11,000 B.C.). It is clearly a reindeer-hunting culture and was discovered and thoroughly investigated through the excavations of A. Rust. It can be demonstrated that the glaciers again penetrated the European continent after the later phase of the Hamburgian culture (Poggenwisch). Near Grömitz, at the steep shore of the Baltic, several meters of glacial till cover a layer of tools belonging to the later Hamburgian culture. Evidently the glaciers advanced into the region of the Bight of Lübeck even after 11,000 B.C.

Also for our knowledge of human habitations (i.e., tents) during this period we are obliged to A. Rust (Fig. 1). Schwantes and Rust see the origin of the Hamburgian culture primarily in an eastern context.

FIGURE 1. Schematic reconstruction of a tent from the Hamburgian culture on the Poggenwisch (*after A. Rust*).

The Ahrensburgian civilization, likewise a culture of reindeer-hunters, was also made known by the work of Rust. The idea that it developed out of the Hamburgian culture has much in its favor (Schwabedissen, 1937) but cannot be proved conclusively. Typological similarities of flint tools do not change this, especially since the Ahrensburgian culture is considerably younger and falls into the upper Dryas (between 9000 and 8000 B.C.). For the present, C^{14} determinations interpose 2,000 years between the Hamburgian and Ahrensburgian cultures. On the other hand, no more evidence demonstrates the immigration of this culture—although certain features point to a southeastern provenance. Thus, for instance, the same reindeer-antler axes occurred plentifully on the Pollau site (Pavlov) in Moravia (Klíma, 1955, 1957); there, however, they are much older (C^{14} determinations of about 26,000 B.C.).

Although the Ahrensburgian culture creates the impression of a unique civilization of the western lowlands, it nevertheless shows a relationship to the Swidérien of the eastern plains, where reindeer-antler axes are known also. The flint instruments from the Ahrensburgian differ in some respects from those of the Swidérien. Aside from other typological differences, the *tanged points* of the Swidérien customarily show a surface retouching of the underside, which is not the case in the Ahrensburgian material. It is possible that the relatedness of the Ahrensburgian culture and the Swidérien nevertheless points to a remote genetic connection with the southeast that we cannot as yet fix chronologically.

A civilization of a different kind could be demonstrated for the period separating the lower and the upper Dryas, especially the Alleröd, with its more favorable climatic conditions. It is characterized by *Federmesser* (penknives), Gravettian points, backed knife blades, etc. It is referred to as the *Federmesser* civilization. Up to the present, it is represented chiefly by a great number of surface finds. A stratigraphic occurrence at Rissen near Hamburg and an excavation near Usselo in Holland led to chronological placement by C^{14} determinations and pollen analysis. Accordingly, the *Federmesser* culture belongs to the Alleröd period, or else to a slightly later phase (C^{14} determinations fall between 9000 and 10,000 B.C.).

Three different, probably rather localized, groups may be distinguished within this civilization: the Rissen group in northwest Germany and northeastern Holland, the Wehlen group in northern Hanover and Schleswig-Holstein, and the Tjonger group of southern Holland and northern Belgium. It is misleading to subsume the three groups as "Tjongerian."

Archeologically the *Federmesser* groups can be allied neither to the Hamburgian nor to the Ahrensburgian, but only to the late Magdalenian in the west. Similarities also exist with the Azilian. It remains to be determined whether the *Federmesser* civilization can still be regarded as genuine, although waning, Magdalenian or should be considered Azilian (Schwabedissen, 1954). C^{14} determinations from western European late-Magdalenian and Azilian sites should provide answers in the relatively near future. At the same time, I am not quite certain that the classical Azilian does, in general, really fall within the Alleröd. However this may be, we are dealing here with offshoots of the western European late Magdalenian; it indicates that this culture expanded with increasing differentiation into virgin lands during the late glacial period, especially during the Alleröd, and advanced even into the northern European plains regions.

While the Hamburgian and Ahrensburgian cultures are at least partially related to the southeast, the *Federmesser* civilization is incontrovertibly connected to the west of Europe. Western European late Magdalenian peoples or their descendants seem to have advanced into the northern plains, making them their home during the late glacial period.

Another culture of the terminal paleolithic remains to be accounted for: it is the Bromme-Lyngby culture, which dovetails with the *Federmesser* civilization in many ways, although its character is still insufficiently explored. Phases of it belong to the Alleröd period (Bromme dating). It is not yet clear where this culture was centered. Among other things, we shall have to consider whether or not it should be sought on the erstwhile dry lands now covered by the North Sea.

MODE OF LIFE AND FORM OF ECONOMY

The bearers of the *Federmesser* civilization might be thought of as relatively localized hunters if we connect the Alleröd period and its open forests with the first occurrence of *Standwild*, game which keeps to established grounds. In contrast, the treeless scrub tundra of the lower and the upper Dryassic period was primarily the range of the incessantly moving reindeer on its continuous seasonal back-and-forth migrations. As the excavations at Meiendorf and Stellmoor have shown, reindeer has been the principal game animal of the Hamburgian and Ahrensburgian cultures. Hunting it must have been a mobile pursuit, and we may assume that an Ahrensburgian reindeer-hunter of the late glacial period led a nomadic life. Tents (i.e., habitations quickly erected and equally quickly moved to other locations) fit well into this image (Fig. 1).

II. THE MESOLITHIC

Core and flake axes (picks and tranchets), as well as microliths, play a decisive role during the northern mesolithic. Where microliths are concerned, the criterion of smallness should not assume central importance. We should like to see especially those small tools called microliths, which are characterized by geometrical form.

How and where microliths originated is an old problem, of course. One can no longer assume them to have emanated from a single center—once said to be the Caspian—but must suppose several centers of origin. For this we have an illustration in several sites of the Ahrensburgian culture, one of which—an important one—was recently excavated by W. Taute (1959) near Deimern in the Lüneburger Heide. When we also keep the triangular microliths of the Magdalenian in mind, we must indeed give consideration to several modes and localities of origin.

The oldest picks and tranchets are found in A. Rust's so-called "Pinnberg" phase and are very primitive. The axes of the Klosterlund site in Jutland, investigated by Th. Mathiassen, are somewhat younger and further developed, as are those that J. G. D. Clark (1954) recovered at Star Carr. C[14] determinations and pollen analysis assign these sites to the Preboreal.

In Schleswig-Holstein sites of the Duvensee phase fall in the early Boreal. The material from Duvensee itself, not yet fully published, has a character of its own. Despite some objections, it embodies for me a separate cultural group, especially because new stations will show a similar cast (Boksee near Kiel, Hohen-Viecheln); those of the Maglemose group exhibit many similarities with the Maglemose group of Denmark. Aside from temporal discrepancy (the Maglemosian sites are of late Boreal and early Atlantic period), the Maglemosian has an individual stamp. It is not justifiable, in my opinion, to combine all finds and sites of the middle mesolithic in northern and northwestern Europe into a Maglemosian culture. It seems to me that in the mesolithic we must count in local differences that result in local groupings. The causes lie not only in individual traditions but in the molding force of the different environments and particular settlement conditions. These will be discussed briefly.

While the flint implements of the Duvensee group show a strong relationship with those of the Ahrensburg (short, broad triangles, Zonhoven points, large blades), those of the Maglemose group exhibit many similarities with the *Federmesser* civilization, and especially with the Tjonger group of Holland, Belgium, and western north Germany, ranged along the southern shore of the North Sea. Since the now submerged land of the North Sea must be accepted as fact, and since we may conjecture that the cultures of adjoining areas had been represented on it, it is very natural to assume that the chronologically younger Maglemose group (Klosterlund, etc.) had migrated from or across this now engulfed region (Schwabedissen, 1951). The Duvensee group, on the other hand, had developed in the Holstein region or in Lower Saxony from the Ahrensburg tradition. As seen from the west coast, the area of distribution of the Ahrensburgian culture was contained in a "dead corner," not part of the movements across the now submerged North Sea land, and was thereby enabled to develop along its own paths.

During the early Atlantic period we find the Oldesloe stage in Schleswig-Holstein. It corresponds to the Gudenaa culture of Jutland. There is no doubt about the correspondence of these two groups. Thus we find a uniform culture on the Cimbric Peninsula during the early Atlantic period. Until recently its chronological placement was more supposition than proved fact. A site of the younger type at Satrup (Fasaneninsel) could be determined at 4200 B.C. by means of pollen analysis and C^{14} count. It is likely that the Maglemosian culture continued to flourish in the Danish Islands into the Atlantic period proper.

Lately it has been possible for Sv. Jørgensen more clearly to define another culture of the Danish Islands, having a different stamp—the so-called Kongemosian culture. It was first recognized by Vebaek and designated as an older coastal culture by Th. Mathiassen, who could trace its development through his excavations at Dyrholm and other places. G. Schwantes calls it the "Bloksbjerg" or "Amager" culture. Sv. Jørgensen's excavations have, however, demonstrated that this culture is not shore-bound but also occurs inland.

The Kongemosian culture is not represented in western north Germany (Schleswig-Holstein, Mecklenburg, and Lower Saxony). Its origin is obscure. A certain relationship to the Ahrensburgian culture exists, but, on the other hand, there are also connections to eastern areas.

Besides the defined region in which picks and tranchets occur, there are groups of mesolithic cultures in western north Germany that lack such axes. They are characterized by microliths alone and, up to now, are known only from open-air stations. They permit ordering into several developmental phases. However, according to the present stage of research, they have not attained significance for the formation of the neolithic but may have been absorbed in essence into several neolithic groups. It is a problem awaiting intensive study.

MODES OF LIFE AND FORMS OF ECONOMY

The transition from the glacial to the postglacial period brought with it an incisive and rather rapid change of climate, thus affecting flora and fauna. The climate of the Boreal was more favorable than that of the present. Extensive hazel groves have been demonstrated for the Boreal, and, at its termination, deciduous forests of oak, elm, and linden began to expand. The dense forest no longer offered proper ecological conditions to the migrating reindeer. It was replaced by *Standwild*, such as red deer, *Ur* (European bison), wild pig, elk, etc. Beaver built dams along the numerous lakes of the northwestern European plains. All kinds of waterfowl lived in the lakes, and the rivers abounded with fish.

Man, of course, also adapted to the altered environment. The dense forests had halted extensive movement. Just as the game held to defined grounds, so did man. The area around certain lakes and rivers became his narrower ecological confine. It was there that he fished and hunted for waterfowl or lay in wait for big game as it came to the shore to drink. Dugouts—found at Pesse in Holland, attested by paddles found at Star Carr in England, at Duvensee in Schleswig-Holstein, and at Holmegaard in Denmark—carried him on fishing trips or to gather water nuts (*Trapa natans*), which were in great demand. The neighboring woods offered opportunities for gathering berries and roots as well as hazelnuts, the shells of which cover the living sites in thick layers. We have remains of habitations, basket-like huts about 2.5 × 3 meters in size. It is to be noted that several huts are systematically grouped (Fig. 2).

The earliest demonstrated occurrence of the axe, which Schwantes thinks so

FIGURE 2. A late mesolithic settlement by the Retlager spring, Detmold province (*attempted reconstruction after H. Schwabedissen*).

significant, may have played an important part in the adaptation to a brushland and forest environment.

Such a detailed picture of life and cultural conditions during the mesolithic could so far be drawn only in northern Europe, thanks to the excavations of bog stations in Denmark and Schleswig-Holstein. They show us that man was no longer a migrating, nomadic hunter. He had become specialized as a hunter of *Standwild* and as a fisherman who rounded out his diet with fruits; he operated from relatively solid huts, which could not readily be disassembled and re-erected farther along the route, and was thus inhibited, just as by the dugouts, from transportation over a wider region.

During the mesolithic we are confronted by a phase of development that, though remaining an exploitative form of economy, differs from that of the nomadizing reindeer-hunter of the upper paleolithic as a really more restricted hunting and gathering mode of life. In my judgment, this fact is of great significance as preparation and premise for a transition to a genuinely settled form of existence. Nomadic reindeer-hunters could never have immediately taken the step to sedentary agriculture.

III. Protoneolithic and Early Neolithic

1. ellerbek culture

The Ertebölle culture, characterized in Denmark by its shell mounds (Kjök-kenmöddinger), extends over north Germany and over Schleswig-Holstein in particular, although not in the form of Kjökkenmöddinger. It has recently become apparent that this culture does not occur only in coastal shell mounds but that it also has a wide inland distribution. Danish excavations at Aamose on the Island of Seeland, as well as my own in the Satrup bogs and Schleswig-Holstein, have shown this. Accordingly, this culture appears divided into two groups: one (having shell mounds) at the coast; the other, inland. It is, however, still not clear whether the shell mounds designate seasonal habitation sites or indicate a distinct, littorine cultural group.

The Ellerbek group can be more particularly defined by the rich find of bone, wood, stone, and pottery excavated from the Satrup bog, and it permits rather exact determination by pollen analysis and C^{14} counts. Accordingly, the Ellerbek group belongs to the time span between 4000 and 3400 B.C. Its pottery includes, according to the Satrup excavations, the well-known *Spitzbodengefässe* (vessels with conical bottoms) and lamps of many forms, some of them beaker-shaped. The ceramic ware thus creates a fully neolithic impression. A few, still incon-clusive, imprints of grain have been found, and at several locations there occur some domesticated animals; at Satrup it was possible to recover almost half a dozen excellent spades made of ash, which were 140–200 centimeters in length. An undisturbed stratum in the Förstermoor near Satrup produced a so-called *Schuhleistenkeil* (Shoe-last celt). All this should at least keep us from continuing to assign the Ellerbek group to the mesolithic. We are dealing with a new type of archaic neolithic or protoneolithic. This finding agrees with the opinion of Troels-Smith, although I can see in the Muldbjerg I site (for archeological as well as chronological reasons) only the complexion of an extended Ertebölle.

2. EARLY NEOLITHIC I

The succeeding phase seems to add further pottery types, including in some areas perhaps the earliest examples of Becker's types A and B. On this score we do not yet see clearly. On the other hand, Ellerbek-Ertebölle elements recede more and more, though they continue on to the end of the next phase.

3. EARLY NEOLITHIC II

Excavations at several locations on the Satrup moor have permitted us to see further developmental stages of the neolithic in stratigraphic superposition. The characteristic nordic funnel-beaker (Trichterbecher) culture begins during these stages. The first phase (*a*) seems not to know of collared flasks (Kragenflaschen) which do, however, appear regularly in the second phase (*b*) along with megalithic flasks and varied, richly ornamented ceramic ware. Phase (*b*) coincides with the earliest dolmen in the north.

4. MANNER OF LIFE AND ECONOMY

Ecological conditions at the time of the Ellerbek culture, that is, during the late Atlantic period, correspond to those of the preceding mesolithic. This applies to climate as well as to fauna and flora. It was already expressed in the notable change in the way of life and the economy of man: a group of hunters, fishermen, and gatherers who established their small, perhaps kin-defined, communities and built their fixed habitations in relatively delineated areas, as, for instance, the environs of one of the larger lakes. Now an undercurrent of further incipient change is suggested. The appearance of *Plantago lanceolata* gives us a first hint, and the sporadic occurrence of grain and domesticated animals gives evidence of the gradual inroads of a new mode of life leading to agriculture and animal husbandry.

The new economy and mode of existence becomes clearly discernible with the early neolithic at the transition to the Subboreal. Numerous grain imprints and increasing numbers of domesticated animals tell us of a new epoch, that of a level of incipient farming society. Solid houses (Fig. 3), not isolated but arranged in groups, prove that the first stage of sedentary life had been attained.

5. CAUSES OF NEOLITHIZATION

How had the initial process of neolithization, first apparent in the Ellerbek group, been triggered? Are we dealing with an indigenous development, with the intrusion of a new population, or with cultural influences?

The Ellerbek culture of Schleswig-Holstein shows many connections with the mesolithic phase of Oldesloe; the Ertebölle culture of the Danish Islands, as already demonstrated by Th. Mathiassen, relates to the older coastal culture, now

FIGURE 3. Attempted reconstruction of a rectangular neolithic house of
the Trichterbecher culture (*from the remains in Huntedorf,
north bank of the Dümmer, Lower Saxony; after K. H. Jacob-Friesen*).

called Kongemosian culture. The strata of Dyrholm, combined with information
from other sites, let us discern a transition from a pure mesolithic to Ertebölle. It
seems, therefore, as if neolithic elements had intruded into the mesolithic hunting
and fishing civilization of the north sometime during the younger Atlantic period.
Judging by the close intermeshing with the preceding mesolithic, we can hardly
reckon with the immigration of a new population. We are in all probability faced
with cultural transmission.

In which direction do these cultural contacts point? Formerly *Bandkeramik*
was considered the transmitter of the oldest neolithic manifestations from southeastern Europe into central and northern European regions; and even today some
investigators like to connect the earliest northern neolithic with eastern Europe
genetically. In my opinion, this view no longer correlates with the finds now at
our disposal.

Finds of the early neolithic phase, including pottery as well as stone implements,
primarily point to the west. In the east there is no cone-bottomed pottery of the
nordic type, nor are there picks and tranchets. The latter occur in the "Campignien
typique" of northern France and Belgium (which is undoubtedly related to the
Ertebölle-Ellerbek culture); cone-bottomed pottery is found in north Africa, in
the Almeria culture of Spain, in south-central France (Roucadour), and also in
the Michelsberg culture. The Michelsberg culture may have older beginnings
than hitherto assumed, though still being younger than the Ellerbek group. They
seem to cross in one horizon. A great number of details, particularly in the pottery, reoccur in the west. Pottery of the older Chassey culture occurs also in the

stone cists of Hessen. It is interesting to note that it is of Briton type (details will be published elsewhere). Western cultural phenomena thus reached also far into middle Europe. New C[14] determinations also aver the possibility of such a relationship.

Thus the impression grows that the "eastern drift" as an impetus to neolithization is paralleled by a "western drift," whose waves penetrated to the north and became the impulse that directed the hunting and fishing peoples of the region toward a new cultural epoch. Even if this event cannot be called "eruptive," on the basis of the presented facts, it signifies, when seen in context, a decisive change in course—a "first revolution," to use Braidwood's term, in the history of mankind.

C. CONCLUDING OBSERVATIONS

Owing to certain conditions, given by geology and the history of scientific investigation, it was possible to demonstrate for northern and northwestern Europe, as for no other area, a rather continuous development from the late paleolithic through the mesolithic to the formation of the first agrarian cultures. We were able to isolate the following stages in the modes of life.

1. Highly mobile, nomadic reindeer hunters on the late-glacial tundra
2. Territorially restricted hunters, fishers, and gatherers in a densely forested mesolithic setting, which permitted only a less mobile form of life
3. Continuation of the previous way of life, but the first beginnings of the raising of grain and breeding of cattle
4. Sedentary agriculturalists and cattle-breeders with subsidiary hunting and fishing during the early neolithic

The beginning of sedentary life, with all its concomitants, doubtless constitutes the foundation for later developments leading to the growth of permanent settlements, the establishment of villages and towns, and thereby to our present culture —the urban civilization of our day. After all, during the neolithic we find not only solidly built houses—whether of wood or stone does not matter (cf. Fig. 3)— but also settlements of village-like character. The great houses of Barkaer in Jutland could shelter a population corresponding to that of a village. If, until now, Barkaer constitutes a special case, we find in the funnel-beaker culture of the Dümmer near Osnabrück a larger grouping of houses with truly village-like character. Corresponding settlements are even better attested in southwestern Germany—as, for instance, at Aichbühl or Ehrenstein. At Köln-Lindenthal, a settlement of the Bandkeramik culture (Fig. 4), we have a complete village protected by rampart and ditch. Conditions in the geographical area under discussion did not change much during the bronze and iron ages (Buchau, Buch, Biskupin, etc.). At the beginning of the Christian Era we find in our area *Colonia Claudia Agrippinensis*, present-day Cologne (Köln), rising as the first city in the modern sense. All other city foundings here are of a later date.

It is possible that the germ of town formation, a sort of urbanization, is latent in certain types of the oppida.

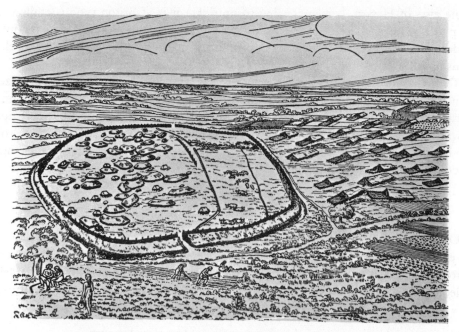

FIGURE 4. The Köln-Lindenthal village, Bandkeramik culture
(*Reconstruction attempt by W. Buttler.*)

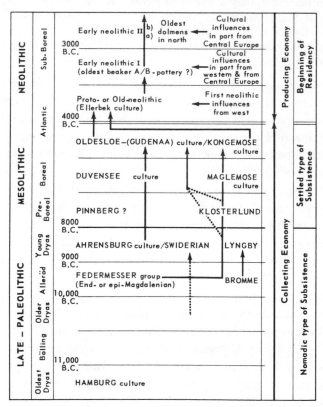

FIGURE 5. Chronological sequence in northern Continental Europe.

At this time, and previously, all settlements and village-like aggregations had nearly the same character as during the neolithic. There is, then, a broad distribution of settlements, ranging far back in time, from which, at different times, at different locations, from totally different constellations, and in entirely different ways, a proto-city or city might arise; unless, of course, it grew forth from entirely different, independent roots. Beyond this, the idea of urbanization or city culture will be difficult to define for and apply to early epochs.

In any event, however, the formation of a city and of urban culture became possible only after foundations had been laid during the neolithic by transition to sedentary life and by the coalescence of defined communities into permanent settlements. Thus, the process of neolithization, as viewed by us, is indeed one of the most decisive *caesurae* in the history of mankind.

BIBLIOGRAPHY

BECKER, C. J.
1947. *Mosefundne Lerkar fra yngre Stenalder*. Aarbøger.

BRAIDWOOD, R. J.
1952. *The Near East and the Foundations for Civilization*. Eugene, Ore.

CLARK, J. G. D.
1954. *Excavations at Star Carr*. Cambridge.

JØRGENSEN, Sv.
1956. "Kongemosen," *Kuml*, pp. 23–40.

KLÍMA, B.
1955. "Prînos navé paleolitcké stanice v. Pavlové k problematice nejstarsidich zemedelskych nástroju, Památky archeologické," 46: 1:1–29.
1957. "Übersicht über die jüngsten paläolithischen Forschungen in Mähren," *Quartär*, 9:85–130.

MATHIASSEN, TH.
1942. *Dyrholmen*. Kopenhagen.

RUST, A.
1937. *Das altsteinzeitliche Rentierjägerlager Meiendorf*. Neumünster.
1943. *Die alt- und mittelsteinzeitlichen Funde von Stellmoor*. Neumünster.
1948. *Die Funde vom Pinnberg*. Neumünster.
1958. *Die jungpaläolithischen Zeltanlagen von Ahrensburg*. Neumünster.

SCHWABEDISSEN, H.
1937. *Die Hamburger Stufe im nordwestlichen Deutschland*, 2:1–30.
1944. *Die mittlere Steinzeit im westlichen Norddeutschland*. Neumünster.
1949. "Die Bedeutung der Moorarchäologie für die Urgeschichtsforschung," 8:46–74.
1951. "Zur Besiedlung des Nordseeraumes in der älteren und mittleren Steinzeit." In *Festschrift Gustav Schwantes*, pp. 59–77. Neumünster.

1954. *Die Federmessergruppen des nordwesteuropäischen Flachlandes: Zur Ausbreitung des Spätmagdalénien.*" Neumünster.

1958. "Untersuchung mesolithisch-neolithischer Moorsiedlungen in Schleswig-Holstein," *Neue Ausgrabungen in Deutschland* (Berlin), pp. 26–42.

1960. "Die Ausgrabungen im Satruper Moor." *Zur Frage nach Ursprung und frühester Entwicklung des nordischen Neolithikums,*" 16:5–28 (18 Abb.).

SCHWANTES, G.

1939. *Vorgeschichte von Schleswig-Holstein.* Neumünster.

1957. *Urgeschichte Schleswig-Holsteins.* Neumünster.

TAUTE, W.

1959. "Neu entdeckte Lagerplätze der Hamburger und Ahrensburger Kultur bei Deimern, Kr. Soltau, in der Lüneburger Heide," *Die Kunde*, n.s., 10:182–92. Hannover.

TROELS-SMITH, J.

1953. *Ertebøllekultur-Bondekultur*, pp. 5–62. Aarbøger.

THE TEMPERATE ZONE OF CONTINENTAL ASIA

A. P. OKLADNIKOV

THE CLIMATICALLY temperate belt stretching from the Urals to the Pacific Ocean across northern Asia encompasses vast areas blanketed by the forest of the Siberian taiga. To the south, these expanses border on the steppes and deserts of Turkestan and those of the Central Asian plateau of Mongolia and Tibet. To the north, the forests gradually give way to the wooded tundra and true tundra of the Far North. Prior to the arrival of the Russians, the taiga area was inhabited by peoples of varying languages and culture: Ugrians, Turkic groups, Mongols, Tungus, and "Paleo-Asiatics." Their history and the past of these portions of Asia, Siberia proper, and the Far East, have been an object of interest to both Russian and foreign investigators since the seventeenth and eighteenth centuries. However, in view of the enormous area involved and its remoteness from the civilized centers of Europe and of the Near and Far East, the history of the woodland tribes of northern Asia was known, until recently, only in part and in its broadest outlines. Written sources dealing with the ancient inhabitants of the temperate zone of northern Asia reach no further back than the period of the Han dynasty (Chinese annals provide information on the land of the Khagyas on the Yenisey and on the Huns of Mongolia and Trans-Baikalia). As a result, archeological materials constitute our basic source of information for earlier times. These same materials retain their importance in many respects for subsequent periods, inasmuch as foreign sources prior to the seventeenth century remain quite limited in scope, while the vast majority of the peoples of Siberia lacked writing of their own. Exceptions to this include only the Yukagir, among whom native pictographic writing was found to exist in the nineteenth century, the ancient Turkic tribes that possessed the Orkhon-Yenisey runic writing system in the seventh to the tenth centuries (and perhaps later as well), and, in part, the Buriat, with their Mongolian script (from the thirteenth century onward). We may understand, therefore, why so much effort has been expended in the last decades on archeological research in Siberia, including the Arctic. Both local and centrally located scientific organizations have participated in this work, which has been sponsored by museums, universities, and regional societies. A leading role among them has been assumed by the Institute of Archeology of the Academy of Sciences, U.S.S.R., which has been organizing systematically large-scale expeditions in Siberia. The most ambitious of the expeditions have been financed from funds allocated by the government for the construction of giant hydro-electric power plants, namely, the Irkutsk and Bratsk stations on the Angara, the Novosibirsk station on the Ob', and the Krasnoyarsk station on the Yenisey.

These researches have broadened considerably our conception of the past of Siberia. Naturally, the expanses of Siberia are too immense to allow full arche-ological coverage. The archeological map of Siberia still retains many "blank spots." Decades will be required to fill these gaps. The historical problems faced by the archeologist are likewise highly complex. Their understanding will require infinitely vaster material than we have at our disposal today.

Archeologists in Siberia are beginning only now to make use of the results of radiocarbon (C^{14}) analysis, though a few initial test runs have been made. As a result, our conclusions still rest, in the main, on the older comparative and stratigraphic methods and remain largely confined within the framework of relative chronology. More or less accurate absolute determinations begin in the middle of the second millennium B.C. (Karasuk burials and the Shang dynasty in China), while the neolithic may be anchored in time from the middle of the third millennium B.C. onward (parallels between burials of the Kitoi type in Baikalia, on the one hand, and pit and catacomb graves in southern Russia and finds in the cave of Sha-kuo-t'un, on the other). Nevertheless, our over-all picture of the Siberian past is in considerably better focus than it was a short time ago. Regional sequences of culture-historical periods have been worked out in the Minusinsk region, in the Ob' area, in the Baikal, in Trans-Baikalia, and in the Far East. A number of syntheses dealing with major areas have appeared, and monographs have been published dealing with major cultural developments. They include the works of S. V. Kiselev on southern Siberia, S. I. Rudenko on the Pazyryk mounds and the ancient cultures of the Bering Sea region, M. P. Gryaznov on the bronze and early iron ages in western Siberia, and A. P. Okladnikov on the neolithic and bronze ages of the Baikal and on the ancient history of Yakutia and of the Far East. Researches on the paleoanthropology of Siberia have been published by G. F. Debets, and M. G. Levin has synthesized the contemporary physical anthropology of the Far East. Valuable researches by ethnographers (S. V. Ivanov, A. A. Popov, L. P. Potapov, G. M. Vasilyevich, and others) have made it possible to amplify the conclusions reached on the basis of archeological materials.

Departing from the results of these researches, it is possible to attempt an outline of the major features of the history of the inhabitants of the temperate zone of continental Asia within the limits set forth by the program of the present symposium, that is, beginning approximately at 15,000 B.C. or somewhat earlier.

The point of departure in such an outline is the existence in Siberia of a distinctive and well-characterized culture of upper paleolithic hunting tribes, as evidenced by remains of their settlements at Mal'ta and Buret' on the Angara, as well as at the site of the "Military Hospital" in Irkutsk. Geologically, they date from the ice age and are marked by a fully developed mammoth fauna, including mammoth, woolly rhinoceros, arctic fox, reindeer, and cave lion.[1] In determining the age of these paleolithic finds, the remains of woolly rhinoceros are of prime stratigraphic importance, inasmuch as they are absent at later habitation sites.

If we compare—both among themselves and with the paleolithic of the European portion of the U.S.S.R.—the three paleolithic sites on the Angara, whose faunal associations include the bones of rhinoceros, we may divide them into two chronological groups. The earlier, representing the early portion of the upper paleolithic in Siberia, would include the habitation site at the Military Hospital, discovered as early as 1871. Its inventory is characterized by bifacially worked laurel-leaf points or knives and by a developed bone industry and includes such items as spheres and rings carved out of mammoth ivory. These traits link it to the Solutrean culture of Europe.

Mal'ta and Buret' may be assigned provisionally to early Magdalenian times, in chronological terms ("bâtons de commandement," perforators of the type found at Mezin, development of decorative art on bone, and appearance of miniature prismatic cores and of small discoidal scrapers).

Unfortunately, the habitation site at the Military Hospital was excavated a long time ago, and the materials obtained were lost in the great Irkutsk fire of 1879. However, the culture of the inhabitants of Mal'ta and Buret' presents a rather clear picture. The sites in question were not temporary camps of wandering hunters, but true settlements, composed of a number of solidly built dwellings designed for prolonged use. At Buret', for example, the remains of four dwellings have been found.

One of these, better and more completely preserved than the others, rested on a quadrangular foundation sunk into the ground that was, without doubt, especially excavated for the purpose. A narrow entrance-way issued from it in the direction of the river. The edges of the depression were first lined with carefully aligned and symmetrically placed thigh bones of mammoth, the lower ends of which were buried in the ground and secured at the bottom with slabs of limestone to insure their stability. These constituted as it were, the "timbers" of this ancient house and formed the structural framework supporting the walls and the roof. The dwelling had about twelve of these "timbers."

In addition to the "timbers," the remains of this paleolithic dwelling retained portions of the frame of the roof. Inside the house, on the floor itself, numerous reindeer antlers were found that gave clear evidence of having been especially gathered and sorted. In a number of instances the antlers were laid out so as

1. Geologists are not in general agreement as to the number of glaciations in Siberia, their extent, or their correlation with those of Europe. The author of a special synthesis on the Pleistocene of the Soviet arctic, V. N. Saks, distinguishes three major glacial phases: a phase of maximum glaciation (which he equates in time with the Dniepr or Riss glaciation), a Zyryanian phase (Würm), and a Sartanian phase (the last stage of Würm).

It is still difficult to relate these sites with any greater precision to specific phases of the ice age. It is clear, however, that they do not antedate the Zyryanian glaciation, and it is likely, rather, that they date from the latest interglacial (Military Hospital site) of the Sartanian phase (Mal'ta and Buret').

to cross at right angles, the tines and main branches being spaced at regular intervals in a kind of grid pattern. It appears from this that the roof of the paleolithic dwelling at Buret' had a frame in the form of a cribwork of reindeer antlers, intersecting and joined not only with lashings but also through the interlocking of their tines. In general, these dwellings and settlements are surprisingly similar to those of the sedentary coastal hunters of northeast Asia in the seventeenth to the nineteenth centuries, the Eskimo and Chukchi.

Hearths were located in the middle of the houses, and the floors of the latter yielded a variety of artifacts of stone and bone. The finds include figures of women and birds carved out of mammoth ivory, engraved representations of mammoths and snakes, a large number of decorated objects of household use, and finely made ornaments.

Apart from the usual female figurines, representing the unclad body, with the head framed in an abundant growth of hair, three figures are outstanding for their depiction of clothing. One of these was found at Buret'. It provides a conventionalized rendering of a one-piece suit with a hood over the head. Two similar statuettes, though miniature and, as a result, rendered more schematically, were found at Mal'ta. In concept, this clothing is analogous to the "airtight" tailored clothing of the Arctic tribes of northeast Asia and North America.

In its totality, this upper paleolithic culture may be described as a continental Arctic culture of sedentary or semisedentary hunters. It was based on the same economic foundation as the contemporary culture of similar upper paleolithic hunters in eastern and western Europe, and flourished in the same environment of the termination of the ice age.

However, the similarity between them is, without doubt, due to more than just convergence. Mal'ta and Buret' have yielded small flint tools, made from thin lamellar flakes, identical to those found at western European sites of early Magdalenian age and at coeval sites in eastern Europe: they include scrapers, a variety of points, and, particularly, perforators of various shapes, including unilateral and two-ended forms.

The similarity between the paleolithic settlements of the Angara and European regions of this period is reinforced further by the similarity of the artistic expression of their occupants.

The connection between the art of the early phase of the Siberian paleolithic and the paleolithic of Europe is apparent, first of all, from the choice of subjects. Foremost among these is the female figure. The basically realistic style in which it is depicted is likewise a definite point of similarity. Particularly significant are the correspondences to be seen in the over-all treatment of these female representations. They are uniformly sculptural and three-dimensional. Nude figures predominate, with arms extended downward and coming together in a distinctive manner in the lower portion of the abdomen. We have here a mother-figure, conceived by paleolithic mammoth-hunters in the periglacial zone of Europe, appearing in the same rigidly traditional form on the banks of the Angara river.

Naturally, it was inevitable that regional differences between the cultures of

Europeon and Asian tribes should arise over the vast expanses of Europe and Asia. Such differences, at times remarkably pronounced, existed within Europe itself. A case in point is the difference between the figurines from Mezin and those of Kostenki. Yet the over-all uniformity of the pattern of paleolithic art in Europe remains an indisputable fact.

For all its distinctive details, the rich art of the Siberian upper paleolithic thus appears as a direct offshoot and local variant of the highly developed and distinctive art tradition of the paleolithic hunters of Europe.

It is quite justifiable, therefore, to suppose that the ancient inhabitants of Siberia came to the shores of Lake Baikal from eastern Europe toward the end of the ice age, bringing with them the basic features of a culture of upper paleolithic Arctic hunters.

However, the process of the population of the expanses of Siberia recently freed of ice was not proceeding solely from the west, from behind the Urals. In Buret' and Mal'ta we already find choppers made from pebbles, the ends of which have been crudely sharpened, which testify to connections with southeast Asia. The Ust'-Kan cave, one of the very early habitation sites of the Altaï region, yielded flakes and points reminiscent of the Moustero-Levalloisian tools of the Syr-Daria basin, in association with the bones of kudu.

There is no doubt that other areas of Siberia, apart from the Angara valley, were inhabited by man at this time. Rhinoceros bones associated with stone artifacts have been found, for example, at a dwelling site near the village of Chastinskaya, in the Lena River valley, as well as at the site of Sannyy Mys on the Uda River, beyond Lake Baikal, in the Buryat Republic.

The finds from these oldest living sites on the Lena and beyond the Baikal differ from the materials obtained in the excavations at Mal'ta and Buret'. Thus, for example, Sannyy Mys yielded miniature blades, as well as miniature core-scrapers, together with massive scrapers reminiscent of Mousterian. However, the data at our disposal are still too scant to allow any idea of the total culture of the dwellers at these sites.

With time, the mode of life and culture of the ancient inhabitants of Siberia— as well, it would seem as their ethnic composition—underwent important changes. These changes were so profound and fundamental that we might ascribe them to some historical catastrophe, such as a replacement of population, if it were not for countervailing evidence of a definite debt of the Siberian late paleolithic to the earlier culture represented at Mal'ta and Buret'.

The late paleolithic period (the later phase of the upper paleolithic in Siberia), represented by such sites as Afontova Gora on the Yenisey, Verkholenskaya Gora near Irkutsk on the Angara, Nyangi and Ust'-Kyakhta on the Selenga, and Makarovo, Shishkino, Nyuya, Markhachan, and other habitation sites on the Lena, was marked by an increase in the size of the population in Siberia. Evidence for this is to be found in the over-all increase in the number of dwelling sites pertaining to the end of the paleolithic. People now occupied the southern reaches of the major Siberian watercourses, such as the Amur, the Selenga, the Yenisey, the Angara, and the Lena. Human occupation extended to the Altaï, formerly buried under a continuous ice sheet.

Changes of even greater significance are to be observed in the culture and mode of life of the occupants of Siberian paleolithic settlements. The earlier dwelling sites, consisting of a number of solidly built permanent habitations, now disappeared. Living sites were in the form of temporary hunting camps, consisting of a few above-ground dwellings, most probably of the tent or *chum* type, of which, except for the hearths, no trace remains to allow a reconstruction of their form or structure. The hearths often have the form of ring-shaped alignments of stone slabs set on end.

The change in house type may be explained by the disappearance of the mammoth and the rhinoceros and the consequent adoption of a new nomadic mode of life.

It is harder to explain the changes in the tool kit, and, generally speaking, in the stone and bone artifact inventory. Stone tool forms now changed abruptly and unexpectedly. Instead of carefully made perforators with thin curving or straight points, miniature scrapers, and flakes worked over by pressure retouch, we now find a widespread class of massive and heavy tools, whose crudity, at first glance, is equalled by their uniformity of type. All of them are, essentially, variants of one and the same tool type, reproduced over and over with amazing uniformity: a massive scraper, semilunar or nearly oval in outline, worked along its steep working edge by retouching in the form of long and broad flake scars. In shape and workmanship, these scrapers are reminiscent in part of Mousterian tools. Stone artifacts at late paleolithic sites include also large scraper-like tools prepared by a distinctive technique from split river cobbles. One end was flaked and retouched to produce a massive cutting edge, while the other was left unworked and provided a convenient grip. Without doubt such implements served specific economic ends. In the main, we must suppose that they were woodworking tools, the forerunners of the axe, as well as implements for butchering game. At the same time, their distinctive form and specific mode of preparation may legitimately bring to mind the choppers of southeastern and eastern Asia and, among them, the tool of *Sinanthropus*.

We must suppose that the prevalence of this technology and of such tools in the Siberian paleolithic marks also a new phase in ethnic history. It is highly probable that this time witnessed closer connections between the local paleolithic population and that of neighboring regions of eastern Asia, above all with Mongolia and China and, indirectly, with more distant areas to the southeast.

Another component in the stone inventory of the late paleolithic settlements of northern Asia is represented by points reminiscent of implements of the Mousterian type and by cores of discoidal form. These artifacts, as noted earlier, appear earliest and in greatest numbers in the west, in the Altaï region and in northern Kazakhstan. It is very probable that they were introduced precisely from these areas, where they were derived from the Mousterian culture of continental Asia.

By comparison with earlier times, bone artifacts appear to recede in importance. Much less care was devoted to their manufacture. Art work in bone disappears altogether. Late paleolithic habitation sites in Siberia as yet fail to yield any decorated implements or ornaments. Yet, this impoverishment of the bone inventory and art was compensated for by the appearance of new types of hunting equipment and a new technique for its preparation. Flat harpoons with numerous barbs were now introduced. Laterally slotted knives and points appeared and served to hold thin inserted side-blades. This is evidence of further improvement in the technology of weapon manufacture through the combination of two different materials in the same object, for example, a flexible and elastic material such as bone and brittle but hard and sharp components of stone.

A remarkable feature of the next phase of the culture-historical process in eastern Siberia was the uninterrupted retention of the paleolithic cultural tradition up to the time of the appearance of fully developed neolithic culture. In Siberia, the term "mesolithic" is inapplicable in its usual European sense. An abrupt break in the technology and form of stone and bone implements did not take place here as it did in the West. There is a complete lack of implements of geometric form and of notched blades, and the typical technique of blade-blunting through retouching is absent. This is due to the fact that we did not have here an intrusion of new populations bearing new cultures, such as the Gravettian and Capsian of Europe.

On the contrary, in Holocene times, that is, when modern woodland fauna was spreading throughout the temperate belt in Siberia, we have continued, at late paleolithic sites, massive stone tools made from split cobbles, and large scraper-like implements or knives of semilunar form, accompanied by composite bone knives and points. Traits of the older mode of life persisted equally unchanged. The evidence for this is to be seen in stone-lined fireplaces, similar to those found earlier and situated, apparently, inside huts of light construction, covered with birch bark or hides. It may be concluded that no major changes in population or mode of life occurred in Siberia at this time, so the ancient late paleolithic traditions were allowed to persist unchanged. It would be more justified, therefore, to term this Siberian culture "epipaleolithic." Its more characteristic habitation sites are those correlated with alluvial deposits of the first riverine terrace of the Angara River at the mouth of the Belaya River, the Biryusa site (lower levels) on the Yenisey, and the Makarovo and Shishkino sites on the Lena. The fauna of these sites is already completely dominated by modern taiga species. For example, roe deer (Capreolus pygargus) is the only animal represented in the lower levels at the mouth of the Belaya River. However, pottery and bifacially worked arrowheads are still absent.[2]

It should be added that the author does not share the view according to which

2. The "mesolithic" age of a number of habitation sites previously so dated has not received confirmation. Thus, for example, level "XI" at Ulan Khada on Lake Baikal yielded in 1959 a flint inventory in no way different from that of the Serovo phase levels above it (as well as a polished adz and typical Serovo pottery).

neolithic culture is to be defined in terms of what has been called the "neolithic revolution" (e.g., V. Gordon Childe), that is, by the beginnings of farming and animal hubandry. In my opinion, we must be guided in the classification of archeological phases by a single, more general, and universally applicable principle, that of the evolution of technology or manner of tool production. On this basis, I hold to the older view that neolithic culture, in contradistinction to the meso- lithic and paleolithic, is founded on the appearance of ground axes and pottery, as well as of the bow and arrow tipped with a bifacially worked point.

This does not exclude the possibility of various types of economy based on a common technology foundation, for example, of hunting, collecting, farming, or stock-raising prevailing locally in response to specific environmental conditions. Likewise, we do not exclude, of course, the possibility of unequal rates of cultural development in different regions, of lag among some ethnic groups and accelerated development among others.

For this reason, the so-called "neolithic revolution" in the Near East should be assigned to the mesolithic. For the same reason, we cannot exclude from the broader framework of neolithic culture those tribes that have retained, over a long period of time within the neolithic, the older forms of hunting and fishing economy.

Two burials on the Angara River, in the Chastyye and Khin'skaya gulches, are of exceptional interest in tracing the beginnings of the new neolithic culture in the Baikal region. The inventory with these burials contains distinctive points of archaic appearance. These points are prepared on narrow blades of regular outline. Retouch is only partial and is confined to the ventral side at the tip and base. The latter is shouldered. Similar points are found occasionally east of the Baikal, but most of them are known from west of the Yenisey, from western Siberia and Central Asia. In Central Asia, such points are characteristic of the Kel'teminar culture of the Aral Sea region. It is in the same area, in the cave of Dzhebel on the coast of the Caspian Sea, that we find the earliest points of this type, dated roughly to the fifth millennium B.C. (judging from the results of a radiocarbon assay of charcoal from the overlying neolithic layer, the age of which puts it in the fourth millennium). On this basis, we may speculate that the fifth to fourth millennia are marked by the movement, out of the steppes and deserts of Central Asia through the wooded steppe of western Siberia and into the Baikal region, of mobile groups of late mesolithic hunters and gatherers, whose culture was related to that of the early Kel'teminar peoples wandering in the area of the Caspian and Aral seas. Their influence may be correlated hypo- thetically with the appearance of the bow and arrow among the Baikal tribes, who had not known formerly this type of weapon. However, in the developed neolithic phase that follows, this southern influence is no longer evident in any way. Apparently, these southerners were assimilated by the local aboriginal population and were absorbed into it without a trace, along with their culture.

In any event, it would seem that the epipaleolithic of Siberia, like the late paleolithic, witnessed the presence in fully developed form of the physical type that is to dominate the subsequent history of the area, that is, the Mongoloid. An indication of this is to be seen in the skull fragment recovered in 1937 at Afontova Gora and in the Mongoloid features of the clothed figurine from Buret'.

The new neolithic period was marked by the definitive establishment of novel environmental conditions that henceforth were to govern the life of Siberia's ancient inhabitants. Instead of the former steppes and tundras, evenly and gently grading into one another, the three environmental zones now prevailing take shape in the form of extended latitudinal belts. More exactly, a new forest belt appears for the first time and separates the two older landscape types—the steppe and the tundra. We now have a vast stretch of Siberian taiga, extending from the Baltic Sea to the Pacific Ocean. A new fauna also appears, its leading representatives being the moose and the bear. Neolithic man comes to occupy more land than his late paleolithic predecessor. Evidence of his presence is found, not only throughout the forest zone of Siberia, but also in the tundra areas of the Kolyma, the Indigir'ka, in the central portion of the Chukchi peninsula (site on the Yakitikiveyem River in the basin of the Anadyr'), on the Popigay and Khatanga Rivers, near the Taymyr peninsula, and in the Bol'shezemel'skaya tundra.

New conditions also mark the end of the cultural uniformity that had prevailed earlier. Several distinct culture areas emerge. Each of these culturally and ethnically distinct areas develops its own pattern, and, in each, culture growth follows a distinct series of stages or developmental phases. The new areas are those of (1) the sedentary riverine fishers and maritime hunters of the Far East, which includes the Amur region and the Maritime Province; (2) the forest hunters and fishers of the Baikal area; (3) the hunters and gatherers of the wooded steppes, steppes, and deserts of Trans-Baikalia and Mongolia; (4) the wandering reindeer hunters and lake fishermen of the tundra and forest-tundra of the northeast; (5) the semisedentary fishermen and hunters of central and northwestern Yakutia; and (6) the fishermen and hunters of western Siberia.

The forest neolithic culture of Siberia exhibits its most typical features in two culture areas that at the same time, stand in marked contrast to each other. These areas are (a) central Siberia, that is, the Baikal region and (b) the Far East, that is, the Maritime Province and the Amur basin. It is with these two cultural entities that we shall now be concerned.

The area of distribution of the Baikalian neolithic *sensu stricto* embraces the littoral zone along Lake Baikal in the south, the whole of the upper course of the Lena River down to the mouth of the Vitim in the north, the entire Angara valley to its junction with the Yenisey, and, without doubt, part of the adjacent territory occupied by the basins of the Stony and Middle Tunguzka Rivers to the west. Since early times the subsistence basis for the inhabitants of this territory has been the hunting of taiga game, supplemented by fishing and the gathering of wild edible plants. In this respect, as well as in many other ways, these peoples continued for millennia the mode of life of their paleolithic predecessors, though they already possessed ground-stone tools and made use of typically neolithic arrow points, retouched by pressure flaking on both faces.

The earliest development phase of the Baikal neolithic is the Isakovo. Burials of this period have yielded large bone lance heads with inserted side blades made from lamellar flakes. They are accompanied by stone arrow points of two types: (*a*) tanged and (*b*) asymmetrically spurred, with basal indentations resulting in a "swallow-tail" outline.

The tools at the disposal of the people in this period included large ground adzes of siliceous slate, triangular in cross section. Slate and nephrite knives were used in female household occupations, along with various scrapers, bone needle cases and needles, awls, and other implements.

The large oval scrapers resemble those of the late paleolithic. The extensive use of mammoth bone and certain types of bone points also hark back to the older culture of the paleolithic hunters.

Pots are of extremely simple shape, parabolic in profile. Their outside surfaces are entirely covered with textile impressions resulting from the application of fine-mesh net, which leaves clear imprints of rather thin, tightly twisted strands and knots. Decoration is similarly primitive. It is limited to a band of punctations along the rim of the vessel.

Subsequently, in the Serovo phase, the older adzes of triangular cross section are replaced by a new type of quadrangular section. Green nephrite is increasingly used, along with siliceous slate, in the manufacture of knives and adzes. The older vessels of simple profile are replaced by a new form with a distinct neck, rim, and body. Distinctive vessels designed for suspension appear in the form of flasks with suspension lugs. Dentate "maggot" and linear dentate[3] decoration become common.

Hunting equipment becomes improved in Serovo times. Graves on the Angara and Lena have yielded long strips of bone that served as backing for bows, which, at this time, are the oldest known bows of reinforced or even composite type in the world. Bow length averages 150–165 centimeters. In all, about 25 bows have been recorded

Graves yield finely made stone fish effigies, most frequently depicting the burbot, less often the whitefish or the sterlet. Similar fish effigies were used as lures in the nineteenth and twentieth centuries by tribes of northern Asia and North America in ice fishing with the fish spear.

Settlements of Serovo times are in the form of "stations," that is, remains of more or less permanent, probably seasonal, encampments consisting of tent-like *chums*, of which the fireplaces remain, in the form of circles of river boulders. Sometimes we find evidence of storage pits and sunken fire pits designed for

3. The Russian term "grebenchato-punktirnyy" (literally, "dentate-punctate"), to judge from available illustrations, applies to what would be described as ordinary dentate stamping in the American literature, or comb-marking in the literature of the European neolithic (Paul Tolstoy, translator).

some special purpose. They may have been used for smoking hides or as steam baths.

A remarkable feature of burials in the Serovo period is the consistency of the burial inventory that accompanies the deceased. No differences between "rich" and "poor" are observed in the burial accompaniments. Such differences appear much later. In most graves we find approximately the same range of objects. It is significant, in this connection, that hunting equipment, such as knives and bows and arrows, occur with male and female burials alike. This brings to mind the women warriors and the active participation of women in the chase among a number of Siberian peoples in the past.

Serovo burials also yield abundant material for understanding the spiritual culture of the neolithic tribes of the Baikal, their art as well as their beliefs. Among art forms, first place must be given to realistically executed representations of animals, principally moose. Moose effigies carved out of antler have been found, for example, in the inventory of a burial discovered by I. T. Savenkov near the Bazaikha River on the Yenisey at Krasnoyarsk. They form, as it were, a tableau of life in the Siberian taiga. One moose is standing with its head lowered. The other is lying on the ground with its legs folded under it. It is stretching its head forward and emitting a call. A third figure represents a moose calf. It stands stock still with its ears perked up, listening.

We may also date to Serovo times certain monumental moose figures in a style related to that of the Bazaikha carvings, pecked out on cliffs near the settlement of Shishkino on the Lena River, on the Kamennyye Islands, in the Angara valley, and at other locations. Here too, the ancient craftsmen managed to convey the essential features of the body and motions of this forest animal. Sometimes we find a single moose figure represented on the cliffs at almost natural scale; at other times two moose figures are shown. They are represented as one following the other, spreading widely their thin gangly legs, the female probably in front, pursued by the bull. Carved representations of bear are also known to occur. A distinctive type of decorative art existed alongside realistic carving. This decoration was essentially geometric and rectilinear, characterized by the combination of horizontal and vertical lines, as well as the rhythmic alternation of "bundles" of short incisions.

We gain some idea of beliefs in Serovo times both from archeological data (burials, art forms) and from comparative ethnographic evidence. The moose and bear representations may be related without difficulty to the beliefs and rituals of forest hunters. All or nearly all of the tribes of the north had concepts of supernatural female beings, on whom, according to these beliefs, depended the life and death of the entire tribe, inasmuch as they had complete control of the food supply. At the same time, these zoömorphic beings were thought of as "animal mothers." They were called "rulers," "mistresses," and the "purveyors of all goods" and, in the northern myths, assumed animal form. The Eskimo conceived them as "walrus women," while other tribes thought of them as reindeer or moose, depending on whether subsistence was by hunting sea mammals or reindeer and moose. The Evenki, the inhabitants of the forested regions of Siberia around Lake Baikal and the headwaters of the Amur, until recently had the concept of such animal mothers or *bugady*, who had the form of a female moose. The cult of the *bugady* was connected with ancient magical rites and a spring festival, *ikonipka*, whose purpose it was to increase the amount of game in the taiga and to insure an abundant game supply. The performances of the shamans involved a journey to the female moose *bugady*, the mother and ruler of the animals. They "brought" with them strands of fur, which were then "transformed" into animals. In their dramatic dances the hunters would represent the multiplication of the animals and the chase.

The myths of the forest hunters of the Siberian taiga are also related to these magic rituals and reflect clearly the outstanding importance of the moose in their economy. In these myths the concept of the moose acquires cosmic importance. The Evenki saw a moose and hunters in the Big Dipper, and the snow-shoe tracks of a celestial hunter in the Milky Way. Likewise, our entire planet was conceived in the form of a moose. According to this conception, men dwell on the back of a giant moose, whose fur is the forest, while the birds flying over the earth correspond to mosquitoes and gnats.

Just as the concept of a mythical moose was directly related to economic life and to production, the bear, another animal of comparable bulk and strength, was also closely connected with the religion of local tribes, though on a different plane. A mythological bear was associated with shamanistic ritual and practice and was viewed as especially concerned with guiding shamanistic ritual and as a shaman helper. The special ritualistic role of the bear led, among many forest tribes, to the gradual emergence of a complex bear ceremony in the nature of a true religious mystery play or "passion" of the sacred animal. At the beginning of the play, the bear, previously raised in captivity, is killed. This is followed by the solemn eating of the meat of the killed animal by the members of the kin group, who honor it according to the rules of hospitality among kinsmen. The third part involved the burial of the bones and certain other parts of the body of the animal, to the accompaniment of a ritual designed to "resurrect" the animal, which was then to return to the hunters of its own free will and even bring along its relatives, allured by the respect and hospitality of the people. Thus the bear ceremony constituted a clear expression of the concepts of neolithic people, who thought of the animal kingdom as part of their own society and who conceived relations between men and animals as those between two friendly clans or tribes.

In turn, the burial rites of Serovo times likewise reflect the concept of the indissoluble ties uniting the members of the kin group. This finds its expression in the fact that the dead were taken care of as if they were living. They were accompanied to the "other world" by a nearly standard inventory of essential personal belongings. These usually included a bow with bone reinforcing pieces, from thirty to sixty arrows, one or two adzes, a bone spear point or dagger with side blades, a ground knife, a hunting knife or dagger, and a needle case with needles and awls. It is indicative that essential and compulsory grave goods were made to include a small clay pot with lugs for suspension, which served as a smudge pot. Thus, in the view of the Baikal hunters, even the world beyond the grave was inconceivable without "bugs," without gnats and mosquitoes. The concept of the link between the living and the dead, a link not interrupted even by death, found expression not only in this elementary concern for the well-being of dead kinfolk in the other world but also in the more profound concept of the inevitable resurrection of souls, of the certain return of the soul among the living, and of a kind of endless "circle of souls." This is the explanation provided by ethnographic data to the orientation of bodies that were placed with their heads toward the "land of the morning." It was there that they would begin life anew as children, so as then to come back to the land of the living and be reborn.

It should be added that the distinctive Serovo culture was not confined to the Baikal region. It had quite extensive connections with other areas. A culture basically related to the Serovo existed at the time on the territory of Yakutia, on the middle Yenisey, as well as beyond Lake Baikal. In addition, one of the more remarkable facts bearing on the history of the cultural and ethnic relationships of the neolithic tribes of the Baikal is the occurrence of net-impressed Serovo pottery, as well as stone objects, far to the east of Lake Baikal, in the Gobi desert (Shabarakh Usu) and also at Linnsi and a number of other habitation sites in Inner Mongolia. Nomadic hunters apparently penetrate at this time from the taiga into the forest steppes and steppes of Mongolia, ranging as far as the Great Wall of China. These easterly ties of the Baikal tribes continue and increase in complexity in later times.

The burials of the Kitoi phase, which follow the Serovo graves in time (third and beginning of second millennia B.C.) stand out, in the first place, as a result of one specific feature of the mode of burial, the custom of sprinkling red ocher over the entire body. A prominent element in the inventory of the graves and of contemporary [refuse] sites are composite fishhooks, which have semilunar protrusions at the extremities of the stone shank or weight. The Kitoi burial ground, located near sources of green nephrite, the most valuable raw material of the period, characteristically yields large numbers of nephrite artifacts and, among them, incompletely worked blanks. The possibility is not to be excluded that trade in nephrite was important in the life of the tribe or clan occupying the valley of the Kitoi river and neighboring regions, in the same manner as the tribal trade, which, in its day, affected so greatly the life of a number of tribes in North America and northern Asia who "specialized," to a considerable extent, in trading specific products of their regions or even in acting as middlemen.

The Kitoi phase of the Baikal sequence (end of the third and beginning of the second millennia B.C.) still fits entirely within the boundaries of the neolithic. No traces of metal are noted for this period. The first metal artifacts appear in Glazkovo times, at about 1800 to 1300 B.C. The oldest Glazkovo burials—in addition to containing various kinds of stone and bone artifacts and pottery that is still completely neolithic in appearance—yield leaf-shaped knives of copper, as well as small thin strips of this new material, used as ornaments. The early Glazkovo burials are succeeded by later ones that begin to yield not only copper but also bronze objects of archaic but already more developed form: leaf-shaped knives with a short spike or tang, massive fishhooks, needles, tubular beads of rolled metal foil, and other small objects. All these metal artifacts imitate the forms of earlier stone and bone objects, thereby providing evidence of local manufacture and of the beginnings of local metallurgy.

The appearance of the first copper objects is accompanied by changes in a number of typologically important artifacts. Flint arrow points acquire straight bases, and there is the appearance of two-prong harpoons (fish spears), biconvex axes of nephrite (symmetrical in cross section), a specific type of stone weight or shank for composite fishhooks, pyrophillite beads in the form of short cylinders (white in color), and disks and rings of white nephrite. The spread of new forms is accompanied by the disappearance of such archaic artifacts as knives with side-blades, spear-shaped hunting knives of asymmetric triangular outline, and early arrow-point types.

The economy of Glazkovo times is marked by a further increase in the importance of fishing. The burials that are richest in artifacts belong to fishermen, to judge from their inventories.

Paired burials of men and women are of interest in characterizing social life. In one of these, a flint arrow point was found embedded in the pelvis of the woman. Judging from its position in the body of the woman, she was hit with an arrow shot from a bow at point-blank range, as she was bending down or had fallen to the ground. The over-all arrangement of the burial justifies the supposition that after the death of the man, the woman, who may have been a wife or a slave concubine, was forcibly put to death and buried with the man in a common grave to be his companion in the other world.

It may be supposed that the social life of the Glazkovo tribes of the Baikal had features in common with the pattern observed by ethnographers in the eighteenth and beginning of the nineteenth centuries in northwestern North America, where the labor-consuming occupation of fishing early became the basis for a distinctive pattern of social structure, in which slavery became widespread and individual "aristocratic" families emerged from the ranks of the wealthy. As we know, the Northwest [coast] achieved in the eighteen century a level of technological development of precisely the same order as in Baikal of Glazkovo times, where use was made of copper objects of archaic type, along with stone and bone. It is thus only natural that the Glazkovo fishermen of the Baikal eneolithic should exhibit consistently the same basic features of mode of life and social structure as the Tlinkit and Tsimshian Indians of the Northwest coast of North America in the eighteenth and nineteenth centuries.

These novel features obviously could not help but find their reflection in the world outlook, religion, and art of the ancient inhabitants of the Baikal.

The appearance of a novel riverine burial orientation (parallel to the river) in the Glazkovo period testifies to a new belief in the departure of the deceased downstream, where the land of the dead was said to be. This is consonant with ethnographic data indicating a belief in the existence of a land of the dead, governed by a loathsome monster, a female deity representing the former matriarchal ruler. This is the period in which the cult of male anthropomorphic spirits develops. The first shamans appear (burials near the village of Anosovo and at Ust'-Uda on the Angara). Conventional and schematic treatments prevail in art.

Relations with neighbors and, above all, trade must have been of considerable importance in the progressive development of culture and society among the Baikal tribes in Glazkovo times. Thus, burials of the Serovo phase already yield blunt bone arrowheads designed especially for hunting fur-bearing animals. On the other hand, Glazkovo burial grounds have yielded beads of seashells and whole shells, brought in from the area of the Sea of Japan and the Moluccas. It is of particular importance that the Fofanovo cemetery on the Selenga River should have yielded pottery similar to the ancient Chinese (from settlements prior to and contemporaneous with Shang times).

Direct influence out of ancient China is even more clearly evident for the period of developed bronze-age culture. The distinctive taiga celts, the "Krasnoyarsk celts" of Merhart's terminology (Krasnojarsk Beile), bearing decoration in the form of eyes and pendant triangles, obviously derive from Shang celts of the second half of the second millennium B.C.

The effects of contact with ancient Chinese civilization were even more profound among the neighbors and relatives of the Baikal tribes living east of the Baikal. Here this contact radically changed the culture pattern and affected the composition of the population itself.

In the regions beyond the Baikal, in the area between Sretensk and Barguzin, and on the northern Baikal, the end of Shang times and the Chou period was marked by the spread of a new culture of developed bronze, the culture of the slab tombs of Mongolia and Trans-Baikalia. The bearers of the slab-tomb culture practiced animal husbandry. They raised horses and both large and small horned stock. Most striking and unexpected in their inventory of traits are pottery tripods of the *li* type, with a threefold division of the container portion and with hollow legs. In J. G. Andersson's opinion, the *li* is the "symbol of ancient Chinese agricultural civilization." The appearance of the *li* in Trans-Baikalia testifies, if not to the penetration of actual Chinese tribes to Lake Baikal in the first millennium B.C., at least to the appearance of stock-raising tribes culturally related to the Chinese from Inner Mongolia and adjacent regions of North China. Apparently, agriculture begins at this time beyond the Baikal, the evidence being the *li* tripods themselves, as well as stone grinders, and a bronze plowshare in the possession of the Kyakhta Museum.

In the second century B.C., Trans-Baikalia becomes part of the sphere of influence of the Huns, who were old neighbors of the Chinese and whose culture bore the imprint of ancient Chinese civilization from the very beginning. The Huns not only wandered over the steppe "depending on water and grass" but also built rather extensive, often fortified, settlements. These served not only as administrative centers and headquarters of tribal princelings but also, where agriculture was practiced, as craft centers. Such, for example, is the fortified settlement on the Ivolga near the city of Ulan-Ude.

A new and important phase in the life of the Trans-Baikalian tribes begins in medieval times, when the empire of the Orkhon or "Blue" Turks, the T'u-k'iu of the Chinese annals, arises. The Selenga at this time was occupied by the Uigur, who developed agriculture to a hitherto unprecedented degree and who established an extensive irrigation network and already made use of the plow instead of the hoe. A branch of the Uigur, the Kurykan, settled part of the Baikal region in the first millennium of our era and occupied the upper Angara region and the Lena-Kuda forest steppe. At the same time, around the eighth to the eleventh centuries, a colony of migrants from Sogdiana appeared in the area, establishing an agricultural settlement on the Unga River near Balagansk, where they buried their dead. The immigrants from Sogdiana also apparently introduced their own mode of life and rituals north of Lake Baikal, as evidenced by the sanctuaries or *chiragi* discovered on the Unga and by representations of Gopat Shah, an ancient Iranian deity conceived as a shepherd king with the body of a bull.

In this manner, the world of the forest tribes of eastern Siberia sees the appearance of the beginnings of agriculture, albeit considerably belated, spreading from two directions, Central Asia in the west, and simultaneously from the east. Agriculture was accompanied by influences of urban civilization. However, these influences were confined, as other events had been earlier, to the steppe and forest-steppe zone. The older mode of life of forest hunters, fishermen, and reindeer-breeders continued in the depths of the taiga itself.

While this distinctive culture followed its own course of development over several millennia on the shores of the Baikal, on the upper Lena, on the Angara, and on the Selenga, other tribes, dwelling in the Amur River valley and in the Soviet Maritime Province, developed a fundamentally different culture.

These areas, where glaciation did not take place, likewise could not support the periglacial culture of mammoth- and reindeer-hunters represented by the paleolithic settlements of the Baikal. Thus, the earliest known sites of the stone age in this area already bear a distinctive stamp.

The earliest traces of man known at the present time in the Maritime Province of the Soviet Union are found in the vicinity of the town of Ussuriysk, in the valley of a small stream called Osinovka, near the village of the same name. The finds here consist of pebbles of dense greenstone. One end of these pebbles served as a grip and retained the original surface. The other was flaked by means of a series of strong, deftly aimed blows and provided thus with a broad, massive cutting edge similar to that of a modern axe or cleaver. Such crude, core-like tools could be used to split bone or wood, to excavate the ground, to dig up edible roots, and to stun game animals. Tools of this kind are unknown west of the Urals. They are absent, for that matter, in adjacent Siberia. It is thus of particular interest that they resemble, in their general form and mode of manufacture, similar chopping tools or choppers, known in the stone age of China and of more distant areas of Asia as far removed as Burma and Indochina. These stone artifacts occurred in a reddish stratum, contrasting sharply with the light-yellow clayey soil above it.

Finds from the vicinity of the city of Khabarovsk, near the village of Osipovka and the railroad trestle across the Amur, pertain to a later period, probably to the early neolithic. Here, on a high ancient terrace of the left bank, a stratum of clayey soil has yielded remains of hearths made of boulders, together with stone leaf-shaped points or knives, splendidly worked over by means of fine Solutrean-type retouch, and also end scrapers, flakes, and distinctive adzes, flaked rather than ground, with indented cutting edges.

The culture of the full-blown neolithic is represented by sites at which pottery appears in the form of vessels of distinctive truncated-conical shape. The rims of these vessels bear an outer band of decoration of diamond-shaped impressions with concave sides. This band imitates a basket or net with lozenge-shaped meshes. Decoration of this type occurs in the neolithic from the banks of the Amur in the north to Vladivostok and the Tumangan River in the south. At the same time, it is identical with that used at the present time by the Ulchi and Giliak tribes of the Amur. The neolithic inhabitants of the Maritime Province and of the Amur in this period had at their disposal ground-stone adzes, convex on one face and flat on the other. They also used bifacially retouched knives and points of stone. Their stone arrow points find their closest analogies among the early points of the Baikal, both because of their general form and because one corner is somewhat more elongated than the other. The stone artifacts also include elongate rectangular blades, elaborately retouched on both faces, which served as inserted side-blades for wooden or bone daggers or knives.

With time, decoration in the form of parallel vertical zigzag patterns becomes equally widespread in the Far-Eastern neolithic. On the Amur, it appears in combination with curvilinear patterns representing variations of a spiral motif. In the Maritime Province, it appears alone and is combined with the meander in the latest phases.

The older type of planoconvex adze is now accompanied by a new type, round or oval in cross section, which gradually supersedes the older form. Sites of this period yield many small, finely retouched arrow points. There are also some rather large knives with "knobbed" stems.

The general appearance of the pottery and of the stone inventory, as well as the art of the neolithic peoples of the Far East and the course of development of their culture as a whole, are in marked contrast to what we have observed in Siberia proper. The Siberian peoples had only round-bottomed rather than flat-bottomed pottery, and rectilinear geometric rather than curvilinear decorative art. The development of stone tools likewise followed a different pattern in Siberia.

The mode of life of these Far-Eastern tribes as a whole was as distinctive as their material culture. They lived not in light above-ground huts, as did their western neighbors, but in solid semisubterranean houses, and built themselves true villages of such dwellings.

The final and most important distinctive feature in the mode of life of the Far-Eastern tribes was their adoption, as early as the neolithic, of agriculture and, apparently, the raising of dogs and pigs for meat. The beginnings of agriculture are evidenced by numerous finds of grinding stones and rubbers. On the Amur, however, these artifacts are not found, and the basis of subsistence in that area, therefore, as contrasted to the Maritime Province, was fishing and, above all, fishing for migratory marine species of the salmon family.

Weaving was linked to the growing and utilization of plants. Its relatively advanced state of development is attested by numerous spindle whorls, both biconical and in the form of disks with shaft sockets on one side. There are also clear imprints of coarse fabrics on the bases of some vessels.

The neolithic cultures of the Maritime and Amur tribes were in contact from early times with the cultures of their Far-Eastern neighbors in Korea, Japan, and China. They were an integral part of a maritime culture area—characterized by the use of pottery vessels of truncated conical form, decorated with patterns of continuous vertical zigzags, as well as by polished axes of round cross section, knives of "Mousterian" shape, T-drills, ornaments of *magatami* type, and other objects.

In turn, all these cultures, and particularly those on the mainland, were subject to the powerful influence of the oldest of the farming cultures of the Far East, the Yangshao culture, which was succeeded by the Lungshan. It is the influence of the ancient Chinese agriculturists that accounts for the early beginnings of farming in the Maritime Province.

This view finds support at sites of the following period, "the shell-mound phase." The broad distribution of these mounds coincides in time with important changes in the culture of the ancient tribes of the Maritime Province.

Small flint and obsidian flaked tools are replaced by tools of rubbed slate, which include stone daggers and spear heads—copies of metal models of Shang and Karasuk type and, in part, types of the late bronze and early iron ages of southern Siberia. Stone axes of round cross section are replaced by quadrangular ones. The simple pottery vessels of earlier times are replaced by new forms of more advanced design. Prominent among these are hitherto unknown vessels of more complex profile, as well as shallow cups on narrow pedestal bases. The decoration and outward finish of pottery was drastically modified. We now frequently find vessels with highly burnished surfaces, sometimes purposefully coated with a thin layer of purplish red pigment. The ancient potters now decorated their vessels with a variety of linear designs, particularly fillets arranged in parallel bands and symmetrically placed appliqué bosses.

The subsistence pattern of the coastal inhabitants developed in the direction of dependence on more elaborate techniques of sea fishing and sea-mammal hunting. A specialized harpoon complex appears. Farming developed at the same time, particuarly among the inhabitants of inland areas far removed from the sea. This is evidenced not only by grinding stones and reaping knives of ground slate but also by charred grains of millet found in 1959 at a settlement in the Suchan river, near the village of Yekaterininskoye, and near the town of Artem in the village of Kirovskiy.

All these new traits in pottery and new types of stone artifacts serve to relate the shell-mound culture of the Maritime Province to the late neolithic cultures of Korea (Tsodo Island) and Liaotung (Pitsuwo). A common foundation for all of them, apparently, is to be seen in the ancient Chinese cultures of Yangshao and, particularly, Lungshan, whence agriculture likewise diffused northward as early as neolithic times. The marked intensification of relations with China in the first millennium B.C. was the result, it would seem, of events connected with the struggle between Chou and Shang and with the movements of population that ensued from the destruction of the Shang state by the Chou tribes.

Subsequently, the T'ang period in the first millennium A.D. is marked by the appearance, in Manchuria, of the state of Po-hai, the earliest local state in the area, born of direct contact with Korea (Koguryo) and China. Its territory extended over a considerable portion of the Maritime Province. Cities were built, among which was Shuai-pin. Civilization in the Far East attained its peak during the existence of the state of Po-hai and that of the state of Ts'in, founded by the Jurchen leader A-ku-ta.

We have examined here the broad outlines of the historical process in the temperate zone of northern Asia. We may now draw some conclusions in a wider context. We see that it is characterized, above all, by an unusually prolonged retention of ancient economic patterns. Hunting and gathering, as basic modes of subsistence, were replaced here very late by stock-raising and agriculture; nor did the replacement happen everywhere, but only in those areas where environmental conditions were favorable and where direct contact existed with more developed cultures. For northern Asia, China played the same role as the higher cultures of the Near East had in the initial development of European civilization.

However, it would hardly be legitimate to view the history of the forest tribes of Siberia from a purely negative point of view, as was done by historians of the eighteenth century, and to think of it simply as providing a background for the history of the more progressive peoples of the world.

In the first place, this branch of humanity followed its own path of historical development, passing from one historical phase to the next over a period of several millennia. The forest tribes were creating their own cultures. They may be credited with many original inventions and discoveries. They created their own distinctive mythology and their own colorful and truly remarkable art.

In the second place, the forest tribes stood in complex relationships with the rest of the world and participated thereby in the world-wide historical process as such. To overlook their contribution to the global culture of mankind would be to impoverish the latter. In failing to recognize the bonds between the forest tribes of Siberia and the rest of the world, we would be belittling the true content of the historical process.

BIBLIOGRAPHY

CHARD, C. S.

1956. "The Oldest Sites of Northeastern Siberia," *Amer. Antiq.*, Vol. 21, No. 4.

1958. "An Outline of the Prehistory of Siberia, Part I: The Pre-Metal Periods," *Southwestern J. Anthrop.*, Vol. 14, No. 7

DEBETS, G. F.

1948. "Paleoantropologiya SSSR" ("Paleoanthropology of the USSR"), *Trudy Instituta Etnografii AN SSSR* ("Trans. Inst. Ethnog. Acad. Sci. USSR), n.s., Vol. 4.

GAUL, J. H.

1943. *Observations on the Bronze Age in the Yenisei Valley.* ("Papers Peabody Mus. Amer. Archaeol. and Ethnol.," Vol. 20.)

GERASIMOV, M. M.

1931. *Mal'ta: Paleoliticheskaya stoyanka (predvaritel'nyye dannye): Rezul'taty raboty 1928–1929 g.* ("Mal'ta: A Paleolithic Site [Preliminary Information]: Results of Work in 1928–1929"). Irkutsk.

GROMOV, V. I.

date? "Paleontologicheskoye i arkheologicheskoye obosnovaniye stratigrafii kontinental'nykh otlozheniy chetvertichnogo perioda na territorii SSSR (mlekopitayushchiye, paleolit)" ("The Paleontological and Archeological Basis of the Stratigraphy of Continental Deposits of the Quaternary Period on the Territory of the USSR [Mammals, Paleolithic]"), *Trudy Inst. Geolog. Nauk* ("Trans. Inst. Geol. Sci."), No. 64; "Geol. Ser.," No. 17.

GRYAZNOV, M. P.

1950. *Pervyy Pazyrykskiy kurgan* ("The First Pazyryk Mound"). Leningrad.

KISELEV, S. V.

1951. *Drevnyaya istoriya Yuzhnoy Sibiri* ("The Ancient History of Southern Siberia"). Moscow.

LARICHEV, V. YE.

1959a. "O proiskhozhdenii kul'tury plitochnykh mogil Zabaykaliya" ("The Origin of the Slab Grave Culture of Trans-Baikalia"). *"Arkheologicheskiy sbornik"* ("Collected Papers on Archeology"), Vol. 1. Ulan Ude.

1959b. "Neolit Dunbeya i yego svyazi s kul'turami kamennogo veka severo-vostochnoy Azii" ("The Neolithic of Tungpeh and Its Relations to the Stone Age Cultures of Northeast Asia"), *ibid.*, Vol. 1.

LEVIN, M. G.

1951. "Drevniye pereseleniya cheloveka v Severnoy Azii po dannym antropologii" ("Ancient Population Movements in Northern Asia on the Basis of the Data of Physical Anthropology"). In *Sbornik "Proiskhozhdeniye cheloveka i drevneye rasseleniye chelovechestva"* (In "The Origin of Man and the Ancient Migrations of Mankind"). *Trudy Instituta Etnografii AN SSSR"* ("Trans. Inst. Ethnog. Acad. Sci. USSR"), n.s., Vol. 16.

MICHAEL, H. W.
1958. "The Neolithic Age in Eastern Siberia," *Trans. Amer. Phil. Soc.*, n.s., Vol. 48, Part. 2.

OKLADNIKOV, A. P.
1941a. "Neoliticheskiye pamyatniki kak istochnik po etnogonii Sibiri i Dal'nego Vostoka" ("Neolithic Sites as Source Material on the Origin of the Peoples of Siberia and of the Far East"). (*Kratkiye soobshcheniya Instituta istorii material'noy kul'tury AN SSSR* ["Brief Communications Inst. Hist. Material Culture, Acad. Sci. USSR"], No. 9.)

1941b. "Paleoliticheskiye zhilishcha v Bureti" ("Paleolithic Dwellings at Buret'"), *ibid.*, No. 10.

1950a. *Osvoyeniye paleoliticheskim chelovekom Sibiri* ("Settlement of Siberia by paleolithic Man"). "Materialy po chetvertochnomu periodu SSSR" ["Materials on the Quaternary Era in the USSR"]), No. 2.

1950b and 1955a. *Neolit i bronzovy vek Pribaykaliya*, chast' I i III ("The Neolithic and Bronze Ages of the Baikal, Parts I and II"). ("Materialy i issledovaniya po arkheologii SSSR" ["Materials and Researches on the Archeology of the USSR], No. 18.) Chast' III ("Part III"). (*Ibid.*, No. 43.) Moscow-Leningrad.

1955b. "Yakutiya do prisoyedineniya k Russkomu gosudarstvu" ("Yakutia Prior to its Merger with the Russian State"). In *Istoriya Yakutskoy ASSR* ("History of the Yakut Autonomous Soviet Socialist Republic"), Vol. 1. Moscow-Leningrad.

1958. "Ancient Cultures and Cultural and Ethnic Relations on the Pacific Coast of North Asia," *Proc. 32d Internat. Cong. of Americanists, Copenhagen, 1956.* Copenhagen

1959a. "Tripody za Baykalom" ("Tripods beyond the Baikal"), *Sovetskaya arkheologiya* ("Soviet Archeology"), No. 3.

1959b. *Paleolit Zabaykaliya: Obshchiy ocherk* ("The Paleolithic of Trans-Baikalia: General Outline"). ("Arkheologicheskiy sbornik" ["Collected Papers on Archeology"], Vol. 1. Ulan-Ude.

date? *Ancient Population of Siberia and Its Cultures.* ("Russian Trans. Ser. Peabody Mus. Archaeol. Ethnol., Harvard University," Vol. 1.) Cambridge, Mass. (See review by CHESTER CHARD in *Science*, Vol. 27, November, 1959).

SOSNOVSKIY, G. P.
1941. "Plitochnyye mogily Zabaykaliya" ("The Slab Graves of Trans-Baikalia"), *Trudy otdela istorii pervobytnoy kul'tury (Gosudarstvennyy Ermitazh)* ("Transactions of the Department of the History of Primitive Culture, State Ermitage Museum"), Vol. 1. Leningrad.

TOLSTOY, P.
1958. "The Archeology of the Lena Basin and Its New World Relationships," Part I. *Amer. Antiq.*, Vol. 23, No. 4.

EASTERN NORTH AMERICA

JOSEPH R. CALDWELL

THE IDEA of diverse culture-historical pathways toward urban life has led me to repeat some previously published arguments about the prehistory of eastern North America (Caldwell, 1958). The region from the Atlantic as far as the Plains can be considered a developmental unity differing in important respects from those sequences in Mesoamerica and southwest Asia reputed to have led more directly to cities and high civilizations. Here a long period of adaptation to forest existence, mostly completed by the end of the so-called "Archaic" stage of about 8000–1500 B.C., culminated south of the Great Lakes during the subsequent Hopewellian phase of roughly 400 B.C.–A.D. 500. This adaptive trend to the establishment of "primary forest efficiency"—represented by changes in hunting methods, emergence of economic cycles and food specializations, and achieving a kind of balanced reliance on almost all sources of natural foods—had a peculiar effect on the course of historical development. It apparently became possible in the forested East to get along very well without agriculture. There are indeed cultigens, probably antedating the beginning of the first millennium A.D. in the Hopewellian and related Adena manifestations, but there is no evidence that these were depended upon more than any single source of wild food. Perhaps it would be unwise to speak specifically of resistance to food production, but there was evidently some time lapse between first knowledge of cultivation and considerable reliance on it among most groups, with some later Hopewellians as a possible exception. Our first reliable indication of a dependence on food production sufficient to have had noticeable social effects is at the beginning of Mississippian times, around A.D. 800. A similar reluctance to depend greatly on food production, even long after its methods were known, has been described in other papers in this symposium dealing with regions outside the areas where the first nuclear civilizations arose. An ethnographic instance of a similar phenomenon may be represented in California, although a climatic reason has been suggested (Kroeber, 1939, p. 211).

Long before these events, both the Great Plains and the forested East shared with a vast region of the North American continent a common economic basis in the hunting of large mammals. At least, such is inferred from the occurrence in the East of fluted projectile points of Clovis type, persisting perhaps as late as 7000 B.C. But on the Plains arose a distinctive development of the bison-hunting specialization of Folsom-Plainview, from perhaps 9000 B.C. until after 6000 B.C., apparently coming to an end at just about the time some of the eastern societies were in the midst of their adaptation to a forest mode of life. We shall have something to say about the Plains in this paper. If some of its developments can be regarded as mainly autochthonous, Plains prehistory on the whole can hardly be intelligible without constant reference to events in the eastern forest area that supplied Plains societies with so much cultural material. For this reason, not lessened by my inability to handle Plains materials with the sagacity they deserve, we shall consider the Plains as an appendage of the forested East.

We said that primary forest efficiency was being reached toward the end of the Archaic stage. An important series of economic innovations took place during that interval. More stylistic elaboration occurred later. Style changes found particular expression in the ceramic and mortuary activities of some of the later societies. We shall refer to these successive expressions as the Hopewellian, Gulf, Mississippian, and Southern Cult "climaxes," using this term in the sense introduced by Kroeber (1939, p. 223): regional situations of relatively greater cultural elaboration and organization from which a radiation of cultural material took place.

What may be an interesting feature of these climaxes is that only in the case of the Mississippian is there any good reason to conjecture an economic cause— that is, increased dependence on food production. And it is in this climax, incidentally, that we have our best evidence for the outward migrations of people from a presumed heartland in the central Mississippi Valley. For the others— Hopewellian, Gulf, and Southern Cult—there is less evidence of movements of peoples and more evidence for the spread of ideas ("cultural material") to peoples surrounding climax areas. These other climaxes, moreover, represent more noticeably at least in part, reworkings of the old eastern ideas of lavish mortuary procedures and the placing of valuable objects and regalia with selected individuals.

All the climaxes recognized here took place in a context of increasing influence from Mesoamerica. There are increasing numbers of discrete recognizable Mesoamerican elements as one moves chronologically from Hopewellian, through Gulf, through Mississippian, to Southern Cult. Yet we cannot guess at the nature of these Mesoamerican connections except to suggest, following Kelley (1955), that the intervening area of low cultural level in Texas and northeast Mexico had a certain effect on what could be transmitted to the East via this route. And it must be said that Mesoamerican elements in eastern North American assemblages are rarely identical with their analogues in Mesoamerica.

On the basis of the foregoing, we may now suggest a little more precisely how the prehistory of eastern North America can be contrasted with the prehistories of such regions of nuclear civilization as Mesoamerica and southwest Asia. The development of a forest efficiency may have slowed down further economic innovation, especially the adoption of agriculture as an economic basis, while offering a sufficient livelihood to permit stylistic elaborations, and such non-economic activity as the building of mounds and earthworks and the disposal of considerable wealth with the dead. Instead of the more direct progress to new levels of "sociocultural integration," such as we imagine to have occurred in regions of nuclear civilization, there was a succession of little-understood cultural climaxes that to some degree represented reworkings of the old eastern idea of elaborate and lavish treatment of certain selected dead.

If we may now regard the East as one kind of culture-historical pathway and the Mesoamerican development that was influencing it as another, we have a framework within which we shall, in the final and most speculative part of this paper, engage the main questions asked in this seminar—whether effective food production and urbanism may have been emerging in eastern North America.

In a vast region east of the Mississippi River a series of forests extended from subtropical Florida to subarctic woodlands. Within this area can be distinguished certain variations in native subsistence. In historic times small tribes of the Atlantic and Gulf coasts lived partly by hunting, partly on seafood, and raised a little maize. Other tribes in the interior put more reliance on maize, beans, and squash, but hunting and gathering were always important. In the upper Great Lakes area there were maize, hunting and gathering, and, where available, considerable reliance on wild rice (*Zizania aquatica*). In the northern forest of the eastern subarctic, where planting was impossible, there was still gathering and hunting, especially of the moose and caribou.

The archeological evidence is that there was once a time when there was no planting at all and that the acceptance of food production as a major economic basis was a long and difficult affair. Even in historic times, food production was

LOCATIONS OF SITES AND CULTURAL GROUPINGS MENTIONED: FIGURE 1

EARLIER SITES:

On Map

A—Bull Brook, Massachuetts
B—Region of Folsom, Yuma, and Plainview assemblages
C—Signal Butte, Nebraska
D—Modoc Rock Shelter, Illinois
E—Ferry Site, Illinois

NORTHERN TRADITION:

N 1—Region of the Adena phase and Cowan Creek Mound, Kentucky
N 2—Ohio Hopewellian sites
N 3—Illinois Valley Hopewellian sites and Brangenberg site, Illinois
N 4—Southern Illinois Hopewellian sites and the Twenhafel site
N 5—Kansas City Hopewellian sites
N 6—"Bluff Culture," Illinois

MIDDLE EASTERN TRADITION:

M 1—Eva focus, Tennessee

M 2—"Round Grave culture" and Watts Bar focus, Tennessee
M 3—Kellog focus, Georgia
M 4—Badin focus, North Carolina
M 5—Baumer and Crab Orchard foci, Illinois

SOUTHERN APPALACHIAN TRADITION:

S 1—Swift Creek sites, Georgia
S 2—Woodstock period sites, Georgia
S 3—Etowah sequence, Georgia
S 4—Kolomoki site, Georgia (later becomes Gulf)

GULF TRADITION:

G 1—Poverty Point, Louisiana
G 2—Lower Valley sequence: Tchefuncte, Marksville, Troyville, Coles Creek, Plaquemine periods.
G 3—Northwest Florida sequence: Deptford, Santa Rosa, Weeden Island
G 4—Middle Baytown period
G 5—Davis site, Texas

FIGURE 1. Location of sites and cultural groupings mentioned:
I. Eastern North America.

only supplementary in many regions and was the sole economic basis in none. Aside from cultivation, subsistence practices seem to be variations on the common theme of hunting and gathering whatever was available. Even the corn-growing Choctaw and Illini might leave their towns deserted to go hunting, and some Illini claimed that they ate maize only when they could not get bison. The Cherokee, whose women annually raised thousands of bushels of maize, regarded themselves not only as warriors but more strictly as hunters, pleading economic necessity to claim several million square miles of land that they did not occupy.

In these eastern forests and somewhat beyond, a number of intergrading culture subareas have been distinguished by ethnologists working with historical data of the native tribes. This lightness of cultural contour, as Kroeber has said (1938, p. 60), has its parallels in the lack of sharp environmental differences. Again the archeological evidence comes to our aid in showing that this was probably always so—that the cultures of the entire region tended more toward uniformity at any particular time than toward subregional differences. The import of this is that we can consider the prehistory of the East as a great interrelated culture-historical structure.

The foundations of this historical structure are represented by the ancient hunting and gathering societies belonging to what is called the "Archaic" stage, a conception co-ordinate with the far-flung "Desert" culture of western North America and other regional manifestations in North and South America.

The interior grasslands were historically involved with the forested East. Tall-grass prairie extended eastward from the ninety-eighth meridian into a kind of prairie peninsula narrowing between the northern and southern hardwood zones of the forest. In the eastern prairies there is little evidence of a particular prairie subsistence until the occurrence of bison bones in assemblages of the historic periods. Settlements were on the rivers and streams. It has been argued that these offered forest environments within the prairie zone. On the western prairies and on the short grass of the High Plains extending to the slopes of the Rocky Mountains there was an early hunting specialization. The Folsom materials, from about 9000 to 7000 B.C., apparently represent societies subsisting mainly on large, and some now extinct, herbivores, especially bison (*taylori*, *antiquus*, and *occidentalis*). For our story, however, specialized plains hunting continued during the time of succeeding Yuma, Eden-Scottsbluff, and Plainview-like assemblages to about the time of the altithermal, perhaps about 4000 B.C. A possible climatic explanation for the disappearance of some of these hunters is supported by the observation that similar flint projectile-point forms persist until 2800 B.C. in Canada (MacNeish, 1959, p. 12.)

Succeeding Prairie materials, such as Signal Butte I in Nebraska at about 2400 B.C., imply greater emphasis on smaller game and hunting, but on the High Plains an impoverished bison-hunting economy was still present in Coronado's time (Eggan, 1952, p. 39).

Developments in the eastern forest area had the most serious consequences for later history in the grasslands. By Hopewellian times, at least, eastern settlements were fingering westward along the major rivers. But correlating cultural manifestations on the Plains with particular eastern contemporaries is a difficult task that has scarcely begun. When the introduction of the horse and gun made a new plains-hunting development possible, the eastern tribes thus attracted to the area provided much of the cultural basis for the famous specializations of historic Plains Indian life.

The plains-hunting Folsom specialization mentioned earlier may be a regional adaptation in an early context of hunting societies, including the slightly earlier Clovis materials of the southwestern United States. Unfortunately, with the exception of Bull Brook in Massachusetts, at about 7000 B.C., there are few early dated materials *in situ* from the eastern forest areas and no associated animal remains. Occupation sites with chipped-stone assemblages are beginning to be recognized, and thousands of characteristic fluted points, more usually resembling Clovis than Folsom, have occurred as surface finds. There is a significant lack of shell heaps representing forest and waterside adaptations; these evidently arose later. In the Great Lakes region during the final retreat of the Wisconsin Glaciation, 10,000–5000 B.C., there was a gradual change in the periglacial forests from spruce-fir to pine and gradual disappearance of such fauna as mastodon and giant beaver. The distribution of fluted points correlated with glacial, lake level, faunal, and vegetational evidence, has enabled Quimby (1960) to make a good circumstantial case that mastodon were hunted in the region, perhaps as a major basis for subsistence.

As the ice slowly retreated from the Great Lakes region, hunting peoples here, no less than on the Plains, found themselves in a changing world. How great were these changes is portrayed in Quimby's admirable little book. The assemblages in this region during 7000–5000 B.C., called "Aqua-Plano" to indicate the similarity of projectile-point forms to the post-Folsom "Plano" assemblages on the Plains, were hunters in a landscape dominated by spruce and pine, lake waters, and glacial ice. Deer, elk, and barren-ground caribou were there to be taken, but it is possible that the mastodon was already gone. By this time, however, the use of boats or canoes is inferable from the same evidence that indicates that, in the summertime, groups of people were probably fishing on lakeshores and islands that could not have supported them in winter months. In the succeeding "Archaic Boreal" period, 5000 to possibly 500 B.C., which witnessed the development of the deciduous forest in the region, there is evidence of continued adaptation to the land and the discovery of its resources. There is now, Quimby tells us, an emphasis on ground and polished woodworking tools, like the axes, adze, and gouge, and there is also the remarkable development of the Old Copper industry.

The record of technological development in the Great Lakes region may be expected to differ somewhat from that in the more southerly parts of the eastern forest, if only because it occurred in a setting dominated by striking postglacial changes. We shall describe the forest adaptation in the southerly regions in slightly different terms, but with an assurance that these events were taking place almost contemporaneously with those in the north and were influencing and/or being influenced by them.

During the general period of from about 8000 to 1500 B.C.—the Archaic stage, in which the Boreal Archaic is a regional development—there is evidence of the development of a forest-hunting pattern. The earlier chipped-stone spear points had been lanceolate, suitable as tips for thrusting-spears. The trend is to shouldered and barbed points better for javelins and ambush hunting (Caldwell, 1958, p. 13), with direct evidence for the spear-thrower (atlatl).

There is evidence for the development of seasonal cycles. Earlier levels going back to 8000 B.C. at the Modoc Rock Shelter in southern Illinois suggest year-round occupation (Fowler, 1959). Later levels of about 3000–2000 B.C. show a greater proportion of deer bones and more restricted artifact assemblages, which could be the debris left by hunting parties. A similar development occurs at a later time in Wisconsin farther north (Wittry, 1959). Various localities in Illinois and Kentucky suggest other specializations; one shows an abundance of acorn hulls, multiple pitted "nutting stones," extensive areas reddened by fire—presumably for roasting acorns—but no storage pits or other features (Fowler, 1957).

Archaic adaptions were not everywhere alike. On the Green River in Kentucky, the Tennessee River in northern Alabama, the upper Savannah River in Georgia, and on the Atlantic and Gulf coasts shell middens are large and numerous. A degree of reliance on shellfish—also an Archaic innovation—may have encouraged a greater degree of *sedentism*: the earliest southeastern pottery—fiber tempered—occurs most frequently on shell heaps.

In post-Archaic ranges of time there were some economic innovations that can be regarded as developments of the hunting-gathering pattern already established. Most later change, however, seems to have been in small things—in the form and decoration of artifacts, especially pottery, and in particularities of burial customs. Change usually represented not technical improvement but stylistic differentiation. As a result, we can discern the existence of several regional traditions: a Northern (Woodland), a Middle Eastern, a Southern Appalachian, and a Gulf.

In the *Middle Eastern Tradition* (Caldwell, 1958, pp. 23–27) there is evidence of continued development of the hunting-gathering pattern. While some Middle Eastern pottery occurs on shell heaps, there is a dependence on acorns and underground storage greater than in earlier or later times, but no evidence of food production. The distinctive pottery of this tradition (cord-wrapped-stick decorated) is characteristic of such manifestations as the Late Eva Focus and "Round Grave" cultures in Tennessee and is spread throughout the acorn-rich central deciduous part of the eastern forest. It stops just beyond the area that includes the Crab Orchard Focus at the edge of the Prairie Peninsula in southern Illinois, at just beyond the edge of the Kellogg Focus in Georgia on the border of the southern pine forest, and includes the Badin Focus in North Carolina on the edge of the pine forest of the Atlantic coastal plain. Small circular storage pits are numerous, and a few show traces of fire. Large burned areas like those found at the Archaic Ferry site have not been noticed. If the bow and arrow was adopted early in the Middle Eastern region, as has been argued (Caldwell, 1958, pp. 26–27), this would be a further development of hunting practices to a stage essentially as known in historic times.

The stylistic distinctiveness of the *Southern Appalachian Tradition* is represented by pottery decorated with impressions of carved wooden paddles. Economy was not dissimilar to that of preceding Archaic times. There is yet no evidence of food production until a relatively late date; carbonized maize has been found in the Woodstock period in northern Georgia—this ought to be roughly equivalent to early Mississippian times, about A.D. 800 (Caldwell, 1958, p. 48).

The *Northern Tradition* includes the Hopewellian assemblages; with less assurance, Adena; and most of the manifestations that have been called "Woodland" except those in the south that do not have cord-marked pottery as the major decorated type.[1]

The Northern Tradition seems to be rooted in earlier Archaic manifestations of the region, including the proposed Boreal Archaic, where there are specific burial practices that showed greater elaboration in subsequent Adena and Hopewellian times (Ritchie, 1955; see also Quimby, 1960, p. 49). The Adena Aspect of the upper Ohio Valley, from about 800 B.C. well into the first millennium A.D., is known chiefly from the contents of conical burial mounds, but with other information from occupation sites. It is partly earlier and partly ancestral to the Hopewellian manifestations to be described in more detail below.

Mortuary practices show considerable similarity. Although the great majority of subsistence remains from Adena sites are products of hunting and gathering, at the Cowan Creek Mound, Ohio, A.D. 445, we find evidence of a cucurbit (pepo), probably pumpkin, associated with a mass of charred goosefoot (*Chenopodium*) seeds (Goslin, 1957). Rock shelters in Kentucky, where plant remains are less certainly associated with Adena materials, have yielded such cultigens as gourd, pumpkin, squash, and sunflower; but no Adena site has yet shown evidence of maize or beans.

It may soon become possible to speak of an Adena cultural climax as distinct from Hopewellian. In addition to the mortuary elaborations of Adena, we find a number of distinctive Adena cultural elements, for example, tubular stone pipes

1. For readers who are new to eastern archeology, it should be explained that most of the students of this region do use the term "Woodland." Specifically, it includes everything that is not Paleo-Indian, Archaic, or Mississippian. The thirty-five hundred years or so of eastern prehistory since Archaic times has been divided into three parts: Early, Middle, and Late Woodland. It is true, however, that all of us are interested in regional differences and more definite dating, and I suppose I differ from many of my colleagues in my inability to understand the additional necessity of using this great threefold scheme. In the present paper the focus is directly upon the developments of particular regions of the East; major regional continuities are regarded as cultural traditions, to be contrasted or examined in their interplay, and from which to infer certain events.

and reel-shaped gorgets, widely diffused to the Northeast and Southeast (Webb and Baby, 1957; Ritchie and Dragoo, 1960).

We are still in the dark as to the kind of sociological reality represented by the Hopewellian assemblages. These date for the most part between 400 B.C. and A.D. 500. The Hopewellian "culture" was first defined in southern Ohio many years ago on the basis of its typical monuments—groups of burial mounds often with extensive earthen enclosures. Since most excavators have not been unmindful of the occurrence of fine museum specimens deposited in graves, most of our information concerns burial customs. Across the northern United States from western New York to Kansas City are other prehistoric sites called Hopewellian, evidently co-ordinate developments, related but not necessarily tributary to Ohio.

The Illinois Valley shows an enormous number of Hopewellian sites, some of which have yielded relatively older radiocarbon determinations. Sites still farther west are thought to have a particular connection with the Illinois Valley (Griffin, 1958). Hopewellian influences appear in the Northeast and the Southeast. There are some specific connections with the Marksville period of the Gulf Tradition.

The culmination of this post-Archaic phenomenon of regional differentiation and stylistic change we shall describe as the Hopewellian climax, subsequently followed by a decline. While Hopewellian shows cultural elements ultimately derived from Mesoamerica—the rare finds of cultivated maize are the best example —the view taken in the present paper is that Hopewellian cultural elaborations were essentially a development of the older Archaic hunting-gathering economy and religious practices organized around the care of the dead in the hereafter.

Some will not agree that the economic pattern was basically hunting-gathering: it has usually been assumed that Adena and Hopewellian, to build large burial mounds and earthworks, must have had an agriculturally based surplus. It is risky, however, to argue from earthworks to agriculture. Preserved food remains are almost altogether mammalian, fish and bird bones, mollusk shells, and various kinds of nuts and acorns. Finds of maize, beans, and squash are more exceptional than for later times. The most we can say is that some Hopewellian societies were practicing mixed economies, with hunting-gathering having the best of it. This, in turn, leads to a view of gradual acceptance of food production in the East, with emphasis on the successive steps by which it may have come about and with separate consideration of the social consequences of food production of each degree.

We know some details of log tombs and round or oval houses made of poles. Relics of costume are occasionally found with the dead, and other details are known from small pottery figurines. Differential placement of burials and grave objects suggests variation in social status. The skill exhibited in fine objects placed with the dead implies full or part-time artisan specialists. A widespread trade supplied the raw materials for mortuary offerings. From the Lake Superior region came native copper, which was cold-hammered into ornaments. Mica from the southern Appalachians was cut in abstract and naturalistic forms and probably attached to costumes. From Florida came seashells for ornaments and, especially, the large *cassis* shells for cups. Obsidian was probably supplied from as far west as Wyoming.

The larger Hopewellian settlements, particularly in Ohio, lend themselves to interpretation as primarily religious or mortuary centers, especially when we contrast them with large sites of subsequent Mississippian times that have more of the character of secularized towns. According to this view, smaller dispersed settlements were occupied for most of the year. At a much later peripheral site in the Southeast, the Irene Mound site, Georgia—which may reflect an older adjustment because it is peripheral—there is a predominance of public over do- mestic buildings. It has been suggested that such sites may have been occupied by caretakers while the populations were away.

By A.D. 500, Hopewellian was being replaced in the extreme northerly and westerly portions of its range by generalized Northern assemblages not greatly different from those that had preceded it. In the old regional centers of Ohio and the Illinois Valley the decline of Hopewellian was probably more complex, and the spectacular features of Hopewellian burial practices were not all at once replaced by simpler rites. In the lower Illinois Valley the Brandenberg site shows late Hopewellian pottery and ceramic features inspired by the Gulf Tradition (Griffin, 1952), which had been reaching its own climax during the Marksville period after A.D. 1. Similar Gulf elements also occur farther south at the Twen- hafel site. Still later in southern Illinois we find smaller sites and simpler, less specialized artifacts (Maxwell, 1951).

The Hopewellian climax was the high point of cultural complexity reached by the Northern Tradition. We regarded this as a largely indigenous development of hunting-gathering and mortuary practices first formulated in Archaic times. Subsequent major developments: the Gulf, Mississippian, and the Southern Cult climaxes occurred with increasing rapidity and show progressively stronger Meso- american features. The role of Mesoamerican influences in these developments may have been to broaden progressively the basis for innovation.

The Hopewellian decline in the North is paralleled by the rise of the *Gulf Tradition* in the South. This occupied portions of the Gulf Coastal Plain on both sides of the lower Mississippi Valley. Here the appearance of ceramics had been slightly delayed, and the regional Archaic is notable for some curious large earthworks at Poverty Point, Louisiana, 1000–500 B.C. (?), evidently not earlier than some of the mound-building developments in the North. The stylistic dis- tinctiveness of the Gulf Tradition becomes noticeable with the common occur- rence of pottery in the Tchefuncte period of about 500 B.C.–A.D. 1 in the lower valley. Burial mounds are possibly derived from contemporary Hopewellian manifestations of the Northern Tradition. During the succeeding Marksville period, from about A.D. 1 to A.D. 500, Gulf features were spread into northwest Florida. It is possible to infer from the presence of a temple mound at Kolomoki in southwest Georgia that this feature may be present in the Gulf Tradition before A.D. 500, and here it is associated with a large village site. Other temple mounds in the central Mississippi Valley have been attributed to the somewhat later Middle Baytown period of that region but are said to resemble ceremonial centers rather than constantly occupied towns (Phillips, Ford, and Griffin, 1951, p. 441). There was a considerable elaboration of mortuary practices, which reached a culmination in the Marksville and Troyville periods (and their equivalents in adjacent areas of this tradition), with a lavishness only slightly inferior to Hopewellian. Mortuary artifacts again suggest some degree of craft specialization. A trade in exotic materials for these could represent a partial continuation of the far-flung trade arrangements of the earlier Hopewellian climax, but which were now serving burial mounds distributed from Florida to Texas. Gulf pottery, in a variety of forms and decorations, shows great similarities from one end of a vast region to the other, arguing a high degree of interaction among Gulf peoples. Ceramic styles also document the eastward spread of the Gulf Tradition into Florida and the slighter diffusion of Gulf elements into Late Hopewellian of southern Illinois. There is evidence of maize cultivation at the Davis site, Texas, dated A.D. 398, but we do not know its importance in Gulf economies.

In the central Mississippi Valley on the border of the Gulf Tradition there somehow emerged a new tradition, the *Mississippian*. A date for early Mississippian at the Eveland site in Illinois is A.D. 939. There is no evidence of a corresponding decline in the Gulf Tradition, as there was earlier for the decline of Hopewellian. Mississippian continued to receive Gulf influences while at the same time surpassing Gulf in some respects. Mississippian shows greater reliance on food production, greater or at least more concentrated populations, and, if we are justified in considering most large Hopewellian and Gulf sites as primarily centers of religious ceremonial, we can say that the Mississippians had more secularized towns, maintaining larger populations for longer periods of time.

A central Mississippi River heartland suggested by geographical distribution of Mississippian sites has not provided evidence for a single origin of the Mississippian Tradition—which in any case would probably be a culture-historical impossibility (cf. Phillips, Ford, and Griffin, 1951, pp. 451–54). Yet Northern [Bluff culture] and Gulf [Middle Baytown] assemblages in this region do provide better evidence of continuity with succeeding Mississippian features than one finds elsewhere. In this matter, the circumstance that the Mississippian Tradition seems to have arisen on the northern border of the Gulf Tradition is interesting in the light of the earlier appearance of Gulf ceramic features in late Hopewellian sites in southern Illinois.

It is the concurrence of temple mounds and plazas; emphasis on plain, painted, and sometimes modeled pottery; reliance on maize agriculture; and semisettled towns that give Mississippian assemblages their Mesoamerican character. All but the last two features are readily derived from earlier Gulf occurrences, perhaps ultimately from Mesoamerican sources. Other supposed Gulf "firsts"—rim-flange bowls, duck-effigy vessels, and elaborate incised decoration—seem to have reached Mississippian assemblages at a later time.

The steps in the development of the Mississippian economy are unknown, but food production assumed a new importance. Not only do we more frequently find carbonized maize, but the size and apparent permanence of settlements implies population aggregations larger than before. Yet, for all this, hunting and gathering are still greatly relied on. There never existed in prehistoric America that fruitful combination of plant-raising and animal husbandry that became the foundation of Old World agriculture.

We should not give the impression that all Mississippian sites were large, but it is probably true that we have more large Mississippian sites than we do of any other period. Regional situations differed. There are many small sites, and some of those in southern Illinois may have been hunting camps. Twenhafel in Illinois shows the unusual condition of a small Mississippian settlement superimposed upon a really large Hopewellian one. In western Georgia there are at least two Mississippian sites larger than anything found earlier or later in the region. Arkansas, Mississippi, western Tennessee, and southeastern Missouri are notable for scores of extensive Mississippian sites with moats or embankments and well provided with platform mounds. In northwestern Florida, Willey has contrasted the intrusive Fort Walton Mississippian with earlier sites of the Gulf Tradition, suggesting that there was a shift of ceremonialism to the temple mound and a disappearance of the old burial-mound ceremonialism (1949, p. 581). His population estimate for Mississippian there is no larger than that for the preceding Gulf period, but he thinks that communities were larger.

The details of the spread of the Mississippian Tradition include migration of peoples, acculturation situations, and the diffusion of ideas to more remote groups. In the early Mississippian range of time far-flung fortified sites like Aztalan, Wisconsin, and Macon Plateau in Georgia indicate outward movements of people. These arrivals interrupted previous cultural continuities, and their survivors, if any, must have participated in the succeeding mixed cultural balances representing the fusion of Mississippian with the older regional traditions. A wholesale acculturation of an original Northern population to semi-Mississippian ways can be suggested if the Fort Ancient Aspect—Shawnee (Central Algonkian) equivalence stands (Griffin, 1952, p. 364). The Owasco Aspect farther east continued to represent the Northern Tradition, while probably adopting some Mississippian features secondhand from Fort Ancient. In the Southern Appalachian Tradition the north Georgia sequence of Etowah I-II-III-IV-Savannah-Wilbanks-Tumlin-and-Lamar suggest that original Southern Appalachian populations received repeated Mississippian influences. In the Gulf Tradition the Plaquemine period of the lower Mississippi Valley, and the Fulton Aspect of eastern Oklahoma show strong Mississippian diffusions. Fort Walton of northwestern Florida, however, may be involved with a migration of actual Mississippian peoples from central Alabama (Willey, 1949). On the prairies and plains of Kansas and Nebraska an intensification of food production, somehow connected with the Mississippian development to the east, gave rise first to semisedentary small-village cultures. Later settlements were larger, fewer, and fortified. The descendants of these peoples were, at least in part, the Village Indians of historic times. In Wedel's words, "in Kansas, as in Nebraska, concentration of the historic tribes—the Kansa, Pawnee, and others—in one or two large villages or towns for each tribe, completed a long sequence of changing settlement patterns" (Wedel, 1959).

The over-all result was the formation of a cordon of mixed cultures on the borders of the Mississippian development. These had certain common features, some of which were not specifically Mississippian but rather a result of this interaction.

During the rise of the Mississippian Tradition it seems almost as if the old Hopewellian and Gulf predilections for lavishing wealth on the dead might have been overcome, with ceremonial revolving around the temple rather than the burial mound as heretofore. Yet the height of the Mississippian development coincides with the spread during A.D. 1100–1400 of what is called the *Southern Cult*—the lavish disposal of costume and ornaments with certain selected dead. Artifact styles and decoration were more specifically Mesoamerican than anything that had been present before. Yet these are thoroughly reinterpreted with other indigenous features, including some evidently present long before in Adena (Webb and Baby, 1957, pp. 102–8). We may also suspect that embodied here is the old eastern idea of lavish mortuary expenditure. The mortuary program required craft specialists and extensive trade in raw materials, copper, mica, flint, and shells as before, but little obsidian. This development may or may not have begun in the Gulf area, but it spread through the Mississippian settlements to the regions beyond. It was once thought that the spread of the Southern Cult may have been as rapid as the much later Ghost Dance on the Plains (Waring and Holder, 1945). Precise similarities in complex designs on shell and copper ornaments and regalia

LOCATIONS OF SITES AND CULTURAL GROUPINGS MENTIONED: FIGURE II

On Map

Some early Mississippian sites far beyond Mississippian boundaries suggest migrations of peoples who later disappeared or became absorbed into surrounding populations.

O 1—Aztalan, Wisconsin
O 2—Hiwassee Island, Tennessee
O 3—Macon Plateau, Georgia

Some "Southern cult" centers outside Mississippian boundaries indicate that the cult need not always be associated with Mississippian cultures or necessarily have originated among them.

* 1—Mt. Royal, Florida
* 2—Hollywood, Georgia
* 3—Etowah, Georgia
* 4—Dallas focus, Tennessee
* 5—Spiro, Oklahoma

Protohistoric archeological manifestations beyond Mississippian boundaries show mixtures of Mississippian traits with those of the respective regional traditions. These are shown on map by upper-case letters:

e.g., *OWASCO*

Historic tribes are shown in lower-case letters:

e.g., *Catawba*

FIGURE 2. Location of sites and cultural groupings mentioned:
II. Eastern North America.

indicate, not only craft specialists whose products were spread over a great region, but the strict contemporaneity of many of the sites where they occur. Nevertheless, some elements may have been used before others. There are derivative designs in immediately succeeding times, but by the historic period only the slightest traces of Cult motifs remained in either material culture or mythology.

The earlier Hopewellian and Gulf climaxes had widespread effects, but the impact of the Mississippian seems to have been the greatest. On all sides of the Mississippian Tradition arose cultural balances showing varying kinds and degrees of Mississippian influences on the respective regional traditions. I wish to impress you with the symmetry of the historical structure here proposed.

1. There was a central region, later consolidated in what archeologists have referred to as "Middle Mississippi Culture," while at the same time the most distant Early Mississippi penetrations (e.g., Aztalan, Wisconsin; Macon Plateau, Georgia; Fort Walton[?], Florida) were being absorbed into the development of the new hybrid cultures surrounding Mississippian.
2. The surrounding hybrid cultures, representing the fusion of Mississippian with the various regional traditions, show significant similarities. Individual towns seldom reached the proportions of the great Mississippian centers, but fairly large sites are numerous, and some of these hybrid cultures—Owasco (in New York, Pennsylvania, and Michigan), Monongahela (Pennsylvania), Lamar (Georgia), and the Upper Republican and Nebraska cultures on the Plains—have been characterized as having the largest populations in their areas up to that time. In other cases, the sites of the Fort Ancient and Oneota aspects north of the Middle Mississippi region, Fort Walton in northwest Florida, and Bossier in Oklahoma are characterized by numerous sites with populations not greatly, if at all, inferior to the other regions. Except in those instances in which indigenous societies in Georgia and Florida adopted the Southern Cult for a time, we find little evidence of excessive ceremonialism.
3. Eventually there was a resurgence of regional styles even in some of the more centrally located areas of the Mississippian Tradition. The Dallas Focus of eastern Tennessee shows the increasing favor of the old cord-marked style of pottery decoration. The increased prevalence of the pottery-type Cahokia Cord-marked in the Upper Mississippi Valley may be a similar phenomenon.
4. By historic times the sites of the Mississippian Tradition from eastern Arkansas to central Illinois had experienced a population decline, and we are having great difficulty in relating the Mississippians to particular historic tribes. In a number of instances, however, it has been possible to connect historic tribes with the mixed regional cultures surrounding Mississippian.

With the closer look that historic ethnology brings, we may here note something that was probably slighted in the archeological evidence of the earlier periods—variability in the economic condition of the eastern tribes. In historic times there was, here and there, a decline of cultivation in favor of hunting. Reduced rainfall may have been a contributing factor on the Plains (Wedel, 1959), and of course the reintroduction of the horse led some tribes away from cultivation to a new Plains bison-hunting specialization. In the first Great Lakes region and northward the fur trade had the effect of diminishing native food production. Trade in deer skins exported from Charleston, South Carolina, to

Europe may have had a similar, if lesser, effect in central Georgia, where Fairbanks noted a decline in cultivation at Ocmulgee Fields (1956, p. 60).

There is a significant contrast between these various situations and the picture Quimby reports of the Huron relying heavily on agriculture (1960, p. 114), and we have other accounts of vast cornfields observed by travelers. In the Cherokee towns thousands of bushels of corn were destroyed by British troops. We shall, then, have to close our story by asking a question that may eventually be answered by a combination of archeological and ethnological evidence. Is it possible that in some sections of the cordon of mixed Mississippian-indigenous cultures surrounding the old Mississippian heartland a new level of agricultural activity was arising? We remember that these areas had been characterized as having achieved their heaviest populations in late prehistoric times, and we should also mention that there is a hint of a new settlement pattern, at least among the Creeks and the Cherokee. Town clusters, which include miles of farmsteads strung along the rivers and streams (Caldwell, n.d.), might be a more effective accommodation to agricultural necessities than the hypothetical major town and tributary villages pattern that some students believe to have been the usual settlement arrangement during Mississippian times.

SPECULATIONS

Perhaps I should have let matters stand at this, claiming that eastern prehistoric development was distinctive—or at least unlike that of the nuclear areas—and hence the forms of food production and settlement might well be different too. But I do not wish to imply that those might have been different simply because they were a result of a particular history. I should rather see them as different as a result of processes we are beginning to understand.

As a primary focus, the conceptions "food production" and "urbanism" allow one to ask interesting questions. Moreover, if we agree that these are bound to take different forms in different cultural developments, there is no reason why one cannot proceed to more analytic terms, more readily transposable from one developmental pathway to another. Steward has attempted this by one means, represented by the idea of "cross-cultural type," and it must be clear to the reader that the idea of separate developmental pathways is just another way of expressing Steward's pioneering conception of multilinear evolution (1955). Here I shall experiment with rather different analytic terms in order to examine the questions of the emergence of food production and settled life in this region. Since we will be dealing with change, these terms will be concerned with "conditions of innovation" and adaptive situations. The result will be to exhibit forest efficiency, food production, and settlement as interrelated in particular ways. To whatever degree these proposed interrelations can be accepted as valid, they can qualify as additional historical "facts." But innovation is undoubtedly limited in determinate ways, and therefore there ought to be some chance, eventually, of using such conditions and interrelations for additional generalizations about historical development.

It is supposed that the major event characterizing eastern North America during late glacial and early postglacial times was a shift from economies based mostly on hunting—represented by fluted-point assemblages—to economies in which hunting and gathering were more nearly balanced—represented by the assemblages we call Archaic. The economic innovations involved in what we called "primary forest efficiency" can be taken together as primarily adaptive, that is, the discovery of new ways to obtain resources in the land, forests, streams, and shore. To call such innovations adaptive, moreover, could help us select situations elsewhere that might involve sequences of similar innovations to see what we could learn from this. We could select geographically—other temperate forest regions—or "processually"—steps leading to plains, desert, or maritime "efficiencies." Either approach should lead to some conclusions as to what kinds of innovations were possible, and what were not, in particular steps in the various sequences and thus help focus on relations among the innovations that actually occurred.

For example, if it turns out, as I think it must, that the regional assemblages that Willey and Phillips classified into a New World Archaic stage (1958, pp. 104–43) represent adaptive situations, it may then become possible to say that the various (and sometimes debatable) proposed hearths of early plant cultivation in the New World appear at the end of such sequences. Tamaulipas, Peruvian Coast, Amazonian lowlands, and the northern Mississippi Valley begin, or may be supposed to begin, cultivation after the development of a hunting-gathering type of economy is well under way or nearly completed. Moreover, these can be claimed to be, on empirical as well as logical grounds, specifically regions where the use of wild plant foods had become important as part of their initial adaptation to the land.

Other presumed consequences of such adaptive situations can be offered as reasonable hypotheses about the conditions under which plant cultivation emerged. In eastern North America one consequence of the adaptive trend toward primary forest efficiency was the ability of some societies to become more settled. This would also probably be an effect to any adaptive trend that did not take nomadism as one of the ways it could be achieved. In short, as more copious supplies of natural foods are attained, it is expectable that people need travel less to obtain them. We can say further that some degree of settled life usually would be a precondition for the acceptance of innovations pertaining to cultivation. Another precondition would be an interest and considerable knowledge of wild plants, something else that must have increased in the change from hunting to economies relying more on plant foods. We may never know exactly how the first cultigens were adopted in eastern North America—whether according to Edgar Anderson's "Dump Heap Theory" (1952, pp. 136–50) or by some other means—but, given the preconditions suggested above and generations of women with an empirical interest in wild plants and their properties, we should be less surprised if we found a possibly independent development of food production in the Mississippi

Valley than if we did not, for the opportunity to innovate along these lines must have occurred innumerable times.

It is possible that early plant cultivation in the East, whether actually indigenous or somehow stimulated by early cultigens from southward, facilitated the introduction of maize from Mesoamerica. It has already, however, become a matter of debate in North America whether the Adena and Hopewellian manifestations, which certainly practiced some planting, actually had an effective food production. My own view is that by and large they did not. Only in later times, especially during the Mississippian period, can we with any confidence state that food production probably had notable social consequences. Even so, food production seems never to have provided as complete a basis for subsistence as is presumed to have been achieved in Mesoamerica by 1500 B.C. or in western Asia some thousands of years earlier. Elsewhere (Caldwell, 1958), I have used this focus on conditions of innovation to suggest that the very efficiency of forest adaptation was a factor inhibiting the acceptance of food production as a major economic basis.

I do not think we can ever assume that a society will automatically turn to food production for its subsistence basis, even where the techniques of planting and harvesting are already known. In the instances in which this has happened we ought to try to discover the means by which it occurred. We can, for example, use a contrast between eastern North America and the nuclear regions to go a little way into problems connected with the change-over to substantial food production in the areas where civilizations arose. Eastern North America provided innumerable sources of wild foods, and its population, for reasons at present debatable (Kroeber, 1938, pp. 148–49), was far from reaching the limits of its wild and cultivated resources. But the nuclear civilizations of southwest Asia and Mesoamerica are somehow associated with dryer lands of less natural abundance. Wild resources ought sooner to have reached their limits in portions of these regions so that some societies, already "experimenting" with cultivated plants, could turn gradually to food production as the older hunting-gathering activities became less and less fruitful. It does not matter for this argument that tropical areas are also found within or adjacent to early food-producing civilizations. The archeological evidence would be whether the areas within the nuclear civilizations that provided the most substantial natural foods were later in turning to food production as the main basis for subsistence.

Turning back to eastern North America, the Mesoamerican plants maize, beans, and squash were involved in the picture here of a gradually increasing reliance on cultivation. Probably these were more productive than the native domestications that had preceded and/or been stimulated by them. Mesoamerican borrowings notwithstanding, cultivation had to be adapted to the social necessities of the eastern forest economy. What this meant, in the first place, was that the cultivators were to be women, for as food-gatherers they probably had a greater knowledge and interest in plants than did the men. Moreover, ordinary domestic duties would keep them daily closer to home and the cultivated crops.

Another consequence of the forest economy is one that has not been clearly delineated in the regions of nuclear civilization. As dependence on food production gradually increased, women maintained their ascendancy in this activity. Even by historic times there was nothing here corresponding to the farmer or agricultural specialist. The men were warrior-hunters or, rarely, "specialists" of other kinds. Agriculture, if we may use this term, was a part-time occupation of women, and its increasing importance was probably reflected in historic times by the prevalence of matrilineal institutions among the more agricultural tribes.

The idea of a "primary farming community," which is coming to be of the greatest usefulness in understanding the emergence of the nuclear civilizations, can hardly have the same meanings when applied to these eastern North American communities of hunters and feminine part-time cultivators. "Forest communities" would be a better term. Increasing cultivation and borrowings from Mesoamerica were, most of us would agree, changing these forest communities to something else. But I am not at all sure that our understanding of the processes of change will be furthered by the assumption that these were leading to the kind of village-farming communities we believe to have existed in contemporary Mesoamerica. Nor do we have any evidence that Mesoamerican communities were introduced bodily into eastern North America. It is entirely likely that Mesoamerican civilization would in time have practically submerged this North American development. But the time was not yet, and Willey's recent statement that "Middle American town life with its temple-mound-and-plaza complex, entered the Mississippi Valley sometime between A.D. 500 and 1000" (1960, p. 84) has an odd ring in terms of the context I have been trying to discover and portray.

Primary forest efficiency had already given these communities a good start toward sedentism, but one that could be carried only so far. Even by historic times, hunting and gathering was still of sufficient importance that the entire population of an average town might in season depart for some other place where the hunting was better. This ease of movement, which offends some of our notions of how a town ought to behave, not only was a reflection of forest economy but also was of no disadvantage under the general conditions of warfare that had come to prevail by historic times, at least, and particularly among those tribes that relied most heavily on planting. Kroeber's view that, because of war, populations were kept down in the East and agriculture kept in the role of only a contributer to subsistence is one that archeology has not quite the sophistication to handle or yet to neglect. This warfare "insane, unending, continuously attritional, from our point of view; and yet . . . so integrated into the whole fabric of eastern culture, so dominantly emphasized within it, that escape from it was well-nigh impossible" (Kroeber 1938, pp. 148–49) may not, as Kroeber suggests, have kept "population down to a point where more agriculture was not needed," but may have kept agriculture down by placing some additional premium on the mobility of forest communities.

In short, food production and settlements in the East took forms that were not, or possibly at least not for long, characteristic of the regions of nuclear civilization. Granted that there may be some similarities—some inherent necessities that could evoke similar institutions among peoples of any background who might choose to bind themselves to the land or live in large aggregations—this had not yet happened in the East. We may never know whether a fully effective agriculture or a massive urbanism would eventually have appeared, but we may learn that the pathway actually taken was different, and therefore interesting. I have emphasized these differences in the hope that they may eventually become illuminating.

BIBLIOGRAPHY

ANDERSON, EDGAR
1952. *Plants, Life, and Man.* Harcourt Brace.

CALDWELL, JOSEPH R.
1958. *Trend and Tradition in the Prehistory of the Eastern United States.* ("Ill. State Mus. Scient. Papers," Vol. 10, and Amer. Anthrop. Assoc. Mem. 88.

n.d. "Appraisal of the Archeological Resources of Hartwell Reservoir, South Carolina and Georgia." ("Smithsonian River Basin Surveys" [mimeographed].) Washington.

EGGAN, FRED
1952. "Ethnological Cultures and Archeological Backgrounds." In James B. Griffin (ed.), *Archeology of Eastern United States.* Chicago: University of Chicago Press.

FAIRBANKS, CHARLES H.
1956. *Archeology of the Funeral Mound, Ocmulgee National Monument, Georgia.* ("Nat. Park Serv. Archeol. Res. Ser.," No. 3.) Washington.

FOWLER, MELVIN L.
1959. "Summary Report of Modoc Rock Shelter, 1952, 53, 55, and 56." (Ill. State Mus., *Report of Investigations*, No. 8.)

GOSLIN, ROBERT M.
1957. "Food of the Adena People." In WEBB and BABY, *The Adena People, No. 2.* Columbus: Ohio State University Press.

GRIFFIN, JAMES B.
1952. *Some Early and Middle Woodland Pottery Types in Illinois.* ("Ill. State Mus. Scient. Papers," Vol. 5, No. 3.)

1952. "Culture Periods in Eastern United States Archeology." In JAMES B. GRIFFIN (ed.), *Archeology of Eastern United States.* Chicago: University of Chicago Press.

1958. *The Chronological Position of the Hopewellian Culture in the Eastern United States.* ("Univ. Mich. Anthrop. Paper," No. 12.)

KELLEY, J. CHARLES
1955. "Juan Sabeata and Diffusion in Aboriginal Texas," *Amer. Anthrop.*, 57:981–95.

KROEBER, A. L.
1939. *Cultural and Natural Areas of Native North America.* ("Univ. Calif. Publs. in Amer. Archaeol. and Ethnol.," Vol. 38.)

MacNeish, Richard S.
1959. "A Speculative Framework of Northern North American Prehistory as of April, 1959," *Anthropologica*, 1:7–21.

Maxwell, Moreau
1951. *The Woodland Cultures of Southern Illinois*. ("Logan Mus. Publs. in Anthrop," Bull. 7.)

Phillips, Philip, James A. Ford, and James B. Griffin
1951. *Archaeological Survey in the Lower Mississippi Alluvial Valley*. ("Peabody Mus. Amer. Archeol. and Ethnol.," No. 25.)

Quimby, George Irving
1960. *Indian Life in the Upper Great Lakes*. Chicago: University of Chicago Press.

Ritchie, William A.
1955. *Recent Discoveries Suggesting an Early Woodland Burial Cult in the Northeast*. (New York State Mus. and Sci. Serv., Circ. 40.) Albany.

Ritchie, William A., and Don W. Dragoo
1960. *The Eastern Dispersal of Adena*. (New York State Mus. and Sci. Serv., Bull. 379.) Albany.

Steward, Julian H.
1955. *Theory of Culture Change*. Urbana: University of Illinois Press.

Waring, Antonio J., and Preston Holder
1945. "A Prehistoric Ceremonial Complex in the Southeastern United States," *Amer. Anthrop.*, Vol. 47.

Webb, William S., and Raymond S. Baby
1957. *The Adena People, No. 2*. Columbus: Ohio State University Press.

Wedel, Waldo R.
1959. *An Introduction of Kansas Archeology*. (Bur. Ethnol. Bull. 174.) Washington.

Willey, Gordon R.
1949. *Archaeology of the Florida Gulf Coast*. (Smithsonian Miscellaneous Collections, Vol. 113.) Washington.

1960. "New World Prehistory," *Science*, 131:73–86.

Willey, Gordon R., and Philip Phillips
1958. *Method and Theory in American Archaeology*. Chicago: University of Chicago Press.

Wittry, Warren L.
1959. "The Raddatz Rockshelter, Sk5, Wisconsin," *Wisconsin Archeologist*, 40:33–69.

NORTHERN EUROPE

CARL-AXEL MOBERG

INTRODUCTION

NORTHERN EUROPE proper was still covered by ice at 15,000 B.C. Glaciation is believed not to have ceased entirely before the seventh millennium B.C. In the northernmost two-thirds of the area nothing that can really be called "urbanization" took place until late historic times, *and then only on a very modest scale to begin with.*

Thus, for the beginning of the period treated by this symposium, there is nothing to be considered in northern Europe at all. And in the same area the last part of the problem, urbanization, must be studied mainly by means of historical documentation, since archeological evidence from these latter centuries is very inconsistent or entirely lacking.

Although the area concerned is small and although systematic research on its prehistory has a relatively long history, the region is by no means thoroughly enough investigated to permit a continuous record of this prehistory. In the southernmost regions the prehistoric record is interrupted because the sea beaches on which the sites of some periods must lie are now submerged below contemporary ones. The actual questions can best be studied within a modest number of small key areas, surrounded by areas about which we have much less knowledge. With few exceptions, these key areas are or were maritime, or at least situated within a short distance from the coast. As a consequence, the history not only of food collection but also of food production and urbanization may at any time have been influenced by maritime opportunities for (*a*) fishing and sea hunting, and (*b*) communications facilitating invasion, diffusion, and trade. In the north, arctic or semiarctic climatic conditions permitting the use of sledges and skis made traveling over very long distances possible—including distances over frozen stretches of lake and sea areas—in quite another way than was possible in the south.

This outline will therefore deal with the problems as they present themselves when one is surveying the different coasts of northern Europe from south to north.

I. CHANGES IN FOOD-COLLECTING BEFORE THE INTRODUCTION OF FOOD PRODUCTION

To get an idea of "varying degrees of intensification of food-collecting" requires a considerable quantity of finds accurately dated and from not too short a period.

At least as far as published materials are concerned, this condition is best fulfilled in two quite different parts of northern Europe: in the southwest in Denmark-Skåne, in the northeast in southwestern and in southern Finland. In the majority of the other regions there is not yet a sufficient background of evidence for a study of this special problem.

In the southwest, food-collecting complexes of different age and/or tradition may in a simplified way be grouped under two main headings, according to their position and size: (1) late glacial cultures + Klosterlund + Maglemose + Gudenå, (2) early coastal + Kongemose; Ertebölle.

The difference between the two groups is, not only that generally the first is represented by inland and the second by coastal settlements, but also that several among the latter are relatively large (Ertebölle sites run up to *ca.* 200 × 40 meters). The earliest of these large settlements appear in the sixth millennium B.C. The interpretation of the general character of Ertebölle is controversial (see below).

The northeastern sequence generally comprises coastal settlements. The valley of Porvoonjoki (east of Helsinki) provides an outstanding instance of how occupation has followed the change of the seashore for thousands of years. Luho (1956) investigated six sites of the earliest Askola stage. From the following Suomusjärvi period he mentions about 100 sites and then numbers of comb ceramic and later sites. Provided that a continuity exists between these groups, the Porvoonjoki complex can be said to testify to a considerable permanency in settlement. Occupations that change in adaptation to a changing natural surrounding can themselves be regarded as stable.

An impression of a special sort of permanency is also given by the late food-collecting sites in northern Norway (Karlebotn), excavated by Nummedal (1935–36) and others, beyond the limits of any prehistoric food production: the permanency depended on repeated use of the same site within a seminomadic seasonal cycle. There were 88 huts in one single settlement area, but all 88 were not contemporary (cf. Gjessing, 1959; Simonsen, 1960).

This instance of food-collecting permanency should be stressed, since forms of primitive food production in many cases seem to have resulted in less-permanent settlement.

II. THE TRANSITION TO FOOD PRODUCTION

A. EARLY AND MIDDLE NEOLITHIC TRB CULTURE ZONE

Within the area where food production was first introduced by the TRB culture (German, *TRichterBecher;* Danish, *TRagtBaegere*: the "First Northern Culture" of Childe), detailed combined archeological and biological studies have been carried out on Sjaelland (Zealand) in Denmark and in Södermanland (southwest of Stockholm) in Sweden.

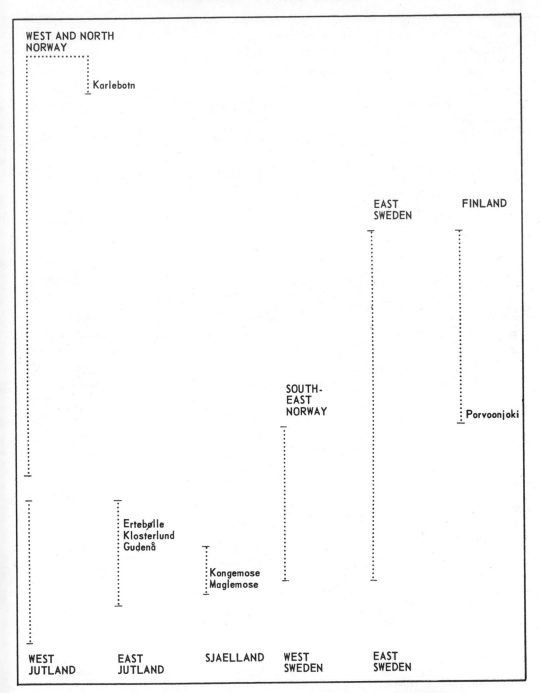

FIGURE 1. Food-collecting before the introduction of food production.

FIGURES 1 to 4 are map-graphs of the coastal stretches of Northern Europe for four phases of their prehistory and history. The scheme is a highly simplified one, with the longitudinal stretches of coastline approximated to north-south lines. Note that since the coasts of Scandinavia north of *ca.* 62° N. run in a southwest to northeast line, the distances indicated for these northerly portions are foreshortened. The localities and zones noted are mentioned in the text.

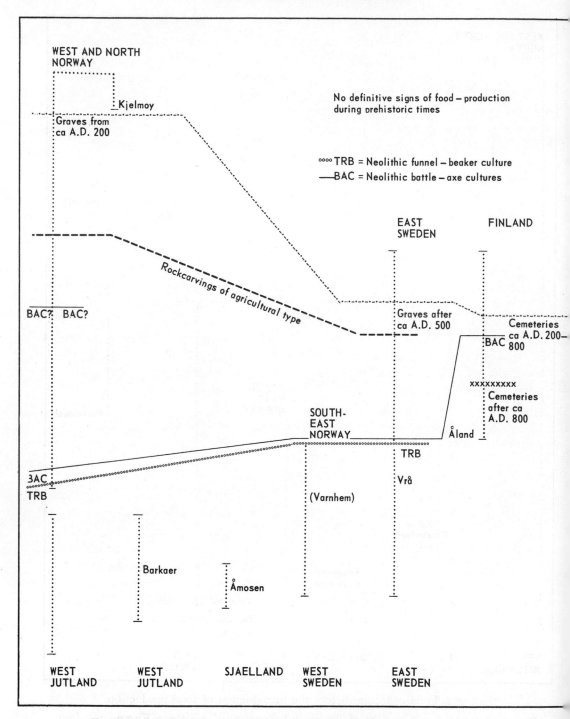

FIGURE 2. Food production appears along the southerly stretches of coast.
(See legend to Fig. 1 for remarks.)

In Denmark attention has been focused on the Åmosen bog, where an exceptional number of rich sites have been given more than usually detailed investigation (Troels-Smith, 1953). There are C^{14} determinations—for example, 2620 ± 80 B.C. According to the investigator's opinion, the finds reflect (1) the classical Ertebölle, beginning as a semifarming culture, with hunting and fishing still an integral part of the economy but with a gradual swing toward a culture chiefly based upon field and animal husbandry, among other things, after presumably receiving strong intrusive additions, and (2) the immigration of a nomad culture. As to the interpretation of the first part, Troels-Smith's view has not been generally accepted. For Becker (1955), Brönsted (1957), and Mathiassen (1959), the introduction of earliest TRB agriculture is at least mainly the result of immigration. For fuller interpretation of this matter we must wait for a definitive publication of the Åmosen finds, and in the meantime it should be observed that the term "Ertebölle" has somewhat different implications for different authorities. (See Schwabedissen's contribution, this volume.)

Denmark is the only Scandinavian region of the TRB culture where there is conclusive evidence of real villages and of organized flint-mining.

North and west of the main portions of Denmark there were at least attempts to introduce the TRB type of food production in southern Norway (Hinsch, 1951–53) and to establish more definitive bridgeheads in discontinuous areas along the west coast of Sweden. There is also an interesting but archeologically very little known inland isolate. Within this, an important pollen-analytical study has been made by Fries (1958) near Varnhem (Fries stresses the probable unreliability of the Varnhem C^{14} determinations; 3330 ± 110, 3630 ± 110 B.C.).

In the southernmost part of Sweden's east coast, a different ecological context may explain an interesting sequence at Siretorp. The site is no doubt of a fishing-hunting type, alternately used by Ertebölle, TRB, and later inhabitants (Bagge and Kjellmark, 1939).

Farther north, isolated TRB settlements of corresponding date are known. In the Södermanland area southwest of Stockholm, Florin (1958) has excavated a sequence of agricultural settlements, the so-called Vrå culture. These settlements belong to the TRB culture, but Florin has emphasized differences from the Danish finds. Radiocarbon determinations exist (e.g., 3400 ± 100 B.C.) but seem to be dependent on a probably controversial interpretation of the quaternary geology of the region. Florin regards it as doubtful whether agriculture could have been introduced by way of invasion and seems inclined to believe in an internal development (as was suggested earlier by Åberg). This opinion is not generally accepted. To the author, it seems to lack convincing support from archeological evidence (Bagge, 1951).

To sum up, Denmark proper seems to be the most outlying of the northern European regions where agriculture was *definitely* established by the time of the TRB culture.

B. The Middle Neolithic Battle-Axe Culture Zone, *ca.* 2000 b.c.

Within the vast outlying area of the TRB culture zone, the introduction of food production was renewed—and outside these limits was initiated by—the battle-axe cultures belonging to the northern European middle neolithic period. As to the character of food production in this culture, it is generally accepted that emphasis was on nomadic cattle-breeding. However, this view seems to be based on rather weak evidence. It is well known that the question of the local or of the extraneous genesis of these groups is a most controversial matter, or at least it has been so. But from what is actually known from the Scandinavian finds, it would be very difficult to find substantial support for the idea of a local development of the battle-axe cultures in Scandinavia.

Graves definitely belonging to these groups have been found from southeastern Norway (Hinsch, 1954) through central Sweden—thus within the region of the earlier TRB expansion—whereas a settlement in the Trondheim district (Marstrander, 1956; Møllenhus, 1958), which is the subject of some discussion, would be outside the TRB region.

The distribution of the battle-axe culture in Latvia, Estonia, and Finland (Kilian, 1955; Gimbutas, 1956, 1958), stretching in to Österbotten (Meinander, 1946, 1950), is evidently far outside this TRB limit. Here, in the east, the first appearance of food production is no doubt connected with the battle-axe culture. In Finland it also eventually provides an exceptional opportunity to study a case of transition from food producing to food-collecting.

C. The South Scandinavian Late Neolithic Culture, toward *ca.* 1500 b.c.

In southern Scandinavia and adjacent regions, the late neolithic period is characterized by a culture with such traits as flint daggers and crescentic implements, ceremonial deposits, and, among other things, stone cist graves. No doubt the connections of this cultural manifestation with earlier groups deserves a more thorough discussion. Its importance as a starting point for the following bronze age development seems evident. Several scholars, especially in Norway, have indicated the role it played in a firmer establishment of agriculture, perhaps of a seminomadic tradition. Archeological and/or pollen-analytical evidence in this direction has been produced, among other places, for parts of the Swedish west coast (Olausson, 1957), southeast Norway (Hagen, 1960; Hafsten, 1958), and the Trondheim district (Hinsch, 1948).

D. Bronze Age (*ca.* 1500 b.c.–500 b.c.) and Later Periods

The post-neolithic spread of food production in Scandinavia mainly affects regions where the archeological evidence is little suited to give information on our problem. For instance, it may be mentioned that from Sweden north of the Mälar region (i.e., for the northern two-thirds of the country) not a single prehistoric grain impression has yet been reported, although one grain itself has been noted (Hjelmqvist, 1955). In Norway only one such impression is mentioned as far north as the Trondheim district. These two regions in Sweden (Florin, 1960; Helmfrid, 1958) and Norway (Larssen, 1953, 1954) are also the northernmost ones where palynological evidence of prehistoric agriculture has been recovered. As to the bones of domesticated cattle, the situation is somewhat brighter, but these are often found in contexts where their close dating remains a more or less open question, for example, in Norwegian coastal rock shelters from late periods.

Rock carvings, mainly of the southern Scandinavian type, which may express an agricultural ceremonialism, can give some impression of how far north agriculture was practiced during the "bronze age" (of course, this term is, per se, a meaningless label for this area and time) and for some centuries following. On the Norwegian west coast, these rock carvings are well represented in the Trondheim district, and isolated cases have been hitherto observed up to about 66° north latitude at least. On the east side of the Scandinavian peninsula, they do not extend north of the Mälar region, apart from one isolated occurrence at 63° 30′ N. (Nämforsen,, intermingled with carvings of so-called Arctic, hunting-magic type [Hallström, 1960; Janson and Hvarfner, 1960]).

The evidence of datable bronze-age graves, which can be taken to express the same spread, seems to agree mainly with that of the rock carvings. In Finland we must rely on graves of southern Scandinavian types. According to Meinander (1954), they can be followed up to *ca.* 63° 40′ N.

For our problem, this hints at one interesting point at least: the expansion of food production was a continuing process along the northern European coasts (Moberg, 1960). But it leaves us unaided as to the question of how this process took place. To the bronze age belong the very interesting villages, excavated by Meinander (1954*a*) on small islands of the Åland archipelago. The inhabitants of these seasonal sites must have been mainly seal hunters and fishermen, but the presence of millstones *might* indicate some form of contact with food production.

The contemporary situation in southwestern Norway must be omitted here. Important investigations have been conducted by Hinsch (1954); we must hope for posthumous publication of his full results.

The decisive expansion of food production to the northern coastal regions took place after the first centuries of our era, but at different periods on the opposite sides of the Scandinavian peninsula. On the Norwegian coasts, graves indicate settlements of southwestern Norwegian type up to the fringes of the Arctic ocean as early as A.D. 200. On the other hand, presumed invasions of immigrants to southern (and inland) Finland initially reach Österbotten, but the late cemeteries of the ninth to eleventh centuries A.D. are only to be found in exceptional cases north of *ca.* 61° 30′ (cf. Kivikoski, 1947–51). Along the Swedish east coast quite a few corresponding monuments can be found up to *ca.* 64° N. The meeting of the zone of agriculture from both the Finnish and the Swedish sides, around the northernmost parts of the Gulf of Bothnia, belongs to historic times, from the fourteenth century A.D. onward.

But this late historical process is evidently characterized by the same feature that we have to presume for all the preceding prehistoric expansions, from late neolithic onward; food production in the form of agriculture was introduced to northern Europe mainly by way of successive migrations. The only phase for which a serious controversy exists on this question is that of the early neolithic and the TRB culture.

But a second and most important feature must finally be stressed, and this is that within these migratory frameworks there are marked differences in the relative roles of food production.

Only in Denmark have real neolithic villages been excavated (e.g., Barkaer). So far, only here and in very limited adjacent areas of Sweden (mainly coastal) is there evidence from the neolithic periods of time that suggests anything like an effective food production, with plant cultivation and/or animal domestication assuming a *major* subsistence role. This is expressed by sites with considerable numbers of grain impressions, by high-level pollen curves of cereals and ecologically related plants that are contemporary and continuous, as well as by major components of domesticated animals within the faunal remains. Outside the area mentioned for Denmark and adjacent coastal Sweden nothing even partly similar appears until the series of iron-age (around and after A.D. 1) villages and farm sites, excavated in Jutland (Hatt, 1937, 1957), on Bornholm (Klindt-Jensen, 1957, 1958a, 1958b, 1959; cf. Becker, 1958; Norling-Christensen, 1958, 1959; Werner, 1960), Gotland (Stenberger, 1955) and in southern Norway (Petersen, 1933, 1936; Grieg, 1934; Hougen, 1947; Hagen, 1953).

From western Norway, central Sweden, and southern Finland northward, it is obviously reasonable to reckon with a continued greater importance of food collection. Cultivation and/or animal domestication here may be "incipient," not only to begin with but up to the present; "supplementary" is a more useful term here. But even in the northern regions food production is of course "effective" in the sense that the domesticates are being utilized far outside their natural habitat.

Between these two main regions, one of more effective food production in Denmark and adjacent coastal Sweden, and one more supplementary region farther north, there is a broad intermediate zone, where the question of "effective" or "supplementary" food production is relevant in any period.

E. Pastoral Nomadism of the Same

In historic times we meet a form of pastoral nomadism in the north, the reindeer-breeding of the Same (Lapps), both inland and along the coastal regions of the Arctic ocean. It would be of great value in our context of interest if we could study the transition from a food-collecting to a food-producing economy of this special kind. There is archeological evidence of iron-age communities, using non-domesticated reindeer, above all at Kjelmö. And on some of the northern Scandinavian hunting-magic rock-pictures, reindeer are represented, although elks are in the majority. So far, however, only hypothetical suggestions

may be made concerning the transition, and it would lead us too far from archeological evidence to enter into a discussion of Same ethnogenesis.

Throughout this outline the profound and complicated changes both in environment and in the practice of agriculture, during the periods *between* the
first appearance of food production and the earliest indications of incipient urbanization, cannot be treated even summarily. It is only possible to stress the fact
of these changes and to admit that our knowledge of them is very incomplete.
As to the agricultural aspects of the situation, recent investigations such as those
mentioned above have yielded valuable information on crucial problems, but
only in certain key areas; outside these areas knowledge is much more incomplete.

III. THE APPROACH TO URBANIZATION

In northern Europe, especially in its northernmost regions, an effective urbanization comparable to that accounted for during this symposium (e.g., for the Near
Eastern–Mediterranean areas or in Mesoamerica) occurred mainly in late historical
times. If one were to use Childe's criteria for an urban civilization, it seems uncertain whether the purely archeological record from any Scandinavian medieval
town would produce fully satisfactory evidence for the existence of such an
urban civilization. Even the term "threshold of urbanization" does not seem very
useful for the prehistory of this area. Instead, one could—for northern Europe—
speak of a certain "approach to urbanization." Urbanization proper did not come
until later in history, but in some regions and in certain particular spots its coming
was prepared for by certain traits. No doubt this prehistoric *approach to urbanization* had an important impact on the patterns and distribution of historic urbanization.

What we have to look for is a differentiation, a specialization among settlement
concentrations. We might speak of an "approach to urbanization" when we have
archeological evidence of a certain "elite" of concentrated settlements within a
group of otherwise run-of-the-mill contemporary sites, within a regionally limited
cultural manifestation. Such an elite site would be characterized by one or more
of such traits as number of inhabitants, fortifications, special ceremonies; it would
be especially valuable if there were evidence pointing toward a special situation
for these centers within a given economic system, for example, concentration of
surplus, importation of materials or products, specialized crafts. The sites might
be bigger, stronger, "more ceremonial," more industrial or commercial, wealthier
than the majority of sites belonging to the same pattern or group of settlements.
Thus the other sites may be assumed to be "dependent" in Redfield's sense.

The evidence from northern Europe does, in fact, show such a situation in some
late cases. But in the main, there is no evidence for the autochthonous beginnings
for such traits in northern Europe. One has to look for external origins for this
approach-to-urbanization situation. There are, however, different potential sources
to discuss for the Continent, outside the Mediterranean world.

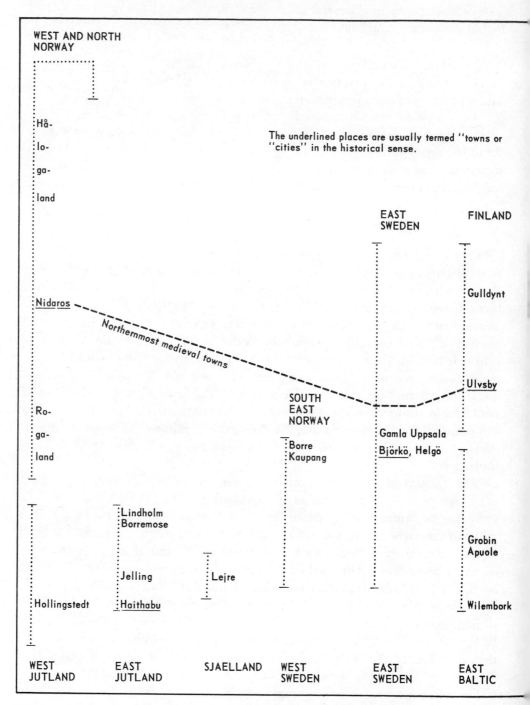

FIGURE 3. The approach to urbanism. (*See legend to Fig. 1.*)

It might seem as if one of the first urban-like patterns within reach of northern Europe was that of the Lusatian culture in Poland *ca.* 500 B.C. It comprises the fortified settlements of, for example, Biskupin, Sobiejuchy, and Izdebno, which lie within 250 kilometers of Bornholm and which are probably related to the northern Polish and east German fortifications of the same period, lying even closer to Scandinavia. But Rajewski (1958) assumes that the sites mentioned above were the only permanent ones of their particular regions and that such other sites as have been excavated in each particular region were only temporary and seasonal "camp sites" of the same population. Consequently, this Lusatian group would have to be ruled out of the "elite"-site–"dependent"-site picture, as there were no controlled rural people and no permanent dependent settlements.

Perhaps, there is an analogy in the partly contemporary eastern European Gorodishtshe culture, branches of which reached to the Baltic and perhaps in some places even crossed it.

Another possibility for consideration is opened by the western and central and southeastern European fortified settlements of the Hallstatt and La Tène periods, *ca.* 500 B.C.–A.D. 1. A few of these (e.g., Mont Beuvray in Burgundy) fulfill the requirements of "specialization of sites" to such a high degree that the prevailing view of them as "the first cities north of the Alps" seems to be very much justified (Moberg, 1950). Others of these sites might rather be fortified manors, important centers for trade, metallurgy, and crafts. In exceptional cases, such sites are encountered near northern Europe (e.g., not far from the mouth of the Elbe), and the Borremose site in Jutland could be regarded as a marginal representative of this group. But in these latter cases there are as yet no signs to indicate other settlements that might be "dependent" upon them.

However, it should be stressed that during the late La Tène period (toward A.D. 1), this Central-European group had a considerable importance for some regions in southern Scandinavia. This seems to have been one of the earliest, more direct contacts of northern Europe with a culture including some distinct urban traits. (As a still earlier case one could discuss the perhaps traceable Hallstatt period relations with the Etruscan area, but this depends upon the interpretation of the relations between Alpine and Italian crafts).

The period of Roman occupation in Central and western Europe brought its Mediterranean type of military urban settlements no closer to southernmost Scandinavia than by about 600 kilometers. It did, however, result in intensified contact for northern Europe with urban civilization. (The author is inclined to guess that the enormous concentration of graves at Wilembork/Willenberg at the mouth of the Vistula could possibly be an indication of a commercial center, and, if so, why not a town? [Moberg, 1941].)

During the post-Roman centuries and in part much earlier, a number of isolated criteria can already be observed, which together could have created an incipient urbanization *if* they had appeared together (which they did not). Such isolated criteria are:

a) Increased size of cemeteries, probably reflecting increased size of settlements (but of course there is nothing to prove that these should have been anything more than villages).

b) Increasing specialization in funeral ceremonies, probably reflecting increased social specialization. This is, sometimes with the aid of historical documentation of an uncertain reliability, interpreted as an expression of "kingship."

c) During some parts of these periods, and in certain regions, increased signs of warfare ("warrior graves," ceremonial bog deposits of military equipment, hidden treasures indicating wars, fortifications).

d) Large public buildings (i.e., some of the fortifications mentioned above, which are especially magnificent on the island of Öland).

e) Remarkable concentrations of surplus (as revealed, e.g., by gold and silver treasures, belonging to the same migration period context as above).

f) Full-time specialists—the only possible explanation for the development of the sophisticated "Germanic" animal styles (Holmqvist, 1955), which are characteristic for the period A.D. 400–1000, although 2,500 years earlier, the archeological record in northern Europe already includes traits suggesting full-time specialization.

g) Writing (runes), even if its first use seems limited almost entirely to magic.

h) Important long-range trade, beginning as early as the third millennium B.C.; from *ca.* A.D. 300 onward occasional connections are also indicated by the use of coins (these are imported; local coinage in the south began on a very modest scale *ca.* A.D. 800).

But at least so far there are no known traces of cities. The only more direct trend in such a direction is seen in the development of a number of village- or manor-sized "community centers," or whatever one chooses to call them, for example:

a) The surprisingly regular "administrative centers" and their subcenters investigated by H. E. Lund (1955, 1960) far to the north in Norway in the ancient Hålogaland, and corresponding settlements in southwestern Norway.

b) Helgö or Lillö near Stockholm, under extensive excavation by Holmqvist (1954, 1959, 1960).

c) Lindholm Høje in northern Jutland (soon to be published by Th. Ramskou; cf. 1953, 1955, 1957, 1960) as well as another site of related type in the same region.

d) It is tempting to mention Gulldynt in Österbotten in Finland in this context; according to Meinander (1946, 1950), it is a Migration period commercial center.

The establishment, in about A.D. 800, of the first more city-like settlements we know of is, however, something very different. One of these "cities," Haithabu/ Hedeby, lies just upon the southern threshold of the actual Scandinavian regions. It seems to have been of overwhelming importance to the entire area. With its 240,000 square meters, surrounded by a 1,300-meter wall as part of a complicated system of area fortifications, Haithabu overshadows all corresponding sites within our region. The number of its graves is estimated at between 3,000 and 5,000 for

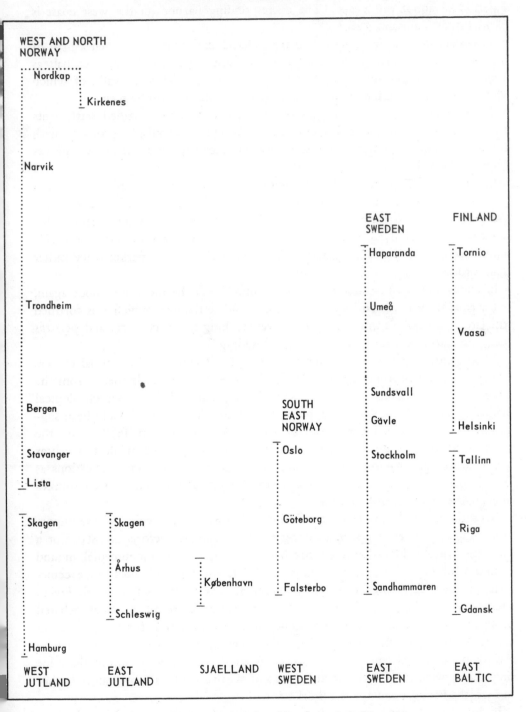

FIGURE 4. Present-day cities. (*See legend to Fig. 1.*)

a period of about 250 years. (The corresponding harbor on the west coast is Hollingstedt [Jankuhn, 1956].)

The island settlement at Björkö in the Mälar Lake (which was then a firth of the Baltic) is identified with Birka of the written sources. It is not even half as large as is Haithabu, measuring 90,000 square meters within its walls, of which 500 meters are still visible. Some 2,000 burial mounds can also be seen.

There has been a strong suggestion that corresponding fortified settlements must have existed in Latvia, for example at Grobin ("Seeburg"), probably with a much smaller area but doubtless with considerably more than 600 graves (Nerman, 1958).

In southeastern Norway, the archeological situation at Kaupang in Tjölling (identified as Skiringssal) seems to have another character (Blindheim, 1953, 1960.) It is known mainly from hundreds of graves, containing a remarkable number of imported objects, and there seems to be no trace of fortifications. It would seem more probable that this was a regularly visited market place rather than a town.

In connection with a later period, Lindholm should be mentioned once again, but seemingly only as an important village-sized settlement, which was fortified still later. Lindholm's grave inventories reflect long-range contacts and *perhaps* there are traces of a small central "public building."

These places are the northernmost, more or less town-like commercial centers of the last prehistoric period of Scandinavia *ca.* 800–1050 A.D. Is there—from the more restricted regions where these sites lie—any particular earlier archeological evidence that might explain the appearance of these sites? It has already been suggested that there is evidence from Lindholm. At Kaupang in Tjölling, on the other hand, there seems so far to be none. It was only later, while this center was in existence, that the adjoining regions present such splendid indications as the famous ship graves of the Oslo fjord district, for which written sources indicate the existence of a dynasty.

Now the Mälar Lake island site of Björkö is situated in a region where important things had been happening during the last centuries before A.D. 800. For a long time, archeological interest has been focused on the monumental mound cemetery of Gamla Uppsala (Lindqvist, 1936), and the rich boat-grave cemeteries of the same district. In recent years the already mentioned enigmatic Helgö site has become known. Also there is renewed reason to recall the much debated problem of early iron metallurgy as one possible explanation for the prospering of the regions northeast of the Mälar Lake (then a firth). Is this the reason why the region attracted continental and even Anglo-Saxon interest, and at the same time the explanation for the accumulation of wealth by local potentates? Is this, in fact, the background for the Björkö town?

In any case, it seems reasonable to assume the importance of foreign elements for Hedeby, Lindholm, Kaupang, and Björkö. As to Grobin, its excavator is inclined to see it as a result of organized colonization from Sweden, but the published finds do not seem to support this view convincingly. Observations at the related site of Apuole, for example, might indicate a local background for this type of settlement.

It is important to note the fact that there is only a very limited correlation between urban and political development in northern Europe. Political centers

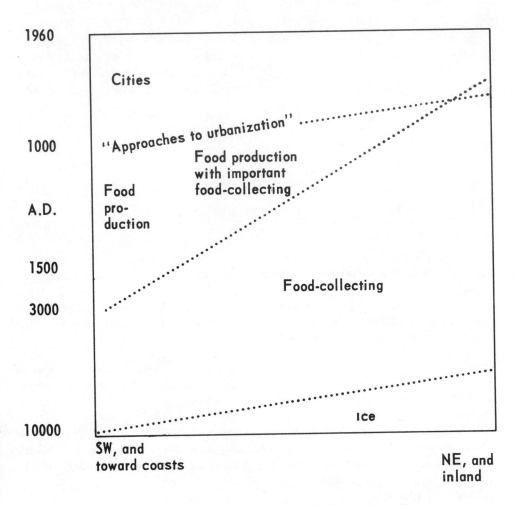

FIGURE 5. Graph to illustrate the main trends in northern European prehistory, as described in the text. The approximate time scale is logarithmic.

in the Scandinavian states, emerging following *ca.* A.D. 800, are not towns, but royal manors. The remaining actual archeological traces of these consist primarily of monumental graves (Jelling, perhaps Lejre [Andersen, 1960], Borre [Blindheim, 1953], and the debatable Gamla Uppsala).

The continuation of urban development in these regions must be studied mainly by means of historical documentation. It reflects organized political and ecclesiastical action and thus falls outside the scope of this summary. But it should be emphasized that during the Middle Ages up to *ca.* A.D. 1500, urbanization is limited to the southern half (and barely that) of Baltic Europe, no towns having been established north of Nidaros (Trondheim) in Norway, Gävle in Sweden, or Ulvsby in Finland (Bull and Steen, 1933). It should be emphasized that even these town were still quite small, often with only a few hundred inhabitants.

One must remain aware of the possibility that medieval archeology may yet change the picture given above, or at least add important qualifications for its later phases. Thus, recent field work in Norway by Herteig has already resulted in much information on medieval commercial centers, almost unknown from the written records.

BIBLIOGRAPHY

This bibliography includes some important papers, etc.,
published after the symposium.

ANDERSEN, HARALD
1960. Hovedstaden i riget. *Nationalmuseets arbejdsmark*, pp. 13–35, Köbenhavn.

BAGGE, AXEL
1951. "Fagervik, Ein Rückgrat für die Periodeneinteilung der ostschwedischen Wohnplatz- und Bootaxtkulturen aus dem Mittelneolithikum, Eine vorläufige Mitteilung," *Acta archeol.* 22:57–118. Köbenhavn.

BAGGE, AXEL, and KNUT KJELLMARK
1939. *Stenåldersboplatserna vid Siretorp i Blekinge. Die steinzeitlichen Wohnplätze bei Siretorp, Blekinge in Schweden.* ("Kungl. vitterhets historie och antikvitetsakademien.") Stockholm: Wahlström och Widstrand.

BECKER, CARL JOHAN
1955. "The Introduction of Farming into Northern Europe," *J. World Hist.*, Vol. 2.
1958. Review of: O. KLINDT-JENSEN (Klindt-Jensen, 1957), *Bornholm i folkevandringstiden og forudsæ tningerne i tidlig jernalder, Fornvännen*, pp. 142–47. Stockholm.

BLINDHEIM, CHARLOTTE
1953. "Borre i lys av Borrefunnet og Nasjonalparken," *Borre bygdebok*, pp. 1–26. Horten.
1953. "Preliminary Report on the Recent Excavations on Kaupang, near Larvik, Vestfold," *Annen Viking Kongress*, pp. 59–67. Bergen.
1960. "Kaupangundersøkelsen etter 10 år," *Viking*, 24:43–68. (A slightly altered edition of this paper will appear in English in *Acta archaeol.*, 1959/60). Oslo.

BRØNDSTED, JOHANNES
1957. *Danmarks Oldtid, 1, Stenalderen.* 2d ed. København: Gyldendal.

BULL, EDVARD, and SVERRE STEEN (eds.)
1933. *Byer og Bybebyggelse.* (Nordisk kultur 18.) Stockholm: Albert Bonniers förlag; Oslo: H. Aschehoug & Co.s Forlag; Köbenhavn: J. H. Schultz Forlag.

FLORIN, STEN

1958. *Vråkulturen, Stenåldersboplatserna vid Mogetorp, Östra Vrå och Brokvarn.* ("Kungl. Vitterhets Historie och Antikvitets Akademien.") Stockholm: Almqvist och Wiksell.

FLORIN, MAJ-BRITT and STEN

1960. *Naturhistorisk utveckling vid Dragby under bronsåldern, Från en påbörjad undersökning över områdets kvartärgeologi.* (Publs. Inst. Quat. Geol., Univ. Uppsala, No. 16, ser. 8.) (Also *Tor. Meddelanden från institutionen för nordisk fornkunskap vid Uppsala universitet,* pp. 87–121; English summary, pp. 116–18).

FRIES, MAGNUS

1958.*Vegetationsutveckling och odlingshistoria i Varnhemstrakten, En pollenanalytisk undersökning i Västergötland.* ("Acta phytogeographica suecica," Vol. 39.) Uppsala. (German summary, pp. 55–58; "Vegetationsentwicklung und Siedlungsgeschichte im Gebiet von Varnhem, Eine pollenanalytische Untersuchung aus Västergötland (Südschweden)"; English abstract, p. 59).

GIMBUTAS, MARIJA

1956. *The Prehistory of Eastern Europe, I: Mesolithic, Neolithic and Copper Age Cultures in Russia and the Baltic Area.* (Amer. Sch. Prehist. Res., Peabody Mus. Harvard Univ. Bull. No. 20.) Cambridge, Mass.

1958. "Rytprusiu ir vakaru Lietuvos priešistorines kulturos apžvalga." In *Mažoji Lietuva, Lithuania Minor, Kleinlitauen.* ("Studia Lituanica," 1.) New York: Leidžia Lietuvos Tyrimo Institutas-Lithuanian Research Institute, Inc. (English summary, pp. 291–94: "A Survey of Prehistory of East Prussia and Western Lithuania.")

GJESSING, GUTORM

1959. "Nordnorske samfunnsorganisasjoner i steinalderen," *Wissenschaftliche Zeitschrift der Ernst Moritz Arndt-Universität Greifswald, Gesellschafts- und sprachwissenschaftliche Reihe, Nr. 3,* pp. 147–52.

GRIEG, SIGURD

1934. *Jernaldershus på Lista.* (Instituttet for sammenlignende kulturforskning, B 27.) Oslo. (German summary, pp. 122–37.)

HAFSTEN, ULF

1958. "Jordbrukskulturens historie i Oslo- og Mjøstrakten belyst ved pollenanalytiske undersøkelser," *Viking,* 21–22:51–73. Oslo. (English summary, pp. 72–73; "Pollenanalytical Investigations on the History of Agriculture in the Oslo and Mjøsa Regions.)

HAGEN, ANDERS

1953. *Studier i jernalderns gårdssamfunn.* (Universitetets oldsaksamlings, skrifter 4.) Oslo: Universitetets oldsaksamling. (English summary, pp. 354–87.)

1960. "Jordbrukspionerer i steinaldern," *Viking,* 24:1–42. Oslo. (English summary, pp. 37–41: "Problems concerning Early Neolithic Agricultural Groups.")

HALLSTRÖM, GUSTAF

1960. *Monumental Art of Northern Sweden from the Stone Age, Nämforsen and Other Localities.* Stockholm: Almqvist & Wiksell.

HATT, GUDMUND

1937. *Landbrug i Danmarks oldtid.* (Folkelæsning, No. 367.) København.

1957. *Nørre Fjand: An Early Iron-Age Village Site in West Jutland.* (Arkaeologisk-kunsthistoriske Skrifter utgivet af Det Kongelige Danske Videnskabernes. Selskab 2, No. 2.) København: Ejnar Munksgaard.

HELMFRID, S.
1958. "Eine pollenanalytische Untersuchung zur Geschichte der Kulturlandschaft im westlichen Teil der Provinz Östergötland, Schweden," *Geografiska annaler.* Stockholm.

HINSCH, HERIK
1948. "Buplass-kulturen på mørekysten i dolktida," *Viking,* 12:89–132. Oslo. (French summary, pp. 130–31: "Les sites de la fin du néolithique à Møre.")
1951–53. "Traktbegerkultur-megalitkultur: En studie av Øst-Norges eldste, neolitiske gruppe," *Universitetets oldsaksamling, Arbok.* Oslo. (French summary, pp. 163–72.)
1954. *Yngre steinalders stridsøkskulturer i Norge.* (Universitetet i Bergen, Årbok, Historisk-antikvarisk rekke 1.) Bergen. (English summary, pp. 223–37.)

HJELMQVIST, H.
1955. *Die älteste Geschichte der Kulturpflanzen in Schweden.* (Opera botanica a societate botanica Lundense in supplementeum seriei "Botaniska notiser" edita, Vol. 1:3.) Stockholm: Almqvist & Wiksell. (English summary, pp. 172–80: "The Oldest History of Cultivated Plants in Sweden.")

HOLMQVIST, WILHELM
1954. "Die eisenzeitlichen Funde aus Lillön, Kirchspiel Ekerö, Uppland, Vorläufiger Bericht über die im Jahre 1954 begonnenen Untersuchungen," *Acta archaeol,* 25:260–71. København.
1955. *Germanic Art during the First Millennium* A.D. *Kungl.* (Vitterhets Historie och Antikvitets akademiens, handlingar 90.) Stockholm.
1957a. "Gårdsanläggningar från yngre järnåldern på Helgö (Lillön) Ekerö socken i Mälaren, En översikt," *Fornvännen,* pp. 97–115. Stockholm. (English summary, pp. 115: "House Settlements from the Late Iron Age on Helgö Island (Lillön) in Lake Mälar in the Parish of Ekerö.")
1957b. "Fynden från Helgö, En översikt," *Fornvännen,* pp. 209–26. Stockholm. (English summary, p. 226: "The Finds from Helgö.")
1959. "Hednisk kult på Helgö," *Kungl. vitterhets historie och antikvitets akademiens handlingar,* 91:203–12. Stockholm.

HOUGEN, BJØRN
1947. *Fra seter til gård: Studier i norsk bosetningshistorie.* Oslo: Norsk arkeologisk selskap.

JANKUHN, HERBERT
1956. *Haithabu, Ein Handelsplatz der Wikingerzeit.* 3d ed. Neumünster. Karl Wachholtz Verlag.

JANSON, SVERKER, and HARALD HVARFNER
1960. *Från norrlandsälvar och fjällsjöar.* Stockholm: Riksantikvarieämbetet.

KILIAN, LOTHAR
1955. *Haffküstenkultur und Ursprung der Balten.* Bonn: Rudolf Habelt Verlag.

KIVIKOSKI, ELLA
1947–51. *Die Eisenzeit Finnlands, Bilderatlas und Text,* Vols. 1–2. Porvoo, Helsinki: Werner Söderström osakeyhtiö.

KLINDT-JENSEN, OLE
1957. *Bornholm i folkevandringstiden og forudsætningerne i tidlig jernalder.* (Nationalmuseets skrifter, Større beretninger 2.) København: Nationalmuseet. (English summaries, pp. 239–77, 314–18.)

1958a. "Nogle bemærkninger til foregående anmeldelse," *Fornvännen*, pp. 147–54. Stockholm.

1958b. "Bemærkninger til Norling-Christensens afhandling: Bidrag til belysning af kulturforholdene på Bornholm i ældre germansk jernalder," *Aarbøger for nordisk oldkyndighed*, pp. 124–28. København. (English summary, pp. 127–28: "Remarks on H. Norling-Christensen article 'Contributions to the Elucidation of the Cultural Relations in Bornholm in the Early Germanic Iron Age.'")

1959. "To detaljer fra udgravningen af Sorte Muld," *Aarbøger for nordisk oldkyndighed*, p. 222. København.

LARSSEN, KARI EGEDE

1953. "Pollenanalytiske dateringer fram Trøndelag," *Det kongelige norske videnskabers selskabs forhandlinger*, 26:94–101. Trondheim.

1954. "Pollenanalytiske dateringer fra Trøndelag," *Det kongelige norske videnskabers selskabs forhandlinger*, Vol. 26, No. 22. Trondheim: F. Bruns bokhandel.

LINDQVIST, SUNE

1936. *Uppsala högar och Ottarshögen*. (Kungl. vitterhets historie och antikvitets akademien.) Stockholm: Wahlström & Widstrand. (English summary, pp. 327–53.)

LUHO, VILLE

1956. *Die Askola-Kultur, Die frühmesolithische Steinzeit in Finnland.* (Suomen muinaismuistoyhdistyksen aikakauskirja, Finska fornminnesföreningens, tidskrift 57.) Helsinki.

LUND, HARALD E.

1955. "Håløygske høvdingeseter fra jernalderen," *Stavanger museums årbok*, pp. 101–7.

1960. En oversikt over: "Håløygske hövdinge-gårder og tun-anlegg fra eldre og yngre jernalder." (Mimeographed letter to Gustaf Hallström, Stockholm.)

MARSTRANDER, SVERRE

1956. "Hovedlinjer i Trøndelags forhistorie," *Viking*, pp. 1–69. (English summary, pp. 56–63: "A General Outline of the Prehistory of Trøndelag." Oslo.

MATHIASSEN, THERKEL

1959. *Nordvestsjællands oldtidsbebyggelse.* (Nationalmuseets skrifter, arkæologisk-historisk række 7.) København: Nationalmuseet. (English summary, pp. 61–64: The Prehistoric Settlement of Northwestern Zealand.

MEINANDER, CARL FREDRIK

1946. "Förutsättningarna för den förhistoriska bebyggelsen i södra Österbotten," *Nordenskiöld samfundets tidskrift*, 6.

1950. "Etelä-Pohjanmaan esihistoria," *Etelä-Pohjanmaan historia*, 1. Helsinki.

1954a. *Die Bronzezeit in Finnland.* (Suomen muinaismuistoyhdistyksen aikakauskirja, Finska fornminnesföreningens tidskrift 54.) Helsinki Helsingfors.

1954b. *Die Kiukaiskultur. (Ibid.,* tidskrift 53.)

MOBERG, CARL-AXEL

1941. *Zonengliederungen der vorchristlichen Eisenzeit in Nordeuropa.* Lund: C. W. K. Gleerup.

1950. "When Did Late La Tène begin? A Study of the Basis of the Current Absolute Dating" (Ornavasso-Horn 1.), *Acta archaeol.*, 21:83–136. København.

1960. "On Some Circumpolar and Arctic Problems in North European Archaeology," *Acta arctica*, 12:67–74. Copenhagen.

MØLLENHUS, KRISTEN ROLSETH

1958. *Steinalderen i søndre Helgeland.* (Det kgl norske videnskabers selskabs skrifter 1958:1.) Trondheim.

NERMAN, BIRGER

1958. *Grobin-Seeburg, Ausgrabungen und Funde.* (Kungl. vitterhets historie och antikvitets akademien.) Stockholm: Almqvist & Wiksell.

NORLING-CHRISTENSEN, HANS

1958. "Bidrag til belysning af kulturforholdene paa Bornholm i ældre germansk jernalder," *Aarbøger for nordisk oldkyndighed og historie,* pp. 109–23. København. (English summary, pp. 119–23: "Contributions to the Elucidation of the Cultural Relations of Bornholm in the Early Germanic Iron Age.")

1959. "Ny bidrag til belysning af kulturforholdene paa Bornholm i ældre germansk jernalder," *Aarbøger for nordisk oldkyndighed og historia,* pp. 217–21. København. (English summary, pp. 219–21: "New Contributions towards Elucidating the Cultural Conditions in Bornholm in the Early Germanic Iron Age.)

NUMMEDAL, A.

1935–36. "Yngre stenaldersfunn fra Nyelven og Karlebotn i Østfinnmark," *Universitetets oldsaksamling, Årbok,* pp. 69–131. Oslo.

OLAUSSON, ERIC

1957. *Das Moor Roshultsmyren, Eine geologische, botanische und hydrologische Studie in einem südwestschwedischen Moor mit excentrisch gewölbten Mooselementen.* (Lunds universitets årsskrift, N.F. Avd. 2, Bd. 53, Nr. 12.) Lund: C. W. K. Gleerup.

PETERSEN, JAN

1933. *Gamle gårdsanlegg i Rogaland fra forhistorisk tid og middelalder.* (Instituttet for sammenlignende kultur-forskning, Bd. 23.) Oslo. (German summary, pp. 120–35.)

1936. *Gamle gårdsanlegg i Rogaland, Fortsettelse.* (*Ibid.,* Bd. 31: German summary, pp. 87–99.)

RAJEWSKI, ZDZISAW

1958. "Arkæologisk forskning i Biskupin," *Kuml,* Årbog for jysk arkæologisk selskab 21–62. Arhus. (German summary, pp. 49–62: "Forschungsergebnisse über die Besiedlung der 'Lausitzer' Kultur in Biskupin und Umgegend.")

RAMSKOU, THORKILD

1953. "Lindholm: Preliminary Report of the 1952–53 Excavations of a Late Iron Age Cemetery and an Early Mediaeval Settlement," *Acta archaeol.,* 24:186–96. København.

1955. "Lindholm Høje: Second Preliminary Report for the Years 1954–55 on the Excavation of a Late Iron Age Cemetery and an Early Mediaeval Settlement," *ibid.,* 26:176–85.

1957. "Et landbrug fra 1000-årene på Lindholm Høje," *Fra nationalmuseets arbejdsmark,* pp. 97–100. København.

1960. *Lindholm Høje.* (Nationalmuseets blå bøger.) København: Nationalmuseet.

SIMONSEN, POVL

1960. "The History of Settlement." In *Norway North of 65,* pp. 100–121. (Tromsø museums skrifter, vol. 8.) Oslo: Oslo University Press.

STENBERGER, MÅRTEN, and OLE KLINDT-JENSEN (eds.)

1955. *Vallhagar, a Migration Period Settlement on Gotland/Sweden,* 2 vols. Copenhagen: Ejnar Munksgaards forlag.

Troels-Smith, Hørgen

1953. "Ertebøllekultur–Bondekultur, Resultater af de sidste 10 aars Undersøgelser i Aamosen, Vestsjælland," *Aarbøger for nordisk Oldkyndighed og Historie*, pp. 1–62. København. (English summary, pp. 47–62; "Ertebølle Culture–Farmer Culture, Results of the Past Ten Years' Excavations in Aamosen bog, West Zealand.")

Werner, Joachim

1960. Review of O. Klindt-Jensen (Klindt-Jensen, 1957), *Bornholm i folkevandringstiden og forudsæ tningerne i tidlig jernalder*, in *Prähist. Zeitschr.*, 38:142–51.

CONCLUSIONS AND AFTERTHOUGHTS

ROBERT J. BRAIDWOOD AND GORDON R. WILLEY

IN THE foregoing sixteen papers, more than that number of regional archeological time perspectives are considered. Seven New World areas—Mesoamerica, Peru, the northern Andean Intermediate area, Amazonia, the Caribbean, the greater Southwest (with its familiar southwestern "core"), and eastern North America—are accounted for. In the eleven Old World papers—southwestern Asia east of the Euphrates, southwestern Asia along the Syro-Cilician and Palestinian strip, China, India, sub-Saharan Africa, southern Central Europe and southeastern Europe, northern Central Europe (Czechoslovakia), the lower Rhine Basin, northern Continental Europe, Baltic Europe, and Soviet Asia east of the Urals—several of the authors have also dealt with more than one discrete environmental region. At the same time, other important areas of prehistoric development have not been covered. What we have here is in no sense a universal prehistory for the time range and problems of our concern, although we take it to be an interesting sampling of various types of developments.

In all regions considered, societies that were either wholly or predominantly native ones passed from a status of food-collecting to one of a more or less effective food production, at least by the time Columbus had discovered America. In two New World areas (Mesoamerica and Peru) and in three Old World areas (southwestern Asia, India, and China), the threshold of civilization and urbanization was also attained at least by the beginning of the Christian Era if not significantly earlier. In other native areas, civilization and urbanization came later, largely as a result of some more effective form of expansion or diffusion, and—in certain regions of some of these areas—is only now being completed. In some areas these thresholds were never attained insofar as native societies are concerned.

Let us review the way in which culture developed in these several areas. What are the similarities and differences in the attainments of "thresholds" or "conditions" such as incipient cultivation, effective food production, and urbanization? How are these phenomena historically interrelated or independently arrived at in the areas under consideration? We will take up these problems in the order of the thematic questions posed in the Introduction to this volume.

I[1]

In late glacial and early postglacial times many of the inhabitants of the New World followed a hunting existence, pursuing large mammals (many of them species now extinct) under Pleistocene environmental conditions quite different from those of the geological Recent. These early hunters shared technological traditions that included the making of well-chipped and distinctive lanceolate spear or projectile points and various knives and scrapers. Finds of these chipped-stone weapons and tools have been made in "kill" and camp sites in North America, particularly east of the Rocky Mountains, in Mesoamerica, and in several localities in South America. In North America they have been dated to a period before 8000 B.C., going back to 12,000 B.C. or perhaps earlier. It is assumed that the spread of the Pleistocene big-game-hunting way of life was, in its general drift, from north to south and that the early lanceolate point and other artifact forms found in Mesoamerica and South America are related to those of North America. The one kind of environmental situation in which evidences of the big-game-hunting pattern has not been found is the tropical forest lowland—of either Mesoamerica or South America.

Coincident with the big-game-hunting mode of existence, at least in certain New World areas, was a different life way, one based on the collection of food plants and the hunting of small game. This subsistence pattern is represented by artifact types quite different from those characteristic of big-game hunters. The North American greater Southwest is, at least on present evidence, the area where the coexistence of these two basic subsistence patterns, big-game hunting and hunting-collecting, can best be examined. Their contemporaneity here, at least for a span of time at the close of the Pleistocene, seems certain. Less definite is the relative antiquity of the inception of the two patterns. Are both offshoots of an earlier and less differentiated American tradition? Or, as Haury suggests, does each have its remote beginnings in quite separate traditions in the Old World? Archeological data are not yet adequate to resolve these questions.

For well back in the late-glacial ranges of time in the Old World, Klíma's Pavlov sites yield us a picture of big-game hunters with a varied and rather spectacular artifact assemblage, and semisubterranean hut settlements. Comparable materials and settlement traces extend eastward beyond the Urals and provide a contrast with the more familiar upper paleolithic of western Europe. Nevertheless, human adjustment to life in Europe and more northerly Asia (including China), at least up to the beginning of postglacial times, remained essentially one in which the hunting of big Pleistocene game played a large part. We feel bound to ask whether the various manifestations of art styles, at least from as far east as Okladnikov's Mal'ta to the Franco-Cantabrian cave art of the west,

1. These Roman numeral subheads are organized following the five "themes" or "questions" referred to in our Introduction. For no other reason than the accident of how we happened to draft these conclusions, we tend to review the New World evidence first and then that of the Old World.

and the present apparent lack of such art styles in Pleistocene contexts south of
the European–northern Asiatic zone, are entirely due to accidents of discovery
or preservation. It is conceivable that these art styles all had a functional place
within the matrices of the various cultures adjusted to the hunting of the great
Pleistocene animals. There does not appear to be a New World counterpart for
this late-Pleistocene artistic flourish in the big-game-hunting cultural context.

As in the Americas, an Old World contrast also presents itself in the now
available evidence from late glacial times. In southwestern Asia the great Pleistocene animals seem already to have disappeared. Sankalia remarks that materials
of this general range of time are only now beginning to appear in India; the
slightly later microlithic complex would not dispose us (if seen elsewhere) to
think of a predominantly big-game-hunting economy. Clark sees his sub-Saharan
Africans of the time of the Gamblian maximum as already food-collectors and
on the way to intensified forms of collective hunting and dependence on vegetable foods. Certainly tropical Africa (and India) may seem an awkward place
to sustain a thesis based on a shift to *small*-animal hunting but the point will
rest with the frequency of large animal bones in the archeological sites of the
time. In southwestern Asia the *Bos primigenius* (wild cattle) seems occasionally
to have been taken, but the usual quarry of the huntsman was now primarily no
larger than the onager (wild half-ass) or wild sheep and goats.[2] This trend
seems to have set in as early as the time of the Mousterian industries of southwestern Asia, and suggests comparison with that in the New World which is
also based on plant-collecting and smaller-game hunting. Also, as in the Americas, very considerable local adaptation now appears to have been in process
in response to different environmental situations.

What is clear in both hemispheres, however, is that the big-game-hunting tradition disappeared or was drastically modified with the end of the Pleistocene
and that a variety of hunting-collecting subsistence adaptations then sprang up
throughout the world. In a subsistence-pattern sense, at least, this change involved the usual present conception of the mesolithic as a cultural readaption
to post-Pleistocene environments. But the conception has become an awkward
one, on a world-wide scale, since, as we have just seen, there is evidence that
the same trends toward readaptation and the intensification of collecting activities had begun to manifest themselves in certain areas before the conventional
date for the end of the Pleistocene. One of us (Braidwood, 1958, p. 1428) is of
the opinion that there was *no* mesolithic, *sensu stricto*, in southwestern Asia at
least.

The proposition for a variety of post-Pleistocene hunting-collecting patterns,
in terms of area and environmental setting, is particularly clear in the New
World. In the greater Southwest a "Desert" cultural tradition of seed and plant-
collecting and small-game hunting was early established. In eastern North America forest hunting and collecting was a somewhat different specialization; and in

2. Elephants persisted in upper Mesopotamia at least until 1400 B.C. but seem to have been
only the prey of royal hunting parties.

some regions of the East, as well as in Middle and South America, a riverine or coastal adaptation developed in which shellfish were an important part of the economy. In other areas, of which the North American plains is an example, a modified pattern of big-game hunting continued with a Recent fauna. For the tropical forest areas of South America we have relatively little information as to what went on in this period. It is probable, though, that a subsistence pattern was in formation that was oriented to hunting, fishing, and tropical-plant utilization but that this way of life left little archeological record in the tropical lowlands.

For many parts of the Old World where we have adequate archeological evidence of early postglacial times, the situation seems to have been almost an exact parallel. The same tendency for a swing toward new adjustments to changing environments, the same diversity of adjustment—environment to environment—may be observed. Thus, at the symposium, Moberg ("Northern Europe") could say that Caldwell ("Eastern North America") had already presented his generalizations for him. Obviously there were detailed differences in the ways in which different human groups adapted themselves to essentially comparable environments in the Old and New Worlds. Nevertheless, in the higher latitudes the tendency seems to have been toward intensified collecting of both plants and animals, fish and shell food, in riverine, coastal, and even oasis (in Mongolia) localities. In the lower latitudes Sankalia's Gujarati sites suggest much the same thing, although in a somewhat more lush environment, with bananas and coconuts. Clark believes settlement in central Africa to have been largely at the zones of contact between gallery forest and savanna, rather than in the then more restricted tropical rain forest; the artifacts of his Lupemban assemblages reflect this.

In certain zones of southwestern Asia, on the other hand, the proposition has been made that a level of incipient cultivation had already begun by the time of the conventional late-glacial–early postglacial boundary line in the North Temperate Zone (*ca.* 8000 B.C.). We thus postpone discussion of this area for our next "thematic" question.

The extent to which these several ways of "settling into" a number of different natural environments were historically interrelated is difficult to appraise. How are we to visualize, for example, the ecumenical yet necessarily unspecific cultural meaning of the spread of the habit of producing microliths on bladelets for the making of composite tools? In some instances, more specific connections are seen in tool and artifact types. In general, however, it seems safe to say that this was a time—roughly from 8000 to 2000 B.C.—of multiple and at least semi-independent responses to post-Pleistocene environmental changes. Man, throughout the world, was becoming adapted to the geological Recent. In most of these adaptations he gradually increased his subsistence efficiency over the millennia. One kind of increase, which came into being only in certain areas, was food production. In its beginnings this means of increase, which had only a minor subsistence role, is referred to as incipient cultivation and domestication.

II

What appears to be a nearly complete chronological record of incipient food production through plant cultivation is seen in northern and central Mesoamerica. The initial cultural context is that of food-collecting cultures in forested or semiarid upland environments of Tamaulipas and the Valley of Mexico. At 7000 B.C. the diet of the Tamaulipas food-collecting societies was made up of wild seed plants, small game animals, and two possible cultigens, the pumpkin, or *Cucurbita pepo,* and the chili pepper. During the next three millennia beans (*Phaseolus vulgaris*) and additional cucurbits, all clearly domesticated, are added to this food complex. A primitive but domesticated maize makes its appearance shortly after these. By 2000 B.C. greatly improved hybrid strains of maize appear; and what had been incipient cultivation—in the sense of minor or limited economic dependence—gives way rapidly to plant cultivation as the established way of life.

Incipient cultivation in the southwestern "core" area of the greater North American Southwest is historically related to Mesoamerica. It is also similar in environmental and cultural contexts. The southwestern Cochise culture—found in both mountain and desert locales—appears to have developed some degree of sedentism by 4000 B.C. through its exploitation of wild plants and seeds. Haury surmises that the Cochise societies also may have had some local plant domesticates, such as chenopods and amaranths. It was in this setting, at about 3000 B.C. that a primitive domesticated maize appeared. We feel bound to ask whether this maize was diffused from Mesoamerica along a highland corridor or whether such southwestern maize sites as Bat Cave lay within the effective boundaries of the primary natural-habitat zone of the plant. The first southwestern maize was probably little better as a food source than many of the wild plants gathered by the people who cultivated it, and its advent appears to have had little immediate effect for culture change. In both Mesoamerica and the Southwest, stone seed-grinding implements were present in the wild-plant-collecting cultures. These became somewhat more numerous and more carefully made with the gradual increase of plant cultivation, but the change is extremely slow. Squash, beans, and improved types of maize are added to the southwestern incipient-cultivation complex by 1000 B.C. Early pit-house sites suggest an increase of sedentism in the last millennium B.C., and pottery and figurines are received from Mesoamerica after this.

The processes of the acceptance of incipient cultivation in Mesoamerica and the Southwest are similar in that in both areas primitive cultigens first appear as minor adjuncts to a plant-collecting economy in societies that were already predisposed to sedentary settlement. With this incipient cultivation neither area reveals immediate radical culture change. Artificial adaptations increased sedentism, and population increase can be measured in both only over the millennia. But there are significant differences between the two areas. In Mesoamerica a swift improvement of the domesticated food plants, with new hybrid strains of maize, took place at about 2000 B.C. and resulted in established food production through agriculture by 1500 B.C. Although the Southwest had a primitive maize at 3000 B.C., it saw no such rapid development of it or other cultigens. Some 2000 years or more later, improved maize strains were brought to the Southwest from Mesoamerica and the threshold of established agriculture was not achieved until about A.D. 500.

Our knowledge of incipient cultivation in Mesoamerica is too sketchy for us to do more than speculate upon the reasons for Mesoamerican priority in this development of food production. We would suggest that Mesoamerica offered more varied natural environmental settings within a relatively small geographic space than did the North American Southwest and that these Mesoamerican regions, ranging from tropic to temperate and from wet to arid, also had a greater wild-plant potential for cultivation. Because of these natural factors there was a multiregional variation in populations of plants of the same species (as well as a variety of species). This variation presumably had a role in humanly stimulated introgressive hybridizations, which led to potentially favorable new forms between 7000 and 3000 B.C. This was followed by further (and perhaps even slightly conscious?) interregional exchange and hybridization between 3000 and 2000 B.C., which resulted in vastly improved strains. These improved plants became the basis of a fully agricultural economy.

In the Central Andes the earlier chronological ranges of incipient cultivation have not yet been disclosed. At least our first glimpse is that of settled food-collectors, fishers, hunters, and part-time farmers living along the Peruvian shore at about 2500 B.C. As Collier emphasizes, the site locations of these people were extremely favorable for taking food from the sea and supplementing it with wild and domesticated plants. The mouths of the Peruvian coastal valleys with their fresh-water lagoons and marshes were, in effect, desert oases. The Peruvian coast is a rainless one with a moderate-to-hot climate and a year-round growing season. Cucurbits, chili, a jack bean (*Canavalia*), the lima bean (*Phaseolus lunatus*), and cotton were under domestication at 2500 B.C. It is likely that these were all local domesticates of wild species and not imports from Mesoamerica. The context of sedentary living of which this incipient cultivation was a part is a more established one than that seen in either northern Mesoamerica or the Southwest at a comparable date. The seashore villages consisted of numerous semi subterranean dwellings of mud-and-stone or adobe-walled structures. At about 1400 B.C. Mesoamerican influence appears in the form of maize. This is a fairly well-developed maize, more advanced and valuable as a food than that of early Tamaulipas or Bat Cave. This maize is followed shortly after (1200 B.C.) by the introduction of pottery. These introductions have little immediate effect on the size and location of coastal settlements, although it is noteworthy that planned ceremonial centers, with artificial mounds and plazas, appear between 1200 and 750 B.C. After 750 B.C. there is a shift of settlements away from the shore to the valley interiors, a change undoubtedly related to the increasing importance of agriculture in the food economy. It is at this point that Collier marks the beginnings of established food production and the village agricultural threshold.

Peru and Mesoamerica are similar in that in both cases a degree of sedentism—although made possible by quite different resources—provided the matrix for incipient cultivation. But the Peruvian coast differs from Mesoamerica in that its incipient cultivation was a part of a much richer economy than that enjoyed by the Tamaulipas cave dwellers. This is not to be ascribed to the early cultivated plants, which appear to have been relatively minor in Peru, as they were in Tamaulipas, but to the marine environmental niche that the Peruvian coastal societies exploited so effectively. After 1400 B.C. the Peruvian coast accepted maize from Mesoamerica. The introduction of this plant as a fairly well-developed food product seems to have been the factor that led to village farming by 750 A.D. This relative swiftness with which the Peruvian coastal societies accomplished the transfer from incipient cultivation to established farming thus appears to be explained by the high degree of sedentary life already enjoyed and by the advanced nature of the corn product that they received from Mesoamerica. But, again, archeological sampling and knowledge are extremely limited.

The other great natural zone of the Central Andean area, the highlands, is almost unknown for the particular centuries we are here considering. It is quite possible that cultivation, incipient or established, was well under way in the highlands before it was on the coast. The coastal sites thus may reflect the influence of highland centers of agricultural development. For example, certain strains of Peruvian maize are believed to be the result of early crosses between Mesoamerican local wild races; however, it is possible that such crosses could have occurred between the Mesoamerican domesticates and a Peruvian maize that had been independently cultivated prior to the arrival of the first Mesoamerican maize on the coast. If so, such an independent domestication might have taken place in the highlands. Also, as Collier brings out, the early history of the domestication of the potato is unknown, but there can be no doubt that that plant is an ancient Andean highland cultigen.

Since the first season's work at Jarmo in 1948, there has been an increasing focus of attention on the later prehistory of southwestern Asia.[3] Nevertheless, such a long and continuous sequence as that seen in the Tamaulipas region of Mesoamerica is not yet available in southwestern Asia. There are still gaps in the chronological and developmental tables of both Kurdistan and Palestine, as we examine the build-up to effective village-farming communities, and south-central Anatolia is just beginning to come into the known picture. The case for

3. With the exception of Arkell's (1949, 1953) work in the Sudan and that of McBurney and Hey (1955) in Libya, this increasing tempo of postwar research in late prehistoric archeology has not had its counterpart in the region of Egypt and northeastern Africa. There are also certain obvious gaps in those countries in southwestern Asia where the prevailing interpretations of national antiquities laws do not permit the complete processing of the bulk categories of artifacts (which demand statistical analysis) or of the laboratory-bound analysis of paleoecological materials. Some of us believe that, where such circumstances prevent the completion of the archeologists' goal of their complete analysis and interpretation, it is better to let the materials remain buried.

a level of incipient cultivation and domestication has had to be made almost entirely by inference and *post facto* judgment.

In Palestine the more immediate antecedents of the Natufian are not known, although an increase in the number of sites—most of them open-air—is now noted for pre-Natufian times, however little their industries are understood. We may be a bit better off in Iraqi Kurdistan, where several open-air encampments of pre-Karim Shahirian aspect have been identified in surface surveys. The relationships between the several aspects of the Zarzian and those of the Karim Shahirian are not yet clear, however; the time difference between the two cannot have been great, but neither does the development from Zarzian into Karim Shahirian appear to have been an absolutely direct one.

With both the Natufian and the various facies of Karim Shahirian, we seem to be momentarily on firmer ground. The various sites grouped as Karim Shahirian are all open-air settlements, with more or less understandable traces of structures. Although the Natufian was first identified from caves and their terraces, Perrot's exposures at Ain Mallaha (and to a degree those of other sites, such as Nahal Oren) indicate the developed extent to which there were Natufian architecture and positive settlement. In both the Natufian and the Karim Shahirian instances, there are one or two categories of artifacts (e.g., sickles, milling stones, celts) that probably point to food-plant manipulation, although not necessarily to cultivation. And, in spite of Reed's (1959) earlier reservations about positive animal domestication, we now hear from Solecki and his zoölogical collaborator, Dexter Perkins, that domesticated sheep are evidenced at Zawi Chemi Shanidar. Nevertheless, it is clear that the preponderant basis for the food supply, in either the Natufian or the Karim Shahirian instances, was one of rather highly intensified food collection. It is our *post facto* judgment, in terms of what is to follow, that firmly prompts us to classify this range of materials as one of incipient cultivation and domestication. On the basis of the very few radiocarbon determinations now available (Tell es-Sultan "Natufian," Zawi Chemi Shanidar), it might appear that this level had been achieved by *ca* 9000 B.C.

We note several things in general about this level. We either know (i.e., from the animal bones) or may reasonably infer (i.e., from the plants, as seen at Jarmo, somewhat later) that the level was attained within a natural-habitat zone, although we do not yet know the exact boundaries of this zone. We have indications that the level began upon the basis of earlier adaptations to food-collecting and some degree of open-air settlement and "settling-in." We also note physiographic and environmental diversity within the natural habitat zone (to the extent to which we can now define it). The Kurdish flanks of the Zagros, especially, may be visualized as a tipped corrugated plane of ridges and intervening montane valleys running from northwest to southeast. Each intermontane valley lies successively a bit higher, each higher mounting ridge tends to be cut at right angles by the main drainage channels or their tributaries, making access from one intermontane valley to another relatively easy. Hence, just as Willey (this volume) remarked for Mesoamerica, a great variety of environmental niches, on both the ridges and the valley floors at a succession of elevations, were already available to the somewhat more generalized food-collectors of the pre-incipient levels.

This diversity doubtless bears on the different complexions of the assemblages within the general Karim Shahirian group. It must also bear on the fruitlessness of any suggestion that the level of incipient cultivation, as a supposed unitary complex, was the achievement of any particular niche or intermontane valley, especially when we have yet to define the effective over-all boundaries of the natural-habitat zone.

It must also be clear that, at the moment, we are not so well off in our understanding of the actual plant elements of incipient food production in southwestern Asia as are our New World colleagues. Wheat and barley are not yet attested in an earlier context than that of Jarmo, which is on the settled village-farming level; nor did Helbaek (Braidwood and Howe *et al.*, 1960, p. 103) appear to anticipate that a long span of time and manipulation was necessary to produce cereals of the form seen at Jarmo.

Basing himself on the Jarmo evidence and its wheats and barley, Reed (Braidwood and Howe *et al.*, 1960, p. 124) believed the development of incipient cultivation and its implications of sedentism to be a basic factor that might lead to animal domestication. Now it appears the animals may have come first, although Reed's implications concerning the trend toward sedentism still hold. It also follows that for southwestern Asia we cannot yet be very specific about the time rate of the build-up, from a more generalized level of food collection, through incipient food production, to the level of the village-farming community. There are, in fact, a pair of radiocarbon determinations for Jarmo at *ca.* 9200 B.C. (Braidwood, 1959) which—on the theory that contamination tends to make the determinations more recent—might still prove to be valid. However, these determinations seem uncongenial with the rest of the evidence and the small Natufian-Zawi Chemi cluster of determinations at *ca.* 9000 B.C. If the *ca.* 6750 B.C. Jarmo cluster is valid, then the time span for the development between the Karim Shahirian and Jarmoan levels seems more reasonable, although it still suggests a slightly greater rate of acceleration than does the development seen in Tamaulipas.

In the Intermediate and Caribbean areas of the New World, Rouse is dubious of any incipient cultivation whatsoever. It is his belief that such cultures as Monagrillo (Panama), Barlovento (Columbia), Valdivia (Ecuador), and Manicuare (Venezuela) followed only a shellfishing, fishing, and collecting subsistence. These cultures date in the range of 2000–1000 B.C. and are thus contemporary with the incipient cultivation of the Peruvian coast. All except Manicuare have ceramics. We are inclined to believe that the lack of evidence for incipient plant domestication in these cultures is a function of preservation or lack of preservation rather than a reflection of a true situation. Without the preservation of the dry Peruvian coast, the remains from the early coastal shell-mound sites of that area might appear much more comparable to those of Valdivia or Monagrillo. The absence of stone grinding implements of the type found in Mesoamerican or southwestern incipient cultivation contexts is not necessarily a crucial argument against plant cultivation. The Peruvian middens, from which the cultivation evidence is indisputable, lacked such stone grinding tools; their presence is probably related to hard seed foods, such as maize, which were not present in the earlier Peruvian coastal incipient cultivation levels. But whether or not incipient cultivation was a part of the economy of the early shell-mound populations of the Intermediate area and Venezuelan littoral, it is obvious that these people were living a life not greatly different from that of their Peruvian contemporaries and that this settled existence probably prepared them for the acceptance of agriculture a few centuries later. As will be seen, two sources of influence are described by Rouse to account for this later agriculture. One of these is Mesoamerican seed-planting and is apparently related to the diffusion of maize southward from Mesoamerica; the other is South American and has its origins in the Amazon basin or in the llanos of Venezuela. This second source of agriculture has as its basis the root crop, manioc. Rouse surmises—and we would agree—that manioc cultivation had an incipience in the tropical South American lowlands in advance of 1000 B.C.

In the Old World our coverage of tropical and subtropical environments is restricted to sub-Saharan Africa, India, and southern China. Nevertheless, Clark's earliest evidence of a trend toward the domestication of African cattle comes from the northern dry belt, where the representations on some rock paintings are ascribed to the mid sixth millennium B.C. Milling stones, with their implications of incipient cultivation, appear only much later—save in the Khartoum sites. Clark is inclined to see the general complex of incipient agriculture and stock-raising as having entered Africa from southwestern Asia late in the sixth millennium B.C. and hints that African readaptation to this new way of life was a slow affair. The spread to the Horn and into the Rift Valley grasslands also appears to have been slow and to have involved animals more importantly than plants, although Clark scouts the idea that certain millets and sorghums may have been taken into use in the grasslands by the so-called stone-bowl people, following the transmission of the idea of plant cultivation from southwestern Asia.

All the foregoing is seen as having taken place within various matrices of intensified collection and "settling-in," and this same picture appears to have characterized the peoples of the forest margins in the tropical zone proper. Clark is, in fact, open to the idea that indigenous beginnings of vegeculture may have taken place here, but he does not follow Murdock (1959) in having this development begin quite independently of the diffusion of ideas from northern Africa.

The central-African savanna and the southern grasslands appear to have persisted on a level of intensified cultivation until about the beginning of the Christian Era.

As regards India, we can only agree with Sankalia that the evidence for (what would be in our terms) incipient food production is "scattered and hence inadequate for understanding the steps by which this was achieved" (this volume).

It is perhaps suggestive that the growing inventory of microlithic-yielding sites of the intensified food-collecting level are being located in situations adjacent to rivers, extinct lakes, or along the coast, but this may only reflect the difficulties of survey in the tropical-forest environments. That there is much in India that may be pertinent to our interests is suggested by the plant complex (which follows the earlier appearance of wheat) at Navdatoli, of which rice is one element. Although Sankalia may in part be right in suspecting that the type of culture represented at the Navdatoli site arrived in India with the Ayran-speaking tribes we are also bound to wonder whether indigenous beginnings in vegeculture (as the result of idea stimulation from southwestern Asia or not?) will yet be evidenced in India or beyond in southeastern Asia. The Navdatoli plant complex could be more readily comprehended were this the case.

We gather from Chang (this volume) that understandings of southern China are, if anything, still more unsatisfactory than for India. At the moment, it appears that we may account for only traces of "Hoabinhian" food-collectors, before a southward push of Lungshanoid farmers who presently adapted themselves to the new southern environment. Again we have the feeling that much more is yet to be learned about this area.

In eastern North America the context of incipient cultivation was a well-integrated and efficient forest and riverine hunting-collecting economy. Caldwell is of the opinion that such a pattern of life was in formation between the close of the Pleistocene (*ca.* 8000 B.C.) and 2000 B.C. and that by the latter date it had crystallized as a condition of "primary forest efficiency." This was a level of subsistence well-being that, in its environment, blocked or slowed the acceptance of plant cultivation. The first evidence of plant cultivation comes in the first millennium B.C. with the Adena culture of the Ohio Valley region. Here *Cucurbita pepo, Chenopodium,* and the sunflower (*Helianthus*) were definite domesticates; the first was probably a Mesoamerican import, the other two were apparently local. Whether or not maize was present at this time is unknown. These plants are believed to have played a minor dietary role in a society that constructed large ceremonial and burial mounds and made pottery. The latter trait was not, as far as archeologists can determine, of Mesoamerican derivation. Hopewellian culture, which overlapped chronologically with Adena and lasted from about 400 B.C. to A.D. 500, represents a peak of mortuary ceremonialism in these older eastern North American mound-building cultures. Maize definitely occurs for the first time in the area, but finds of it are rare. Caldwell sees it as being of little economic importance in what he believes is only a climax to a rich forest hunting-collecting tradition. Some archeologists would disagree with this interpretation and place more emphasis upon maize as a dynamic factor in the Hopewellian efflorescence, but virtually all would admit the strong bias of a forest hunting way of life in the Archaic-Adena-Hopewellian continuum.

In the more temperate parts of the Old World, at least in the west and north, our sources do not yet appear to indicate a counterpart for the indigenous and most probably independently achieved domestication of such plants as the *Cheno-*

podium and *Helianthus* in eastern North America. This does not, of course, exclude the proposition that the trend toward an increasing use of wild plants was now marked. Does Klíma's plant-like engraving (Fig. 2) fit simply with this increasing use or with something more comparable to the *Chenopodium* and *Helianthus* instance of plant manipulation?

Much is still to be learned from the preceramic horizons in west-central Anatolia and Thessaly. The question at issue here is whether these establishments are to be considered within the level of incipient food production or within that of the following level of village-farming communities. The resolution of this question will bear on the further one of the exact boundaries of the natural-habitat zone in southwestern Asia and of whether diffusion outside this natural-habitat zone was a possible characteristic of the level of incipient food production. And this, in turn, will bear on some of the issues that Pittioni raises. It has been claimed, for example, that einkorn wheat (although not emmer) has been noted in the wild in the Balkans; it has also been maintained that both these wild wheats are not tolerant of summer rainfall. Clearly the whole matter of establishing the existences and boundaries of natural-habitat zones depends on the archeologists' providing evidence for and enlisting the interests of highly competent paleoecologists. However, since Pittioni does not—as we understand him—explicitly claim the appearance of an independent level of incipient cultivation in southeastern and Central Europe, but rather an unspecific achievement of the "neolithic," we postpone our discussion of the issues he raises until our next section.

As a generality, it would appear to us that the peoples of Europe and Siberia continued the tempo of their readaptations to the succession and variety of post-glacial environments on an intensified food-collecting level. This went on, we ourselves believe, until such times as their readaptations were impinged upon and —to a degree "captured"—by influences stemming from the level of the primary village-farming communities. In this sense, it has been with considerable interest that we note the increasing usage, by our European colleagues, of the word "neolithization," with its implications of process. To what degree this process was blocked or slowed by the achievement of highly intensified "primary forest efficiencies," as in eastern North America, is a matter we shall return to in the next section.

There remains the problem of northern China and of assessing the likelihood of an independent appearance of incipient food production in Chang's "nuclear" Huangho Basin. The evidence for a trend toward intensified collecting and "settling-in" beforehand is available. Nevertheless, for the moment, Chang feels constrained, through lack of evidence, to make his case a speculative one and must allow for uncertainty as to whether food production came about through local "invention" or by "adopting plant cultivation and animal domestication." Chang hints that his own "era of incipient cultivation has been assumed on the ground of necessity," and certainly the complex of plants he lists is not a southwestern Asiatic one. Again the question arises of a natural-habitat zone for a peculiar set of plants and animals, and of its natural boundaries, along with the matter of whether diffusion out of this zone characterized the level of incipient cultivation and domestication.

We may also, of course, ask whether the major plant complexes seen both in northern China and in India (e.g., Navdatoli) represent vectors from some portion of southeastern Asia, just as we may wonder whether at least some elements of the animal complex (and probably the wheat in India) represent vectors from southwestern Asia. Satisfactory evidence for answering these questions is certainly not yet available to us.

We have now reviewed when and where and how incipient cultivation appears in the world, insofar as the papers of this symposium cover the matter. Let us summarize briefly the conditions under which our instances of this level seem to appear.

First, the perplexing question of what kinds of natural environmental settings were most propitious for the early development of incipient food production is by no means solved. Nevertheless, the data on hand suggest that generally semiarid regions (of temperate to tropical latitudes) with adequate but not overabundant collectible food resources were the hearths of the most important beginnings of cultivation and domestication. There is some suggestion that localized environmental diversities within a given generalized natural-habitat zone may have favored incipience. The semiarid-region part of this proposition does not rule out certain cases of plant-cultivation incipience in tropical-forest environments where significant food resources were developed through vegeculture. The single clear instance of this is the rise of manioc and other root starch crops in the Orinoco-Amazon basins of South America. (Lack of firm archeological evidence prevents us from going beyond sheer speculation as regards this type of incipient cultivation in southeastern Asia). Whether or not this South American root-crop development was truly independent or was stimulated by the traditions of incipient seed cultivation in adjacent areas remains undetermined. What appears to be a very minor incipient-cultivation pattern, based upon such plants as the sunflower and *Chenopodium,* arose in the temperate woodlands of the Mississippi Valley; but the effective food-supplement value of such cultigens as these never seems to have been of significance.

Second, we ourselves do not understand the spirit of the symposium to have favored environmental determinism in any explicit sense. Clearly, within the long range of climatic changes, environmental fluctuations, and renovations within the Pleistocene, the favorable conditions for incipient cultivation and domestication must have obtained at least several times previous to the time in which they were taken advantage of in the various instances that we cite. Why did incipient food production not come earlier? Our only answer at the moment is that culture was not yet ready to achieve it.

Third, at the present moment in our understanding of the evidence, we face the question of whether incipient food production is bound to the natural-habitat zones of its potential domesticates (plants or animals) or whether these domesticates and the associated cultural patterns are viable elements for extra-zonal diffusion. In this connection, for example, is the early and primitive cultivated maize of Bat Cave, New Mexico, the result of diffusion from incipient-cultivation centers in Mesoamerica? Or is it a parallel development within the habitat zone of wild maize and the same ecological-cultural area? Was Haury's highland corridor also a natural-habitat corridor?

Fourth, incipient food production appears in a context of some degree of pre-existent sedentism. This may vary considerably, but it would appear to be a very strong positive correlate. Beyond this, how far can we generalize; what were the other cultural conditions favoring incipient cultivation or domestication? Certainly there is nothing in the archeological record to indicate that those few instances of cultural build-up and elaboration, as manifested by the varying art styles of the upper paleolithic from western Europe into Siberia, or the contents of such developed mesolithic assemblages as the Maglemosian of north-western Europe, or the late Archaic assemblages of eastern North America provided a favorable ground for incipient food production. On the contrary, those instances of incipient cultivation or domestication of greatest potential are found in contexts of a much less spectacular character. Again, a possible exception might be cultures in which a tropical-forest root-crop cultivation had its origins; but, again, this is an *argumentum ex silentio*.

Fifth, in the only instance in which the archeological record approaches completeness—because of the preservation factor and the chronological range subsumed—namely, northern Mesoamerica (Tamaulipas), the trend from more generalized food-collecting to incipient cultivation is seen as a slow process. Nowhere else in the world are the archeological data sufficient to allow us to draw further definitive conclusions on the matter of relative slowness or rapidity of this process; however, speculatively, it seems probable that the build-up and increase of incipient food production was also slow in southwestern Asia.

Sixth, in no case does incipient food production appear to have had a marked effect on culture change—at least in any sudden or immediate way. The Meso-american sequences reveal only a very gradual build-up of material culture and trends toward greater sedentism .The most reasonable interpretation of the available evidence from southwestern Asia suggests the same thing. Two New World situations imply exceptions: the coastal collecting and incipient-farming populations of the Peruvian coast and the Adena culture of eastern North America. However, in the first of these it seems quite apparent that cultivated plants had but a relatively small economic role in a subsistence oriented to the sea. A similar interpretation—a forest hunting intensification and "efficiency"—has been advanced to account for the Adena build-up (although in this case it can be oppositely argued that maize cultivation, by way of diffusion from Meso-america, was of real importance). In the Old World there appear to be no such exceptions to our generalization that incipient cultivation and domestication had little immediate effect on general cultural development.

III AND IV

In Mesoamerica we have observed that food production by plant cultivation became a reality by about 1500 B.C. This is based upon data from the northern and central parts of that area; perhaps the event was slightly earlier in the south. The criteria adjudged by archeologists as indicating the established agricultural threshold in Mesoamerica are settled village life and ceramics. As we have seen in other areas, either of these traits may occur independently of agriculture, so we cannot be absolutely sure that they were correlates of successful farming whenever they are found in Mesoamerica; but, by extrapolation from the Tamaulipas sequence, it is a reasonable working assumption that the currently known early village-ceramic sites represent agricultural establishments. It is, of course, entirely possible that this linkage of pottery + settled village life + established cultivation will dissolve as archeological sequences are carried back in time, particularly in the southern part of Mesoamerica; however, we would hazard the guess that these three elements will all be found to have their Meso-american origins at approximately the same time and that this span of time will be in the range of 2000–1500 B.C. Insofar as we can see, effective food production by cultivation is indigenous to Mesoamerica and is the result of a long, slow process of cultivation incipience. In this sense, it does not give the over-all effect of having been "explosive" or "revolutionary." However, it is quite possible that effective farming was diffused or carried to certain marginal regions or localities of Mesoamerica as a well-knit complex and that it replaced previous incipient cultivation practices in these regions with "revolutionary" speed.

Incontrovertible evidence for the beginnings of a village-farming community way of life in southwestern Asia is already manifested at Jarmo, at least in its preceramic levels, with the presence of two wheats, a barley, domesticated goats, and probably sheep. The matter of dating this complex is more troublesome, however; for the moment we rest with the excavator's preference for the *ca.* 6750 B.C. cluster of determinations. Perrot, while noting Zeuner's inclination to consider the Tell es-Sultan P.P.N.A. as a level of intensified food collection (Perrot, this volume, n. 3), is himself of the opinion that a "reasonable level of food production" must have obtained, even if there is still very little direct evidence of it. Since he cannot conceive of an independent achievement of effective cultivation in the Jericho oasis—and we agree—Perrot sees Tell es Sultan P.P.N.A. as our first hint now available in Palestine of the social and economic consequences that followed when it became possible to cultivate the cereals beyond the limits of the natural-habitat zone.

Of the other occurrences of preceramic village establishments in southwestern Asia, the basal levels of Ras Shamra and of Haçilar are bound to be of pertinence when details concerning them become available. We do not yet know whether they were properly *farming* villages, however, and the general complexity of Sarab—apparently without cereals, at least in any quantity—gives us pause in pushing inferences too far. Nevertheless, the general trend of the evidence appears to be in a direction that would suggest that effective village-farming communities were probably established in southwestern Asia by *ca.* 7000 B.C., and there is even Perrot's hint that an expansion outside the natural-habitat zone had already begun. Do the establishments at Khirokitia on Cyprus, the pre-ceramic Thessalian sites, and even basal Haçilar pertain to this expansion, or to some earlier moment in the previous level of incipient cultivation? Again the lack of definition of the natural-habitat zone and its boundaries plagues us. But by 6000 B.C., or soon thereafter, we may see, at such sites as Hassuna and Matarrah (in the piedmont flanking the upper-middle Tigris) and at Baghouz and Samarra (along the lower-middle Euphrates and Tigris margins), that the movement out of the natural zone was an accomplished fact.

In the southwestern United States, Haury places established agriculture at 500 A.D. This is about 1500 years after the spread of improved maize into the Southwest from Mesoamerican sources. As we have noted, these diffusions were accepted into a context of incipient cultivation and at least the beginnings of settled village life. In this rather complex situation, should we consider the "event" gradual or explosive? A thousand or more years is obviously gradual when measured against the span of human generations; but, projected against the long chronological ranges of the food-collecting and incipient-cultivation eras that preceded it, the changes might justly be called explosive.

On the Peruvian coast established agriculture became a fact a good deal earlier than in the North American Southwest. Incipient cultivation began to be modified at about 1400 B.C. with the advent of Mesoamerican maize. Pottery, probably also coming into Peru from the north, arrived at 1200 B.C. Both these elements entered a pre-existing context of settled village life. By A.D. 750 a switch to an inland-valley settlement pattern documents the attainment of village agricultural status. As in the Southwest, the ground had been prepared by a long history of previous incipient cultivation and a tradition of sedentary living, but, once improved maize reached the area, it moved much more rapidly to full agriculture.

Data on village agriculture are few in the Caribbean and Amazonian areas. On the lower Orinoco River, Rouse places established agriculture, based on vegetative planting (manioc), at 1000 B.C.—the Saladero phase. It is likely that a similar chronology is applicable to Amazonia. As noted earlier, the incipient cultivation history leading up to these events is unknown.

To the west, in the Intermediate area, the Momíl culture seems to reveal an early root-crop agriculture, followed later by maize. This evidence suggests a prevalence of influences, first from lowland South America and afterward from Mesoamerica. Both Momíl and Saladero are pottery-using cultures with stable village settlement; both represent a marked departure from the earlier coastal shell-mound cultures such as Barlovento or Manicuare; yet in each instance, there is a previous resident tradition of settled living and, possibly, of incipient culti-vation.

In reviewing the case for possible beginnings of incipient food production in sub-Saharan Africa and India, we were also forced to consider the earlier phases of village life in these regions. Clark (this volume) places the first effective food production in East Africa in the second millennium B.C. with the appearance of the "stone-bowl" group, with their derived millet cultivation and animal domesticates and their open village settlements. In western Africa the so-called Nok culture, placed at about the beginning of the first millennium B.C., seems to have also practiced cultivation, probably including millet. Agriculture was also practiced in Katanga (the Kisalian culture), but cattle-raising appears to have been characteristic south of this. With certain exceptions due to population movements at about the beginning of the Christian era, Clark sees the African adaptations of predominantly borrowed plant and animal elements into local food-producing patterns as a terminal stage in a long and gradual developmental process.

The Indian case appears to have been an exasperatingly complex one; again we have a vast subcontinent with great environmental variety to deal with and, as Sankalia emphasizes, far too little archeological evidence. What led to the formation of the Indus valley civilization, the effect it had on the regions to the east and south during its brief flourish (and Sankalia can at least suggest that there were some effects), the nature and effects of the invasions of Aryan speakers, and the imponderable southeast-Asian problem, are all matters that must remain in limbo for us. It is a consolation to note that Sankalia and his colleagues appear to be very conscious of these problems and that problem-oriented research is under way.

Caldwell dates established agriculture, based on maize, at A.D. 800 in eastern North America. If we assume that maize first entered the East in Hopewellian times, at about 400 B.C., this rate of change from incipient to established cultivation is about the same as that for the Southwest but much slower than that for Peru. Even after A.D. 800 Caldwell is hesitant to accept Mississippi Valley village and town life as quite the functional equivalent of the Mesoamerican farming village. He attributes this to the strongly competing subsistence and culture patterns already well developed in the area.

We noted in our discussion of the level of incipient food production, and earlier, that the process of the "neolithization" of Europe evidently took place on a basis of a variety of locally intensive adaptations to the succession and variety of postglacial environments and that the new elements of food production apparently stemmed from sources within the village-farming community level rather than from that of incipience. Pittioni's proposition that there was an independent development of food production in Central Europe is, of course, at some variance with our own views. Unfortunately, we do not yet have radiocarbon determinations for the preceramic horizons of Thessaly. However, in view of Mellaart's (1961) reckoning that basal Haçilar lies within the seventh millennium B.C., it would not surprise us if the Thessalian material may date to the mid-sixth millennium. A pair of determinations for Starčevo village materials in Yugoslavia run at 4915 ± 150 B.C. and 4440 ± 75 B.C. (Mellaart, 1960, p. 277). Waterbolk is able to point to a very respectable cluster of determinations for his Dutch Bandkeramik sites, at ca. 4200 B.C. Thus, while entering into the controversy concerning "neolithic diffusion rates" (Edmonson, 1961) is furthest from our minds, it would appear to have taken effective food production about 2,750 years (*ca.* 7000 B.C. to *ca.* 4250 B.C.) to move the *ca.* 2,000 miles from Syro-Cilicia to the Rhine Delta, and about 2,250 years (*ca.* 1500 B.C. to *ca.* A.D. 750) to move the *ca.* 2,000 miles from the vicinity of Mexico City to the head of the Ohio River at Pittsburgh.

This again raises the question as to whether the intensified food-collectors of certain parts of Europe were not at a level of "primary forest efficiencies," in Caldwell's sense, and whether they tended at first to reject the spread of the new elements of the food-producing way of life. The other side of this coin, of course, is the matter of how quickly the plant and animal domesticates, and the artifactual techniques for their manipulation, could be adjusted to a succession of new environments. In this sense, the problem is an environmental as well as a cultural one and so must have been in the New World as well. It is our guess that the Troels-Smith—Becker *et al.* controversy concerning the semifarming nature of the Ertebölle may be resolved in such terms as these.

Clearly there are many questions still unanswered here. *How* did the new elements spread into Europe (unless Pittioni is right, they did so spread); how shall we conceptualize the nature of the cultural mechanics of "diffusion" and the spread of new "influences" through a vast area of already functioning cultural and environmental adaptations? Which particular channels served to bring the new elements to the extremes of northwestern Europe, and how complicated was the cross-cutting and intermingling of these channels? A simple picture of the march of many peoples up the Danube or Rhone into a vacuum is certainly not congenial to the way our European colleagues understand their evidence. It is in this connection, indeed, that all members of the symposium noted our misfortune that none of our invited participants from the western Mediterranean lands, Britain, and the Soviet Union were able to attend.

It is our inability to answer the foregoing questions (and many others) convincingly that makes difficult our response to Pittioni's view of an independent origin of food production in southeastern Europe and the Danubian area. Clearly this question cannot be resolved without much more evidence. Also, clearly, the beginnings of its resolution would be dependent on the establishment—by competent paleoecologists—of the likelihood for either a separate but similar biotic and natural-habitat zone or the natural extension of a lobe of the southwestern Asiatic zone up into southeastern Europe. A second step, we believe, would need to be the delineation of the archeological and natural traces of a level of incipient cultivation and domestication in southeastern Europe. Both the artifactual and non-artifactual elements of this level of incipience (*if* it should prove to exist), and of the subsequent village-farming community level, would need to be demonstrably and significantly different from those of southwestern Asia; not alone in detail but in general form and function. Finally, as Pittioni also clearly realizes, the degree of chronological assurance for the proposition would need to be much more elaborate than is the present random scatter of available radioactive carbon determinations.

In our opinion, Pittioni has not accounted fully enough for the general shift backward in time of our chronological notions (granting these notions depend on the present threads-and-patches fabric of the now available radiocarbon determinations). As the determinations in Europe have generally given us an apparently longer chronological span, so have those of southwestern Asia. We believe Pittioni, in asking for very explicit elements with which to demonstrate diffusion and in rejecting the proposition for stimulus diffusion, is over-strict. Nor do we feel bound by Pittioni's ideas that some finite (but undefined) amount of cultural "potential" is necessarily possessed by a culture before its elements may be successfully diffused—perhaps we do not fully understand him, however. In our opinion, the diffusion of elements of the new way of life was under way well before the Halafian phase began, even if the lower levels of Halaf itself may now be said to be "fixed" by the single C^{14} determination of *ca.* 5500 B.C. (an unpublished Groningen determination, Gro 2660, not available to Pittioni when he wrote).

Siberia is clearly an interesting case and, perhaps not too surprisingly, appears to parallel the eastern North American instance in some ways. Had Okladnikov been able to attend the symposium, his reaction to Caldwell's "primary forest efficiency" notion might have been interesting. Perhaps Okladnikov's preference for the older usage of "neolithic" (this volume)—the presence of ground axes, pottery, and the bow and arrow, but without cultivation—is best understood in these terms. Some degree of rejection of the new plant and animal domesticates must also be at issue, although how much this blockage might have been due to natural environmental factors and how much to the completeness of the cultural adaptations to the Siberian environments on an intensified level of collecting is not clear to us. When food production did appear, it seems in large part to have come from China.

Whatever our difficulties may have been with the case for the establishment of a level of incipient food production in China and with China's little-known earliest ceramic Shengwen phase (Chang, this volume), the Yangshao horizon puts us on very firm ground. Clearly, this was no earliest phase of effective village-farming community way of life, nor may we see it simplistically as the result of outside "influences" alone. Chang is certainly not against the idea that some elements may have been "loans" to the people of the Huangho basin, but he rightly (we believe) takes the point of view that the whole complex was functionally defined or redefined in Chinese terms.

What generalizations may we draw?

First, with the advent of an effective village agriculture it would appear that the natural environment quickly comes to have a less confining influence. In fact, this is probably the point in all human history at which man commences to manipulate seriously and to control the environment. The archeological record in both the Old and the New World indicates that, very shortly after the attainment of the village agricultural threshold in those primary areas of previous incipient cultivation or domestication, an agricultural and/or animal husbanding way of life is propagated to new environmental zones.

Second, concerning this propagation of the new way of life, we are unclear as to the balance between the cultural impulsions and the natural genetic tolerances of plants and animals that made this spread possible. Although it was a move of relative and explosive suddenness, it must be remembered that agricultural and food-preparational techniques had to change and adapt to new and different environments, just as did the plants and animals. A simple example of these attempts at adaptations would be the cutting and burning of forest lands to transform them into agricultural terrain, as happened in many parts of native America and in central and northern Europe.

Third, we have referred to the spread of a village agricultural way of life as "sudden and explosive." These are relative terms. Specifically, we note that, in the New World, village life based on maize farming diffused from Mesoamerica to Peru between 1500 and 750 B.C. and from Mesoamerica to the southwestern United States between 1500 B.C. and the beginnings of the Christian Era. In the Old World the spread seems to have been at about the same rate. Assuming 7000 B.C. as a fair date for the earliest effective farming villages in southwestern Asia, this mode of life reached Atlantic Europe at about 4250 B.C.

Fourth, it is a problem as to what degree village agriculture diffused, or was carried, as a total entity or complex. There is evidence that it did not always so move. For example, in the Americas an improved Mesoamerican strain of maize reached Peru about 1400 B.C., some six or seven hundred years before full village agriculture could be said to have resulted from cultural and social changes set in motion by this innovation. Similarly, new improved Mesoamerican maize hybrids arrived in the southwestern United States more than a thousand years before village agricultural communities can be said to have come into being in that area. On the European scene, it occurs to us to wonder whether the controversy over the apparently tentative appearance of food production in the Ertebölle culture may not have some similar explanation in manner of diffusion of agricultural traits. Otherwise, we see no direct European counterpart for this New World phenomenon.

Fifth, it would appear that, if the elements of established cultivation are diffused into a context in which existing subsistence and cultural traditions are firmly set, successful, and even in a state of climax, these preconditions may act to brake or to delay the usual rapid spread and acceptance of village agriculture. In these situations it is, of course, realized that natural environmental conditions, and their influences on the resident receiving cultures, are a part of the deterrent or barrier. In the Old World there appears to be relatively little evidence to allow us to assess the issue as regards agricultural diffusions from southwestern Asia into southeastern Europe. In the more northerly and westerly forested portions of Europe successful adjustments on an intensified food-collecting level probably inhibited the ease of spread of the agricultural way of life. Certainly in the case of Baltic Europe the long prehistory and history of semisuccessful and supplemental agriculture in an essentially food-collecting context is evidence of this resistance (we are fascinated with Moberg's curious Finnish instance of a transition from food production back to food collecting). In eastern North America it is believed that a somewhat similar forest collecting and hunting economy acted as a brake to the acceptance of fully agricultural patterns as these were diffused from Mesoamerica. The same also appears to have been the case in Siberia, where the diffusion seems to have come most strongly from China when it took effect.

V

In both Mesoamerica and Peru a kind of incipience to urbanization and civilization is seen in the rise of the ceremonial or temple centers. These are special sites, or precincts within sites, marked by mounds or other "public" structures. In Mesoamerica such centers appear in the southern part of the area at the beginning of the early Preclassic period (*ca* 1500 B.C.). Thus they appear to be as early as village agriculture. In Peru we have already noted the presence of such sites as far back as the end of the level of incipient cultivation. In Mesoamerica such ceremonial centers are of imposing size by the middle Preclassic period (after 1000 B.C.), and in Peru they are of comparable grandeur after about 750 B.C. From this point forward, the centers are foci of the elements of civilization, that is, great art rendered monumentally, organized priesthoods and governing officials, long-distance trade, craft specialists, and (especially in Mesoamerica) astronomic science and writing or (especially in Peru) metallurgy. Actual urban clusterings of population definitely appear in Mesoamerica by the beginning of the Classic period (as at Teotihuacan). This appearance is foreshadowed by somewhat less definite indications of urbanism dating back into the Preclassic period. For Peru, Collier dates the emergence of true urban zones somewhat later than this. But in each area the urban center appears as the end product of the ceremonial-center development. In both Mesoamerica and Peru, urbanism is preconditioned by intensified food production through agriculture and by high population densities. In Peru, this intensified agricultural production is traced back and verified by Formative period irrigation canals and agricultural terraces. In Mesoamerica irrigation, terracing, and "floating garden" techniques have not been archeologically identified before the Postclassic period, but their earlier presence is reasonably inferred in such a region as the Valley of Mexico.

The picture is apparently a somewhat different one in southwestern Asia, and also possibly so (although our evidence is very scanty) in India and China. If the Protoliterate period in southern Mesopotamia (*ca.* 3600–3200 B.C.) is taken there to be the very threshold of urban civilization, ceremonial centers do not appear to have preceded it by more than *ca.* 750 years, in the Ubaidian sequence of temples at Eridu. Although numerous small structures with earlier contexts (especially in Palestine) have been called "temples" or "shrines" by some excavators, there would not be general agreement that such was actually their function. Even if the early extreme of the Eridu temple sequence were to be 4500 B.C., at least two and a half millennia lie between this and the beginnings of effective village-farming communities. This takes for granted, certainly, that our still relatively insignificant exposures in such pre-Ubaid phases as the Halafian, Samarran, Hassunan, and Jarmoan have given us a nearly fair representation of their assemblages and that such structures as the Halafian *tholoi* are not bound to be interpreted as "shrines."

Further, it would appear—from our present understanding of the evidence in southwestern Asia—that few of the usual concomitants of urban civilizations (e.g., monumental art, officials, and specialists, trade, writing) made their appearance in any very formal sense before the Protoliterate period. Naturalistic art, for example, especially as seen in life-sized attempts in sculpture at rendering the human head and face, is not manifest before the beginning of the Protoliterate. It is true that there was some previous build-up in the development of metallurgy and that a bulk carrying trade in obsidian was already evidenced even at Jarmo; but in general the appearance of the usual concomitances seems to have been sudden. Hence Frankfort (1951, p. 16) supposed that Near Eastern civilization was born, ". . . the outcome of a sudden and intense change, a crisis in which its form—undeveloped but potentially a whole—crystallizes out. . . ." We must, however, insert one caveat to this image of a sudden crystallization of urban civilization in southwestern Asia. The exposures made so far in the Ubaidian phase of southern Mesopotamia are quite restricted, and those of the intervening phase between the Ubaidian and the Protoliterate, the Warkan, are woefully inadequate. The image of a sudden crystallization *might*, at least in part, be an artifact of the incompleteness of the archeological record.

It is perhaps worth mentioning again that recent research in southern Mesopotamia (Adams, 1960, p. 27) has very seriously tended to downgrade the role of irrigation as a determinative factor in the achievement of sociopolitical communities of the urban civilizational level.

Chang sees considerable continuity from his Lungshan materials into those of the Yin-Shang dynasty, but it also appears that predynastic Chinese ceremonialism did not run toward ceremonial centers. In any case, the long sequence of developing ceremonial centers of Mesoamerica and Peru is not evident. And Sankalia explains the relatively sudden appearance of the complex Harappan materials by reference to Mesopotamian influence upon a number of local and possibly Iranian derived, but environmentally readapted, developments (e.g., Amri, Kot Diji I, and Harappa I). Again, a long build-up is not to be inferred from the present evidence in India.

Hence—*if* our focus of attention is on ceremonial centers—it might appear that in the Old World there is a step up to the threshold of urban civilization, while in the New World it is approached by a more gradual ramp. The reasons for this difference are not manifest in the now available evidence. In southwestern Asia we could speculate that the rather rapid crystallization followed upon a new and successful adjustment to food production in the basin of lower Mesopotamia by a man-plant-animal symbiosis originally developed in the natural habitat zone of the hill flanks. It is probable that greater acreage yields for the cereals (at least in the beginning) plus the important addition of dates and fish to the diet were contributory elements toward a new upswing in lower Mesopotamia (Adams, 1960, pp. 27–30).

Nevertheless, the proposition seems to hang too heavily on one item alone—the relatively early and gradual development of ceremonial centers in the New World and their apparently much more rapid start at a relatively later phase of development in the Old World—to give us much to build upon. It remains for us to see whether other differences also appear.

With reference to an observation in our Introduction, however, even this one apparent difference in the manner of approach to the threshold may explain Braidwood's timidity to make the direct step up to a range of evidence that has traditionally (in the Old World) also been the concern of another branch of scholarship. Willey, on the other hand, more sure-footed on his ramp and uninhibited as the result of lack of academic departmentalization, sees little reason not to proceed with the story.

One further observation on the difference might be the question: Would Gordon Childe have found the phrase "urban revolution" so congenial had he understood the New World evidence more completely?

In the southwestern United States large towns follow the threshold of village farming by about 500 years. Pueblo Bonito, one of the largest ruins in the Anasazi region, is a prime example, and Haury has estimated its population as 1,000 people. These southwestern towns incorporated formalized religious architecture; the earlier ceremonial chamber, the kiva, was now reproduced on a grander scale. The towns were also centers of trade, although trade was never of the magnitude that it was in Mesoamerica. But the criteria of civilization, as these have been described for Mesoamerica and Peru, were largely lacking, including the criterion of formal urbanism. Haury notes that the necessary foundation for civilization—village-farming—had been laid down but that "innate cultural factors more than environmental restrictions set the boundaries of high accomplishments." Perhaps this is so, but it seems to us that "environmental restrictions" are still to be explored as a basic limiting factor. The Southwest, even in its favorable "core" regions, is a land precariously on the edge of water shortage. Unlike Peru's desert coast, which is fed annually by run-off from Andean rains and snows, the rivers and irrigation systems of the Southwest are less sure of an abundant and regular water supply. This is true today, and there are evidences of long droughts from Precolumbian times. This limitation may have been a molding force in the development of the non-expansive cultural patterns of the area.

Ceremonial centers—great earthwork enclosures and burial mounds—are an old tradition in eastern North America. They begin with the Adena cultures of the first millennium B.C. and continue through the Hopewellian cultures of the early centuries A.D. Thereafter, temple-type mounds, usually arranged around courts or plazas, mark ceremonial centers in the area. The style and layout of these later centers is such that Mesoamerican stimulus is suggested. For the most part, the temple mounds characterize the period after A.D. 800, when maize cultivation had become a significant socioeconomic force. Large towns are found around some of these centers, and these represent the point of eastern cultural development that approaches nearest to urban civilization, although does not attain it.

The northwestern part of the Old World, at least, also had its elaborate ceremonial centers within the matrix of a food-producing but precivilized level of culture. Stonehenge and Carnac are famous examples of this, although the matter has not been touched upon heretofore in this symposium. Unlike the New World instances, however, these do not appear to stem from much older localized traditions, as we have no trace of such. The likelihood seems rather to be that such traditions of ceremonialism stem from somewhere in the eastern Mediterranean. How such great concentrations of ceremonial activity became integrated into a socioeconomic level based upon hoe agriculture, herding, and collecting is a question upon which there is hardly the space or available information for speculation here.

Large towns around temples or chief's houses, territorial kings or paramount chiefs, formal priesthoods, class differentiation, and some craft specialization are all found in the late Precolumbian periods in the Intermediate area, the Caribbean, and in parts of Amazonia. Of the three areas, the Intermediate moved closest to the status of civilization and urbanism, particularly in the late-period cultures of the Ecuadorean coast or the late prehispanic Tairona culture of northern Columbia. Yet, in general, true cities were lacking, as were great art styles, imposing architecture, complex governments, capital wealth, and intellectual pursuits on the order of those of Mesoamerica. The societies of the Intermediate and Caribbean areas tended to be richer, in material goods, than those of eastern North America; but otherwise they did not differ greatly in the magnitude and complexity of their social and political forms from, say, the Natchez tribe of the lower Mississippi Valley.

We have been provided with very little to justify consideration of indigenous levels at the thresholds of civilization in the semitropical and tropical portions of the Old World. What little is known of tropical India and southern China suggests derivative and delayed developments, but again lack of knowledge of southeastern Asia plagues us. The spectacular Nok terra-cotta sculpture of west Africa should not be overlooked, but the assemblage with which it had context is very little known, and ironworking—which Clark takes as a trans-Saharan importation—appears at least with the terminal Nok phase. Nor is Zimbabwe apparently without its "exotic" influences from the East Coast. In neither case should these implications of outside influences detract from the culture-historical importance of these antiquities; their form and style is quite African. The main trouble is that we know too little about the once-functioning cultures of which they were parts.

What are the causal correlates of the attainment of civilization and city life? In both the Old World and native America food production through agriculture was a prerequisite, but, as we have seen, urbanism and civilization do not necessarily follow it. Nor does length of time under conditions of village agriculture seem to be a crucial factor. In Mesoamerica some of the qualities of civilization— for example, the great arts, hieroglyphic writing, and monumental architecture— all begin to appear within five hundred years or so after the village agricultural threshold. In Peru both the monumental architecture and the major arts come in with the village agricultural threshold. Contrast this with the Intermediate area, where village agriculture dates back almost as early as it does in Mesoamerica and perhaps earlier than in Peru and where such features are entirely lacking at these same times. This also holds true for southwestern and eastern North America, where several centuries of experience with village agriculture, following 500 and 800 A.D., respectively, did not result in urban development in either area. Given more time, in the Southwest, at least, might more have happened? Certainly the case in southwestern Asia took much more time than it did in Mesoamerica and Peru. Probably the eastern North American sequence would have been like that of Europe (barring the discovery of America): gradual development up to the time of the establishment of a Mexican or southwestern counterpart for Imperial Rome.

What possible factors or forces making for the development of civilization are there that might be examined archeologically? Let us first turn to the natural settings of society and culture. What environmental potentials are shared by the two areas of New World civilization, Mesoamerica and Peru? We have already suggested that regional variation within a single area might have been a crucial circumstance in the development of cultivated plants and the subsequent achievement of village agriculture. Could this regional variation have also operated to aid later development in a more strictly cultural rather than a cultural-botanical sphere?

Both Mesoamerica and Peru have an internal variety of regional climates, soils, and vegetation. In Mesoamerica tropical climate is varied and modified by elevation. Upland basins lie within a few miles of lowland forests. Peru has somewhat less internal differentiation, but here the numerous coastal desert oasis valleys back up to, and are connected by passes with, highland valleys and basins. From early times interchange of produce and cultural items went on between these two strikingly different but closely juxtaposed natural zones. We suggest that each Mesoamerican environmental region, some of which had very definite natural boundaries, such as the Valley of Mexico, provided a kind of niche to which a local culture became adapted. Also in Peru highland basins and coastal valleys or groups of valleys offered similar regional niches. Within both Mesoamerica and Peru the cultures of their various regions constantly stimulated but did not overwhelm each other. Each regional culture retained its local uniqueness and integrity. These conditions prevailed throughout the respective Preclassic and Formative periods of the two areas and resulted, in each area, in the multiple developments of the brilliant regional civilizations of the Classic period. Teotihuacan, Classic Maya, and Classic Monte Alban are the outstanding Meso-american examples; for Peru we have Classic Tiahuanaco, Nazca, and Mochica. Interestingly, in both Mesoamerica and Peru the Preclassic period was character-ized by a quite early interregional sharing of a great art style and perhaps a religious ideology. For Mesoamerica this was the Olmec style; for Peru it was the Chavín. In the geographically adjacent Intermediate area it may be signifi-cant that there is no such early interregional stylistic phenomenon.

In sum, we argue that the cultural-ecological configurations of Mesoamerica and Peru in the epoch between village agriculture and the threshold of civiliza-tion were very similar. Each had considerable natural regional variation within the framework of a larger area. Regions were closely juxtaposed. Regional cul-tures developed in these several settings. In each area there was a regional inter-communication and interstimulation; this "symbiosis," as Sanders (1957) has re-ferred to it, promoted cultural growth. At this time no single region in either area exerted dominance over the others, although in each area the presence of a great multiregional art style (and an attendant religious ideology?) is observed. Under these conditions of cultural regionalism both Mesoamerica and Peru at-tained to the threshold of civilization and urbanism. It was not until after this had happened that the regionalism of each area was broken down by what ap-peared to be the beginnings of attempts at area-wide empires.

In the Old World the southwestern Asiatic instance might, at first sight, appear to have had a different nature. Urban civilization developed not upon the site of the earlier achievement of the village-farming community level in the environ-mentally varied hill flanks, but rather upon the generally uniform semiarid alluvial plain of southern Mesopotamia. Here "the settlements followed closely the shift-ing braided channels of the major rivers" (Adams, 1960, p. 281). The Indus valley instance must have been approximately similar (granting that we do not under-stand its build-up in detail), although Chang's description of the Huangho basin hints at less area and uniformity and certainly at less aridity than the Indus or Mesopotamian cases. However, it is clear in both the Mesopotamian and the Indus valley instances that interchange of both things and ideas obtained with their surrounding territories. As is well known, the alluvium is completely lacking in good stone, metal, and other important raw materials. It is further clear that there was not absolute cultural uniformity throughout the generally uniform alluvial plain of southern Mesopotamia and that in Susiana—which is the uniformly con-tiguous extension of the alluvial Mesopotamian landscape and environment into lowland Iranian Khuzestan—the complexions of the successive archeological yields show curious differences from those of their contemporary equivalents in Meso-potamia proper. Nevertheless, the available sites of northern Iraq along the pied-mont and hill flanks and in the hill flanks of the Iranian Zagros, from the Ubaidian phase onward, all yield archeological traces of a generalized commonalty of understandings and traditions. This commonalty, regardless of the detailed re-gional differences that certainly do exist, suggests the growth of an *oikumene*, with southern Mesopotamia as its central focus, and indicates the same features of interregional sharing that we note for Mesoamerica and Peru in their Pre-classic periods. In this connection, the spread of the Mesopotamian-type cylinder seal might be cited as one parallel to the spread of the Olmec style.

Of all the instances we might note, Egypt is perhaps the most curious. The growing *oikumene* of southern Mesopotamia reached it and affected it at a very critical moment, as Frankfort (1941, 1951) demonstrated some years ago. Various Mesopotamian traits were at least temporarily accepted and rather quickly given an Egyptian form or style. Even so, they seem eventually to have been found uncongenial to the matrix of Egyptian culture, and their vogue ended after not too many generations. Characteristically, Egypt was, relatively speaking, both geographically isolated and self-sufficient, and it has, of course, often been suggested that this contributed to the remarkable uniformity and persistence of the Egyptian cultural tradition.

There is not much to say, in our present understanding, of the cases in India and China, save to remark that both Sankalia and Chang—while realizing the possibilities and even probabilities of outside influences upon their areas—would also insist that these influences were quickly assimilated into styles and forms that were characteristically Indic or Chinese.

We have no reason to believe that Sanders' (1957) "symbiosis" proposition would not obtain as well for Mesopotamia and probably also for the Indus and Huangho basins as is suggested for the New World. The Egyptian case is peculiar, but we note that it was touched by the Mesopotamian *oikumene* during its formative phase, and we must also note that even Egypt did not persist in its vacuum throughout its history. More than bare planks reached Egypt from the Lebanon, as cedar was imported for coffins and construction purposes, and we also know that the flow was not entirely one way.

How do these conditions of natural environmental and cultural regionalism compare or contrast with those other Old and New World areas that did not become the settings of native civilization? We have already offered the opinion that the southwestern United States was severely limited by the precariousness of its water supply, but what of eastern North America, Amazonia, the Caribbean, or the Intermediate area and of temperate Europe and Asia and tropical Africa? All these areas have sufficient rainfall and zones of adequate soils for successful cultivation. But several of them, particularly eastern North America, Amazonia, western Europe, and the more tropical portions of the Old World, lack the regional climatic and terrain variation in the way that this variation obtains in Peru or Mesoamerica and in southwestern Asia at least. To be sure, climate varies in Amazonia and in tropical India and Africa as well as in eastern North America, western Europe, and southern Siberia on a north-south axis, but this is variation on a very gradual continuum. Temperate upland basins are not interspersed with tropical or semiarid valleys. Instead, there are long stretches of monotonous woodlands, jungles, or savannas. Thus, following the thesis presented above, opportunities for regional cultural specialization, interstimulation, and development are not the same as they are in Mesoamerica and Peru and at least in southwestern

Asia. In addition, the woodlands of North America, Europe, and Siberia and of tropical Asia, Africa, and Amazonia have extensive navigable river systems. Such systems, with the canoe transportation available in each area, made for easy, rapid, and long-distance movements of peoples. These things taken together—a uniformity of natural environment, a uniformity of cultural contour, and ease of movement through the area—may be the preconditions of what Kroeber (quoted by Caldwell) described as the endemic warfare of the North American East: "insane, unending, continuously attritional." This description could apply equally to the war patterns of the Brazilian tropical forest Indians. Warfare of this nature among tribes of equal strength and very similar culture would have provided a drain on manpower, interests, and energies. Such a drain may well have served as an effective deterrent to the development of civilization. These conditions of natural uniformity and ease of transportation also apply to the Caribbean area and perhaps also to the Mediterranean region from the Aegean to the west, but with somewhat less strength than to either eastern North America, western Europe, or Amazonia and the Old World tropics. Perhaps significantly, the cultural contour is more varied in these two areas than in the opposing instances.

But what of the Intermediate area in South America? Here regional environmental variation is notable. The Ecuadorean coast has sections of semidesert, savanna, and tropical forest. These are juxtaposed to uplands. In Colombia the Andean chain is splayed into four parts, each separated from the next by deep river valleys. Throughout the area regional culture is marked. Moreover, close proximity to both Mesoamerica and Peru resulted in a sharing of many traits with these two areas of native New World civilization. Nevertheless, the cultures of the Intermediate area did not advance to an urban level or, in the broader sense, to a level of civilization. Rouse is at a loss to explain this, as are we. His suggestion of low population density and simplicity of social stratification and religious complexity impress us, as they do him, as symptoms rather than causes of the fundamental situation; and absence of irrigation seems unlikely as a cause.

As an example of a further area of perplexity for us, one of the many not considered in detail by the symposium, we might note northwestern Africa, the breadbasket for Imperial Rome. Again regional variation up to the heights of the Atlas obtained; again there was an environmentally differentiated piedmont and coastal plain. Perhaps the environment, like that of California, was in fact too favorable to the persistence of intensified collecting, and again the factor of rejection is at issue. Still further, northwestern Africa was perhaps rather too isolated—by sea and desert—to have been affected by the "symbiosis" proposition.

Irrigation, hitherto so often cited as a causative factor in bringing about the sociopolitical and economic conditions that underlay the appearance of urban civilizations, was never widespread in Mesoamerica. For Mesopotamia, there is a growing realization that the implications of the word "irrigation" are far too grand to describe the facts, until civilization had been under way for some time. Even in Peru, where it became very important, it should be noted that civilization, at least on the Chavín horizon, was under way before the construction of large irrigation works.

It is possible, of course, that the very factors of natural regionalism and cultural regionalism, which we have put forward as vital elements for the development of civilization in our key areas, may have been a block to culture development in the Intermediate area and perhaps in northwestern Africa. A corollary of this might be the absence in the Intermediate area of a "universal" art style on the order of Olmec or Chavín. Thus, the Intermediate area seems to have lacked that nice balance between regional cultural semi-independence and mutual area-wide participation in ideas that appears as the background of civilization in Mesoamerica and Peru. Although we are far from being so well informed in the matter, we might tentatively suggest the same for northwestern Africa.

But this is a descriptive statement of what did happen rather than an explanation of cause. Although cause, or situations causally predisposed, within limits, may be sought for and found in prehistory, the archeologist is still far from an awareness of all the elements in any equation of social and cultural behavior.

BIBLIOGRAPHY

ADAMS, ROBERT M.
   1960. "Factors Influencing the Rise of Civilization in the Alluvium: Illustrated by Mesopotamia" and "Early Civilizations, Subsistence, and Environment." In CARL H. KRAELING and ROBERT M. ADAMS (eds.), *City Invincible*, pp. 24–34, 269–95. Chicago: University of Chicago Press.

ARKELL, J. A.
   1949. *Early Khartoum*. London: Oxford University Press.
   1953. *Shaheinab*. London: Oxford University Press.

BRAIDWOOD, ROBERT J.
   1958. "Near Eastern Prehistory," *Science*, 127:1419–30.
   1959. "Über die Anwendung der Radiokarbon-Chronologie für das Verständnis der ersten Dorfkultur-Gemeinschaften in Südwestasien," *Österreichische Akademie der Wissenschaften, phil.-hist. Kl., Anzeiger, 1958*, 19:249–59.

BRAIDWOOD, ROBERT J., BRUCE HOWE, *et al.*
   1960. *Prehistoric Investigations in Iraqi Kurdistan*. Chicago: University of Chicago Press.

EDMONSON, MUNRO S.
   1961. "Neolithic Diffusion Rates," *Current Anthrop.*, 2:71–102.

FRANKFORT, HENRI
   1941. "The Origin of Monumental Architecture in Egypt," *Amer. J. Sem. Lang. and Lit.*, 58:329–58.
   1951. *The Birth of Civilization in the Near East*. Bloomington: Indiana University Press.

McBurney, C. B. M., and R. W. Hey

1955. *Prehistory and Pleistocene Geology in Cyrenaican Libya.* Cambridge: Cambridge University Press.

Mellart, James

1960. "Anatolia and the Balkans," *Antiquity*, 34:270–78.

1961. "Two Thousand Years of Haçilar—Starting from Nine Thousand Years Ago . . . ," *Illustrated London News*, 238:588–91.

Murdock, George Peter

1959. *Africa: Its Peoples and Their Culture History.* New York: McGraw-Hill.

Reed, Charles A.

1959. "Animal Domestication in the Prehistoric Near East," *Science*, 130:1629–39.

Sanders, W. T.

1957. "Tierra y Agua ("Soil and Water"): A Study of the Ecological Factors in the Development of Mesoamerican Civilizations." (Ph.D. diss., Harvard Univ. [Peabody Museum Library].)

INDEX